D1462455

THE CHURCHES AND THE LABOUR MOVEMENT

THE CHURCHES AND
THE LABOUR MOVEMENT

by

Stephen Mayor

LONDON
INDEPENDENT PRESS LTD
LIVINGSTONE HOUSE SWI

Ⓒ INDEPENDENT PRESS LTD.

First published 1967

261
M454

MADE AND PRINTED IN GREAT BRITAIN BY
THE GARDEN CITY PRESS LIMITED
LETCHWORTH, HERTFORDSHIRE

CONTENTS

Foreword   5

Preface   7

Introduction: The Mid-century Scene   9

1   The Church and the Working Classes   19

2   Trade Unionism   80

3   Some Other Forms of Working-class Organization   152

4   Christian Socialism   165

5   Relationships of the Churches and the Secular Socialist
      Movement   242

6   The Churches and the Political Organization of the
      Working Classes   304

7   The Contribution of the Churches to the Labour
      Movement down to 1914   334

Epilogue   357

Appendix I: *Lux Mundi*   389

Appendix II: Works of Andrew Reid   390

Bibliography   397

Index   403

FOREWORD

EW QUESTIONS PROVE more controversial than that of the part religion should play in great political issues. Over the centuries religion and politics have found it impossible to keep apart. This is inevitable since the overwhelming majority of political issues have essentially a moral content.

Christianity is an all embracing faith which claims pre-eminence in every field of human endeavour. That is why inspired Christians have been to the fore in every great struggle for the advancement of human rights.

Christianity's revolutionary teaching concerning man and God is a dynamic political gospel in itself. It has certainly inspired Christian Socialists who believe that there are no unimportant people in the world and that things and institutions must therefore be controlled in the service of mankind as a whole.

Christian Socialism has been the driving force of the Labour Movement ever since it began. It has provided the dynamism for courageous leadership on such issues as race relations; living conditions for the submerged tenth of our society; education and health of the masses; and above all on questions associated with peace among the nations.

Today in Westminster there is a solid core of Labour Members of Parliament who are in politics only because they see it as a proving ground for their faith.

It would be misleading to pretend that this is any longer true for the majority of Labour Members of Parliament, but Christian Socialism is still a mighty influence both in the Parliamentary Labour Party and in Constituency Parties.

A growing danger to the Labour Movement is that of being so wrapped up in the challenge of current affairs that it may forget its Christian heritage. The reality of power sobers many an idealist into accepting a half of the loaf for which he campaigned. Yet it is when responsibility for Government is in the hands of the

Labour Movement that it most needs to be reminded of its Christian heritage.

This book serves as an important and informed reminder of the way that Labour has come to where it is today. It holds an unspoken challenge to Labour leaders in the 1960's and in the 1970's to prove worthy of the heritage they have received. Because I believe that knowledge of our past is important if we are to behave rightly in the present I hope that this book will be widely read.

GEORGE THOMAS
Minister of State (Commonwealth Office)

COMMONWEALTH OFFICE
DOWNING STREET, LONDON, SW1
JANUARY 1967

PREFACE

IT IS USEFUL to be told at the beginning of a book—and sometimes at the end as well—what it is about. This book is about religion and the Labour movement in England since 1850. It is not in the main about the Labour movement and religion: that is to say, it is concerned more with the attitude of the Churches to the activities and ambitions of the organized working classes than with the attitude of the working classes to the Churches. Obviously there is no rigid line to be drawn, if only because those who belonged both to the working classes and to the Churches can be entered on both sides of the account, and it would be largely a matter of definition whether their views were regarded as religion influencing Labour or Labour influencing religion. But the distinction is significant in so far as it determines my approach to the subject. Thus I have drawn a good deal of material from the religious press, as representative of vocal opinion in the various denominations. For the Church of England I have used the *Guardian* (not the daily newspaper which in recent years has become reticent about its birthplace, but a religious weekly which perished a decade or so ago), the *Church Times*, and the *Church Family Newspaper* (now the *Church of England Newspaper*). For Nonconformity I have used the *Nonconformist* and the *British Weekly*, and for the Roman Catholics chiefly the *Universe*, supplemented in the early period with the *Tablet*.

My thanks are in a very high degree due to Dr W. H. Chaloner of Manchester University for his interest, guidance and advice over a number of years. I am also grateful for advice from Professor W. H. G. Armytage of Sheffield University. Finally I must express my gratitude for many things to the members of the two Congregational churches which I have served as minister while writing this book: Handbridge, Chester, and Westminster Road, Liverpool.
S.M.

INTRODUCTION:
THE MID-CENTURY SCENE

THERE IS A COMMON misapprehension that the age of faith ended fairly recently, somewhere on the horizon of living memory. The truth is that by the middle of the nineteenth century a very large section of the English people had only the most formal link, if even that, with organized religion. The educated sceptic had been known from classical times, and had maintained his attitude of sceptical detachment from vulgar enthusiasms in all but the most fervent epochs. A much newer phenomenon was the urban proletariat, increasingly indifferent, or even hostile, to religion; but even this was nothing new by 1850. During the French Revolution the doctrines of atheistic democracy had ventured across the Channel, and the Evangelical Revival had only stemmed, rather than reversed, the tide. As the Industrial Revolution brought together more and more wage-earners in the factory and the slum, the contagion of infidelity spread.

So far as the Established Church was concerned, one obvious and immediate cause of the failure to win the urban masses was the rigidity of the parish system, for the Anglican parishes were of ancient origin and by now quite out of touch with demographic reality. Local anomalies could not easily be remedied, since until 1843 a special Act of Parliament was required in order to divide a parish. The consequence was that while some country parishes were virtually sinecures, in urban areas there was sometimes a huge population within the boundaries of a single parish. In 1840 the parish of St Paul's, Knightsbridge, had a population of 73,000; but even this was dwarfed by the parish of Leeds, which in 1841 numbered 150,000. At Leeds a conscientious incumbent promoted an Act of Parliament to divide up the parish, with a serious reduction of his own income. Such a procedure was likely to be rare.

In such parishes the parson could know only a minute section of his nominal flock, however diligent he might be. In the middle

9

of the century the Church of England was still a countryman's church, at home in the life of the countryside, and holding for the moment the loyalty of most classes of the agrarian population, but uncomfortable in the new industrial areas. Nothing is more striking to the modern reader of the Anglican press of the period than its rural bias. The same bias reappears in the distribution of buildings. By 1851, 51% of the population lived in towns with over 10,000 inhabitants, but these towns included only 38% of the church accommodation. A generation before, in 1818, Parliament had voted £1 million for new churches, but since then there had been further great shifts of population. To meet the situation campaigns for the building and endowment of churches were periodically launched, often to the accompaniment of a vigorous debate as to whether the church building or the congregation should be the first aim. The greatest such campaign was the work of Bishop Blomfield of London, who appealed for the building of fifty new churches in his diocese. The appeal was more than answered: by 1846, forty-four new churches had been completed, ten were being built, and nine were about to begin, with the effort concentrated in Bethnal Green, Islington, St Pancras, Paddington, and Westminster. Such a campaign represented a great effort of energy and sacrifice, for funds had to be provided for the maintenance of church and incumbent as well as for building, yet it could only keep pace for a few years with the influx of new population.

The Establishment was not unpopular; indeed, with the masses of the population it was probably the target of less hostility than either earlier or later in the century. The hunting parsons of the eighteenth century, whose life and interests had been identical with those of the secular gentry among whom they lived, had in the main gone. The burden of tithes had been lightened by the slow decline in the value of money over a very long period, and the state was now responsible for their collection, so that bitterness against them was no longer so automatically directed against the incumbent of the parish But none of this made much difference in the towns, where the clergyman was a remote and irrelevant figure.

Among the clergy themselves social distinctions were marked. In 1850, 174 clergy received an income of over £1,000 a year; a 1,000 received over £500; and 8,000 received over £300. There were about 12,000 livings and 5,000 curates. Inquiries by the Ecclesiastical Commissioners had revealed the existence of what has been called, perhaps with some exaggeration, 'a veritable proletariat among the Anglican clergy, hidden among the hills of Wales and Cumberland, uncultured, of worse than indifferent morals, and recruited from the children of the scarcely civilized farmers of these poor districts.'[1] The Church of England reflected the hierarchical character of the nation, though the social divisions in the ministry did not constitute a caste system, since it was possible to rise from one social grade to another, and there was none of the bitterness between the upper and lower clergy which marked the *ancien régime* in France.

Of the various parties in the Church of England the most prominent was at this stage still constituted by the Evangelicals. As a theological force they had passed their peak, but they were strongly entrenched in the Episcopate, in the universities, and in the parishes, and as a social influence they were at their height, under the leadership of Lord Ashley, who succeeded to the earldom of Shaftesbury in 1851. It is important to remember that the Evangelicals retained their predominance until the closing years of the century, and during the whole of the reign of Victoria the odds were very high that anyone criticizing 'religion,' and anyone defending it, meant not only the Christian religion, but even more precisely, the Evangelical Protestant interpretation of it. Surprising consequences followed: for example advocates of a more liberal attitude to Sunday observance tended to be regarded as hostile to Christianity, although Roman Catholics and many Anglicans were with them. Sunday was important to the working classes, and this was typical of the kind of misunderstanding which arose.

The Evangelicals formed one limb of the rather strange tripartite alliance which brought about most of the important mid-century reforms—Evangelicals, Dissenters, and Benthamites. Yet as a social force the Evangelicals had severe limitations. They were individualists; they believed in self-help, but not in combination, and hence not in trade unions; and their Calvinist theology might well inspire sermons preaching the duty of submission and contentment with one's lot. Shaftesbury was typical, except in the ways in which any great man must be untypical—in the single-mindedness of his enthusiasms, for example. He gave his life to the assistance of the unfortunate, yet the joint action of the

[1] E. Halévy, *A History of the English People in the Nineteenth Century: IV. Victorian Years 1841–1895* (1951), 344.

unfortunate through trade unions he condemned, so that, like Wilberforce before him, he failed to win the affection of many of those whose cause he had at heart. The Evangelicals had too an ambiguous attitude to wealth. Worldliness and other-worldliness went hand-in-hand: hard work and thrift were Christian duties, and God rewarded their fulfilment with wealth; yet material considerations ought not to dominate life, for the world's injustices would be recompensed later, in heaven. Successful businessmen were welcomed into the ranks of the prosperous Evangelicals, but for a class or a group to attempt to overturn the social order was an offence against the Creator. Despite the reforms to the credit of the Evangelicals, and above all of Shaftesbury, their achievements were largely vitiated by these aspects of their belief. They were limited too by the class character of the Evangelical leadership, which became lukewarm when reforms threatened its own position. To the intolerant, such as Dickens, the Evangelicals were hypocrites, who justified their own privileges and the oppression of the poor by theological arguments, and their services to the poor were simply a sop to safeguard an unjust order.

The other Anglican groups were for the moment of less importance. The High Church party was dominated by the Tractarians, and the Tractarians themselves were absorbed in defending the narrow isthmus which Newman had called the *via media* against the assaults on the one hand of militant Protestantism and on the other of former colleagues now in the Roman communion. When left in peace they were concerned with matters of ritual and doctrine, though they were potentially important for two reasons: they emphasized the corporate element in religion and in social life against the prevalent individualism, and they rejected the current *laissez-faire* Liberalism. But they opposed the nineteenth century from the point of view of an idealized middle age, not on the basis of a hope for the future. Pusey, the real leader after the defection of Newman, did express some social judgements, but his idea of social justice was essentially the restoration of the hierarchy of classes, in which each man knew his place and possessed both rights and duties belonging to it. This was not what the working classes wanted.

There was no Broad Church 'party' in the middle of the nineteenth century, and this particular Anglican tradition was overshadowed first by the Evangelicals and then by the Tractarians, though in a rather obscure way it lingered on, and through a few outstanding individuals continued to influence religious thought, until it came to the fore again in a modified form later in the century, through the rise of the new Biblical scholarship. In 1850 Thomas Arnold had been dead eight years, but his ideas had a long life before them, not least through the works of Thomas Hughes. Arthur Penrhyn Stanley was to became a Canon of Canterbury the next year, and later a national figure as Dean of Westminster. James Fraser was still in his early thirties and a parish priest. F. D. Maurice, who was forty-five, was about to be plunged into unhappiness by becoming the centre of a theological controversy. But this was normal.

Like the Church of England, organized Nonconformity was out of touch with the working classes in the middle of the nineteenth century. The religious census of 1851 showed that Nonconformity was slightly stronger than the Church of England, a fact which many Dissenters quoted joyfully as the conclusive argument for disestablishment, and which some Anglicans could not bring themselves to believe. But the strength of Nonconformity was in the lower middle classes. Except for Methodism, which was strong in some rural areas, it was concentrated in the towns, but not particularly in the working-class districts of them. Of the 'three denominations' of historic Dissent, the Presbyterians had deviated from orthodoxy into Unitarianism, and had seriously declined, to be succeeded in time by a new Presbyterianism derived from Scotland. The two denominations with an 'Independent' polity, the Congregationalists, or Independents proper, and the Baptists, were both flourishing, but they were ill-equipped in various ways to evangelize the poorer areas of the cities. Their system of government, according complete independence—at least in theory —to each local church, made the organizing of large evangelistic efforts difficult, and the founding of churches without sufficient funds to run themselves almost impossible. Moreover each church was democratic internally, and in the Church Meeting each member was expected to play his part, with the deacons almost corresponding to company directors in the coming era of limited liability. Methodism was in some ways similarly organized, but there was a check on democratic control through the authority of Conference, ministers, and class-leaders. The result of the Independent system was that the pure Independent church, as distinct from the later development of the mission church, had little place for the uneducated or unvocal member, and the appeal of these churches tended to be to the lowest grade of the middle classes rather than to the working classes. It has been suggested that Nonconformity played some part in limiting the influence of revolutionary Chartism, by robbing the workers of their natural allies, the educated lower middle class.[1] Such a class, near to the upper strata of the proletariat in some ways, might be very far away in others, for it was the class of the small employer and merchant; if the upper classes could afford to look with a good deal of indulgence on the poor, the *petit bourgeois* saw no reason why the poor should not enrich themselves by the practice of *bourgeois* virtues. The High Churchmen of the Young England school and Anglican aristocrats such as Ashley espoused the workers' cause, according to their own interpretation of it, while Dissenting Liberals were often uninterested in the protests of the working class. But the Independent type of church did give scope for the active participation in its government of men of any class who were willing and able to take such a part; persuasive oratory could find there a wide field of influence, and it is not altogether surprising to find later in the century Labour leaders such as Keir Hardie and Ben Tillett among the Congregationalists. But working-class Dissenters were not always prominent in their own denominations; there is evidence that throughout the century many of those who attended Nonconformist places of worship were not formally members, and there may have been a social distinction between members and mere attenders. Thus while Dissent maintained strong contacts with the working classes, including the politically active leadership, some social factors tended to limit the effectiveness of such contacts. Moreover the Independent type of churchmanship had all the limitations, from the present point of view, of the Anglican Evangelicals, with a still stronger emphasis on individualism. Even before 1850 some Congregationalists were worried by the absence of the working classes from their chapels, but others prided themselves on the middle-class character of the denomination, regarding their own class as the soundest.[2]

The range of social classes represented among the Baptists[3] is

[1] Halévy, op. cit., 395.

[2] e.g. Thomas Binney. See F. R. Salter, 'Congregationalism and the "Hungry Forties",' in *Transactions of the Congregational Historical Society*, xvii, 115 (1956).

[3] For the Baptists see Underwood, *A History of the English Baptists* (1947).

shown by the fact that they included among their ranks Sir Morton Peto, a typical Victorian capitalist (except that he went bankrupt), and also Thomas Cooper, the Chartist, but the main support was again lower middle class. Of the three outstanding leaders of the Baptists in the later nineteenth century, Spurgeon was the son of an Independent minister, Maclaren of a Glasgow businessman, and Clifford, who began work at the age of twelve, of a factory worker. Significantly it was the last-named who emerged as the Radical leader in late-Victorian Nonconformity. In the middle of the century the Baptists were still strongly divided over their two historic controversies, one on Calvinism, and the other, to some extent bound up with it, on the admission of the unbaptized to Communion.

The Methodists are more important from the present point of view. The Wesleyans, the largest group, experienced in 1849 another in their series of violent schisms over the question of whether the laity should share effectively in the government of the denomination, which John Wesley had vested in a Conference composed wholly of ministers. Dr R. F. Wearmouth points out that this demand was 'a reflex of the political struggle,' and as in the wider sphere, reforms were not readily granted. The Wesleyan hierarchy, firmly middle class, as always opposed reforms and suppressed the reforming movements, with the result that the Wesleyans lost 97,419 members in the five years 1850–1855.[1] The second largest group, the Primitive Methodists, were contrasted with the parent body not least in social class, for Primitive Methodism was preeminently the religion of the industrial north and midlands. From its birthplace in Staffordshire it spread north into Lancashire and Yorkshire, and flourished especially in the mining villages of Durham and Northumberland. Alone among the Nonconformists the Primitives, with some smaller Methodist churches, could claim mass support among the workers. Three features of Methodism as a whole must be noted. First, despite the checks on popular control, all types possessed many democratic features, even the Wesleyans: for example, the use of the referendum to settle disputed issues. Second, Methodism alone of the Nonconformist churches was strongly entrenched in the countryside, and was in rural areas the most formidable rival of the Established Church, a fact of importance in the rise of agricultural trade

[1] R. F. Wearmouth, *Methodism and the Struggle of the Working Classes 1850–1900* (1954), 91.

2-TCATLM

unionism. Third, all Methodists were fervently devoted to evangelism, sometimes by eccentric and sensational methods. Least of any denomination were they likely to survey unmoved the alienation from religion of large masses of the population.

It has sometimes been claimed that Methodism was responsible for saving England from revolution in the first half of the nineteenth century. This period lies outside the scope of this book, but the point is not irrelevant in considering the background to Methodist thought in 1850. E. J. Hobsbawm has given reasons for thinking that the claim is much exaggerated.[1] Though the Methodists, or at least the largest body of them, the Wesleyans, were hostile to revolutionary ideas, there seems to have been little correlation between periods and places of Methodist success and either the presence or the absence of revolutionary feeling. Many Wesleyans, when economic stresses affected them, ignored the warnings of their leaders and took part in combinations and even riots. The smaller Methodist groups were even less unanimous, and from the start tended to be a socially radical force. In any case the whole body of the Methodists was too small to have the effect with which it has been credited. In 1851 they may have totalled about 500,000 members in a population of 18 millions, but this was after a generation's rapid growth. In the first decade of the century they were only 1% or 2% of the population, and even by 1850, and even in their strongest centres, they were only a minority. According to Hobsbawm, 'Methodism advanced when Radicalism advanced and not when it grew weaker . . .'[2] On the other hand statistics quoted by Dr W. H. Chaloner show that of 425 persons imprisoned in Lancashire for their part in the riots of 1842 only one-seventh were Methodists, compared with half who were Anglicans.[3] This supports the view that there was no very rigid relationship of either a positive or a negative kind between Methodism and subversive feeling, but it does seem that as they entered into the second half of the nineteenth century the Methodists were not inhibited by the tradition of Wesley's conservatism from taking their place with the forces making for change. In their contacts with other Nonconformists, who already had strong connexions with the Radicals and reformers, and in their prominent part in the creation of workers' organizations, they would not feel too

[1] In *History Today*, February 1957, 115–124.
[2] Ibid., 124.
[3] Ibid., May 1957, 335f.

strongly the restraints of a tradition they had already shown themselves ready to forget when circumstances so demanded.

The Roman Catholic Church was still at this stage in the background. For a long time Catholicism had been the preserve of a comparatively few wealthy families, maintaining the old religion through all the vicissitudes of three centuries of religious strife; but by the middle of the century two causes were bringing the Roman Catholic Church prominently before the eyes of Protestant England: on the one hand the Catholic revival represented by the Oxford Movement, with the spectacular conversions of Newman (1845) and Manning (1851) and other prominent Anglicans; and secondly, perhaps in the long run more important, the rising tide of Irish immigration. A Church composed of English titled families and Irish labourers faced a problem of great difficulty, and mid-century Catholic thought and effort was largely devoted to welding together these disparate factions. Compared with other denominations the Roman Church had an abnormally low proportion of middle-class adherents. For example the 1832 Reform Act brought in very few Catholics. At this stage the main Irish influx still lay ahead, and in the 1851 census of religion only 3·5% of the worshippers were Catholics. The total Roman Catholic population of England and Wales that year is estimated at 679,000, very unevenly distributed over the country. In the south of England, outside London, there were hardly any. If the attendance at Mass is expressed as a percentage of total population (not total church attendance) the figure for most of the Catholic dioceses is around 1%. At one extreme is Plymouth with a figure of 0·2%, at the other are Salford with 2·8%, and, very strikingly, Liverpool with 7·8%. The Irish-born population varied in proportion to the Catholic worshippers: in most dioceses it varied from 1% to 3%, while in Salford it was 6·7% and in Liverpool 12·7%. The census showed that of the towns the least Catholic were Oxford, Plymouth, Norwich, Exeter, Ipswich, Northampton, and Merthyr, in all of which the Roman Catholics amounted to less than 2% of the church attenders; at the other extreme were Liverpool (30·6), Preston (30·6), Wigan (26·6), Manchester, with Salford (25·0), Newport (15·5), Carlisle (15·2), Newcastle (13·7), Stockport (12·5), Bolton (11·0), and Bradford (10·6).[1]

In 1850 the Roman hierarchy in England was suddenly restored,

[1] For the Roman Catholics see G. A. Beck (ed.), *The English Catholics 1850–1950* (1950).

to the great alarm of Protestant feeling, which was placated with legislation relating to the use of episcopal titles. The restoration of the Episcopate was a sign of the Church's confidence of its future in this country, a confidence justified by the rapid growth of the next few decades. The outstanding feature of the growth of the Roman Catholic Church in Victorian England was that, being Irish, it was overwhelmingly working class. Although for Protestants and freethinkers the Roman Church was the very embodiment of reaction, Manning in particular saw that its future in England was bound up with the progress of the working classes, and socially he emerged to the Left of the old-style Radicals. Even before the rise of Manning the English Catholics were moving into an extraordinary alliance with the already widely divergent coalition which made up the Liberal Party. The outburst of feeling over the restoration of the hierarchy and the Liberal support for Italian unification interrupted this relationship, but thereafter it remained fairly constant. Especially when Irish Home Rule became a live issue, the priesthood and the Catholic press encouraged Catholic voters to support the Liberals, and because the legal supremacy of the Anglican Church, both in England and in Ireland, was obnoxious alike to Dissenters and to Roman Catholics, the priesthood was even prepared to give its support to bigoted Nonconformist candidates for Parliament sponsored by the Liberation Society. In return the great bulk of the Nonconformists remained faithful to Home Rule to the very end, unmoved by the telling argument of the Ulster leaders that Home Rule meant Rome Rule. The alliance of Roman Catholicism with Radicalism was an almost unique phenomenon in Europe for most of this period; it rested upon the sound foundation of a common discontent with the existing order.

CHAPTER I

THE CHURCH AND THE WORKING CLASSES[1]

1 *The Secularist Challenge*

THE 'FIFTIES AND 'SIXTIES of the nineteenth century were a critical time for English religion. The initial bitterness stirred by the Oxford Movement was dying down a little, but as the attention of the Anglo-Catholic party turned from historical and theological debate to the reform of the Liturgy there was new opportunity for dispute. Roman Catholicism was advancing, under the leadership of Wiseman (Archbishop of Westminster 1850–1864), and after him of Manning (1864–1892). The science of Biblical criticism was beginning to develop, especially in the work of F. C. Baur and the Tübingen school in Germany. The geological researches of Sir Charles Lyell were still the subject of controversy, and in 1859 came the shock of Darwin's *Origin of Species*. The next year the composite volume with the innocuous title *Essays and Reviews* indicated a marked advance of liberal and rationalistic tendencies in the Church of England, and there was something like a panic. In 1862, while feeling was still at its most sensitive, J. W. Colenso, Bishop of Natal, published the results of his researches on the Old Testament, with radical conclusions concerning Moses and the Pentateuch. Open hostility to religion became more prevalent. In 1851 Manning was not the only convert: there was also Joseph Barker (1806–1875).[2] In his earlier years he had moved from Wesleyanism into the Methodist New Connexion, and then, experimentally, among the smaller Dissenting bodies. In 1846 he had entered politics, advocating republicanism, repeal of the Union, and land nationalization; he supported Chartism, was imprisoned, and was elected to Parliament. In this year, 1851, he turned his back at once on Christianity and England, becoming a Deist and

---

[1] On the issues covered in this chapter see K. S. Inglis, *Churches and the Working Classes in Victorian England* (1963).

[2] John Thomas Barker (ed.), *The Life of Joseph Barker, written by himself* (1880).

removing to Ohio. In 1860 he returned to England, and for a short time was active in anti-religious propaganda, before drifting back to his earliest faith.

G. J. Holyoake was eleven years younger. He had come from a strict Evangelical home, but by now was nationally known as an enemy of religion, having to his credit a term of imprisonment (in 1842) for blasphemy. He was an outstanding figure in the history of the workers' movement, especially in the field of co-operation. He was a remarkable example of the association of religious and political radicalism, for while his origins were similar to those of other leading Victorian Radicals, men like Edward Miall remained firm in their support of Nonconformity, while for Holyoake Christianity was merely a point of departure against which his later life was a continuous reaction. As a boy he attended Carrs Lane Congregational Church, Birmingham, with his mother, under the ministry of John Angell James, the predecessor of R. W. Dale, and he recorded his boredom there. Yet for a time he was almost to be counted among the Christian Socialists, for he came to politics through religion: 'The habit I had acquired of frequenting chapels and missionary meetings led me to attend political assemblies. This further enlarged my views of life and duty, which the religion taught me had hidden from me.'[1] In the Birmingham Political Union, in which he served his political apprenticeship in the early eighteen-thirties, he found a colleague in a Unitarian minister, the Rev Hugh Hutton, and comments, neither truly nor grammatically: 'Only Unitarian ministers at that time would pray for Liberals, or who would pray among them.'[2] In some contradiction to this is the fact that he also records among the members a Roman Catholic priest, the Rev T. M. McDonnell. Gradually he found the atmosphere of Carrs Lane alien to his beliefs:

> For five years I was a scholar in the Carr's Lane Sunday Schools, yet save Watts's hymns and reading in the Bible, I had learned nothing . . . Once the Rev John Angell James, the pastor, delivered a week-night public address, in which he counselled young men to be content in the station and with the lot which Providence had assigned them. Dissent was no better than the Church as regarded secular progress. When I heard Mr James's counsel, I believed it.[3]

[1] G. J. Holyoake, *Sixty Years of an Agitator's Life* (4th impression 1900), I, 33.   [2] Ibid., I, 30f.   [3] Ibid., I, 33.

Later than this, however, he taught in a Unitarian Sunday School 'at the new Meeting House, locally known as Dr Priestley's Chapel,' at the same time retaining his 'Trinitarian belief with which they never interfered.'[1] Throughout his whole career Holyoake was in active co-operation with Christians, from alliance with Miall in the agitation for the abolition of the newspaper tax in 1855 to a long association with Hughes and other Christian Socialists in the co-operative movement, but his rationalistic views remained firm to his death in 1906.

Charles Bradlaugh[2] was younger still, but already launched upon his life's work of denouncing superstition, and while still in his teens (in 1849) he had been expelled from his home for his beliefs. After service in the army he became leader of a movement, largely working class, combining free thought in religion and republicanism in politics.

These three men represented different points of view, and Bradlaugh and Barker quarrelled, partly because Barker's unorthodoxy was more strictly confined to matters of religion than Bradlaugh's. But all of them had a wide following among the working classes, Bradlaugh for example attacking religion for regarding the misery of this world as nothing more than a preface to the blessings of the world to come. His atheism was intimately related to his political creed, and he 'always insisted that even in his purely theological disputes he was fighting for the poor of England.'[3] He was hostile to Socialism, a fact which ultimately led to his breach with his ally Annie Besant and alienated him from the leaders of the working classes; but for the moment he enjoyed wide support. It was symptomatic of the change which was occurring that the exponents of scepticism were beginning to address themselves chiefly to the working classes.

2 The Drift from the Church

But the activities of rationalists were only peripheral, and a far more important feature of the age was the spread of simple indifference to religion. From the very beginning of this period there were repeated laments at the decline of the Church, and

[1] Holyoake, op. cit., I, 47f.
[2] Hypatia Bradlaugh Bonner, *Charles Bradlaugh: A Record of his Life and Work* (7th Edition, 1908).
[3] C. Brinton, *English Political Thought in the Nineteenth Century* (1933), 242.

above all at the absence of the working classes. In 1851, when the only national census of church attendance was carried out, more than two-fifths of the population were in church. A series of private investigations in 1882 gave the following estimates of regular church attenders (as percentages of population) in various towns:[1] Sheffield 23, Nottingham 24, Liverpool 26, Bristol 31, Southampton 38, Hull 41, Portsmouth 41, Bath 52. The social contrast between the first-named and last-named towns was thus reflected in figures of church attendance. It was estimated that about 37% of those who did attend were to be found in the parish churches, compared with about half in 1851. The Roman Catholics were gaining ground and the Nonconformists were holding their own better than the Church of England.

In the great industrial centres the working classes were already largely absent from the churches before 1850. In 1840 St Philip's, Sheffield, a 'million' church[2] was the only Anglican church serving a parish said to contain 24,000 'labourers and mechanics,' and until recently it had had only one clergyman. It possessed 800 free seats, but far from being crowded these were 'too often thinly tenanted.' Rather remarkably the incumbent attributed the utter indifference to religion of the working classes to the example of their parents, who had been just the same.[3] Another clergyman taking part in a survey in 1843 gave evidence that very few of the parents of his Sunday School scholars attended church, and another survey published the same year stated:

> The artisans generally are not frequent attendants on a place of worship. It is stated, on authority which is the result of inquiry, that not one family in twenty is in the practice of visiting either Church or Chapel, indeed it is a duty in the performance of which the working classes are exceedingly lax, and the evil is not to be cured by the creation of religious accommodation.[4]

In the Bishop of Middleton's excellent book on Sheffield, from which this passage is quoted, the heading 'The Estrangement of the Common People' refers to the period 1800–1850: so early was the fact realized. One cause often quoted to explain this estrange-

[1] R. Lloyd, *The Church of England in the Twentieth Century*, Vol. I (1946), 59f.
[2] i.e. one provided by the fund of £1 million voted by Parliament in 1818.
[3] E. R. Wickham, *Church and People in an Industrial City* (1957), 87.
[4] Ibid., 92.

ment was the system of pew-rents. Even though the charges made might not seem heavy to the middle classes they could bear heavily on the poor, and in any case the system was a very plain demonstration of social distinctions at the very heart of the Church's life, a demonstration made all the plainer by the fact that often the free seats for the poor were those so badly situated that it would have been difficult to let them. There was often a complete gradation, from large and prominent pews near the front, through cheaper lettings in less eligible positions, down to free seats in remote corners or behind pillars. The number of free seats available bore no relation to the size of the working-class population, and the Nonconformist churches were often worse than the Anglican in providing for the poor, this being especially true, at any rate at Sheffield, of the Congregational churches. In 1841 the parish of Sheffield contained 112,492 persons. For them the thirteen Anglican churches provided a total of 15,000 seats, of which 6,000 were free. Thirty-seven Nonconformist churches seated 25,000, less than one-third without charge.[1]

In mid-Victorian times the drift from religion increased. The shocks of scientific progress were now felt throughout the whole social system, and disbelief, if it was still sometimes regarded as a misfortune to be endured rather than as a liberation, became the attitude of many intellectual leaders. Hitherto anti-religious views had been themselves a sort of religion, a prolongation of traditional anti-clericalism, but now many people were simply uninterested in religion, or else regarded it as a curious historical phenomenon, destined like others to pass away. Darwin, who lost interest in religion, Huxley, who invented agnosticism, and Matthew Arnold, who surveyed with dispassionate and analytical curiosity the alleged revelations of the traditional religions, represented the new mood. But these were the doubts and denials of intellectuals, and a better key to the age was the phenomenally successful novel *Robert Elsmere*, by Mrs Humphry Ward, who thought that the time had come for religion to give way to social service. Florence Nightingale, who kept fairly quiet about her antipathy to the official religion of England, was another example. This outlook conditioned the thought of the age.

An indication of the declining influence of the Church lies in the statistics of ordination to the Anglican ministry. These are

[1] Wickham, op. cit., 80. On class-feeling and its relation to pew-rents see pp. 112–119.

available in full only from 1877, when 678 deacons were ordained. The number rose year by year till 1886, but only in proportion to the rising population. In that year a peak was attained with 814 ordinations. Then the decline began.

In the 'nineties there was another change in atmosphere. There was little growth of hostility to religion, but there was a marked growth of indifference, and something of a reaction against the earnestness of the mid-Victorian period, an earnestness which had been fully shared by dissenters from all current beliefs. A generation earlier railway hotels had provided Bibles for use by businessmen on journeys, and three successive Lords Chancellor—Cairns, Hatherley, and Selborne—taught in Sunday Schools for most of their lives. The move away from a Puritan outlook on life affected the religious world itself. The severity particularly associated with the Evangelicals had marked every type of churchmanship; it reappeared in the asceticism of the Tractarians; it was characteristic of Maurice and Westcott, and it was continued in Gore. But other churchmen regarded the Puritan attitude of mind with open mockery—among them Stewart Headlam, Scott Holland and J. G. Adderley: 'Plain living and high thinking had given way to plain speaking and high spirits.'[1] But in the religious realm most people continued in the old vein, and the rebels against mid-Victorian moral seriousness often turned against the Church and inclined to a careless Epicureanism. The devotees of the cult of hedonism believed that they had the open sympathy of the Prince of Wales himself.

The Churches were largely absorbed in internal matters, and after 1870 the education question came to be a favourite topic for dispute between the denominations. In earlier times the Nonconformists had co-operated happily with the Evangelicals in the Church of England in the work of social reform, but now the rise of Anglo-Catholicism had broken the good relations with the Established Church, and the quarrel over education brought back a degree of bitterness which it had been thought belonged to the previous century. This dispute over education, ' a controversy which of all Victorian controversies is perhaps the hardest to recall with patience,'[2] harmed the Church because it seemed that religious leaders and their firmest supporters were

[1] M. B. Reckitt, *Maurice to Temple* (1947), 141.
[2] G. M. Young, *Victorian England: Portrait of an Age* (1936), 115.

primarily interested in matters of little concern to the working population: 'Anglicans and Nonconformists were quarrelling before the eyes of a public uninterested in religion of any kind.'[1] Moreover at a time when the income of the clergy was declining the advance of education offered increased opportunities of alternative employment for intelligent young men. Both the quantity and the quality of recruits to the ministry were affected, and the Nonconformists were touched as much as the Church of England.

By 1900 parish priests in the great cities were lamenting a 'slow but steady decline in church attendance.'[2] In 1903, when Randall Davidson became Archbishop of Canterbury, a census of worship in London had just been carried out by Mudie Smith and published in the *Daily News*. Compared with a similar census in 1886, the population having increased by half-a-million, gross total attendance (i.e. including double-counting of those who attended more than one service) had fallen from 1,167,321 to 1,003,361. The decline in the Church of England was much more severe than among the Nonconformists: Anglican worshippers went down from 535,715 to 396,196, while Nonconformist worshippers, excluding the Salvation Army and missions, declined only from 369,349 to 363,882. In London at least Nonconformity was much nearer to holding its own than the Established Church. Excluding dual attendances worshippers numbered 832,051 out of a population of 4,470,304, a proportion of $\frac{2}{11}$. In 1851, over the whole country, not very much less than half the population were to be found in church. In some places church attendance was apparently increasing. In Liverpool censuses taken by the *Liverpool Post* in 1881, 1891, and 1902 gave totals as follows: 149,469; 157,846; 178,477. But this advance fell below the growth of population, and Liverpool was exceptional in the influx of Irish Roman Catholics. One figure which was certainly increasing was that of Anglican communicants. In 1891–1892 they numbered 1,437,719; in 1896–1897, 1,886,059. But this reflected a changing attitude to Holy Communion: 'These figures are really a testimony to the devotion of the Anglo-Catholic movement.'[3] In Sheffield the Churches made

---

[1] Halévy, op. cit., *V. Imperialism and the Rise of Labour* (second edition, 1951), 169.
[2] Lloyd, op. cit., Vol. I (1946), 59.
[3] Ibid., 60.

very large gains in the period 1851–1881, but only kept pace with the rapidly rising population, and by 1900 they had passed their peak and begun to decline. Such progress as they had achieved was not with respect to the working classes: 'However impressive the years of growth, and however imposing the congregations of those days as we picture them in the imagination and compare them with the reduced numbers now worshipping in those same buildings, in respect of the working-class population the churches had made negligible gain.'[1]

In London clergy in various parts of the metropolis vied with one another in lamenting the paganism of their own particular areas. In 1900 an anonymous pamphlet about the St Pancras area protested against the subdivision of parishes, with the provision of the 'cheapest possible churches' lacking endowments. In the area four old churches had split into thirty new ones, and the author appealed for the whole area to be treated as a mission district, with large churches, each having a specialized staff of clergy. Such schemes were operated with success at various places, for example at Yarmouth, Leeds, Stepney, and in the very large parish of Portsea, but the Act of 1838 against pluralities still stood in the way of experiments, and exceptions still needed a special Act of Parliament.

In the great cities there was a marked shortage of clergy, and

---

[1] Wickham, op. cit., 150. Figures of church attendance in Sheffield in 1851 are given on page 109 and for 1881 on page 148. With the population up from 135,310 to 284,410 the following were the attendances for various denominations:

	1851	1881
Church of England	14,881	33,835
Independents	4,550	7,847
Baptists	2,344	3,206
Unitarians	1,000	1,188
Wesleyans	10,561	11,848
New Connexion	2,183	2,726
Primitive Methodists	2,527	5,402
Wesleyan Reform	130	2,526
United Methodists (in 1851 the Wesleyan Association)	402	7,146
Roman Catholics	4,000	5,473

The high figures for the minor Methodist groups are abnormal in that Sheffield was one of their strongholds.

where living conditions were least congenial the income was apt to be lowest. The thirty new parishes in St Pancras had incomes varying from £700 to £173. Anglo-Catholics, unwelcome elsewhere and ready for martyrdom, were in general the only clergy prepared to go to the worst areas: 'The Anglo-Catholic curate normally went to a slum parish. By 1900 that had become a tradition.' Such men worked hard, and they tried to identify themselves with their people.[1]

The working classes, if they read at all, read the *Clarion*, a paper edited by Robert Blatchford and bitterly hostile to Christianity. It is described as

> One of the most ably edited weeklies which had ever existed . . . The Church had nothing, nothing whatever, to put against it. The only interesting Church weekly papers were too busy denouncing other Christians to give much space to answering attacks on Christianity as such, and the other Church papers were scholarly but dull.[2]

The cost of training for the ministry meant that the clergy still constituted a 'class priesthood with a money qualification,' until a supply of poorer men began to flow through the Anglo-Catholic foundations at Mirfield and Kelham.

If Nonconformity was more successful at holding its own at this time, its success was only relative, for during the 'nineties it was steadily losing the hold it had had on the working classes. Charles Booth had found the worship of Congregationalists to be personal, with little social significance. The middle-class character of this denomination had become more marked, and this was what most struck Booth about it:

> The Congregational Church is more than any other the Church of the middle classes, its membership being practically confined within the upper and lower sections of those included under that comprehensive title. Where these classes prevail Congregationalists are to be found in force; where not, their Churches lead a struggling existence; and when owing to some change in the social character of a neighbourhood, old supporters leave, the chapels fall into disuse and one by one are either closed or pass into other hands.[3]

[1] Lloyd, op. cit., 136f.
[2] Ibid., 153.
[3] Quoted in John W. Grant, *Free Churchmanship in England 1870–1940* (no date), 171.

Nonconformist leaders were willing to substantiate Booth's testimony, and R. W. Dale considered that Congregationalists had a special mission to the middle classes. On its social side and in politics Nonconformity showed little sympathy with the aspirations of the working classes and was allied with the Manchester School of *laissez faire*.

3   *Efforts to recover the Working Classes*

However nostalgically twentieth-century church-goers may look back to a Victorian golden age when the churches were full, the clergy and leaders of the denominations at the time were quite aware of the fact that very many working-class people never went to church at all, and they made considerable efforts to find a cure. Some of these efforts were as follows:

(*a*) Increased church accommodation. One of the most obvious features of the age was the accumulation of population in the developing industrial areas, and some students of the situation thought that the all-important need was for more churches. The work of Bishop Blomfield was continued in the Church of England and in every other denomination, and the churches built in the industrial areas in Victorian times, whatever their architectural merits or defects, represent a remarkable achievement. In Sheffield the places of worship in 1851 and 1881 were as follows:[1]

	1851	1881
Church of England	23	50
Independent	10	22
Baptist	4	6
Unitarian	1	2
Wesleyan	16	29
New Connexion	5	12
Primitive Methodist	1	25
Wesleyan Reform	2	15
United Methodist (in 1851 Wesleyan Association)	2	15
Roman Catholic	1	6

The number of seats provided increased similarly:

	1851	1881
Church of England	19,562	32,751
Independent	4,486	10,900

[1] Wickham, op. cit., 148.

Baptist	2,220	3,200
Unitarian	900	1,100
Wesleyan	10,479	14,917
New Connexion	1,952	5,342
Primitive Methodist	1,000	8,904
Wesleyan Reform	(not given)	3,720
United Methodist	670	8,178
Roman Catholic	950	2,715

The figures of buildings erected or brought into use, analysed into three roughly equal periods, are also of interest:[1]

	1841–1865	1866–1890	1891–1914
Church of England	10	16	11
Independent	6	8	4
Baptist	3	3	4
Wesleyan	1	17	18
New Connexion	3	4	2
Primitive Methodist	9	18	9
Wesleyan Reform	12	5	3
United Methodist	4	11	3
Roman Catholic	3	4	3

These figures reveal a certain falling-away in the last period, although the population continued to rise rapidly. The denominations listed opened eighty-six churches in the period 1866–1890, but only fifty-seven in the period 1891–1914. In some denominations the slowing down was obvious: in the first thirty-seven years of the period the Independents opened thirteen churches, in the last thirty-seven only five; while the New Connexion opened only two new churches after 1878.

Further statistics were provided by the newspaper, the *Nonconformist*. It is worth mentioning here that this journal provided the medium for the most vigorous expression of the political and social convictions of the Nonconformists, representing the standpoint of Edward Miall and bearing on every issue the ebullient motto: 'The Dissidence of Dissent and the Protestantism of the Protestant Religion.' It was in effect the voice of the Liberation Society (officially the Society for the Liberation of Religion from State Patronage and Control), which had been founded in 1844 to campaign for the disestablishment of the

[1] Wickham, op. cit., Appendix V (b), 281ff.

Church of England. It was therefore from the start a highly political journal, though for many years it gave comparatively little attention to the working classes. Sometimes its propaganda against the Church of England had a wider interest than usually attaches to sectarian polemics. In 1872–1873 there were several articles collecting statistics of church accommodation in the towns of England and Wales. The purpose was threefold: (1) to show that the Church of England was only a minority Church; (2) to show that the provision of church accommodation was keeping pace with the increase of population, and this not only in the case of the Church of England, so that it might be argued that the great endowments of the Established Church could not be defended as the necessary means of catering for the rising population; (3) to show that in fact non-established churches were actually doing *better* in this respect than the Church of England, with all its privileges. This approach had the great advantage, from the point of view of the disestablishment movement, that the Roman Catholics could be added to the Nonconformists, which naturally was a great help in proving the points involved. The interest from the point of view of social history is in the changing pattern of the religious life of the towns, though the change is measured only by the comparatively imprecise standard of seating accommodation, not membership or attendance.

The first of the statistical supplements[1] dealt with fourteen towns with populations of over 100,000. Since the census of 1851 their population had increased by 42·4%, the church sittings by 44%. The Church of England accounted for 42% of the sittings in 1851 and 40·2% in 1872. The biggest proportionate increases were in the case of the Roman Catholics (63·7%, which was attributed to Irish immigration) and in those of the Primitive Methodists, the United Methodists, and the Presbyterians, which had all about doubled. In the second supplement there was a similar survey of twenty towns with populations of between 50,000 and 100,000. Here the proportion of Anglican sittings had gone down from 38% in 1851 to 33% in 1872; the biggest increases were of Roman Catholics, Congregationalists, and Primitive and United Methodists. The third supplement dealt with thirty towns of 20,000 to 50,000 people. As in the previous cases, the accommodation had increased more than proportionately to

[1] The supplements were published with the issues of October 23rd, November 6th, and December 4th, 1872, and January 8th, 1873.

population. The Church of England share had fallen from 48·7% to 43·6%, with the largest increases by the Presbyterians and then by the same smaller Methodist bodies. The fourth supplement covered a further twenty towns in the 20,000 to 50,000 range (for which the results were similar) and also included a general summary of the investigation. For all the towns covered where full figures were available the population was up by 34·4%, the seating by 49·2%. The Anglican sittings were up by 34%, the others by 59·1%. The non-established Churches now provided 60% of the seats. The largest increase of all was for the Presbyterians (151%); then came the Primitive and United Methodists (over 100%). It was noted that these two smaller denominations (though the Primitives were fairly substantial) were predominantly working class, so disproving the allegation that Nonconformity as a whole was losing its hold upon that class. The Roman Catholics showed an 80% increase, again attributed to immigration; the Congregationalists and Baptists 50–60%; and the Church of England and the Wesleyans each 34%. When allowance is made for the fact that the United Methodists and the Presbyterians were small denominations the most striking fact was the 80% increase in Roman Catholic accommodation; certainly the increase of Catholics was overwhelmingly due to the influx of Irish, but, bearing in mind that many of these were very poor, it was a great achievement to have increased so greatly the church accommodation available to receive them. It is also plain that in the urban areas, where the main body of the working classes was to be found, Nonconformity was doing better than the Church of England, though the Wesleyans, the most moderate body within Nonconformity, were a marked exception. In the towns and cities Nonconformity was becoming stronger relatively to the Anglican Church (though not relatively to the Roman Catholic Church), and it was becoming more Nonconformist—a discovery calculated to give immense satisfaction to the kind of Dissenters who took their lead from the *Nonconformist*.

(*b*) An attempt to dispel the conviction that the Church was the preserve of the more prosperous classes. This was a theme often recurring in the press—and in this case it was the Anglican press which was most closely concerned. Among the newspapers of the Church of England the *Guardian* was outstanding. It was the creation of R. W. Church, whose name may be coupled with Liddon's as those of the most influential of the second-generation leaders of the Anglo-Catholic party. Its foundation dated from 1846, and it was designed to rally Tractarianism after the shocks of Newman's conversion and the onslaught of indignant Protestantism, but it was never merely a party paper, and never kindled a very warm enthusiasm among the more extreme Ritualists, having in some ways the flavour of the old, pre-Oxford Movement High Anglicanism. Politically the *Guardian* was Gladstonian until Gladstone became undeniably a Liberal, and even afterwards he remained for it the most respected English statesman; it had no time for Disraeli. A generation later the more thorough Anglo-Catholics founded a distinctly party paper, the *Church Times*. Later still the latter followed the example of its predecessor and sank into respectability.

The *Guardian* was not likely to suggest drastic changes in the Anglican system for the purpose of attracting the missing classes, but it did give a lukewarm recognition to the fact that something needed to be done. It was thought possible, for example, that the labours of the clergy might be supplemented by the appointment of lay assistants by a kind of 'minor Ordination.'[1] In 1856 two articles discussed the question of the 'social position of the clergy.' The first[2] offered a general defence of the selection of the clergy from the upper classes, on the grounds of their 'refinement,' and included a section which, with a change of tone, might almost be from the writings of Marx:

> There is also a political advantage in a clergy of gentlemen. Most men of any thought must occasionally have wondered how the masses, as they are called—not religious enough to be contented with any road to heaven—not shrewd enough to see that men who live by labour will never get much by violence—not good-natured enough to take everything as it comes—yet go on, year after year, submitting without a struggle to the unmerited inequality of lot, which by God's will, is the law of this world. It is no small security for the peace of this nation that 17,000 men scattered throughout the country, in positions which give them access to the poor at all times when they are most open to influence, are connected in habits and prospects, by blood and acquaintance and prepossessions, with what has been called the upper 10,000. And this is not merely advantageous to the rich, it is an advantage to all, if, at least, it is an advantage that all should be encouraged to labour quietly in the vocation to which God has called them.

[1] *Guardian*, April 24th, 1851.
[2] Ibid., December 10th, 1856.

But then the article goes on to admit that the Church has not the influence over the 'manufacturing classes' which it has over the upper classes and over the agricultural labourers; and among the causes of this failure 'it is impossible not to place the social and political position of the clergy.' The conclusion is that more diversity is needed, and it emerges at the end that one purpose of the article is to give a rather cautious defence of the introduction of celibate orders into the Anglican ministry.

The second article[1] answers objections which might be made to the admission of members of the lower classes into the ministry, denying, for example, that this would discourage the entry of wealthy persons, who contributed more, financially, than they took away. The creation of a diaconate of lower-class clergy from the parish schools is advocated; it does not appear that such deacons could rise into the priesthood, so that such a plan, if it had been adopted, would indeed have introduced a caste system into the clergy.

Later the debate shifted to the pages of the *Church Times*. An article entitled 'No Coppers Taken' (referring to the alleged rejection of copper from a church collection) dwelt on the failure of the Church of England to attract the poor, and on the importance of this question,[2] while a leading article sympathized with protests that members of the working classes who attended the Working Men's Meeting at the Church Congress were not allowed to speak.[3] In the autumn of 1871 there was an interesting discussion arising out of the suggestion made by a correspondent that advertisements should be inserted in *Lloyd's Weekly News* assuring the working classes that the High Church clergy were their best friends, and the *Church Times* took up this issue in two articles. The first quoted Taine, to the effect that it was an advantage to the English clergy that they were drawn from higher social levels than the French, agreeing with his judgement and rejecting the argument that the success of Dissent was due to a working-class ministry. Dissenting ministers were alleged to be the servants of the laity, and their success was attributed to 'shrewdness' and 'plain speaking' rather than to their social origins. A 'peasant clergy' would alienate the upper classes. The following week it was claimed that the *Church Times* had always

[1] *Guardian*, December 17th, 1856.
[2] *Church Times*, August 13th, 1869.
[3] Ibid., October 21st, 1870.

tried to 'fight the battle of the people,' and now the time had come for the foundation of a new political party. The duty of the Church was to protect the poor, to secure for everyone 'a fair day's wage for a fair day's work,' and to 'maintain the great maxim of Christian economy, the equality of all men in the eyes of the Creator.' Such a programme would rouse a cry of 'Communism,' but one ought not to be frightened by mere names. The sources of contemporary distresses were 'Puritanism and political selfishness,' and the great reform needed was the creation of 'communes' like the ancient guilds.[1]

This debate reveals two characteristic features of the *Church Times*. First, it was much freer than the *Guardian* from the current economic shibboleths, and spoke of a 'Christian economy,' implying that there should be a theological or ethical criterion by which economic systems might be tested. But second, this relative independence of judgement was restricted by a narrow party outlook, for usually the *Church Times* was more concerned with seeking advantages for the Anglo-Catholic party than with anything else.

(*c*) Special services and lectures. At the very beginning of this period an effort of this kind was responsible for involving the Christian Socialists in one of their many controversies. On the occasion of the Great Exhibition a series of sermons was arranged at St John's, Finsbury Square, on the message of the Church to the rich and the poor. The first sermon was preached by F. W. Robertson of Brighton, the most fashionable of mid-nineteenth century preachers, yet something of a Christian Socialist himself. Robertson denounced the submissiveness of the Church to the rich and its failure to demand justice for the poor. The second sermon was even stronger meat; it was preached by Charles Kingsley, who insisted that it was the duty of the Church to preach Liberty, Equality and Fraternity, and at its close the incumbent stood up to express indignant disapproval. In protest F. D. Maurice, who had been invited to preach the third and final sermon of the series, now refused to do so, and in fact Maurice defended Kingsley so vigorously that Bishop Blomfield was involved and for a time forbade him to preach in London.

The Evangelicals sometimes organized services in theatres, a method most of them would regard as carrying the war into the enemy's country, but it was not a method approved by all Angli-

[1] *Church Times*, October 13th and October 20th, 1871.

cans. In 1860 Viscount Dungannon moved a resolution in the House of Lords condemning the holding of services in Sadler's Wells and other theatres, conducted by Anglican clergymen. There was of course a valid objection from the point of view of the Church of England, in that any such service necessarily fell in the parish of some incumbent who might himself be far from enthusiastic; but it was an attempt to meet a difficulty which constantly inhibited efforts at mass evangelism in this period, as in that of John Wesley, the rigidity of the parochial system. In the debate the Archbishop of Canterbury (J. B. Sumner) said that he did not approve of such services, but was not prepared to forbid them, and Lord Shaftesbury, who was the chief force behind this campaign, as behind so many Evangelical activities, said that not 2% of the working men of London attended church. The incumbent of St Thomas's, Lambeth—on Sumner's own doorstep—had said that the moral and spiritual condition of the district was worse than that of Sierra Leone. The Bishop of London, who was the dignitary most directly involved, followed the Primate's lead, saying that while he was not in favour of the services he would not agree to the institution of legal proceedings against them.[1]

In a later period, A. W. Thorold, Bishop of Rochester from 1877 to 1891, an Evangelical, whose diocese included most of south London, established mission districts in the great working-class areas, with services held in any available place till a church could be built.

The press was not very interested in this kind of approach. Typically, a long report in the *Guardian* on a service for the working classes at St Paul's Cathedral gave more attention to the music than to anything else.[2] A volume of sermons designed to stir up the wealthy to remedy the distresses of the East End, and a book giving an account of the Church's work in large towns received favourable reviews.[3]

(*d*) An alternative approach was the establishment of special places of worship for the working classes, not merely as a short-term measure till an ordinary church could be built, but as an expression of the belief that even from the long-term point of

[1] R. Sandall, *History of the Salvation Army* (1950), I, 13f.
[2] *Guardian*, August 15th, 1877.
[3] Ibid., August 17th, 1870; and June 12th, 1872. For an account of measures adopted in Sheffield see Wickham, op. cit., 150–158.

view the working classes needed special treatment. The *Guardian* carried a lengthy article in 1857 describing the opening of a 'Poor Man's Church' in Stepney, at which the Bishop of London, the Dean of Westminster, Mr Gladstone, and F. D. Maurice were present.[1] As might be guessed from such a list a number of long speeches were made, and several resolutions were carried. Another method often recommended was the abolition of pew-rents, which were indeed increasingly a source of dissension, for they seemed to create a private property in religion, and the increase in the proportion of free seats in churches was a prime object of reformers, in Nonconformity as well as in the Church of England.

(*e*) In late Victorian times the conviction increased that in order to bring the workers to church the Church must go to the workers, not merely in adapting its own procedures to attract them, but in concerning itself with those social questions which pressed daily upon the lives of the poor. In the *Guardian* a leading article called attention to the pamphlet *The Bitter Cry of Outcast London*, which dealt with the slums, and said that in tackling this particular problem 'the principle of *laissez faire* should be thrust somewhat rudely to the wall.' The plea that the Church itself should become an agency of social reform was rejected: 'The Church, as a Church, is not directly concerned with these matters.' An article rather like a sermon, by Llewelyn Davies, on 'The Rich and the Poor,' aimed to rouse the Church to awareness of the dangers of riches and also of the virtues of the poor. A leader was called forth by a memorial published by a group of London clergy on the duty of the rich to the poor, though the *Guardian* thought that the appeal to share was not always practicable, and that the demand that Christians should refuse to buy goods produced by sweated labour was contrary to economics. This increased interest in the relations of the Church and the poor significantly coincided with concern about the spread of atheism among the poor, but the *Guardian* was inclined to agree with an article in the *Fortnightly Review* which denied that it was widespread.[2]

(*f*) Such interest in the lower orders was all very well, but it did not establish contact with the active leaders of the organized working classes, who belonged to a very different stratum of society from the depressed elements of the slums. Some attempt was made

[1] *Guardian*, February 4th, 1857.
[2] Ibid., November 7th, 1883; February 18th, 1885; August 11th, 1886; March 2nd, 1887; June 13th, 1888.

by the Church to talk with this class too, particularly by the Nonconformists. Among the Dissenters Miall's *Nonconformist* took the lead, with a letter in 1866 from the Rev Edward White, proposing a conference on the subject of Christianity and the Working Classes. The newspaper supported the idea, admitting that the working classes 'are almost wholly beyond the range of our religious institutions,' and refusing to find comfort in the fact that this might well have been true for several generations. When the suggested conference was held the *Nonconformist* gave it a report of the kind which died out with the Victorian leisured class: three pages of the main issue and four pages of a supplement were filled with fine print. Many leaders of the Church of England and Nonconformity were present, including Maurice, and Miall himself was in the chair. The *Nonconformist* was very satisfied with it:

> It was tolerably conclusively established, we think, that the ordinary arrangements, methods, habits, and work of our religious organizations are essentially middle class in their character, having but an oblique and very secondary reference to the sympathies and wants of the daily or weekly wage-earning class of the community. It is not, indeed, excluded—it is not wholly neglected—but it is not cared for and dealt with in a brotherly spirit . . . Our social system which is a relic of feudalism, has intruded itself into the sacred precincts of the Church . . . On the whole religion, as administered amongst us, has been preponderantly on the side of worldly power, rank, and wealth, and has been too little known as the friend of the friendless, the helper of the helpless, the protector of the oppressed, the lifter-up of the down-trodden, the champion of man's rights, the tender mother of all.

On the other hand it was felt that many of the criticisms of the Church made by members of the working classes at the conference were no more than excuses. The *Nonconformist* was pleased at the widespread interest the conference had aroused, and believed that the ice had been broken, though there could not be any such thing as a Gospel adapted to the working classes. The growth of Ritualism was one obstacle to the evangelization of the workers. The Church of England itself came in for some rare (but still very grudging) praise for the attention given to this topic at the Lambeth Conference and the Church Congress in 1867.[1]

A generation later the same issue was still debated. There had

---

[1] *Nonconformist*, October 31st, 1866; January 23rd, March 20th, October 9th, 1867.

been a time when it had seemed a good idea to hold a working men's meeting at the Church Congress, but by 1897 the *Guardian* was advocating its abolition, because it had been found to have a patronizing character.[1] This is a significant comment: often it happened that some individual or group would feel strongly about the alienation of the working classes and adopt some means of ending it, only to find that these means themselves underwrote the separation of classes by treating the working classes as something distinct and peculiar. Sometimes well-meant efforts at contact with Labour leaders made matters worse. Thus in 1890 an invitation was given to Ben Tillett to address the Church Congress, but the project fell through, with considerable ill-feeling, after protests that he was not an Anglican. The *Church Times* had a leader on this incident, regretting its occurrence, and rejecting Tillett's allegation that the Church of England was a Church of Capitalists, as well as his appeal to Anglicans to 'democratize the Church' and forget about theology.[2] The *Nonconformist* had by this date fallen on evil days, and in September 1890 it changed its name to the *Independent* and became the official organ of Congregationalism, though without very long delaying its demise, but it could not let pass an occasion when the Church of England had made itself look silly. It claimed Tillett as a Congregationalist, and of course blamed the Anglican authorities for the fiasco, welcoming a conference between Tillett and a group of London Congregational ministers:

> In these days of trade organizations it is of extreme importance that leaders in our churches should have personal, and, if possible, intimate acquaintance with the leaders of local Labour. They are worth knowing, and worth knowing well. They are often the very pick of their class. They are far more interesting than the rank and file of what are called 'good families.'

There were plenty of working men in the churches; they should be given responsible office—and indeed they often were. Tillett's appeal to the churches to support the Labour movement was largely sound, though material progress was not everything. Congregationalists ought to pay special attention to the working classes, if only in self-interest: 'The upper layers of Independency are continually scaling off. Piety is not so hereditary as wealth . . . Verily, how hardly shall they that have riches enter—for more

[1] *Guardian*, October 6th, 1897.
[2] *Church Times*, October 3rd, 1890.

than one generation at least—into a Congregational chapel!' There was a welcome for a conference of Nonconformists and Labour leaders, chaired by the Rev K. C. Anderson.[1]

In the middle of the 'eighties the Nonconformists gained a more powerful voice than they had hitherto possessed with the foundation of the *British Weekly*. The character of the new journal was indicated in the first issue, which announced its belief in progress, and its dedication to the ends of 'Advanced Liberalism.' Like the *Independent* it blamed the Church of England for the Tillett incident, and as late as 1892 it was back again on the old question of how to attract the working classes to church, favouring the establishment of working men's churches in poor districts. It was true, as some people said, that Christ was the friend of the rich as well as the poor, but for the *British Weekly* it was a different kind of friendship in the two cases: 'He wished to help both by altering their position; but the rich he would bless by making them poorer, and the poor he would bless by making them richer.' In the next few issues twenty-six letters on this theme were published, disagreeing as to whether there was in fact class-feeling in the Churches.[2]

A related matter was the intervention of the clergy in trade disputes, of which more will be said later. The *Guardian* denied that it was sufficient merely to urge 'forbearance and charity,' for sometimes, as in the case of the 1889 dock strike, it was a positive duty to 'interfere,' and Cardinal Manning had been quite right to intervene 'outside his province.' The Church was said to have a 'grave responsibility' in social matters, though the clergy were not to imagine that social reform was their whole duty.[3] In the *Church Times* similar arguments appeared in letters. Leo XIII's Encyclical of 1891 on social issues raised the question again, and a leader in the *Church Times* criticized it for rejecting all forms of Socialism. Not all Socialists were Communists: 'Many of the most fruitful thinkers in the ranks of the economists of the day are Socialists.' This article went on to attack Roman Catholics, and especially Manning, for political irresponsibility: 'With him the labourer is

[1] *Independent*, January 16th, February 6th, March 13th, 1891; September 2nd, 1892.

[2] *British Weekly*, October 2nd, 1890; October 27th, November 3rd, 1892; correspondence November 10th to December 8th, 1892.

[3] *Guardian*, July 23rd, 1890; January 27th, April 20th, August 17th, 1892.

ever in the right as against his employer, the tenant as against his landlord, the poor as against the rich, the Radical as against the Conservative, the Socialist as against the individualist.'[1]

In discussing the Church Congress of 1892 the *Guardian* confessed to a 'confused weariness' occasioned by reading the debates on the Labour question, and was moving away from belief in clerical 'interference,' criticizing speeches which seemed to suggest that the Church existed merely for social reform. The Lambeth Conference of 1897 was praised for having adopted the principles of the Christian Social Union in its discussion of social problems, and in 1899 it was denied that the influence of the clergy was declining because they were no longer called upon as frequently as before to arbitrate in disputes, for it used to be 'assumed that a great many things were the business of the clergy which are now seen to be the business of the Church, that is, of expert Christian laymen.'[2]

The *Independent* offered a quite penetrating criticism of the Papal Encyclical. It was late in the day for a pronouncement of this kind, and Leo 'has done little, if anything, more than to remind all parties to the employment of labour of their respective individual duties; in other words, he takes existing relations as he finds them, without inquiry or criticism, and enforces the duty proper to each.' But there was need also to criticize the basis itself.[3] The *British Weekly* pointed out that it was not generosity but justice which the poor were demanding. The question was asked whether ministers should preach about politics, to which the answer was a reserved affirmative, and a sympathetic sermon by R. F. Horton, on the demand for an eight-hour day, was printed. On the death of Manning the *British Weekly* gave the highest praise to the Roman Catholic Cardinal for his relations with the working classes, while a sermon preached at St Paul's to the poor (mostly absent) was ridiculed as a collection of platitudes.[4]

4   *Bishop Fraser*

In these efforts to recover the allegiance of the working classes the dominant figure, at least within the Church of England, was

[1] *Church Times*, July 25th, August 1st, 1890; June 5th, 1891.

[2] *Guardian*, October 12th, 1892; October 18th, November 1st, 1893; August 18th, 1897; October 25th, 1899.

[3] *Independent*, May 22nd, 1891.

[4] *British Weekly*, September 12th, 1890; November 5th, 1891; January 21st, 1892.

James Fraser (1818–1885) whose prominence was chiefly in the 'seventies. He became well known in 1867 when Rector of Ufton Nervet, Berkshire, as a member of the Royal Commission on the employment of children in agriculture, devoting himself assiduously to this work and interviewing large numbers of workers, with whose problems he showed a wide sympathy. In his report he described the system of co-operative farming in use at Assington and advocated agricultural co-operation. In 1870 he became Bishop of Manchester, at first sight a curious choice of a man with a rural background. As Bishop he felt that 'the great function of Christianity is to elevate man in his social condition.' On his becoming Bishop it

took him only a few weeks to make up his mind that the Church in Lancashire, if she was ever to fulfil her mission as he understood it, must take quite new ground with the two most numerous sections of the people, the factory operatives and skilled mechanics, and the mass of unskilled labour and destitution below, which is commonly known as 'the residuum.' Accordingly, always with the consent, and generally with the hearty approval, of the great employers of labour, whom he approached through the local clergy, he attended at such establishments as the St John's Carriage Works, the Atlas Iron Works, and the Gorton Railway Works in the dinner hour, and gave addresses, prefaced by two or three collects and the Lord's Prayer, to such of the mechanics and labourers as chose to attend. In the same way, and for like purposes, he gathered the boatmen on the canals, the scavengers, and the night-soil men, in any suitable room which could be borrowed or hired in the neighbourhood of their work . . . The factory hands, and working people generally, were taken as it were by storm, and had installed him long before the end of the year in a place in their hearts which he never lost.[1]

Fraser's connexions with trade unionism and the co-operative movement will be noted below. He also had something to say on the 'evangelization of the masses,' taking part in a discussion under that heading in Convocation in 1884. He urged the extension of the diaconate and the use of lay helpers, but withheld judgement on the Church Army, protesting against a 'tendency to lawlessness in their work.' But he realized the need for the Church to break away in an imaginative manner from past traditions in order to attract the poor, and in urging the giving of more instruction on

[1] Thomas Hughes, *James Fraser, Second Bishop of Manchester* (1887), 194f.

the liturgy he commented: 'The poor cannot find their way about our prayer book.' He also hoped to see a breaking-down of class barriers: 'Again I think the rich have still far too much influence in parochial arrangements. I want to see agricultural labourers and artisans appointed as sidesmen in parishes.' He was worried at 'the increase of the dangerous, that is to say the idle, classes at both ends of the social scale.'[1]

5   The Slum Ritualists

Fraser was a Low Churchman, and one of the outstanding features of his episcopate at Manchester was his friendliness with Nonconformists. He tried to break down the barriers of denominationalism as well as of class, and he made little of the established and privileged position of the Church of England. At the other extreme were the Anglo-Catholics, with their emphasis on the vital importance of church order, and in some cases a sympathy with the Roman Catholic Church. But extremes sometimes meet. After the first few years of the Anglo-Catholic movement an extraordinary change came over it. Its founders, especially Newman and Pusey, were the intellectual *élite* of the Church of England, while many of their followers were busy parish priests with no scholarly pretensions. The Tractarians were originally thorough Anglicans, looking back to the neglected teachings of the High Church tradition, especially of the seventeenth century; and those who, like Newman, went beyond the Laudian divines, made the whole journey to Rome. The new generation went farther in a number of directions than earlier Anglicans; they were eager to disown the name of Protestant and were filled with an unrequited affection for the Roman Church; yet most of them remained in the Church of their upbringing. Most striking of all was the emergence of Ritualism. The Tracts were primarily concerned with church order, the dignity and authority of the ministry, and the validity of a 'Catholic' interpretation of certain doctrines, such as those relating to Baptism; but now those who had learned from them to emphasize the catholicity of the Church of England added the rediscovery of ornate symbolism in worship. The Anglo-Catholic revival began in the senior common rooms of Oxford, in earnest and acrimonious debate on credal minutiae, but a couple of decades later it was centred in East End churches where Protestant

[1] Hughes, op. cit., 324f.

susceptibilities were offended by the celebration of High Mass with full canonicals.

The ritualistic clergy are important in Church history partly because they ministered to the population of the slums. It is one more contrast with the Tractarians that the latter were not socially conscious, except in emphasizing the traditional duties of the prosperous to the poor, though there was a partial exception in W. G. Ward, who argued that the Church must be a 'poor man's Church,' and claimed that theology had more benefits to offer to large towns than political economy, which he meant to be a considerable claim. But at this stage a social theory to stimulate and regulate practice was lacking. To a certain extent the choice of a slum parish was forced upon the young ritualist curate, for on the whole he found no welcome except in a parish no one else wanted; but the choice was accepted gladly. Service in the most difficult and least desirable neighbourhoods was a kind of martyrdom for the cause; it was a witness to the sacrificial devotion inspired by the Catholic faith, and it made possible the introduction of radical changes in forms of worship. For in the typical country parish a wealthy patron might intervene decisively to defend old ways. There was also a feeling that the colour and pageantry which the Reformation had eliminated were all the more needed in the drab and sordid surroundings of the slums.

Perhaps the best-known ritualist parish was St George's in the East, in London. Alexander Mackonochie and Charles Lowder were curates there together in the 'fifties and 'sixties and they combined two offences against the established order by introducing elaborate ritual and by denouncing sweated labour. They experienced the same mild persecution which fell on ritualists everywhere, and it was alleged that Jewish employers encouraged outraged Protestants to take action against the innovators. As a High Churchman of more moderate views Septimus Hansard was appointed to the parish, on the recommendation of Thomas Hughes, but he brought little comfort to the local employers, being an active Socialist. The same parish attracted Arthur Stanton (1839–1913), a fiery ritualist and politician, who, at the time of the Paris Commune of 1871

> rejoiced with Lacordaire to see Liberty, Fraternity, and Equality on the walls of Paris and, thus inspired, founded among his parishioners 'The Brotherhood of Jesus of Nazareth,' which aimed at

uniting men of different classes in the love and service of their Divine Master.[1]

Stanton's protégé was Robert Dolling (1851–1902),[2] who before his ordination was warden of the St Martin's Postmen's League, founded by Stanton. Dolling was ordained in 1883 and worked in Stepney, later moving to Portsmouth. There, in 1890, he was involved in a vigorous controversy with the Bishop of Winchester after inviting Stewart Headlam to lecture for him, and two years later he preached a sermon on 'The Clergyman's Place in Politics,' defending his support for a Radical candidate for Parliament. He was active in Labour politics, being associated with the trade union movement and such familiar campaigns as 'the land for the people' and the 'living wage.' He once preached a sermon at Notting Hill for the Christian Social Union with a title neatly expressive of the feelings of the working classes: 'Justice first, Charity afterwards.' But he was essentially a parish priest, unafraid of public controversy but chiefly concerned to minister to the needs of the poor around his church.

This group was the most prominent succession of slum ritualists, but other parts of London and some of the other large cities received similar devoted service. Obloquy, riots, and even imprisonment (for ignoring court injunctions to cease certain ritualistic practices) were often their fate and also the basis of their growing success and reputation. Thus in 1875 the suspension of Mackonochie from his parish of St Alban's, Holborn, produced several leading articles and a considerable correspondence in the *Church Times* referring to protests by working men and the consequent formation of the Church of England Working Men's Society.[3]

Parallel to the slum ritualists was the work of the Anglican religious Orders. The revival of conventual Orders, which did more almost than Ritualism to offend Protestant feeling, was a direct, though delayed, consequence of the Oxford Movement. Some of the Orders, mainly among women, were especially formed for work in the slums, and it is perhaps not cynical to say that this work served as good propaganda when the Orders were attacked, for to some people it might seem difficult to condemn men and

---

[1] G. C. Binyon, *The Christian Socialist Movement in England* (1931), 101f.

[2] J. Clayton, *Father Dolling: A Memoir* (1902).

[3] *Church Times*, July 2nd to November 12th, 1875.

women who selflessly gave their whole lives to the service of the outcasts of society. In debate it was this aspect of their lives which was stressed rather than, for example, the vows of chastity and obedience.

It is doubtful how important from the point of view of working-class advance the Anglo-Catholic work in the slums really was. Devotedly as the ritualist clergy gave themselves to the service of the working classes, very few active leaders of the workers were High Anglicans. One reason is that the class which Lowder and Stanton served was not the intelligent and ambitious 'aristocracy of labour' from which leaders arose. But two other reasons can be added. These priests, despite their active interest in politics and their realization, which the Evangelicals had often lacked, that religious and social advances were necessarily associated with each other, were too medieval in outlook. They were reformers, perhaps revolutionaries, but they could not be progressives, or Liberals in the broad sense, and they did not believe that social reform and the breaking down of class barriers were matters of overriding importance for the Christian. Despite 'Young England' and Hyndman, the English working classes obstinately refused to believe that the Liberals were as bad as the Tories. They shared with Gladstone, as against Tories and Marxists and all types of 'Catholics,' the conviction that peaceful and continuous secular reform was possible and desirable. The other limitation of the Anglo-Catholics was their paternalism: the more they strove to identify themselves with their people the more they stood out as priests, shepherding their flocks with a degree of authority not possible for a thorough Protestant. They were saintly men, but the leaders of the working classes needed more scope for self-assertion than they permitted to their parishioners.

6   *The Position of Nonconformity*

For a large part of this period Nonconformity was at least holding its own relatively to the Church of England and still keeping a fairly firm grip on the sections of society which had traditionally been Nonconformist, but two changes were rapidly modifying its character. First, it was becoming secularized. At one time some Dissenters had been noted for a pietist detachment from the affairs of the world, but now they were more and more politically minded. The protagonist of this transformation was

Edward Miall (1809–1881).[1] Significantly, and untypically of his denomination, Miall, who was native to Portsmouth, came from a poor background. He entered the Congregational ministry at Leicester—again perhaps significantly, in view of the traditional Radicalism of that city—where he took an interest in working-class conditions, though for the moment without entering politics. But once he had found his feet he wrote bitterly against the Church of England, the Tory party, and the aristocracy. He was one of a small group of Radicals who tried to establish links between the Chartists and the more respectable middle-class reforming organizations, on a platform of manhood suffrage, and by supporting the Anti-Corn Law League he persuaded Joseph Sturge, John Bright, and other League leaders to join in conferences in Birmingham in 1842 with the Chartist leaders Lovett, O'Brien, and Henry Vincent. In 1845 Miall stood for Parliament for Southwark on a Chartist programme, opposing the Liberal Sir William Molesworth, who was elected. In 1847 he stood for Halifax, in partnership with Ernest Jones, who was soon to be almost the last of the Chartists, when all the other leaders had given up the cause for lost. Indeed Jones was so thorough a Chartist as to be the only one to receive the full approval of modern Marxists. Neither Miall nor Jones was elected, but Miall was successful at Rochdale in 1852 and sat in Parliament till 1857, when he was one of the Radicals to lose their seats for opposing Palmerston. In 1869 he returned to Parliament as one of the members for Bradford, and in the House of Commons he continued his Radicalism and his support of working-class causes. Miall controlled the *Eclectic Review*, of which it has been said:

> Readers of this excellent periodical will look in vain for an article of mystical aspiration or religious meditation. Under colour of making war against clericalism, embodied in the worship of the Establishment, it spoke of nothing but Free Trade, the franchise, and the individual's political rights, and thus, instead of making Radicalism Christian it ended by secularizing Christianity.[2]

For a time Miall was looked upon with some suspicion by his co-religionists, but in time he won their complete support.

In the 'seventies a more marked secularization began, and the movement for disestablishment, ostensibly based on spiritual

---

[1] Arthur Miall, *The Life of Edward Miall* (1884). See also Albert Peel, *The Congregational Two Hundred 1530–1948* (1948), 172f.

[2] Halévy, op. cit., *IV: Victorian Years 1841–1895*, 390.

principles, became increasingly confused with the struggle for social equality. The achievement of this equality was the second main tendency of the period among the Nonconformists. Oxford and Cambridge were opened to them in 1854, and tests for posts there were abolished in 1871. Church rates were abolished in 1868 and churchyards were opened to Nonconformists in 1880.

The two tendencies, to secularization and to social equality, were closely allied, since it was by the vigour of 'political Dissent' that social progress was made. Yet from the point of view of the working classes the two trends were opposed to each other: politically minded Dissenters like Miall were natural allies of working-class Radicals, but once Nonconformity had secured a broad equality with the Establishment it became more conservative in outlook.

Another leading Nonconformist of the Victorian age, the wealthy industrialist Samuel Morley (1809–1886),[1] seemed to possess the same natural Radicalism as Miall, and he was likewise deeply involved in the working-class movement. His home at Stamford Hill became a rendezvous for Nonconformists and Radical politicians. In the Chartist troubles of 1848, though he was opposed to disorder, Morley thought it necessary to frighten the aristocracy to make them 'give up the prey on which they have always been disposed to fatten.'[2] There was in Morley that extreme of Liberalism which insists on a hearing even for views it does not itself share, and on one occasion he acted as chairman of a series of debates on Christianity and Secularism in which Holyoake was one protagonist, taking great care to secure fair play for the unpopular view. In a similar way he chaired a meeting for Ernest Jones in 1867 in the conviction that his views ought to be heard, and for this he was vigorously attacked in the press. He was returned to Parliament in 1868 and was a firm supporter of Gladstone. His concern for the working classes is shown by the fact that he provided the money for several 'labour candidates' to stand for Parliament (as Liberals), and when the National Agricultural Labourers' Union was formed Morley was one of the most active of its prominent supporters. He served on the consulting committee of the Union from its foundation, and at

[1] Edwin Hodder, *The Life of Samuel Morley* (second edition 1887). Hodder omits Morley's association with William Booth and his support for the Salvation Army.

[2] Ibid., 109.

the Exeter Hall meeting in 1872, when Manning was on the platform, he took the chair. He was also an active member of the Artisans', Labourers' and General Dwelling Company. He took charge in the Commons of Lord Stanhope's Bill prohibiting the payment of wages in public houses.

The *Nonconformist* was inclined to take it for granted that the working classes were strongly sympathetic to Liberalism and Nonconformity. Working-class support for Ritualism must be a fake, but support for disestablishment was of course genuine. Even the best of the Bishops—Fraser—was no use on the subject of 'The Evangelization of the Masses': 'He feels free to speak much more positively as to the methods which he rejects, than in dealing with those which he prefers.' That the Congregational Union should concern itself with the 'Labour Question' was good—and natural enough, for: 'The elevation of the people, and therefore every means to that end, has always been a matter of deepest interest to the Free Churches.' The Church should help the workers to 'improve their social and industrial position,' though in judging means to this end it had 'no peculiar advantage,' and did not, as Hugh Price Hughes imagined, have the answer to all problems.[1] But when all was said and done the traditional Radicalism of the working classes, fitting in so well with the Radicalism of Dissent, was showing signs of turning into something else, something much more extreme and much less desirable:

> Their leaders are mostly Comtists, and with this cold and negative creed have been largely imbibed the characteristics of French democracy—discontent at institutions because they are settled, intolerance of freedom of opinion, a readiness to substitute names for things, and the absence of any adequate sense of responsibility in relation to political action.

But of course the real source of the trouble was the Church of England, 'with its Tory electioneering agent in every parish.' Many years later than these comments an article entitled 'Our Artisans and Christianity' referred to efforts to win back the working classes:

> The fact cannot be disguised that a certain amount of alienation has taken place between the body of working men and the community of Christian believers . . . The most conspicuous popular leaders of

[1] *Nonconformist*, November 8th, December 6th, 1871; August 11th, 1881; July 31st, October 2nd, 1884; May 21st, 1885; March 21st, 1889.

our day—the men from whom the vast army of industrial England take their cue—the men whose names elicit the most deafening cheers at the working men's meetings—are men who repudiate Christianity.

Some workers were active Christians, but it was far from a majority. It was necessary to direct their attention back from the distortions introduced by the Church to Christ himself, and to avoid 'too much of a coaxing attitude, of a compromising tone, of a diffident and deprecating air . . .'[1]

Such comments showed doubts and uneasiness at the growing power of the working classes and a recognition that they might not always prove faithful allies for political Dissent.

7   The Salvation Army

In the approach of Nonconformity to the poorer classes the most important development of this period was the foundation of the Salvation Army by William Booth (1828–1912).[2] Booth was brought up in the Church of England, but drifted in boyhood into Wesleyanism, and in 1842 he heard O'Connor speak and threw in his lot with the Chartists.[3] Four years later he was converted, after suffering from a guilty conscience over some sharp practice in a pawnbroker's shop where he worked, and the possible effect of this conversion was to rob Radicalism of a powerful spokesman. Booth became a local preacher, but was expelled, with his future wife, as an agitator. For a time he preached at a chapel belonging to the reforming group, but in 1854 he transferred his allegiance to the Methodist New Connexion, resigning from this in turn in 1862. The root cause of these successive disillusionments was the lukewarm support Booth found in each body in turn for his own peculiar and rather authoritarian methods of evangelism. As early as his Wesleyan days he found the Nonconformists at times as socially exclusive and rigid as the Established Church:

> The respectable citizens who attended Wesley Chapel . . . were one Sunday morning astonished out of their senses by such a scuffling of broken boots, such a rustle of shoddy rags, and such a stertorous breathing of congregated misery as never before had desecrated their brick-and-mortar habitation of Wesleyanism. William Booth had

[1] *Nonconformist*, February 15th, 1871; December 26th, 1888.

[2] Harold Begbie, *The Life of General William Booth* (2 vols., 1920).

[3] The story has often been told. But its importance should not be exaggerated, since Booth was after all only thirteen years old. See Begbie, op. cit., I 49f.

made himself an apostle to the lads of Nottingham slums . . . But the effect of this invasion was not what he had hoped. The young enthusiast was called before Authority, was argued with, was instructed, and was finally told that he might bring these outcasts into the chapel only if he entered by the back door (invisible behind the pulpit) and seated his converts in obscure benches reserved particularly for the impecunious and shabby.[1]

In 1865 Booth launched the work which was to bring him world fame by opening a tent in Mile End in which he conducted what was at first known as the 'Christian Mission,' with financial backing supplied by Samuel Morley. Booth's biographer is critical of the founder's rather naïve approach to the situation: 'He speaks . . . of the *moral* degradation and the *spiritual* destitution of East London. There is not one word, not a hint anywhere, of the *economic* degradation and the *physical* destitution which are only too often the direct causes of spiritual torpor.' And again: '. . . He was blind and deaf to the political question.'[2] But within its limits the work flourished, and progressed from the tent to a succession of buildings, until in 1868 a market-hall on White-chapel Road was purchased. By 1875 there were about a dozen branches in various poor districts of London and a similar number scattered about the country, including branches as far afield as Stockton, Middlesbrough and Cardiff. The 1878 report was notable for a quotation from Shaftesbury, at first a supporter, but later a bitter opponent: 'The working classes will never be reached but by an agency provided from among themselves.'[3] It was notable too for an expressive term descriptive of the work of the Christian Mission and reflecting, with Booth's genius for publicity, the contemporary war scare over the Eastern Question, namely, the 'Salvation Army.' As is so often the case, the nick-name displaced completely the duller official name.

Thus Booth found himself launched on a very large operation, and his increasing success brought imitators into the field. The conscience of the Church of England was stirred and the Church Army created in 1881 by Wilson Carlile and F. S. Webster. Similarly at Richmond, Surrey, the Vicar of Holy Trinity, Evan Hopkins, founded the Church Gospel Army, and at Bristol Canon Atherton the Church Mission Army.

[1] Begbie, op. cit., I, 71.
[2] Ibid., I, 364f.
[3] Robert Sandall, op. cit., I, 262. See plate facing p. 228.

In the later years of Booth's generalship a complete change came over his outlook, in that so far from rigidly confining his work to purely 'spiritual' efforts he came to see the need for large-scale measures of social relief work, though without in any way modifying his basically conservative attitude. Here Booth was influenced by his friendship with the Congregationalist J. B. Paton of Nottingham. Another prominent figure in the same denomination, W. T. Stead, was even more influential in this connexion, and it was commonly said that Booth's famous book, *Darkest England*,[1] which provided the blueprint for the social programme, was more by Stead than by Booth, an allegation refuted by the historian of the Army.[2] The new programme began with the provision of accommodation for men sleeping in the open air in London, in 1888, when in what Booth called 'elevators' food and accommodation were provided in exchange for work. The 'Darkest England' scheme, dating from 1890, went much further, and included, for example, a system of 'labour bureaux' throughout the country, similar to the labour exchanges ultimately established by state action. In the first year 15,697 unemployed and 14,045 vacancies were registered, and by 1897, 81,831 unemployed had been registered and 69,119 had been found jobs, while 18,039 had been received into the 'elevators.' In 1891 Booth 'declared war' on sweating, and opened a match-factory to make matches without phosphorus, paying the workers 4d. per gross instead of 2¼d. or 2½d., until methods of manufacture were improved. Another plan was for farm colonies, and in 1891, 800 acres were purchased in Essex, this being later increased to 3,200 acres. Market gardens were laid out, and there were established a poultry farm, brickfields, cattle, sheep, pigs, workshops, and glasshouses. This colony, at Hadleigh, was favourably mentioned in both the 1909 Poor Law reports, and during the first twenty-one years of its existence 6,870 persons were admitted. In addition a smallholding scheme operated for a time. Booth received a great deal of support for all this work. The influential Archdeacon Farrar was a warm supporter, and Manning wrote to Booth giving his approval:

[1] General Booth, *In Darkest England and the Way Out* (1890). See Pamela Search, *Happy Warriors. The Story of the Social Work of the Salvation Army* (1956).

[2] Sandall, op. cit., III, 77.

I hold that every man has a right to bread or to work. The modern economists say 'Society must adjust the demand and supply of labour until all are employed.' I have asked 'How many years are required for all this absorption, and how many weeks and days will starve an honest man and his children?' To this I have never got an answer.[1]

But there were also critics. Socialists angered Booth by attacking plans they regarded as mere palliation, while at the other extreme Thomas Huxley condemned them as a disguised Socialism, and because they placed great power in the hands of a man he regarded as a religious fanatic, issuing a warning against 'despotic socialism in all its forms, and more particularly in its Boothian disguise.'[2] There were also more detailed grounds on which Booth could be criticized, for the finances of the 'Darkest England' scheme were inefficiently managed, and Booth recklessly spent money on the assumption that he would get it back. Moreover his remoteness from the world of organized Labour and his ignorance of fundamental economic theory meant that he paid little regard to the argument that his measures of relief work also served to undercut the market and to create as well as relieve destitution. A still deeper criticism, made by Booth's biographer, is that the whole scheme was based on sympathy, not justice. As always his methods were autocratic and he put little trust in the classes with which he was dealing: 'I am not sure that he had much faith in democracy's rightful use of political freedom.'[3] In both phases of his work, the 'spiritual' and the programme of social relief, Booth remained what he had always been:

. . . He was a monarchist, a constitutionalist, a conservative, and certainly not a lover of radicals and socialists; he kept his eyes averted from the political problem, he never once was tempted to make himself the leader of revolution, the captain of an angry and avenging democracy; his whole emphasis was on religion, and the only war he understood . . . was the war against sin.[4]

On Booth and the Salvation Army one's conclusion must be similar to that on the slum ritualists: they both alike showed a sincere and urgent concern for the working classes, but as agents of social change their influence was restricted by their paternalism.

[1] Sandall, op. cit., III, 79f.
[2] Begbie, op. cit., II, 129f.
[3] Ibid., II, 84.   [4] Ibid., II, 22f.

The more worldly wing of Nonconformity, represented by Miall, despite its middle-class affiliations and its absorption with the special concerns of Nonconformity itself, found it easier to co-operate with the main stream of the workers' movement at this time. Perhaps its tendency to talk in terms of rights made such co-operation easier, since it was the demand for justice rather than relief which was significant.

8   The Settlement Movement[1]

A very different attempt to establish contact with the working classes was the settlement movement. The original inspiration, as in the case of so many of the movements described in this book, went back to the Christian Socialists, and those who led the settlement movement and their historians paid tribute to this influence. The pioneers of the new movement took for granted the established system of social classes and tried to create a harmonious relationship between people of different classes. The movement aimed to persuade the workers that

> A sound Liberalism must hope, not to raise the working man out of his class but to produce a community of mental outlook between classes . . . Thus the Settlement movement was partly, at least, the reply of the intellectual middle class to the attitude of the artist-socialists.[2]

It was in fact a continuation of the efforts made by the original group gathered by Maurice. The pattern of the settlement, which became conventional, was a building in a poor district, serving as a social and educational centre—and in many cases also as a re-ligious centre—for the local population, and at the same time as a hostel for undergraduates, in which they could learn to live and work with the working classes. There would be a warden in charge, probably an ordained man. The first settlement seems to have differed from this pattern. This was the Ancoats Brotherhood, founded in 1877 by a devoted Manchester citizen, Charles Rowley. In this case the work was not carried on only by University men, but the service of any suitable person was welcomed. However, this effort was isolated and not part of a general movement.

In the greatest area of poverty and distress, the East End of

---

[1] See J. A. R. Pimlott, *Toynbee Hall* (1935).
[2] R. H. Gretton, *A Modern History of the English People, 1880–1922* (1930 edition), I, 112.

London, various efforts were carried on with the aim of raising the standard of life, mostly with a specifically Christian basis. Bishop Blomfield had remedied to some extent the shortage of churches, but it was a different matter to get people into them. Societies had been formed to provide lay assistance, especially district visitors, but some of these did more harm than good, by adopting a superior and patronizing manner. Father Lowder, the ritualist, had started his mission in the docks in 1856, but its progress was hindered by the liturgical controversies. The Salvation Army had begun work in 1865, Anglican sisterhoods were at work, and in 1879 Walsham How was made Bishop of Bedford,[1] with special responsibility for the East End. Missions multiplied, and in 1887 Charles Booth found 100 at work, attended by 40,000 people, but even this only touched the fringe of the problem. A dispassionate observer of these efforts was the Vicar of St Philip's, Stepney, the famous historian, J. R. Green, and he was not impressed with them. The provision of indiscriminate charity he attacked with vigour, regarding William Booth as a 'ranting preacher' who combined 'enormous breakfasts' with 'Revivalist effusions,' and he poured scorn on the district visitors. He knew the East End well, having settled there in 1860. Three years later he took charge of a derelict parish in Hoxton, but had to leave through ill health, and in 1864 he became curate in Stepney, serving from 1866 to 1869 as Vicar of St Philip's. Influenced by the Christian Socialists, and also by Carlyle, he carried on extensive social work, assisted by young friends, who found their stay in the slums useful experience for themselves as well as a service to the local population, and wondered if others might share the work. Some of them discussed the matter with Ruskin, and the possibility of settlements of University men was raised. Nothing immediately came of this, though one of the group, Edward Denison, was an almoner in Stepney, and after he settled there permanently in 1867 he took classes of men and boys and brought abuses to the notice of the authorities. From 1868 to his death in 1870 he was a Radical M.P. Much social work was also carried on by other clergy, such as E. C. Hawkins of Hackney, and Brooke Lambert, first Curate and then Vicar of St Mark's, Whitechapel. Lambert founded a penny bank, a soup kitchen, a working men's club, and a mutual improvement

[1] The titles of suffragan Bishops were at this date still restricted to an ancient list.

society, and in the elections of 1868 he arranged lectures on the duty of electors.

But the settlement movement really began with the arrival in the East End of Samuel Barnett (1844–1913).[1] Barnett came of a wealthy Tory family, and was educated at Wadham College, on the grounds that the Warden, B. P. Symons, was a strong Tory and Protestant, but according to Barnett himself a visit to America knocked the Toryism out of him. In 1867 he became Curate of St Mary's, Bryanston Square, where he assisted with relief work, the Charity Organization Society, education, and a club. By now he was a Christian Socialist and a Broad Churchman. In 1872 he secured preferment to the parish of St Jude's, Whitechapel, though preferment is perhaps hardly the word, since it was considered by the Bishop to be the worst parish in the whole diocese. The following year he took another decisive step and was married, and his wife, Henrietta, was his faithful companion in all his subsequent enterprises, though she was no mere follower, but in many things the leader. In Whitechapel, Barnett announced, his aim was 'to decrease not suffering but sin.' Like Booth, who had similar ideals, he found much scope under both heads, for the parish was a savage and half-civilized area, and the Church without influence, having a congregation consisting of six or seven women. The Barnetts at once showed their readiness to adopt any method of work which held out the prospect of making contact with the local population, ignoring the stream of criticism from the orthodox. On Sunday evenings from 8.30 to 9.30 they gave performances of music and readings from literature, with the warm approval of the suffragan Bishop, How. Barnett frankly called his programmes 'The Religion of Amusement'; he lacked the earnestness of many social reformers, and always thought entertainment a benefit in itself. In a more conventional way he also opened schools, penny banks, a maternity society, and a library. If by some of his methods he provoked distant churchmen, by his strong advocacy of the complete abolition of outdoor relief he infuriated the pauperized population on his own doorstep, almost to the point of riots. By his personality he was able to attract the assistance in his social work of members of the wealthy classes, such as Beatrice Potter, Alfred Milner, and the retired head of Haileybury College, Dr Bradby. In 1877 he helped to found the East London Branch of the University Extension

[1] H. O. Barnett, *Canon Barnett: His Life, Work, and Friends* (1918).

Society, an idea taken over from the Christian Socialists. He also took an active part in politics—for once against the opposition of his wife—becoming President of the Whitechapel and District Liberal Association. He maintained a connexion with Oxford, and accepted an invitation in 1875 from Gertrude Toynbee to visit Oxford and talk about his social work. The ground was well prepared at the time, for Jowett of Balliol, Ruskin, who was Slade Professor of Art, T. H. Green, the philosopher, and Arnold Toynbee all had a strong interest in social affairs. Toynbee in particular was the centre of an admiring group of young men— Alfred Milner, Alfred Grey, T. H. Warren, L. C. Phelps, A. C. Bradley, R. L. Nettleship, F. C. Montague, and Philip Lyttleton Gell among them. This was the beginning of a regular supply of young men from Oxford to the East End, for Barnett gave an open invitation to them to assist in his work.

In 1883 two events gave a new stimulus. First was the publication of the little pamphlet entitled *The Bitter Cry of Outcast London*, variously attributed to Andrew Mearns, G. R. Sims, and even Stewart Headlam, but in fact written by W. C. Preston. Mearns (1837–1925) was appointed secretary of the London Congregational Union in 1876, and, struck by the distress of the East End, he carried out a survey, submitting his conclusions to William Carnall Preston, a Congregational minister (1837–1902),[1] who had held a pastorate in Wigan during the cotton famine and had been active there in relief work. He had also had experience as a journalist, which was no doubt why Mearns chose him to write up his report. Preston's obituary describes his little work as 'epoch-making,'[2] which is scarcely an exaggeration, for although the facts related were not new, it had the advantage of coming at the right time, when public attention was already beginning to concentrate on social problems, and it caused a great sensation. It was the direct origin of the first major effort in slum clearance, and it encouraged the growth of Socialism by advocating legislative and municipal intervention to better the condition of the people. An immediate effect was the appointment of the Royal Commission on Working-Class Housing. Like other good causes it benefited from vigorous publicity provided by W. T. Stead.

The same year, in April, Arnold Toynbee died, and his friends discussed the most appropriate form for a memorial. Barnett made

[1] *Congregational Year Book 1926*, 170.
[2] Ibid. (1903), 193f.

the most of the opportunity of the time when in November he read a paper on University settlements in the rooms of Sidney Ball, himself closely associated with the Christian Socialist movement, at St John's College. A remarkably distinguished company was present, including C. G. Lang, the future Archbishop of York, J. A. Spender, the novelist 'Anthony Hope' (A. H. Hawkins), Michael Sadler, E. T. Cook (later editor of the *Daily News*) and A. H. D. Acland. Cambridge was also represented with distinction by William Cunningham and Sedley Taylor. The idea of a College mission was discussed, but rejected because it would exclude the co-operation of Nonconformists. There was great interest throughout the University, and a little later a working man, Frederick Rogers, was brought in and also spoke in Ball's rooms. A cleavage of opinion soon appeared, to the distress of Barnett, between those who wanted a settlement definitely committed to the Church of England and others who sought a wider basis. This latter group quickly took steps to advance their plans. A building was purchased and renamed Toynbee Hall, and, with some difficulty, Barnett was persuaded to become warden. The opening received nation-wide publicity, mostly approving, though the *Spectator* satirized the superior attitude of middle-class reformers. Toynbee Hall was opened on January 10th, 1885, when J. R. Seeley came along to represent Cambridge, and Bishop How was there, and had the satisfaction of being referred to by a Nonconformist minister as 'our Bishop.' Leading figures of the intellectual world, such as Seeley, W. J. Ashley, James Bryce, and Alfred Marshall, became 'Associates' of Toynbee Hall and gave useful help.

The new venture was strongly imbued with the spirit of Christian Socialism. Lambert referred to Maurice as a 'modern Socrates.' Of the first fourteen residents five besides Barnett were in, or later took, orders: 'The religious motive undoubtedly weighed considerably in inducing young men to come to East London.'[1] Among these pioneer settlers were Thory Gardiner, the Curate of St Jude's, later sub-warden, who with another original, T. H. Nunn, later served on the Poor-Law Commission, and J. M. Macdonald, later M.P. for East Falkirk Burghs, and Bolton King, who were interested in education.

Toynbee Hall brought the intellectual middle classes into contact with genuine representatives of the working classes, not

[1] Pimlott, op. cit., 46f.

specially selected specimens, and it brought them into contact with the questions agitating the working classes at this time. Conferences held there included such subjects as old-age pensions; 'The Essentials of a good Friendly Society'; co-operative credit banks; co-operative difficulties; 'The Possibility of extending Trade Unions'; 'Labour Homes and Farms'; 'New Openings for Co-operation'; the unemployed; and 'The Utility of Strikes'— which brought together a dock director and a member of the dockers' union. Other discussions were of course on Socialism, of which Barnett, despite his thorough Radicalism, was suspicious. In May 1889 he commented: 'On Monday Haldane and Sidney Webb dined and discussed Socialism. The latter won the fight, but nothing was said to instruct or to inspire.'[1]

Toynbee Hall made little attempt to stand outside the conflicts of Capital and Labour. In 1888 a committee of A. P. Laurie, Arthur Rogers, H. Llewelyn Smith, and Mrs Barnett 'interviewed the managing body of Bryant and May's' about the conditions of employment. On the outbreak of the 1889 dock strike the Barnetts were in Switzerland, but, records Mrs Barnett,

> We immediately came home, and with the men who could be mustered in August, Mr Barnett did all he could to support the strikers in their demands for better organization of unskilled labour, aiding by relief those who would have been, without it, starved into unrighteous submission. On September 21st of that year the Central Strike Committee were entertained at supper in Toynbee Hall. Mr John Burns, Mr Ben Tillett, Mr Tom Mann, and about sixty other guests were with us, and it was a great occasion, but not, as my wise husband said in his speech, 'to be considered as one to identify the Settlement with the strike,' for Oxford would have indeed been alarmed at that policy.[2]

But the sympathies of the Barnetts are sufficiently obvious. Writing to his brother, Barnett expressed his feelings for the strikers and his hatred for 'the sympathy which does nothing.' The Toynbee Hall Report for 1893 spoke very highly of the value of trade unions and revealed the relationships between the unions and the Settlement:

> The Tailoresses Union has continued to hold its meetings here, and the Women Cigar Makers in St Jude's schools. Meetings have also been held by members of various trade societies, including the

[1] Barnett, op. cit., II, 63.
[2] Ibid., II, 66.

Stick Makers, Cigar Makers, Tailors' Cutters and Pressers, Railway Servants, Furriers, Shop Assistants, Fellowship Porters, and Dock Labourers ... Committees of Conciliation, representing smack owners on the one hand and the fish porters on the other, have also met at Toynbee Hall. But meetings are only the more formal outcome of the many new friendships that have been made with officers and members of trade societies . . .[1]

Barnett frequently intervened in trade disputes—fourteen times in one year; and the Hall 'was constantly lent to aggrieved employees, and when part of the injustice consisted in such long working hours as to prevent the men meeting at a time when halls could be hired, Toynbee was available even for midnight conferences.'[2]

The settlers joined working men's clubs in the East End, and one led a study in one club of *Progress and Poverty*. In May 1894 Barnett, by now a Canon of Bristol Cathedral, gave a series of lectures there on 'Christ and the Workman's Problems.' The titles were 'Christ in relation to: (1) Wages and Work; (2) Short Hours and Leisure; (3) The Educational Ladder; (4) Women's Position; (5) The Sick and the Old; (6) The Unemployed.' The lectures were strongly criticized in the local press, one newspaper accusing him of teaching that a man's duty was 'to be discontented with his lot in life, to covet and desire other men's goods, and to go on strike if his wages or the conditions of his employment do not suit him.'[3] But there was also some favourable comment. On other occasions he preached at the Cathedral on 'strikes, trade-unionism, white slavery, prison-made goods, shoddy socialism, free trade, housing reform, wealth, Sunday observance, class divisions, war, and poverty.'[4] He was eloquent on the virtues of co-operation; speaking at the anniversary meeting of the Bedminster Co-operative Society in 1894 he said:

> Co-operation and trade-unionism are the two forces which will make the twentieth century. The twentieth century will be the working men's century, and they must take their place in it . . . What will co-operators be in the twentieth century? They may be the merchant princes of that time gathering up all that was great in the merchant princes of the past and dropping all that was mean and bad.[5]

---

[1] Barnett, op. cit., II, 67.
[2] Ibid., II, 67f.   [3] Ibid., II, 206.
[4] Ibid., II, 212f.   [5] Ibid., II, 219.

Even Barnett's admiring wife felt that he was stating the case rather strongly, and questioned in her biography:

> Was it honest to speak of them as if they possessed the virtues he believed them devoid of? He argued that imputed righteousness was not only a great but a vivifying doctrine, and that in painting what they might be and do, he by implication pointed out what they really were and did.[1]

He was exceedingly vague and general in some of his ideals, and curiously selective in others. When in 1892 he was asked: 'What would be your message to the great body of industrial workers?' he urged the need for libraries, baths and wash-houses, art galleries, public performances of plays and music, 'free air, free water, free literature, cheap trains.'[2] In such a programme he showed himself refreshingly free from cant, but one is surprised at the total absence of any reference to working-class politics, or, even to religion. His enthusiasm for social reform did not extend to Socialism proper. To Mrs Dawson of the *Clarion* he wrote in 1902:

> I am always glad when the quiet waters of ignorance are troubled, and I know how many whole-hearted people engage in your cause; but my own Socialism has always been limited by the desire to provide for everyone equality of opportunity and to give to everyone only those things he does not want.

When his correspondent wrote to ask what he meant by this last curious phrase he replied:

> I am a Socialist in so far as I desire for everyone equality of opportunity, an equal share of a healthy life, and of enjoying the best gifts to this age. I put it another way by saying I would give to everyone only that which he does not want. By this I mean that I would give to people those advantages approved by the best minds of the day, which they themselves have not learnt to appreciate. I would give, for instance, the use of abundant water, books, pictures, open spaces, etc., etc., but I would not give food and money, which they have the will to get for themselves. I make an exception indeed as to old-age pensions, because a lax administration of the Poor-law has made the provision impossible out of wages.[3]

The problem of poor-relief, especially in the case of the unemployed and in that of the old, absorbed a great deal of his time and attention. He shared the attitude of the Charity Organization

[1] Barnett, op. cit., II, 220.   [2] Ibid., II, 11f.
[3] Ibid., II, 221f.

Society, with which he was closely associated, that the existing system of charity had gone far to pauperize the English poor. He was much concerned with the problem of the loafers and the idle, and wanted an extension of the workhouse system. For the 'deserving poor' he advocated training schemes, trade unions, and the discouragement of casual labour and of indiscriminate charity. Like William Booth, he favoured resettlement on the land, in the form of a training farm, on which men would remain for six months, after which they would be found a permanent place on the land, or would be enabled to emigrate. He was interested in the scheme for which Joseph Fels put up the money (in 1905), for a labour colony at Hollesley Bay, which he was unable to turn into a training establishment owing to lack of co-operation from the Local Government Board under John Burns. An investigation by the Webbs showed that only 17% of those passing through Hollesley received any permanent benefit. As a remedy Barnett suggested removing it from the control of the Local Government Board.

As early as 1883 Barnett wrote an article in the *Nineteenth Century* advocating non-contributory old-age pensions, and because he did not believe it possible to discriminate fairly he argued that such pensions should be universal. In the same journal in 1886 he described the social cleavages of the time:

> The nationalization of luxury must be the object of social reformers ... On the one hand there is disease from the want of food and doctors; on the other side there is disease from too much food and doctors. In one part of the town the women cease to charm from the want of finery; in the other they cease to please from excess of finery ... Generally it is assumed that the chief change is that to be effected in the habits of the poor. All sorts of missions and schemes exist for the working of this change. Perhaps it is more to the purpose that a change should be effected in the habits of the rich. Society has settled itself on a system which it never questions, and it is assumed to be absolutely within a man's right to live where he chooses and to get the most for his money.[1]

With other clergy he drafted and issued a letter in 1887 to the incumbents of rich parishes:

> The rich, as a class, offer an example of living which is contrary to the Christian profession, though the lives of some of their numbers

[1] Barnett, op. cit., II, 260f.

are striking protests against such an example. They neither give to the poor, nor deny themselves, nor follow Christ. They do not first seek the Kingdom of Heaven, but quote the laws of political economy, or the decisions of the doctor, or the demands of society, to show why they cannot obey God. Nevertheless the rich, as a class, go to Church and are typical Christians. As long as this is so, it is vain for us to expect that the poor will seek in Christianity help or solace.

We would ask you, therefore, to make those who commit any of the following offences and attend your church understand that they cannot call themselves in any full sense followers of Christ.

(1) Possessors of knowledge, beauty, or luxuries who do not share them with the poor. Owners of houses or parks; givers of dinners who never invite to their best those who cannot ask again.

(2) Women who carelessly wear fine clothes, not having inquired the cost in a sister's shame or death at which they have been made. Some 'cheap' things are too dear for 'human' use.

(3) Employers who take their profit and do not concern themselves to know how the employed live; those who think that 5 per cent is a law of God; and that the body he created to be the temple of his Spirit can be fed, clothed, and recreated on a few shillings a week.

(4) All who, having earned or inherited a livelihood, say they have no time to make friends among the poor or to perform public duties.

The contrast between the lives of those who are equally God's children becomes striking in the light of modern days. Many are driven to think that only by force will the poor obtain from the rich the means to develop their capacities for knowing, feeling, and doing, the means, that is to say, by which they may live their lives as God's children.

Our belief is, that by the use of force, the poor would grow in greed and selfishness; gaining with the wealth some of the vices which have gone with riches. Our hope is therefore that the rich, moved to live the Christian life may so give of themselves and of their substance that there shall be no longer sorrow which love could comfort, and no longer weakness which patient teaching could strengthen.[1]

In such a passage the spirit of the settlement movement is summed up—a spirit Radical but not Socialist, religious but not theological. It was understanding, and far from ineffective, but it lacked something of the drive and force necessary to bring about great changes. Barnett himself was the most typical figure in the movement, and in some ways he is representative

[1] Barnett, op. cit., II, 261f.

of the age—far more representative than, say, the convinced Socialist Stewart Headlam. If Anglo-Catholicism was in the ascendant, it was a far more characteristic aspect of the time that men were indifferent to theological issues, even men who counted as theologians; in the jargon of the age deeds counted for more than creeds. The settlement movement was well-meaning, and such a term expresses both its virtues and its weaknesses. Barnett himself was an amiable figure; not everyone agreed with him, but he did not make enemies, and he was quite free from self-display and the arrogance which often accompanies the ambition to set the world to rights. Yet, as with William Booth—so far as he is regarded from the point of view of his social service, that is— one suspects that all the time great and worthy efforts were being directed to symptoms rather than to underlying causes. The solution to the basic problem of the time—the alienation of social classes—could only come through the economic emancipation of the working classes by their own efforts, and by the combination of political and economic methods. To mix together diverse social classes, for their mutual benefit, though of real value, could not be more than a mere palliative, and the fact that the more socially minded Christians, including some of the most outstanding figures in the religious life of the time, placed such emphasis on the settlement movement increased the impression already held by the leaders of the working classes, that the function of the Church, even at its most progressive, was to provide first-aid behind the fighting lines, while more worldly minded agencies led the advance.

At Toynbee Hall the religious nature of the settlement movement became rather less apparent after a time. In the early days the 'Grand Committee' of all the residents put a ban on Sunday tennis and dancing. The clerical influence remained strong for a time:

> The strength of the religious impulse is shown by the fact that at least sixteen out of the eighty odd residents of the first ten years went into the Church or were already clergymen, whilst another became a Jewish rabbi. The weakening of the religious sentiment in the next generation finds reflection in the figures for the next twenty years, when, so far as can be ascertained, only two residents entered the Church, though this is far from indicating that a large proportion of the residents of this period were not fundamentally religious in outlook.[1]

[1] Pimlott, op. cit., 51f.

T. E. Harvey, who was Warden from 1906 to 1911, was a Quaker. In 1904 he introduced Sunday evening religious discussions, which had an average attendance of 200 and were said to be used as an opportunity for expounding atheism. The keynote of them was 'hostility to religion,' with many attacks on the class-bias shown by the Churches, but 'every creed and religious point of view' was heard. An influential clerical supporter was the Rev W. Robinson, who was 'Dean' of Balliol House (one of the constituent hostels) from 1898 to 1905. Toynbee Hall became involved in a controversy with the Lord's Day Observance Society over Sunday art exhibitions, and Barnett wrote to the Bishop of London justifying the Sunday opening. Archbishop Benson visited the exhibitions, an act regarded as giving his approval.

Toynbee Hall, though the most famous of the settlements, was widely imitated. Oxford House differed from Toynbee in its stronger emphasis on doctrinal religion and in its denominational basis, and in the dock strike it took more care to maintain neutrality. Other settlements were founded in London, Edinburgh, Glasgow, Bristol, Middlesbrough, Manchester, and elsewhere. The movement received the widespread support of Nonconformists, and the Congregationalists alone instituted settlements as follows: Browning Hall, Walworth; two settlements in Canning Town, one a women's settlement and the other run by students of Mansfield College, Oxford; Lancashire College Settlement in Hulme, Manchester; Yorkshire United College Settlement in Bradford; and others at Sheffield, Ipswich, and Middlesbrough. There was also a strong tendency among the Nonconformists to establish 'Institutional Churches,' largely under the stimulus of Charles Silvester Horne (1865–1914), a Congregational minister and Liberal M.P. Examples were Whitefield's Tabernacle, Tottenham Court Road, and Zion, Manchester. These institutional churches of the Edwardian era were a belated extension of the settlement idea. The usual custom was for the leadership to be provided by comfortably-off middle-class people coming from a distance, while the general support consisted of the population of the surrounding poor district. Another well-known Congregational minister, J. H. Jowett (1863–1923), is said to have had 'wide social interests, founding the Digbeth Institute at Birmingham in 1906.'[1] Less well known was P. J. Turquand (1826–1902), whose only pastorate was a ministry of thirty-seven years in

[1] Peel, op. cit., 272.

Walworth, where 'the chapel which had been even for that day exceptionally dark and ugly, was transformed into the light attractive structure now worked as a Congregational settlement under the the name of Browning Hall.'[1]

The settlement movement received the warm support of the Anglican press, though there was a natural tendency to prefer Oxford House to Toynbee Hall. Commendatory articles and appeals for funds often appeared in the *Guardian* and the *Church Times*, and also in a new, Low Church, journal founded in 1894, the *Church Family Newspaper*, later to be known as the *Church of England Newspaper*.

The tradition of Barnett was continued by the Methodist Scott Lidgett, who came from a Church Methodist (i.e. High Wesleyan) background.[2] After pastoral service in various places he went to London in 1891 'to found, build and direct the Bermondsey Settlement,' and there he remained for the almost incredible period of fifty-nine years. In 1908 he was President of the Wesleyan Conference, and in 1932 he achieved the unique honour of becoming the first President of the Conference of the newly united Methodist Church. He was active in educational work, and continued a Nonconformist tradition in leading the Progressives on the London County Council from 1918 to 1928. In the establishment of the Bermondsey Settlement Lidgett was given the support of the Methodist Biblical scholar W. F. Moulton, and an official status was conferred by the authority conveyed by Conference in 1891 for its foundation. It differed from some other enterprises of this type in that the residents were mostly office workers, and there were few students. Lidgett was a convinced Liberal, though he had friends in the Labour Party. He was influenced much by Maurice, and his educational work in particular was guided by Maurice's philosophy.

Lidgett was also inspired by the example of Toynbee Hall, and another offshoot of the general movement of which Toynbee was part was the Workers' Educational Association. Albert Mansbridge edited a magazine for the Junior Civil Service Prayer Union and wrote to Bishop Gore for an article. Gore declined, but invited Mansbridge to his house and encouraged him in his ambitions, and Mansbridge was impressed by the Bishop.[3] He went to work for

---

[1] *Congregational Year Book 1903*, 205.
[2] Rupert E. Davies (ed.), *John Scott Lidgett* (1957).
[3] M. Stocks, *The Workers' Educational Association* (1953), 21.

the Co-operative Wholesale Society, and its economic principles
and Gore's interest in it 'satisfied his Christian social conscience.'[1]
Barnett was at first a source of discouragement rather than the
reverse, since he assured Mansbridge that to establish the
association he had in mind would need £50,000: it did in fact
begin with 2s. 6d. and two members, Mansbridge and his wife, in
1903. But once the die was cast Barnett gave warm support, and the
first meeting was held at Toynbee Hall. Dr Percival, Bishop of
Hereford, and Dr Kitchin, Dean of Durham, took turns as
chairman of the association in the early days, and the Fabian
Sidney Ball of St John's College, Oxford, was a useful supporter.
(There was a legend about him that he responded, *sotto voce*, to
the College toast 'Church and King' with the words 'Religion and
the Republic.') From 1905 a distinguished supporter was William
Temple.

9   The Labour Church Movement

The settlement movement represented a new kind of co-operation between the religious and the secular reformers. A move to set
the Church itself more firmly in the context of the secular life of
the working classes can be seen in the Labour Church movement.
The founder of the movement was John Trevor, the minister of
Upper Brook Street Free Church in Manchester, who had been
influenced by the prominent Unitarian, P. H. Wicksteed.[2] In 1891,

> finding his preaching and principles unacceptable to his congrega-
> tion, he decided to start the new movement, prepared to go into the
> wilderness, but discovering to his surprise and pleasure a quite
> unlooked-for amount of support. The Labour Church began as an
> organized effort to develop the religious life inherent in the Labour
> Movement, and to give that Movement a higher inspiration and
> sturdier independence in the great work of personal and social
> regeneration that lay before it. It appealed especially to those who
> had abandoned the religious traditions in which they had been
> brought up, but could not be satisfied to abandon religion altogether.
> Its message was that without obedience to God's laws there could
> be no Liberty; that God was behind the Labour Movement, working
> through it for the further emancipation of man from the tyranny both
> of his own half-developed nature and of those social conditions
> opposed to his higher development; that men were to become
> fellow-workers with God ... The Movement attained a certain

[1] Stocks, op. cit., 23.
[2] Henry Pelling, *The Origins of the Labour Party 1880–1900* (1954), 140.

measure of popularity for some fifteen years or so; thus in 1907 there were thirty Labour churches in different parts of the country, some (possibly all) equipped with Sunday Schools.

From January 1892 onwards for some years John Trevor edited the *Labour Prophet*. In the first editorial he expressed his conviction that the spirit then working in the hearts of the people towards emancipation was essentially a religious spirit, and that in the great social awakening of the early 'nineties was to be found the basis for a new conception, not only of men's relations with each other, but also of their relations with the God of all life. His book *My Quest for God*—at once interesting and disappointing—shows him as one who lived, inwardly, in a religious atmosphere. But the inevitable result of his creedlessness was a vagueness that was a source of weakness to the Movement. It is instructive to compare successive versions of the Statement of Principles; by 1912 all reference to God had been dropped; the purpose of the Labour Church was described as that of giving expression to the religious and general principles of Socialism —it was definitely said not to be theological . . .[1]

The vague but fervent atmosphere of the Labour Churches suited the mood and temperament of some of the outstanding leaders of the Labour movement. The most popular speaker at their meetings was Keir Hardie. But they made little distinctive contribution, not so much because they soon went into decline, as because they developed into just one more kind of meeting place for ordinary Socialists. Some so-called Labour Churches were mere political clubs; for example the William Morris Labour Church at Leek was in memory of a man who did not even believe in God.

The Labour Church movement spread a little further than the Unitarians and the non-denominational and non-theological elements in the I.L.P. Among the Congregationalists the Rev J. B. Wallace founded a 'Brotherhood Church' in London, and the Rev B. J. Harker converted his church into a Labour Church without severing its connexion with the Congregational Union. The extension of the movement to the Congregationalists had an interesting consequence in that the Rev G. S. Barrett devoted to it his two chairman's addresses to the Congregational Union in 1894. In the first, entitled *The Secularization of the Pulpit*,[2] he pointed out the increasing prominence of social questions, and claimed that religion had brought this about, having emboldened

[1] Binyon, op. cit., 182f.
[2] Printed in *Congregational Year Book 1895*, 19–33.

Labour 'to ask, not for the doles and charity of the rich, but for a larger and juster share in the wealth which labour helps to create.' The change was welcome, but there were dangers too. Ben Tillett said that the Church ought to secure for everyone such benefits as 'good wages, equal rights, and . . . temporal good,' but the great work of the preacher was 'not to save the body from suffering, but to deliver the soul from sin.' Social regeneration could only be obtained as a by-product of strictly religious teaching.

This address gave great offence to Tillett, who made a violent personal attack on Barrett, for which he was rebuked by the *British Weekly*.[1] Undeterred, Barrett returned to the theme in his address to the autumn assembly of the Union at Liverpool, under the title of *The Secularization of the Church*.[2] He dealt largely with the 'appeal to the churches that they should cease to be impassive spectators of the great political and social movements of the age, and should take a prominent part in the struggle for the economic and social welfare of the people.' He made three concessions to this demand: that Christians should be active in social movements, that the Church should exercise philanthropy, and that the Church should by example and teaching influence the conscience of society. But direct interference he condemned as not the Christian way. Then he turned to the Labour Churches, and after a criticism of their theology passed to the main grounds of his attack: that they were socially sectional bodies: 'A Labour Church has no more right to be than a Capitalist's Church, or an educated man's Church.' His opponents might have replied that the 'Capitalist's Church' was not unknown, and indeed Barrett admitted that the new movement was a reaction to class prejudice:

> It is a rebuke as well as a warning to many of us. If there are churches where the poor man is not welcome and is not made to feel at home, where the evil system of pew-rents accentuates within the Church those social distinctions which ought to have been left outside, where the man with the gold ring is treated exactly as the Apostle James says he ought not to be treated, they at least ought not to wonder at this attempt of Labour to vindicate its right to a place in the Church of God.

Barrett then quoted the interesting saying of Dr Fairbairn that the Labour Church was

[1] *British Weekly*, May 24th, 1894.
[2] *Congregational Year Book* (1895), 34–51.

a creation more of despair than hope, an attempt to sanctify an evil rather than to cure it. The terms, master and servant, capital and labour, denote relations the Church ought not to know and may not recognize, and to embody such distinctions in her very name is but to run up the flag of surrender.

Barrett saw similar dangers in the 'Pleasant Sunday Afternoon' movement, despite its good work.

Another, and rather surprising, objection to the name was made by the *British Weekly*, in an article on an election at Halifax, claiming that the title 'Labour Church' belonged to all the Nonconformist Churches, since their members were largely drawn— so it was claimed—from the working classes.[1]

10   *The Edwardian Period*

The early years of the twentieth century seem in some ways to show a reaction against the hedonistic attitude of the late Victorian era. Towards the end of the peace a new bitterness entered English life, exemplified by violent strikes, the militant suffragist movement, the Irish troubles, and the uniquely fierce debates in Parliament centring around Lloyd George. There was also a strong sense of responsibility, for many prosperous people had absorbed something of the earnest desire of recent prophets of social reform to raise the standard of life of the poor, and the discussion tended to confine itself to the means of doing so. Things which had not been regarded as serious abuses a generation or two earlier were now felt to be tolerable no longer—especially the twin evils of 'sweating' and slums. No one believed that social conditions were getting worse, except in the matter of unemployment, where successive troughs were tending to be deeper, but few were satisfied that the growing prosperity of the nation was being fairly distributed. The sense of responsibility made people ready for much larger inroads of corporate action than would have seemed possible not long before. The prosperous were well represented in the settlements, the very embodiment of the idea that the fortunate classes had a duty to the less fortunate, and the settlements seemed to set the tone of the times. The mood even overflowed national boundaries, and there is an analogy between the 'mission' or 'settlement' idea in the East End and the new Imperialism, sung by Kipling, which regarded the maintenance of British authority and rule in Africa and Asia as the 'white man's burden.'

[1] *British Weekly*, February 16th, 1893.

The religious life of England was coming to have a more corporate character. If Charles Booth had found the Congregationalist services of the 'nineties lacking in social significance, in Edwardian times a new phrase had arrived: the 'Social Gospel.' Like the revivalism of previous years, which still recurred in English—and still more in Welsh—Nonconformity from time to time, it drew its inspiration from America, but it was quickly acclimatized: 'By 1907 Nonconformists had come to have an intense interest in the social conditions of the people of England, and the doctrine of the Church was being discussed in terms of their betterment.'[1] This new movement had

> three basic tenets: first, the Christian ideal is not the salvation of a remnant but the redemption of the world, therefore Churches are not to be arks of refuge but centres of aggressive activity; secondly, the redemption of humanity is equivalent to the coming of the Kingdom of God and is to be achieved in this world, and the Churches are to bring it about; and thirdly, this is a social ideal, therefore the Church is to be a social agency.[2]

The new generation identified the Kingdom of God with a new social order. Such an outlook found a natural expression in the settlement movement, and Nonconformist settlements already existed. But it was in the early years of the new century that the movement reached its peak, not merely as an empirical measure for tackling the distresses of slum areas, but as the expression of a philosophy. The Broad Plain (Congregational) settlement, at Bristol, was under the wardenship of George Leonard, who 'traced the inspiration of its foundation to the social movement initiated by Maurice.'[3] At the same time the Institutional Church was advancing under Silvester Horne:

> In 1903 he accepted a call to Whitefield's Chapel on Tottenham Court Road, then in rather a derelict condition, and immediately began to transform it in accordance with his progressive ideas. The Church was provided with accommodation for a number of social and educational clubs, even with a billiards room and a bar for non-alcoholic drinks. A men's meeting to discuss topics of the day filled the Church every Sunday afternoon. The experiment was successful beyond all hopes; crowds flocked to the Church and a notable improvement was made in the social conditions of the district. Horne wrote a short book on *The Institutional Church*, telling Churches how they might get away from the 'dear old antediluvian methods' of the

[1] Grant, op. cit., 170.   [2] Ibid., 171.   [3] Ibid., 175.

saints and adopt means that would get results in competition with
music halls and theatres. There was, of course, a purpose in all this.
Horne was not multiplying organizations for their own sake, but
endeavouring to create a new type of Church in which not merely
the religiously inclined of the middle class but all classes and races
could feel at home.[1]

But many who were attracted to the Church in this way did not
form a firm attachment, and were later lost. In the years before
the first world war Horne's methods did achieve great success.
Many Nonconformists were supporters of the Brotherhood
movement, and Horne remarked

> before his last trip to America in 1914 that he intended neither to
> return to the ministry nor to remain in public life, but to devote his
> time to this movement. The supporters of Brotherhood sought, by
> conforming their manner of life to that of the poor, to bring into
> relation with Christianity, those who would be altogether outside.
> The Brotherhood movement was not closely related to the Church,
> although its sponsors hoped to recruit new strength to the Church.[2]

Such movements showed an increasing sympathy with the
workers. The idea grew that the purpose of the Church was social
reform, and the secularization of Nonconformity, already far
advanced in the closing years of the nineteenth century, proceeded
further. The social Gospel tended to become 'a baptism of the
Labour movement into the Christian spirit.'[3] A more profound
corporate emphasis was that of the theologian, P. T. Forsyth,
who had 'learned too much from F. D. Maurice' to think of
Christianity individualistically, and believed that there was a
'social quality inherent in redemption . . . The influence of the
new collectivist social philosophy upon Forsyth's criticism of
individualism is evident.' He was severely critical of the social
Gospel, but he was liable to be misunderstood: his terse and
epigrammatic style lent itself to quotation out of context, and the
wide difference between these two forms of corporate emphasis
may not always have been clear to contemporaries.

The social Gospel fitted in much better with the theological
trends to which Forsyth was most strongly and eloquently opposed,
the 'Modernism,' with a strong emphasis on progress and the
immanent presence of God in man and society, which brought
together a new version of traditional liberal Protestantism and the

---

[1] Grant, op. cit., 176f.   [2] Ibid., 178.   [3] Ibid., 182.

teachings of the Catholic Modernists Loisy and Tyrrell. Such
trends were suddenly presented as a party-line in 1906 under the
tendentious title of the 'New Theology.' The founder of the group,
R. J. Campbell, announced that the New Theology was the
religious counterpart of Socialism, for Campbell was a Fabian. In
1907 a summer school was held at Penmaenmawr, 'with the object
of linking the movement more closely with social reform.'[1] But
Campbell was a superficial thinker with little knowledge of Socialism
or social reform, and it has been alleged that the basis of the relationship aimed at was little more than the mere fact that the New
Theology and Socialism were both new and both in the 'spirit of
the age' and so must be in fundamental agreement, and it has also
been alleged that 'almost every work by the school bears the word
"new" in its title.'[2] The purpose of the churches was said to be
the betterment of the social order, and since many bodies not
normally considered to be churches carry on this work, the scope
of the term had to be widened—sufficiently, according to Campbell, for the Labour Party to be defined as a church. With
Campbell there was Dr K. C. Anderson, who was minister at
Bradford from 1885 to 1892 and at Dundee from 1892 to 1919.
Anderson considered that 'the socialist indictment against modern
society is a true bill; we cannot answer the charge.'[3] He seems to
have derived his ideas of the Church from Comte and given them
a Christian colouring. Another prominent member of this Congregational group was T. Rhondda Williams, who like Anderson
was a minister for a time in Bradford, and indeed Williams was
one of the few members of the group to remain a Congregationalist.
He contributed an article to the *Hibbert Journal* in 1912 entitled
'Syndicalism in France and its Relation to the Philosophy of
Bergson,'[4] denying that the anti-intellectualist tendency of
Syndicalism could be traced back to Bergson. The whole record
of the group illustrates the extent to which Socialistic tendencies,
albeit of a very vague kind, had penetrated the thinking of religious
leaders in the years before the first world war as a result of their
attempt to keep up with the latest ideas of the leaders of the
working classes.

With the coming of the new century the religious press was past
its heyday, for it was no longer read with close and informed

---

[1] Grant, op. cit., 139.   [2] Ibid., 132, note 1.
[3] Fenner Brockway, *Socialism over Sixty Years* (1946), 31.
[4] *Hibbert Journal*, xi, 389.

attention by a fair number of men who were in a position to mould public opinion, and it tended to become absorbed in merely denominational interests. This was especially true of the *Guardian*, which had had the widest scope of any. A leader on the 1906 election results, with the familiar title: 'The Church and the Working Classes,' lamented the alienation from religion of the working classes generally and of the Labour Party, which was 'certainly uninfluenced by any very close sympathy or alliance with the aims and hopes of the National Church.'[1] This divorce was the favourite topic at the Church Congress of this year, and the *Guardian* considered Gore right in insisting that the Church must not belong only to the upper and middle classes, but must begin to draw its clergy from the workers.[2] Years later the social unrest before the first world war was blamed on agitators and 'academic Socialists,' and the Church was said to have no message on social problems, which were intellectual, not moral.[3] The *Church Times* now seemed to have nothing to say on these topics, and the *Church Family Newspaper* very little beyond a somewhat optimistic assertion at the end of the period: 'A gratifying and remarkable change has taken place during the last decade or so in the attitude of the Church towards Labour and social problems.' It was now realized that Labour leaders were not mere agitators, though the Church was still not showing enough 'practical sympathy' on such matters as housing, sweating, and so on.[4] The same article noted with satisfaction that working-class critics were often hostile to the Church but never to Christ; this is a point which serves as a reminder that while the Anglo-Catholic party was always sure that it understood the working classes better than the readers of the *Church Family Newspaper*, its emphasis on the Church was an additional obstacle in the way of the reconciliation it sought.

The *British Weekly* had equally little to say on the Nonconformist side. The anticlericalism and atheism of the Spanish working classes was naturally attributed to the fact that the religion they knew was Roman Catholicism.[5] But on the relations of religion and the workers in England there was virtually nothing.

[1] *Guardian*, March 21st, 1906.
[2] Ibid., October 3rd, 1906.
[3] Ibid., June 14th, 1912.
[4] *Church Family Newspaper*, December 19th, 1913.
[5] *British Weekly*, August 25th, 1910.

11   *The Roman Catholic Church and the Working Classes*

For a great part of this period the Roman Catholic Church was regarded as a totally alien element in the English scene, and indeed was frequently referred to (especially by Anglo-Catholics) as the 'Italian mission.' For some years any English Roman Catholics belonging to the working classes who wished to read a newspaper reflecting their own outlook were badly served, for the main Catholic newspaper was the *Tablet*, which was published in Dublin until September 1858, when it removed to London. It was remote from the life of industrial England and had nothing of interest to contribute on the present theme. But in December 1860 the *Universe* was founded, aiming at the new mass circulation becoming possible among the English Catholics. It was born in the middle of the crisis of Italian unification, an issue which directly involved the Pope and so tended to emphasize the divergence of sympathy between Protestant and Roman Catholic Englishmen, but after a few years it discovered that there were other matters of importance beside Italy and even Ireland with her perennial grievances. The social question was 'far superior to the Italian question and to the Irish question.' The solution was 'either Catholicism, or socialism, disorder, plunder, and ruin.'[1]

The *Universe* soon discovered an argument which was often to be heard henceforth from the Roman Catholic Church: that it alone had a place for the lower classes of society, and that the Protestant Churches were no more than conventicles of the middle classes:

> Anyone who has ever attended the services of the Church of England in any of the large towns of this country cannot fail to have remarked how conspicuous the poor are—by their absence. A few old women, pensioners of some society, and the charity children, are their sole representatives. A ragged coat, or a shoeless foot is a thing utterly unknown, and the better classes of working men are, as a rule, about as intimately acquainted with the interior of their parish church as they are with the geography of the moon, and know as much about their parson as they do about the King of Siam or the Emperor of China.

To stand outside a Protestant church was to see only the respectable, self-satisfied middle classes.

> Then stand, some other Sunday, outside the Catholic Church. Go to the cathedrals of Moorfields and St George's and watch mass after

[1] *Universe*, April 1st, 1865.

mass, and see them coming forth in their poverty, in their rags that threaten every moment to resolve into nakedness, in hunger and in want, not ashamed of their poverty, and not fearing to show themselves in the house of God, because they have learned to look upon it as their own Father's house.

The working man had never taken to Protestantism. The article ended with criticism and ridicule for Sabbatarians who were trying to suppress all the working man's enjoyments.[1] The same note recurred a decade later, when in again attacking Sabbatarianism the *Universe* commented that the working classes did not go to church in England as they did in Dublin; the poor were notably absent from Anglican and Nonconformist churches alike, and notably present in the Catholic Church. The *Universe* did not share Manning's enthusiasm for the Salvation Army and its founder, sharply criticizing the Queen for sending a polite reply to an appeal from Booth—even though she did not go so far as to send any money; the hostile tone is also an interesting comment on the ebbing of respect for the throne. The *Universe* commented sardonically: 'The Queen is getting altogether too gracious.' With characteristic violence of expression it abused the Salvation Army: 'Away with it to the slums from which it sprung.'[2]

By the early years of the twentieth century a change had occurred, in that the Roman Catholic Church had become a major factor in English life. In the approach to the working classes the best-known figure of the period was Bernard John Vaughan (1847–1922),[3] a Jesuit priest of a Catholic family, whose brother was Archbishop of Westminster. Bernard Vaughan was noted for his sensationalist methods of preaching and for his activity on behalf of the poor of London. He opposed Socialism, but engaged actively in social reform, and in visiting large cities made a habit of examining the slum areas and denouncing any apparent injustices. His wildly emotional preaching drew large crowds during his service at the Holy Name, Manchester, and again after his removal to London.

Less sensational methods were used by Charles Dominic Plater (1875–1921),[4] whose father had been converted in 1851, while his

---

[1] *Universe*, February 2nd, 1867.
[2] Ibid., May 10th, June 14th, 1879; July 15th, 1882; July 14th, 1883; May 24th, 1884.
[3] C. C. Martindale, *Bernard Vaughan, S.J.* (1923).
[4] *Dict. Nat. Biog.* (1912–1921), s.v. Plater.

mother's family had always been Catholic. He too became a
Jesuit, and cherished the ambition of creating retreats for working
men. He was active in all Catholic social work from about 1904,
conducting many retreats and writing on social subjects. He
enjoyed great influence among the working classes.

But the Catholic press had still not a great deal to contribute to
discussion of the working classes—indeed its comments on this
topic in general reduced to one repeated assertion: that the Catholic
Church is the natural friend of the working classes. Protestantism,
the *Universe* claimed, 'instinctively sides with wealth against
poverty, and is fast losing the hold till of late possessed by some of
its sects over the artisan class,' whereas there were few Catholic
Capitalists, and 'the field of labour of the priest is especially among
the poor.'[1] Labour politicians in London

> know that their Catholic constituents are amongst the most
> advanced enthusiasts of the claims of Labour to full recognition in
> the legislation of the State. They are workers. They earn their bread
> by the sweat of their brow, or by the slavery of their hands, and of
> their lives. . . . The working men of England have only to be taught
> the humanity of the Church to lead them to conversion.[2]

It was more and more insistently proclaimed that the Catholic
Church was of and for the working classes as it became less and
less true, in at least two senses: less and less could that Church
identify itself with the ambitions of the politically conscious
working classes as these ambitions were increasingly along the
lines of secular Socialism; and less and less was it true—though
for a very long time it would still be largely true—that the Roman
Catholic Church in England was a Church of proletarians. Already
a change was in progress, and in industry and commerce, in
politics, in the Universities, in the armed forces, in the Law, and
elsewhere men of Irish names and Catholic faith were moving
upwards.

12 *Conclusions*

The relations between the working classes of the industrial
towns and the Churches during the period here considered was
consistently uneasy, and the topic of frequent debate. From mid-
Victorian times the alienation of the proletariat was recognized by

[1] *Universe*, August 27th, 1904.
[2] Ibid., October 28th, 1905.

both the Church of England and the Nonconformists, though there is no indication that except perhaps in degree it was a new development—indeed there is evidence that it was already a well-established social fact. The gradually increasing emphasis given to this subject suggests that the various attempts to recover the workers were not proving successful, a conclusion towards which evidence from various directions converges. The Roman Catholic Church had a proportionately larger number of working class and poor supporters, but its total strength in England was for a long time not comparable with that of the Protestants, and the continuing predominance of Irish in the Roman Catholic population made it seem as much as ever an alien element in the English religious scene.

In the 'seventies and 'eighties a note of urgency crept into discussions of this theme, and at times already the alarm verged on despair. Two obvious reasons can be suggested for the increased attention: the alienation of the working classes had proceeded further, and the importance of those same classes had greatly increased with their enfranchisement under the second Reform Act. But the change ought not to be exaggerated: the journals of the various religious bodies were still far more concerned with internal matters and with mutual controversy than with winning the workers. And a large proportion of the working classes themselves were still firmly attached to the Church, despite all the witnesses who insisted that this figure should be placed at only one or two per cent. The slum Ritualists achieved results; there were many Anglican and Nonconformist agencies at work in the cities, the Salvation Army being only the most obvious; and the rapid progress of the smaller Methodist bodies showed that Nonconformity could still make considerable gains in working-class areas. The mid-Victorian era was a time of religious boom; never in the memory of anyone living had so large a proportion of the population been in church and the religious leaders exercised so large an influence in the national life. If active participation in church life, and a sincere and earnest attempt to live by the teachings of the Church day by day, are marks of religious vitality, there has rarely in the modern world been a country so religious as late nineteenth-century England. The flourishing Protestantism of that age has so impressed its mark on English history, and even on the obscure but perfectly real corporate memory of the people, that the crowded churches and silent Sabbaths of three generations ago still seem to a great number of English men and women the normal, and the present social code either a temporary aberration or a welcome revolution, according to taste.

There has never been a generation in English history like the mid-Victorians for getting things done, for good or ill. It was the same generation which covered England with railways, many of them from the start nothing more than a mere speculation, which also dignified the growing industrial towns and cities with the monuments of the Gothic revival, at first a part of that nostalgic affection for the Middle Ages which lay behind much of the programme of the Oxford Movement, but ultimately favoured as much by Primitive Methodists as by Anglo-Catholics. The increase of church accommodation was no mean achievement; from 1851 to 1872 even the Anglican and Wesleyan efforts, lagging behind other denominations, amounted to an increase of one-third in two decades, largely in places near to the working-class populations of the large towns. The steady increase in the Roman Catholic strength meant that in certain places there were now considerable numbers of industrial workers owing allegiance to the Roman Church, with churches springing up to accommodate them, though for a time they were almost entirely confined to one or two fairly small areas.

The attempts to reconcile the workers to the Church did not achieve much. The methods adopted, such as the University settlements, the Institutional Churches, special services for the working classes, and the Labour Church movement, tended to accept the existence of a gap between those classes and the main body of the Church, and in their attempt to meet the workers were inclined to turn into social activities only faintly tinged with religion. In the years that followed they showed signs of losing contact with the mainstream of English Church life without establishing much of a contact with the mainstream of the Labour movement.

In the early years of the twentieth century the familiar topic of the relationship of the Church and the working classes almost disappeared from the pages of the religious press. This was certainly not the consequence of a return of the working classes to the Church; quite the converse was the case. Nor was it altogether a simple loss of interest in social affairs; the *Church Times* and the *Church Family Newspaper*, for example, dealt voluminously with Socialism and various questions relating to trade unionism, as will appear below. But the old question 'Why don't the working classes come to church?' was no longer asked so urgently. It may not have been a sudden despair, in the superficial sense, but an aspect of a more profound and general loss of confidence on the part of Anglicans and Nonconformists alike—a loss of confidence, that is, in their ability to influence decisively the trend of social development. In mid-Victorian times the *Guardian* and the *Nonconformist* reviewed scientific publications and works on the arts because they took it for granted that it was the duty of the Church to pass judgement on all issues of public significance; but by the early twentieth century the religious press largely ignored works outside its own special sphere of interest, except for books of popular religious appeal, and the queen of the sciences acknowledged in this manner her dethronement. Similarly a generation earlier Churchmen were puzzled to find that large sections of the community were quite outside the Church; by Edwardian times they would have been astonished to find them inside—and where they were it was news, and eagerly reported. This was the real decline of religion—not merely the declining statistics of church attendance, but the contraction of interest and scope. From being the regulative principle of society—even if one often challenged—religion had shrunk to nothing more than one of the more important aspects of public life. Nothing had taken its place, and the idea of a regulative principle was no longer accepted, for the age of cultural anarchy was at hand. The narrowing of scope did not prevent the religious press giving the most comprehensive advice to Labour leaders, as to statesmen, but it was advice from one estate of the realm to another; not the somewhat imperious instruction of a mother for her prodigal offspring.

CHAPTER 2

TRADE UNIONISM

1 *The Struggle for Recognition*

AMONG WORKING-CLASS ORGANIZATIONS pride of place must be given to the trade unions: a fact often deprecated by idealists to whom the struggle for better wages and conditions seems sordid, and by some Socialists, for whom the trade union movement in England has been fatally contaminated with revisionism. Yet it is a fact, nevertheless. The 'Labour Movement' has been pre-eminently the trade union movement, for better or worse, and the political organization of the working classes has followed belatedly on their industrial organization. The attitude of the Church to the trade unions is therefore a matter of central importance; it is little use Christian idealists expatiating on the possibilities of Utopia if they scorn the practical steps taken by the mass of the people to bring about piecemeal improvements in their daily lives.

The failure of Robert Owen's ambitious schemes for the organization of the working classes led to a profound reaction after 1848. The leaders of the 'New Model' trade unions which now began to emerge were moderate men, fully accepting the doctrine of self-help, and anxious to secure for their members a fair share of the great harvest which industrial Capitalism was beginning to gather. For nearly two decades the unions increased in strength and gradually won the esteem of the propertied classes, until the Sheffield outrages heralded a more troubled era.

The services to the trade union movement of the Christian Socialists will be noted later; but the Christian Socialists were by no means typical of the Church—even of the Church of England. The *Guardian*, remote from the world inhabited by the industrial workers, hardly noticed the change which was taking place until the Royal Commission report of 1869, by which time it was fairly complete. Thus it had little to say directly about the principles of trade unionism during these years, though a good deal to say about strikes, which could hardly be ignored. Most of the time there was an attempt to be unbiased, and while strikes were always condemned the blame was not usually put wholly on one party.

There was a first wave of strikes early in the 'fifties. On the engineering dispute of 1852, the *Guardian* considered the Amalgamated Society of Engineers unreasonable in objecting to overtime and piecework, and inopportune in its efforts to organize a producers' co-operative, and the Christian Socialists were criticized for their support.[1] The *Nonconformist* in contrast took the side of the men and explained their objections to piecework, though admitting that 'strikes rarely, or never, answer the end proposed.' It also congratulated the union on the attempt at co-operation.[2] On the Roman Catholic side the *Tablet* was at first more warmly in support than the *Nonconformist*, on the grounds that the union was defending a traditional position while the employers were attempting an innovation.[3] But this enthusiasm cooled rapidly when it was found that the A.S.E. had a leaning towards a 'Socialism of the very worst species and spirit' and was hostile to private property.[4]

A very long cotton strike in 1853–1854 brought an appeal for arbitration from the *Nonconformist*,[5] while the *Guardian* made some rather naïve comments.[6] A strike could only bring temporary advantages, and the very frequency of strikes proved that they were unjustified, for 'is it possible to believe that the wages of every class of workpeople are everywhere too low?' The assumption here was that there was a fixed 'just wage,' if only it could be discovered. The threat of action against blacklegs was particularly unfair: 'What would be said if a workman were forbidden to change his master? And ought not the master, in common justice, to be allowed to change his labourers?'

The other industry which attracted most attention in this period was building, subject to recurring disputes. In 1853 the *Guardian* strongly criticized the employers, who would not concede wage increases until they were coerced by a strike, and lamented the end of the old system of personal relationships in the industry. It had been replaced by a 'spurious political economy' which

---

[1] *Guardian*, January 14th, 1852.
[2] *Nonconformist*, January 7th, 1852.
[3] *Tablet*, January 10th, 1852.
[4] Ibid., January 31st, 1852.
[5] *Nonconformist*, April 5th, 1854.
[6] *Guardian*, October 24th, 1853.

'consecrates simple selfishness under the name of a principle.' The
workers aimed only at 'righting themselves' after a period in which
'the capitalists oppressed the workmen.'[1] But by the end of this
decade the *Guardian* was less friendly, and protested that it was
unfair for other trades to help the building workers, inviting the
public to help the employers to redress the balance. The parties to
this strike should learn compromise from the moderation shown
in the Italian question by Napoleon III.[2] In 1861 the men were
'clearly in the wrong,' especially in refusing payment by the hour,
and the unions were accused of 'tyranny' over the workers.[3] But
in 1865 it was said that the continual trouble in this industry
should not be blamed on the unions, for 'the demands of Labour
are apt to seem exorbitant and unjust to Capital, even when they
are really most legitimate.'[4] The *Nonconformist* was inclined to be
more critical of the employers. Unions were necessary, but dangerous, and the building union had 'aimed at what they cannot
possibly accomplish by means of combination, without trampling
individual claims under foot'; but the employers had also acted
unwisely, and some form of arbitration was needed.[5]

This last point was much in mind. The *Guardian* pointed out
that strikes harmed both sides, and recommended councils of
employers and employees, quoting the example of a 'Council of
Prud'hommes' at Lyons.[6] It was a mistake to consider relations as
purely an economic question, just as it was 'unreal—unsuited to
the persons concerned—Utopian' to hope to cure poverty by
recommending delayed marriage and abstinence from drink and
tobacco.[7] The union of Labour was inevitable and 'in obedience
to its own instincts,' and the real problem was to teach Labour not
to use its power despotically. No good could come of strikes, and
workers were ignorant of economics if they imagined that Capital
could yield a profit on a nine-hour day—and in any case the
achievement of this much-discussed object would only lead to
demands for a further reduction. Producers' co-operatives might
be the cure—but only because by this means the workers would
realize that they could not defy the laws of political economy. It

[1] *Guardian*, May 19th, 1853.
[2] Ibid., October 5th (letter) and October 26th, 1859.
[3] Ibid., April 3rd, 1861.
[4] Ibid., January 18th, 1865.
[5] *Nonconformist*, August 17th, 1859.
[6] *Guardian*, August 10th, 1863.
[7] Ibid., July 19th, 1854.

was true that 'a strike, as things now are, is the sole defence of Labour against the tyranny and oppression of Capital,' and indeed the demand for nine hours was a good one, but it was inopportune.[1]

The *Nonconformist* too was much concerned with possible cures for strikes. Perhaps limited liability opened the way to co-partnership.[2] The laws of economics were 'true and inflexible,' but left room for humanitarian action such as that of the great Yorkshire Nonconformist employer, Sir Titus Salt, which was described very enthusiastically.[3] On the demand for legislation on working hours this newspaper had a divided mind. Earlier, when the discussion centred around the Ten Hours' Bill, it seemed fully committed to *laissez-faire*:

> To legislate on the hours of labour, we hold to be as unjustifiable as to fix the rate of wages; and that, again, as futile as to decree what shall be the aspect of the sky, the state of the atmosphere, and the condition of the soil, through any given season . . .

Yet, in contradiction, it was worth trying this method, and the Liberals ought not to try to evade their commitments by amendments to the Bill.[4] Perhaps the strikes might prove to be only the transition to a better system of economic relations. The widespread combination of both sides in an iron trade dispute in 1865 suggested that such complete organization might make it easier to avoid open warfare.[5]

The *Universe* strongly protested its sympathy for employees: 'One of our principles has been the improvement of the social conditions of the working men. The labouring men of this country have many grievances to be redressed,' such as bullying by foremen and long walks to work. The strikes for a nine-hours day should be ended by a compromise. There was some general advice for the workers: 'We do not advise the workmen to persist in the system of "strikes." Nothing is more calculated to demoralize and lower their social condition than "strikes." '[6] For the guidance of other Roman Catholic readers the *Tablet* found the strike a convenient weapon with which to attack the Government's

[1] *Guardian*, August 10th, August 31st and October 5th, 1859.
[2] *Nonconformist*, November 23rd, 1853.
[3] Ibid., September 24th, 1856.
[4] Ibid., May 8th, 1850.
[5] Ibid., March 15th, 1865.
[6] *Universe*, April 6th, 1861.

Italian policy. Just as strikes might possibly be caused by the
intimidation of agitators, so all the troubles in Italy were quite
certainly due to this cause.[1] Those who supported sedition abroad
could not object to it at home. Sometimes trade unionists became
dangerous, like Italian rebels, and neither kings nor employers
could be expected to give away their rights.[2] The *Universe* had
some particularly critical remarks on Thomas Hughes in respect of
disputes:

> To be sure, on the occasion of the strikes and disputes between the
> operatives and their employers, Mr Hughes said many things gratify-
> ing to the working men. But did he ever say anything clear, original
> and intelligible on this most difficult subject? Not a word. He talked
> warmly, generously, poetically; but (we appeal to the working men
> to endorse what we say) he did not utter a single thought that could
> help to solve this the most important (perhaps) and difficult question
> of the age—the relation between the employers and employed.[3]

During the 'fifties and 'sixties, the period when the trade unions
were struggling for recognition, the Roman Catholic press had
little of interest to say about them. The *Nonconformist* was inclined
to be critical of the employers, as of all classes it considered to be
privileged, but its support for the unions and their demands,
though clearly proclaimed, was usually rather lukewarm, and fell
short of what the working classes felt was due. The *Guardian*,
though chiefly a Conservative paper circulating among the clergy,
many of them in rural areas, gave more attention to industrial
relations than any of the other papers. Of its two phases of active
interest during these years the earlier, in the early 'fifties, is rather
reactionary in tendency and out of touch with facts. Regret at the
depersonalization of industry, hostility to the 'spurious political
economy' of the time, the tendency to maintain in veiled terms the
doctrine of a 'just price' for Labour, such terms as 'master' and
'labourers' in antithesis, all suggest a backward glance at patriarchal industrial organization, or perhaps at the surviving
patriarchal character of agriculture, where most of the *Guardian's*
readers must have felt more at home than in the affairs of heavy
industry. The paper's sympathy was at least as much with the men
as with the employers, but trade unions were looked upon as in

---

[1] *Tablet*, August 13th, 1859.
[2] Ibid., June 2nd, 1860.
[3] *Universe*, July 15th, 1865.

some sense exceptional and abnormal, a consequence of the employers' refusal to be 'fair.' They were approved and recognized as necessary in existing circumstances, but not envisaged as a permanent institution contributing to the working of the economic system. By the end of the 'fifties the unions were accepted at least as necessary evils and to a certain extent valuable to society, but more emphasis was laid on the attendant faults, such as the imposition of union rules on workers in general, willing and unwilling alike, and the serious possibility that the unions might not 'understand' economics, that is to say, might not accept the implications of the existing system. To this system the *Guardian* itself appears to have been converted in the interval, and it was no longer a 'spurious political economy.' The more complete acceptance of the unions was therefore compensated by the more complete acceptance of the Capitalist system, though this is perhaps concealed to some extent by the fact that the unions were themselves increasingly ready during this period to take their place within Capitalism.

It has been suggested that the Evangelical party had exercised some influences on the development of unions: 'It was among the atoms of labour that the phrase to be "in union" had first gained a half-sacred meaning: indeed it had religious associations.' There was the influence of Evangelical hymns; for example: 'Thus may we abide in union with each other, in the Lord,' from John Newton's benediction hymn. 'Evangelical hymnology is never irrelevant to nineteenth-century labour history.'[1] Newton was an Anglican clergyman, but the Evangelicals were tending to become individualistic and socially conservative. Even among the Nonconformists a distinction must be made, for the older Dissent of the 'three denominations,' Presbyterians, Congregationalists, and Baptists, was often too middle class to be actively interested in trade unionism, though this was less true of the Baptists than of the others. Even the Unitarians, who prided themselves on their progressive outlook and sympathy with reforming movements, played very little part in the growth of trade unionism: 'They failed to realize either the necessity of it or the contribution it was later to make to English life.'[2] In the middle of the century the

---

[1] J. H. Clapham, *An Economic History of Modern Britain* (1932), II, 178f.

[2] Raymond V. Holt, *The Unitarian Contribution to Social Progress in England* (second edition, 1952), 204.

Rev H. W. Crosskey 'took a prominent part in the Derby Ribbon Weavers' strike,' and George Dawson supported the shop assistants' claim for eleven o'clock closing on Saturday night, while the Rev Henry Williamson founded the Dundee Mill and Factory Operatives' Union. But the main Nonconformist support came from the Methodists. Of Wesleyanism it has been said that by

> providing a far larger sphere of action for the laity than the Church or the older denominations furnished, it brought romance and ambition into a class which, under the pressure of the new civilization, was losing both purpose and aspiration; and the Wesleyan organization—the class meeting, the circuit, the conference, the Legal Hundred—has powerfully affected the constitution of political parties and Trade Unions.[1]

This comment must be amended to the effect that it was not Wesleyanism in the strict sense, but the smaller Methodist bodies, which made the main contribution. The Wesleyan Church took no action to assist the Tolpuddle martyrs, although five of them were Wesleyans and three of these local preachers: 'Trade Union leaders could not be born in an atmosphere of official indifference, and in consequence the Mother Church of Methodism gave practically nothing to the birth and development of the Trade Union movement.' There were some exceptions, but they were later. The share of the Methodist New Connexion in the trade union movement was insignificant: 'No outstanding Trade Unionist of any sort emerged from its ranks.' But the Primitive Methodists present a very different picture:

> From the beginning the Primitive Methodists were enthusiastic supporters of the Trade Union movement. Some of the local preachers, pioneers in Trade Unionism among the miners, suffered hardship and imprisonment because of their leadership and service. Primitive Methodism, being a working-class religion, often felt the adverse effects of strikes and lock-outs.[2]

Dr Wearmouth gives many examples of miners' leaders on the north-east coalfield who were Primitive Methodists. Most of them flourished later than this period, and some note will be taken of them below, but at the local level it was already significant that Primitive Methodism was the religion of the Durham miners.

In the relationship of the Churches and the trade unions during

---

[1] Young, op. cit., 65.
[2] Wearmouth, op. cit., 172–175.

the years when the unions were struggling for recognition two men deserve special mention. William Prowting Roberts was an active member of the Church of England and the son of a Vicar of Chelmsford. Born in 1806, he qualified as a solicitor, and in 1838, through acquaintance with Henry Vincent and other Chartists, he became involved in the Chartist movement, agitating for the reform of the franchise. He became legal adviser to O'Connor's 'Land Bank,' to his own financial loss. From 1843 he was 'concerned in nearly all the law affairs of trade unions,' and in 1844 he was appointed legal adviser to the Miners' Association of Great Britain and Ireland at a salary of £1,000, becoming known as the 'miners' attorney-general.' In 1867 he defended the Manchester Fenians. He was well known in religious circles in that after visiting the Holy Land in 1862 and 1863 he became popular as a lecturer to Anglican societies and Churches on Biblical subjects. His son entered the Church.[1]

Joseph Rayner Stephens (1805–1879) was by origin a Wesleyan, whose father became a Methodist preacher in 1792 and was President of the Wesleyan Conference in 1827. His brother George was a linguistic scholar, and another brother, John, the editor of the *Christian Advocate*. Rayner Stephens was educated at Manchester Grammar School and a Methodist school. In 1825 he became a preacher, serving with a mission in Sweden, and in 1829 he was ordained. At Ashton-under-Lyne he at once associated himself with the factory reform movement led by Sir Richard Oastler, and for this and other offences he was suspended by Conference in 1834. His response was to resign from the Wesleyan ministry and to form a small secession Church at Ashton and Stalybridge. Stephens was now well known as a Tory Radical, who, according to Francis Place, 'professed himself a tory, but acted the part of a democrat.' In the north of England the attack on the factory owners, led by Oastler, Stephens and Michael Sadler, naturally took a Tory form, since it was against the rich Whig millowners that it was principally directed, but it was a continual problem to this group to convince the Left of the Liberal Party that they were real Tories, supporters of the Crown and the Constitution, and when they combined insurrectionary agitation with professions of loyalty they were watched with suspicion by both sides.

When the new poor-law took effect, the same group were

[1] *Dict. Nat. Biog.*, s.v. Roberts.

equally hostile to this new manifestation of *laissez-faire* Liberalism, and the speeches of Stephens in particular became increasingly violent. In one, delivered in 1838, he was reported as urging every man to arm himself with 'his firelock, cutlass, sword, pair of pistols, or his pike,' every woman with 'her pair of scissors' and even every child with pins and needles, and the men to go out (over-equipped, it would seem) 'with a torch in one hand and a dagger in the other,' against the workhouses. He supported Chartism, though openly indifferent to most of its political aspects, because the suffrage was a 'bread and cheese question.' Not surprisingly, Stephens was arrested, and in 1839 sent to prison for eighteen months. In the years that followed he continued to take a prominent part locally in agitation for factory reform, though gradually mellowing, and he took an active interest in trade union affairs, for example opening the miners' conference at Leeds in 1863 with prayers. In 1867 he presided at a Lancashire trade union meeting to agitate for an eight-hour bill.[1]

Stephens was an extreme example of the Radical parson, who saw no contradiction between preaching a fervent and somewhat apocalyptic Christianity and urging arson and massacre in the interests of revolution. He died widely honoured as a sincere and devoted servant of the people, who flocked in numbers to his funeral. He belonged essentially to the last phase of the struggle of the trade union and allied movements to exist, and when the advancement of the interests of the working classes could take a more pacific form new men were needed.

2   The Crisis in Trade Unionism

About 1867 feeling turned for a time against trade unionism, especially with the revelation of the 'Sheffield outrages,' the far-from-gentle persecution by disreputable union leaders of non-union workers. The debate on the proposed enfranchisement of a large section of the working classes was a further reason why feelings were stirred at this time. The *Guardian* considered unions an evil, which could not be expected (as some thought) to disappear with the enfranchisement of the workers. In America they had forced up wages 'beyond their natural level.' They indulged in restrictive practices and ought not to have special legislative

---

[1] J. T. Ward, *Revolutionary Tory: The Life of Joseph Rayner Stephens of Ashton-under-Lyne (1805–1879)*, in the *Transactions of the Lancashire and Cheshire Antiquarian Society*, Vol. LXVIII, 1958, 93ff.

protection. Far from restoring the balance of power in industry, they tipped it in favour of the employee. Much attention was given to the Sheffield outrages, and the unions in general were blamed; yet they could not be suppressed, and the best hope lay in 'the union of all classes in the organization of labour on a sound basis,' an unusually vague recommendation even by the not very exacting standards of social panaceas. The Sheffield unions were violently attacked for condoning the outrages, and troubles at Manchester were linked with Fenian disturbances. The future was dark when political power lay in the hands of the classes which in America were planning class-legislation and at the 'International Conference at Lausanne' seemed 'to have drifted very far towards Communism'—in these terms the First International made its appearance on the *Guardian's* horizon. The vigorous enforcement of the laws against intimidation of non-strikers was approved, though it was thought that action would have to be taken to prevent trade disputes continually ending up in the law-courts.[1] In 1870 a review of Charles Reade's novel *Put Yourself in his Place*, dealing with the Sheffield outrages, shared the author's antipathy to trade unions.[2] In some contrast the *Nonconformist* defended the unions against the more immoderate criticisms. It would be 'an extreme of injustice to cast in the teeth of the artisans of this country any insinuation that this is the sort of conduct which has their sanction, or that it is the kind of outcome which is encouraged by their trade organizations,' though Sheffield was a useful reminder that trade unions could sometimes be tyrannical.[3]

The immediate consequence of the Sheffield outrages was a vigorous public discussion of the law relating to trade unions, and the setting up of a Royal Commission on this subject. The *Guardian* now began to show considerably more sympathy. A review of several books on the working classes argued that at a time of public hostility to unions it was useful to hear the case for them, and there was a welcome for the Master and Servant Act of 1867, which reduced breach of contract on the part of the employee from a criminal to a civil cause.[4] When the Royal Commission reported in 1869 the *Guardian* thought that the minority report, produced

---

[1] *Guardian*, April 24th, May 29th, June 26th, July 10th, September 18th, September 25th, 1867 and August 19th, 1868.

[2] Ibid., August 17th, 1870.

[3] *Nonconformist*, June 26th, 1867.

[4] *Guardian*, August 21st and September 4th, 1867.

by Thomas Hughes and Frederic Harrison, was argued 'with great ability' and deserved 'very careful attention.' General support was given to its recommendations, with the conclusion: 'The most hopeful remedy is the frank concession to the workmen of every constitutional claim, joined with the stern repression of every act of criminal aggression.'[1] The *Nonconformist* referred to the report in a leader entitled 'A Representative Trade Union,' dealing very enthusiastically with the Amalgamated Society of Carpenters and Joiners. Those of the commissioners who even considered banning trade unions 'might as well speak of exiling the whole industrial class from this country.' There was room for improvement in the unions, but 'they must be led, not driven.'[2] The *Nonconformist* had a divided mind on the demand for changes in the law. In 1867 no change was needed, except for additional protection for union funds. Trade unions were sometimes treated like gods: 'It is well, therefore, that their claim to a monopoly, which is "against reason and justice," should be repudiated in the name of the public.' Yet the same year there was 'entire approval' for the draft of a bill drawn up for the T.U.C. under the guidance of Hughes and Harrison, though trade unions were only 'temporary, even if indispensable, expedients,' which must ultimately give way to co-partnerships.[3] In 1869 an article was content to demand that the law should be clarified, and by way of making a start it went on to trace the history of the labour laws from the time of Edward I. The main necessity was for a law which was fair to both sides. The demand that what was legal for one man should be legal for a combination of men was at first sight unreasonable, in view of the very different character actions assumed under varied circumstances, but it was reasonable enough—because the law was ineffective, because professional groups already acted in combination, and because prohibition bred bitterness and resentment.[4] There was support for the demands of a conference at Nottingham for the repeal of the penal clauses of the Criminal Law Amendment Act, for the Common Law was sufficient to prevent violence.[5] But doubts remained, as was indicated by an article following the well-publicized prosecution of supporters of the agricultural union at

[1] *Guardian*, April 7th and July 14th, 1869.
[2] *Nonconformist*, April 14th, 1869.
[3] Ibid., August 28th and November 13th, 1867.
[4] Ibid., February 17th and July 7th, 1869.
[5] Ibid., January 17th, 1872.

Chipping Norton in 1873. The law of conspiracy badly needed reform, and the intervention of the criminal law in what was really breach of contract was anomalous, but actions for breach of contract would be ineffective against strikers, so some form of punishment must be retained.[1]

3 Trade Unionism Accepted

After the uneasiness caused by the Sheffield outrages had died down, and the public had made a more balanced estimate of the virtues and failings of the trade union movement, a number of religious leaders were active in Parliament in advancing current demands of the unions. Shaftesbury, despite his hostility to trade unions, Thomas Hughes, and Samuel Morley were leaders in the campaign for a fifty-four hour week. These three may be listed, respectively, as Evangelical, Broad Church, and Nonconformist.

In the Church of England the most vigorous clerical support for the unions came from Bishop Fraser of Manchester. Something of his general importance with regard to the relations of the Church and the workers has been indicated above, but he was particularly important in the matter of trade unions. It is true that he tended to speak of them only as necessary evils: 'I am no lover of the principles of trade unionism, but they have been forced upon the working classes by the inequitable use of the power of capital.' But at least he did accept their necessity. In the spring of 1874 the master painters of Manchester and Salford and their men appealed to him to act as umpire in their dispute. His award brought peace for two years, though his biographer, Thomas Hughes, thought him unwise in giving reasons for his decisions. His ruling was that the minimum wage was to be 7½d. per hour, overtime on full working days to begin at 9 p.m. and to be at the rate of time-and-a-half, and 1s. a week to be paid to men away from home on Sundays. In March 1876 the dispute was renewed, the men asking for an extra 1d. per hour, and Fraser was again asked to arbitrate. To the plea of the men that they could not 'live in comfort' he replied that they averaged £1 6s. 2d. a week and were better off than many workers, and that in the distressed state of business the higher wages could not be paid without still further depressing trade. He called attention to the fact that the rate fixed was only a minimum and that it was possible to earn a higher rate, but in view of the slight rise in rents he fixed the rate a little higher,

[1] *Nonconformist*, June 11th, 1873.

7¾d. But he did not enjoy his experience as an industrial umpire: 'His experience with the painters made him rather shy of the office of umpire in trades disputes for the future.' He had found that much time was absorbed in examining doubtful statements and accounts, and the usual result was only to 'split the difference.' In 1878 in a strike in the cotton industry over the question of a proposed reduction of 10% in wages, the operatives, after seven weeks, proposed to refer the matter to him in order to avoid an unconditional surrender, but the employers refused. Fraser delivered a vigorous appeal to both sides to end trade disputes, which he alleged were threatening to destroy the country's prosperity: 'The prosperity of fools shall destroy them,' he quoted. He continued to be hostile to strikes, and when, three years later, during a strike in the Bolton area, he sent £20 to the relief fund, and this was acknowledged by Henry Broadhurst, he wrote to Broadhurst condemning strikes in general, and referred to the 'luxury and extravagance' which he claimed was growing in some districts, 'instancing the case which had come to his knowledge of a factory girl giving three guineas for feathers.'[1]

As the unions became more conservative in outlook and methods, press support for them increased. The *Guardian* regretted that no working-class M.P.s were elected in 1869, and referred to this as 'an error of tactics' on the part of the Liberals—not, it is to be noticed, of the Conservatives. It was a good idea for the unions to use their funds to encourage co-operation, and they now wisely recognized that strikes harmed the workers as well as the employers. When engineers struck at Newcastle in 1871 the *Guardian* was alarmed at support from the International, and urged the concession of a nine-hour day to prevent the acceptance of Communistic doctrines. The *Guardian* thought the T.U.C. mistaken in seeking legislation for one class of society, but praised it for pursuing its object by constitutional means. In a South Wales coal strike the employers objected to the intervention in a local matter of the Amalgamated Miners' Association, but the *Guardian* thought that nowadays this was taken for granted and helped to secure the keeping of agreements. On the other hand, it would be good for trade unionists to be elected to Parliament only in order to make them more responsible, and the demand for peaceful picketing was rejected. There were fears of an increasing conflict of Capital and Labour, yet once again a few weeks later the unions were praised

[1] Hughes, op. cit., 225–230.

for their moderation, and later in this decade the T.U.C. was favourably contrasted with the International, with its Utopian ideals.[1]

The *Church Times* was much slower to become reconciled to the unions, attacking them for having 'chastised with scorpions every artisan that has had enough of manliness to think and act for himself.' It was 'deplorable to see the utter ignorance of the most elementary truths which seems to possess the artisan mind.' There would be no job for the workers but for the Capitalist. 'Nor is it true that the toll which the capitalist and the master take is exorbitant.' Because of competition 'great profits for the master and low wages for the workman can never be more than a transient combination. The folly of supposing that any organization can possibly extract more out of capitalists or masters will now be apparent.' An increase in wages would simply devalue money, and there would be no gain, while foreign markets would be lost. The wage-earners most familiar to readers of this paper were domestic servants, and women were criticized for going into traditionally male jobs, so 'drawing from domestic employment more women than could be spared from it.' The most profound comment on the economic situation of which the *Church Times* was capable was no more than a lament over the servant problem. The only servants who would accept 'the old wage of £8 or £9 a year' were the 'sluts.' Women would not dare to marry and produce children if they could not find servants: 'This is what the votaries of Women's Rights have brought women to!' The clergy and schoolteachers should

> impress on girls in national schools the advantages of domestic service over every other method which presents itself to them of earning a livelihood—the really liberal rate at which it is remunerated, its greater becomingness, and the opportunity which it affords them of being brought in contact with persons of superior education and refinement.[2]

It is interesting to compare with this the comments of other papers on the same subject: the *Nonconformist* proposed a quite opposite solution to the servant problem: employers must learn to treat

[1] *Guardian*, September 8th, 1869; September 27th, 1871; January 17th, 1872; January 15th, November 26th, December 24th, 1873; January 24th, 1874; September 26th, 1877.

[2] *Church Times*, August 23rd, 1872.

their servants better and expect less of them.[1] The *Universe* was even more Radical, urging the need for training women so they might find better jobs, and reporting sympathetically on a women's trade union conference: 'To obtain a fair day's wage for a fair day's work is a reasonable desire on the part of women who have made up their minds to earn a livelihood by other means than the precarious drudgery of the needle or by domestic service.' The latter they detested as a petty tyranny.[2]

Its attitude to domestic service was only one example of the reactionary views of the *Church Times*. It regarded the T.U.C. as an organization 'of a most formidable and possibly dangerous character,' though not without some signs of 'sobriety and good sense.' A reference to a meeting of clergy and trade unionists at the time of the Church Congress in London was perhaps a little more friendly: 'The Church Congress meetings have hitherto been chiefly held at great trade centres, where the question of Trades' Unionism has been suppressed by the influence of capitalists.' But there was little change of emphasis. It would be disastrous for the Church 'to take the side of capital, and order as a religious duty the ducking of delegates from Trades' Unions in the nearest horsepond,' but this concession to the workers did not go very far:

> Unfortunately, however, there is grave reason to think that the good which they have derived from unionism is illusory, and that the evil it has wrought them is of a very serious character . . . The great mistake of trades' unionism is to assume that the laws of demand and supply can be interfered with by artificial expedients . . .

The Capitalist was not the enemy of the worker, who would not be employed at all without Capital, 'nor is it true that capital takes more than its fair share.' It was not in the interest of the working man 'to create great organizations for the purpose of trying to repeal what might almost be termed the laws of nature.'[3]

It is difficult to imagine more questions begged in so short a passage as this; to select only two, it was assumed that workers' combination was in some way a breach of the law of supply and demand, whereas it was precisely a response to the operation of that law and an attempt to regulate its working to the greater

[1] *Nonconformist*, May 2nd, 1872.
[2] *Universe*, January 11th and March 22nd, 1879.
[3] *Church Times*, January 23rd, 1874; December 15th, 1876; January 25th, 1878.

benefit of the class which had only its labour to offer for sale; and it unquestioningly identified the 'Capital' without which Labour could not be employed, as informed trade unionists would of course have known perfectly well, with the 'Capitalists' who happened at that moment to control Capital. The slum ritualists, reading their favourite newspaper in their uncomfortable presbyteries in Bethnal Green or Miles Platting, could not have found much useful guidance about the real working classes, and least of all about their most ambitious leaders, who were continually asking the questions conservative Anglicans thought needed no answer.

An incident revealing similar attitudes towards trade unions on the part of some Anglicans arose when the T.U.C. protested against a passage in a National Society reading-book accusing the unions of tyranny. The *Guardian* was prepared to concede that the allegations were exaggerated, which was undoubtedly true, since the passage alleged that trade union members were worse off than 'Russian bondsmen or serfs' or 'negro slaves,' and the newspaper took the occasion once again to urge that the Church must dissipate the idea that it was on the side of the rich.[1]

More than the Anglican press the *Nonconformist* was interested in strikes at this time. In a London shipbuilding strike (1868) both sides were reminded that trade was being driven elsewhere;[2] in a cotton strike (1869) the employers' severity was condemned, and the workers' moderation praised;[3] a gasworkers' strike (1872) was very ill-judged;[4] an ironworkers' strike against piecework was condemned, although the possible abuses of the system were listed;[5] another cotton strike was the fault of the workers, but also due to the example of 'arrogant self-will' set by the Conservative Government.[6] The *Guardian* was strongly critical of this last strike, in face of foreign competition, and Bishop Fraser's warning of the danger of ruining the industry was welcomed.[7] With its mediating position on most industrial disputes the *Nonconformist* was often ready to advocate conciliation and arbitration, and on various occasions it praised the work of A. J. Mundella, treating conciliation as a useful stepping-stone to co-partnership, which it thought

[1] *Guardian*, September 24th, 1879.
[2] *Nonconformist*, February 1st, 1868.
[3] Ibid., May 19th, 1869.
[4] Ibid., December 11th, 1872.
[5] Ibid., January 19th, 1875.
[6] Ibid., May 22nd, 1878.
[7] *Guardian*, May 22nd and June 19th, 1878.

the real cure for disputes. Mill saw the latter as itself a stage on the way to producers' co-operation, but the *Nonconformist* thought the last step unnecessary.[1] The *Universe*, in its Radical mood, came out strongly in favour of Samuel Plimsoll, violently attacking the shipowners and blaming their greed on Protestantism, and heaping abuse on Disraeli for obstructing the efforts of 'honest, fearless and outspoken Mr Plimsoll.'[2] Another representative Capitalist was John Bright, who posed as a 'tribune of the people' while looking after his own interests rather than theirs:

> Perhaps he could explain to the nation how it is that the profits of our enormous trade have gone almost entirely into the pockets of the upper and middle classes; why the producers of all this wealth should have failed to receive something like a fair proportion to reward them for their incessant hard labour; why have they not had a fair share of the prevailing comfort, contentment and happiness; why should there be strikes, destitution and starvation? Sad spectacle, truly, for a civilized, wealthy nation to present. Our wealthy classes ought to look to it. It is in their interest to do so. No wonder that our fair land should be overrun with Internationalists and discontented spirits of every description.[3]

Such a passage was in a sense conservative in tendency; it presupposed the existing class-system while trying to initiate changes in the basis of the distribution of wealth between the classes; and doubtless it was motivated largely by hatred of the Radical Capitalist Nonconformity of which Bright was an outstanding representative. But it revealed the possibility of a new kind of Tory Radicalism, deliberately taking sides with the workers and with the critics of the contemporary social scene, against the leaders of industry, commerce and finance who were accepted as spokesmen of Radicalism alike in politics and in religion.

Such an attitude was not likely to be found in the Anglican press, but the *Guardian's* support for the principle of employers' liability did produce some quite Radical comments. The Bill was wrong to give compensation only when the employer could be shown to be at fault, and still worse was an amendment by the House of Lords further restricting its scope. Indeed, the *Guardian* went so far as to accuse the upper House of being 'unduly biased in favour of wealth,' and called Lord Beaconsfield's amendment,

[1] *Nonconformist*, September 9th, 1874.
[2] *Universe*, July 31st and August 21st, 1875.
[3] Ibid., January 11th, 1873.

setting a two-year limit to the operation of the Act, 'a sop to the unreasonable cowardice of capital.'[1]

Thus after the period of alarm caused by the Sheffield outrages the religious press reveals a fairly rapid acceptance of trade unions as part of the industrial system, even if little enthusiasm for them. The *Nonconformist* and the *Universe* had in common a tendency to attack the employers and to blame them for many industrial disputes, while the *Church Times* continued to live in a world of its own, dreaming of the collapse and disappearance of trade unions.

One of the most important facets of the history of the trade union movement in mid-Victorian times was the growing influence of Nonconformity, and especially of Methodism. There had been a time, not so long ago, when the outstanding leaders of the working classes had included a large proportion of men critical of Christianity of any kind, and Methodism had been notoriously a conservative body. But now not only the Primitive Methodists, but even the Wesleyans themselves, were awaking to social concerns. Henry Broadhurst (1840–1911) was at his most active. In 1872 he became the leader of the stonemasons' union and the following year secured for all masons an increase in wage-rates and a reduction of hours. In 1873 also he became secretary of the Labour Representation League and among other positions he held were membership of the Parliamentary Committee of the T.U.C. and the secretaryship of the Congress. From 1880 to 1906 he was M.P. for various constituencies and served for a time as Under-Secretary at the Home Office. He stood on the extreme Right of the Trade Union movement, being a firm Liberal and an opponent of the agitation for a legislative eight-hour day, and in his later years he was increasingly isolated by the rise of the independent Labour movement.

Apart from Broadhurst the Methodist contribution continued for a time to be made chiefly by the Primitives. The *Primitive Methodist Magazine* took a lively interest in all industrial disputes, taking, as would be expected, the side of the workers, but it was rather defeatist about the prospect of successful strikes. Dr Wearmouth has made a careful survey of comment in the *Magazine* on Labour relations from 1854 to 1898.[2] One's impression is that it sympathized with the workers, and advocated legislation which would benefit trade unions, but that it was essentially

---

[1] *Guardian*, September 1st, 1880.
[2] Wearmouth, op. cit., 175–184.

conservative—in the same sense as Broadhurst and the Wesleyans—
on wider social issues. It was inclined to minimize the real conflict
of Capital and Labour and to appeal to a spirit of reasonableness
on both sides, as exemplified by the great Primitive Methodist employer, W. P. Hartley. Whether Thomas Burt (1837–1922)
should be classed among the Primitive Methodists is doubtful,
though he was brought up in a Primitive Methodist home and was
always influenced by this background.[1] His uncles, Robert and
Andrew, were officials in the Primitive Methodist Connexion, the
former a class-leader and the latter a local preacher. On the other
hand he is also claimed as a Unitarian.[2] Burt can perhaps be put
down as a product of Primitive Methodism if not a very faithful
adherent. Like Broadhurst among the Wesleyans he belonged to
the old school of trade unionists. At the age of thirty-seven he was
elected to Parliament, he and Alexander Macdonald becoming the
first working-class M.P.s. He became President of the National
Union of Mineworkers, President of the T.U.C., Parliamentary
Secretary to the Board of Trade, and 'Father' of the House of
Commons. He too was a steady Liberal. Many other Methodists
who were trade union leaders on the north-east coalfield are
named by Dr Wearmouth, though it is not always easy to decide
when they were at their most active. John Wilson (b. 1837),
John Johnson (b. 1851), Peter Lee, and John Bell all held high
office in the Durham Miners' Union and were all devoted local
preachers, Lee also becoming Chairman of the Durham County
Council. Primitive Methodists were also prominent in the Yorkshire coalfield, where Ned Cowey was President of the Yorkshire
Miners' Federation for thirty years from 1873 and an outstanding
force in the Miners' Federation of Great Britain, the T.U.C., and
international miners' conferences. Many other Primitive Methodists gave local leadership to the miners both in the north-east and
in Yorkshire. In the Midlands Enoch Edwards (b. 1852) became
treasurer of the Miners' Federation, and S. Finney (b. 1857)
served on the Federation Executive. There were Primitive Methodist miners' leaders in the north-west and Lancashire too, but
few of these were as prominent.[3]

It will be noticed that Dr Wearmouth's account of Methodist

[1] Thomas Cox Meech, *From Mine to Ministry: The Life and Times of
Thomas Burt, M.P.* (N.D.)
[2] Holt, op. cit., 205.
[3] Wearmouth, op. cit., 188ff.

contributions to trade unionism in the period 1850–1900 is very largely confined to the miners' unions, the main exception being in the organization of the agricultural labourers, which will be noted below. The trade unionism of the Methodists—even of the Primitives—was therefore of the old-fashioned type characteristic of the early 'Lib.-Lab.' M.P.s and the Miners' Federation to which they belonged. The Primitive Methodists of Durham were part of the aristocracy of Labour, and the spirit of the 'New Unionists' was quite different. Within these limits the contribution was important:

> Not only did Methodism give pioneers and advocates to the Trade Union movement but it also gave atmosphere and fervour, spirit, tone, and method. It permeated the movement with religious earnestness and ardour and the belief that God's blessing would be experienced in the service of the oppressed. Occasions were not rare when local trade union meetings began with prayer and were conducted with a sense of worship and awe . . . The Methodists in seeking to save men's souls in the next world gave a new distinction and importance to the energies and emotions and circumstances of this world.[1]

4 The Agricultural Union

The outstanding event of mid-Victorian times, so far as the relations of trade unions and the Church are concerned, was the emergence of agricultural trade unionism in 1872, which calls for special comment. There had been a feeling among conservative-minded churchmen, fearful and suspicious of trade unionism, that at least it was a purely urban phenomenon, and indeed largely centred on such semi-civilized areas as the coalfields and the industrial regions of Lancashire and Yorkshire, rather than, for example, London. It has been noted several times above that the Church of England was stronger in the rural areas than in the towns, and the parish church in the village remained the norm in the minds of most Churchmen, even when such villages had come to represent only a minority of the population. The shock of the unionization of the submissive country labourer was greater in the religious world even than the great dock strike of 1889.

The founder of the agricultural union, Joseph Arch,[2] was a

---

[1] Wearmouth, op. cit., 209.

[2] Joseph Arch, *The Story of His Life, Told by Himself*, edited by the Countess of Warwick (second edition, 1898).

bigoted Nonconformist, and it is hardly a misrepresentation to say that the struggle of farmer and labourer in 1872 was an episode in the agelong contest of Church and Chapel in rural England. The association of denomination and social class is illustrated with startling clarity in the life of Arch. His autobiography is full of prejudice against the Church of England and the upper classes, which he identified with each other. He relates with satisfaction the battles between his mother, apparently a dominating personality, and the rector's wife. He grew up in the parish church and learned to hate its class divisions: 'In the parish church the poor were apportioned their lowly places, and taught that they must sit in them Sunday after Sunday all their lives long.'[1] From childhood he revolted: 'I never took the Communion in the parish church in my life.' He refused to do so because the worshippers went up to communicate in order of social class, with the poor last. Like his mother, but unlike his father, he preferred to stay away from church altogether. 'Like my good mother before me,' he records, 'I was a Nonconformist by nature and by conviction.'[2] There was no chapel in the village, but Dissenters held meetings in a lane, and those who attended them were refused charities by the parson and the farmers, and the same combination, when a friendly society was founded, 'did their very best to put it down,' lest it should encourage too much independence.[3] Arch goes on to record a number of instances of resistance to the pretty tyranny of the rector. When a Wesleyan chapel was built in 1840 Arch took an active part in its work. It was supported by local preachers, and soon after his marriage at the age of twenty-one Arch began to preach. Till he was approaching middle age there was nothing remarkable about his career, and he knew nothing about trade unions. 'But he was a born orator. His practice as a local preacher had given him confidence, self-reliance, freedom of gesture, and a flow of language.'[4] When in 1872 the effective unionization of labourers occurred almost spontaneously in Warwickshire the organizers sent a deputation of two of their number to ask Arch to take control, and the middle-aged farm worker suddenly found himself a national figure, and his National Agricultural Labourers' Union a formidable power throughout large areas of the countryside.

[1] Arch, op. cit., 17.   [2] Ibid., 48.   [3] Ibid., 34.
[4] George Howell, *Labour Legislation, Labour Movements, and Labour Leaders* (1902), II, 257.

Hitherto the attitude of the Church of England towards attempts to form agricultural trade unions had been mixed. The clergy were often accused of opposing reforms. But there were exceptions, and outstanding among them Edward Girdlestone (1805–1884), whose parochial service brought him into close contact with agricultural labourers. Like Arch, he achieved fame late in life. In 1862 he became Vicar of Halberton, Devon, and showed so warm an interest in agrarian conditions that he became known as the 'agricultural labourers' friend.' From 1867 he carried on a campaign for improved conditions, and in 1868, addressing the British Association, he urged the need for agricultural unions. This was later regarded as the first step leading to the formation of N.A.L.U., though there had been some agricultural unions before. He took a leading part in promoting the migration of distressed labourers to other parts of the country, meeting strong opposition from farmers in his own parish and from fellow-clergy.[1] The Rev E. J. Green, Vicar of Leintwardine, Herefordshire, was an active supporter of the West of England Labourers' Improvement Association, founded in 1870.[2] The Secretary of this Association was a Nonconformist, but the President and twenty Vice-Presidents were clergy. It was a moderate body with limited aims, and quite successful. The warm interest in agrarian conditions of James Fraser, especially during his service on the Royal Commission of 1867, has been mentioned.

But the formation of Arch's union and the strike of the labourers created a sensation in the Church of England, and for many months the Anglican press could think of little else. The issue was confused, so far as the more sympathetic clergy were concerned, by the strong vein of anti-clericalism in the movement, led by militant Dissenters. Most of the leaders were Methodist local preachers, and none were Anglicans. The influence of the Christian Socialists had not reached the remote villages of rural England, and the reaction of the clergy to the agricultural movement was consequently largely antagonistic. The *Spectator* accused the clergy of being unanimously hostile to N.A.L.U. and the strike. Two incidents achieved a notoriety which astonished those responsible. Bishop Ellicott of Gloucester, referring to the strike, hinted, rather indirectly, that the best way of dealing with Arch

[1] *Dict. Nat. Biog.*, s.v. Girdlestone. See also Donald O. Wagner, *The Church of England and Social Reform Since 1854* (1930), 149ff.
[2] Wagner, op. cit., 153f.

would be to throw him into the village pond. He thereby became a symbol of clerical reaction, rather unjustly, for he was more sympathetic to the labourers than many clergy, and inclined by temperament to say sweeping things which perhaps did not deserve to be remembered against him. The other incident was much more serious and sinister. At Ascot in Oxfordshire the farmers introduced non-union labour, and a crowd of women used threats and a little ineffectual violence against it. Sixteen of the women were brought before the Chipping Norton magistrates and sent to prison with hard labour. Both magistrates were clergy, and the result was a widespread outcry against clerical magistrates.

But there is a good deal to be said on the other side. Girdlestone publicly gave his support to the strike. Arch himself mentions some clergy who supported him.[1] There was also J. C. Cox, 'landowner, colliery proprietor, magistrate, son of a clergyman, and later a clergyman himself, who gave full and eager support'.[2] The Christian Socialists, especially Llewelyn Davies, were prominent. Some clerical spokesmen for the labourers, such as Henry Jones of St George's in the East, had urban livings, where they were not likely to encounter the astonished anger of the farmers, but some of the country clergy were ready to brave the wrath of influential parishioners. Many tried to adopt a neutral attitude, believing that the Church had no concern with secular conditions such as wages and hours. In the Church Congress of 1873 clerical, but not lay, speakers were found ready to take the side of N.A.L.U.[3] Among them were Davies and Girdlestone.[4]

The most influential Anglican supporter was Fraser. In his diocese of Manchester he might seem to have been cut off from agricultural life, but he knew more about it, from his work on the Royal Commission, than almost anyone else on the Bench. He was not a wholehearted supporter, in that he advocated moderation on both sides, and sometimes Arch proved too much even for the tolerant Fraser. He was moved to protest when Arch, perhaps carried away by his own oratorical powers, launched a more than usually savage attack on the landlords, proclaiming that he would

[1] Arch, op. cit., 102, 109, 135.
[2] Wearmouth, op. cit., 203.
[3] Wagner, op. cit., 163ff.
[4] M. B. Reckitt, op. cit., 115.

have no regrets if some foreign invader landed and decapitated them all. Arch replied to Fraser by quoting the example of Moses, who rejoiced and showed no regrets over the fate of Pharaoh and his army, a Biblical parallel which seems to have satisfied, or at least silenced, Fraser. Yet Fraser was perhaps the only clergyman who moved Arch to enthusiasm. He called him a 'wonderfully liberal man',[1] and referring to a demonstration in Manchester in 1874 he wrote: 'Even the Bishop, Dr Fraser, took sides with us, which in my opinion was a very brave thing for a prominent dignitary of the Church of England to do, but then he was a man as well as a bishop.'[2] If Fraser was sometimes irritated with Arch, this was nothing to the fury to which he was roused by the attitude of the farmers. In April 1874 he wrote a highly aggressive letter to the *Times*, asking the question: 'Are the farmers mad?' In this he asserted:

> Fair wages will have to be paid to the labourers. If farmers can't afford fair wages at present, rents must come down—an unpleasant thing no doubt for those who will spend the rent of a 300 acre farm on a single ball, or a pair of high-stepping horses, but nevertheless inevitable.[3]

This letter brought down much criticism on his head, but raised his popularity among the workers to new heights, and his portrait, inscribed 'A Friend of the People,' was carried in procession through Manchester.

Fraser was not the only leading churchman who came out frankly on the side of the agricultural labourers. There was also Cardinal Manning, and his vigorous expression of his sympathies startled even his friends. He called for a Royal Commission to investigate the men's grievances. Writing to Gladstone he condemned Anglican leaders who had shown so little understanding of the position of the labourers:

> As to the agricultural affair, the Bishop of Peterborough was as bad as the Bishop of Gloucester. How is it they do not know the day of their visitation? . . . Why cannot you do these things for the labourer? Prohibit the labour of children under a certain age. Compel payment of wages in money. Regulate the number of dwellings

[1] Arch, op. cit., 226.
[2] Ibid., 222.
[3] Hughes, op. cit., 229.

according to the population of parishes. Establish tribunals of arbitration in counties for questions between labour and land.[1]

He sent subscriptions to N.A.L.U. in 1878 and 1879.

Manning's social radicalism sometimes brought about the apparently curious spectacle of Roman Catholic-Nonconformist alliance, opposed by the majority of the Anglican clergy. Support for N.A.L.U. was a marked example of joint action. Apart from the movement's having originated in rural Methodism it drew a good deal of support from Nonconformity at large, and when N.A.L.U. held a famous mass meeting at Exeter Hall the chair was taken by the Congregationalist Samuel Morley, who had donated £500 to the union. Manning was on the platform, as was Thomas Hughes, but Anglican clergymen were 'conspicuously absent.'[2]

The *Guardian* gave a great deal of attention to the agricultural movement.[3] A first article on the strike thought that the labourers would win higher wages and that this would not harm the farmers. The men were unthrifty, but that was no reason to refuse their demands. The next article took up a position of benevolent neutrality towards the strikers, urging the clergy to try to ensure that increases were not wasted, and holding out the somewhat optimistic hope that from being 'half-fed, badly clothed, and uneducated clowns' the labourers would become capable of 'theological enlightenment and high religious aspirations.' The labourers were more intelligent than people thought, and only wanted a fair share in current prosperity. An article by Llewelyn Davies outlined the advantages of trade unionism, and urged the clergy to support the agricultural union and to take the part of the poor. A little later doubts began to creep in, and there were fears that too big a rise would damage national prosperity. The intervention of Fraser provoked the comment that it was good to have a bishop of Liberal opinions—he seemed to be regarded as something of a phenomenon—but that he should be more moderate in expression. It was unreasonable to call the farmers 'mad' merely for fighting back with a lock-out. A reasonable wage ought to be enforced 'either by law or by public opinion'—surprising invocation of the possibility of legislative interference with wages.

[1] Shane Leslie, *Henry Edward Manning*, (1953 edition), 149f.

[2] Wagner, op. cit., 156.

[3] *Guardian*, April 10th, April 17th, June 5th, August 14th, September 4th, 1872; April 8th, August 5th, August 26th, September 30th, 1874.

When the farmers won their struggle the *Guardian* appealed to them to be generous. The first charge on the produce of the soil should be the maintenance of the worker, and smallholdings would be a help. The farmers ought not to try to reverse increases.

There was much correspondence on this subject throughout the 'seventies, but the only further leader on it told the clergy to stop treating agricultural labourers like children and to learn some economics. They should distinguish the Radical politics and anti-Anglican feeling of N.A.L.U. from its economic value.[1] Long afterwards, the 1885 election results produced big gains for the Liberals in the country areas, interpreted as the expression of hostility to the Church on the part of the newly enfranchised labourers, itself explained as revenge for clerical hostility to Arch in 1872. A crop of letters disputed whether this was the right explanation, or whether cheap bread had not counted for more than disestablishment. The *Guardian* repeated that the clergy must learn to accept the new independence of the labourer.[2]

In contrast the *Church Times* had virtually nothing to say. A few correspondents grew heated on the subject of the relations of Church and labourer,[3] and a most hostile leader described the movement as 'a very serious calamity.' Wages had already been as high as possible, and trade unionism, 'disastrous and absurd' in towns, was worse in the countryside. That there had not been violence was only due to the spread of Anglo-Catholicism.[4]

The *Nonconformist* naturally regarded Arch and all his works with enthusiasm, treating the formation of the union as a historic event and appealing for support. Descriptions of rural poverty were no exaggeration. Bishop Ellicott's cure for trade unionism was treated in characteristic manner: 'It is perhaps not surprising that bishops should fail in the obligations of Christian charity, for it is a part of their creed to teach men to be satisfied with the condition in which they have been born.' The right was 'almost invariably on the side of the labourers, who . . . have been wretchedly paid.' At the end of 1873 the *Nonconformist* and the *Labourers' Union Chronicle* had a sharp dispute about the value of emigration, but the former continued to support the labourers and to condemn

[1] *Guardian*, September 5th, 1877.
[2] Ibid., January 13th, 1886.
[3] *Church Times*, August 30th, September 6th, September 20th, 1872.
[4] Ibid., September 11th, 1874.

the farmers.[1] Later, in 1878, the *Nonconformist* wanted to see a combination of farmer and labourer against landowner, a typical expression of Radicalism, but not very appropriate when the labourers were united in a struggle against their immediate employers and the aristocracy was increasingly remote.[2] Later references were enthusiastic for smallholdings.[3] The rise to political eminence of Arch offered the occasion for lavish praise for so splendid a Dissenter, who was the second 'most interesting' man in Parliament, after Gladstone. He was like John Ball, and, rather inconsequently, 'a conspicuous illustration of what England owes to the Free Churches. In the Establishment there was no place for such as he except in inarticulate attendance on the ministrations of the priesthood.'[4]

The *Nonconformist* was biased, of course, but there was a good deal in what it said. Once again its attitude was not altogether dissimilar from that of the *Universe*, and though all the facts were interpreted differently there was at least agreement that the Church of England was in the wrong. The *Universe* was delighted at Manning's enthusiasm for N.A.L.U., and especially delighted at his prominence at Exeter Hall, traditionally associated with militant Protestantism. Ellicott's language 'cannot check a good movement, though it may irritate its promoters,' and Manning's attitude showed that 'the labouring man who seeks for the redress of his grievances by open and honest agitation will find his best and truest friends in the Catholic Church.'[5] Several years later an article attacking low agricultural wages went on to sum up the rather Radical point of view to which the Roman Catholic Church in England had been led by Manning:

> Reform, retrenchment, the readjustment of the relations between capital and labour are great economic questions which can not for long be wisely put off; the day of reckoning will surely come, and the sooner the better for the working classes of the United Kingdom.[6]

5   *The Zenith of the Old Trade Unionism*

In the 'eighties there was a shift of emphasis. The discussion of

[1] *Nonconformist*, April 3rd, April 10th, August 28th, 1872; May 21st, December 17th, 1873; April 1st, April 15th, May 7th, October 7th, 1874.
[2] Ibid., November 27th, 1878.
[3] e.g., January 14th, 1886.
[4] Ibid., January 21st, 1886.
[5] *Universe*, December 14th and December 21st, 1872.
[6] Ibid., August 26th., 1882.

the legal position of the unions passed into the background, and public attention concentrated on the problems of poverty, long hours, and unemployment. There was a demand now for an eight-hour day. The doctrine of *laissez-faire* was out of favour, and the *Guardian* was to be found protesting against the excessive hours worked on the North Metropolitan Tramways routes, and specifically rejecting the reply that there was no difficulty in filling vacancies, so that conditions must be satisfactory.[1] The *Church Times* also condemned long hours, but in characteristically half-hearted terms, and dissociated itself from 'agitators, who profess to be the real friends of what are called the "Masses." ' It had 'no taste for legislative interference in such a matter,' but things were so bad that it was prepared to welcome 'some judicious remedial measures.'[2] The *British Weekly*, the new Radical and Nonconformist journal, was at first not very advanced on this issue. The miners, who had taken the lead, it considered well able to look after themselves, without legislation.[3] But gradually it was realized that the Liberal Party could no longer turn a deaf ear to the demands of Labour,[4] and on the occasion of the Fifeshire election, won by Augustine Birrell, the comment was that neither candidate would have polled 'a solitary miner's vote' without supporting this particular aim.

Much was heard at this time about 'sweating' in London, the *Guardian* putting the blame on foreign Jews.[5] The *Church Times* experienced its usual sense of helplessness: 'If public opinion were already right on this subject, the law would not be wanted, if the law contradicted or even went beyond public feeling, it would be inoperative'—a sufficient answer to any reform proposed.[6] It did however go so far as to recommend a system of lists—'white' and 'black'—of good and bad employers, and the *Universe*, anxious to show that it was up-to-date with the latest slang expression, wanted a 'boycott' of the latter. It rejected legislation, but repeated the useful suggestion of training facilities to increase the 'marketable value' of female labour,[7] and it also condemned the selfishness of people who did their shopping late in the day, so imposing

[1] *Guardian*, August 12th, 1885.
[2] *Church Times*, July 11th, 1884.
[3] *British Weekly*, August 26th, 1887.
[4] Ibid., July 5th and July 12th, 1889.
[5] *Guardian*, December 7th, 1887.
[6] *Church Times*, August 5th, 1887.
[7] *Universe*, July 8th, 1882.

long hours on shop assistants.[1] The Industrial Remuneration
Conference in 1885 brought from the *Guardian* the comment that
the workers might be better off than formerly, but they were still
not getting their fair share of the increased national prosperity,[2]
while the *Nonconformist* thought it disappointing, except in
revealing the opinions of the workers.[3] In the same paper there
was a rebuke for a speaker at a Congregational Union meeting (on
Christian Economics) who was angry at the suggestion that the
poor were partly to blame for their own poverty.[4]

This was an old, indeed a positively antiquated, debating topic,
but a new problem, in terms of scale, was unemployment. The
Guardian disliked the new word 'unemployed' for classing
together industrious and shirkers, and thought Manning's
suggestion of 'national workshops' (not his own term) amounted
to indiscriminate charity.[5] The *Church Times* too was very indignant about this—but then it was always ready to tilt at Manning,
perhaps to emphasize the gulf between real Catholicism and the
Roman heresy. He was guilty of self-display and of talking 'clap-
trap,' and his 'economics and his social ethics' were even worse
than his theology. Much relief had been given by 'Christian
feeling' and most of the poor were responsible for their own misfortune. If each congregation cared for 'three or four old or infirm
people' and 'three or four orphans . . . there would be comparatively
little chance of people who ought not to be in the workhouse
finding their way thither.' It was no use threatening property, 'for, unless property is held absolutely sacred, commerce and
industry cannot thrive.'[6] This was a new doctrine of property from
a 'Catholic' source. The *Nonconformist* had no good word for
Manning either, and was pained at attacks on 'political economy,'
which issued no commands, but only sought to show how things
worked. Manning's suggestion would create paupers, and he was
wrong to think that poverty was the source of crime. On the
other hand Lord Salisbury was reprehensibly indifferent to the
social question.[7] The *Universe*, in Manning's own Church,
criticized the workers for trying to increase employment by

[1] *Universe* June 3rd, 1882.
[2] *Guardian*, February 4th, 1885.
[3] *Nonconformist*, February 5th, 1885.
[4] Ibid., October 25th, 1888.
[5] *Guardian*, February 8th, 1888.
[6] *Church Times*, February 17th, 1888.
[7] *Nonconformist*, February 9th, 1888.

restricting production,[1] but agreed with him that work ought to be created for the unemployed. The press should concern itself less about foreign politics and more about the 'condition of our working people.'[2] Employers should accept lower profits rather than reduce wages and thereby cause strikes.[3]

For the moment the great issues involved in the growth of the trade union movement had passed into the background, and attention was concentrated on the condition of the people.

6 The London Dock Strike of 1889

For some time strikes had not been attracting much notice, though the *Guardian* noted troubles in various parts of the world from time to time, usually attributing them to the unsound character of foreigners. But in 1889 the London dock strike suddenly proved that large-scale and highly organized strikes might occur at home too. The *Guardian* had already attacked the casual labour of the docks,[4] and now it quoted Charles Booth on the poor conditions. It was impressed with the achievement of organizing such workers, and noticed 'another idea, fraught with far-reaching consequences—the solidarity of labour.' There should be 'wise and disinterested arbitration.' It was feared that the strike would harm London as a port, and that the 'solidarity of labour' might be used to secure a general eight-hour day, which would ruin industry, yet by the end of the strike it was anticipated that the workers' victory would benefit the country, and that a general union 'to keep up wages in all trades, or otherwise artificially to advance the interests of the labourers' was unlikely.[5] This was an interesting survival of the archaic word 'artificially' and a contradiction of earlier fears.

More surprisingly, the *Church Times* abruptly changed its mind about trade unions, and came out warmly in favour of the dockers, who were behaving 'with an admirable quietness and self-restraint' and had won public support. Organized thus 'labour may be enabled to do much to diffuse, by the only way in which it can be diffused, more equally than at present, the wealth which under prevailing conditions is apt to accumulate for the

---

[1] *Universe*, November 8th, 1879.
[2] Ibid., January 10th, 1880.
[3] Ibid., February 7th, 1880.
[4] *Guardian*, November 10th, 1886.
[5] Ibid., August 28th, September 4th and September 18th, 1889.

benefit of some fortunate persons, while others starve, or have a fearful struggle for a livelihood.' The Church had no time for 'Communism and Socialism proper,' which suppressed the individual 'for whom all else exists,' but it had authority to teach about social conditions, and to say that an employer had no right to pay the lowest wages possible, or to act as if he had absolute rights over other people. It was gently hinted that Burns and Tillett were rather uncompromising, and less gently that the Bishop of London had shown up badly in returning to his holiday while Manning still laboured for a settlement.[1]

The Nonconformist press reacted similarly, both the leading papers starting non-committally, and the *Nonconformist*, anxious to help, recommending 'wise concessions on the one hand and moderation and forbearance on the other.' But it was already noticing that the men were 'very orderly,' while the directors, 'most unwisely, as we think, are resolute in rejecting arbitration.' The *British Weekly* also found fault with the directors, who were 'wrong alike in their action and in the manner of their action,' though the strike leaders were also very wrong in trying to widen it. Christians should speak out plainly, like Manning and Scott Holland. By mid-September the two papers had diverged. The *Nonconformist* was worried that a deputation of Free Church ministers had urged the directors to give in, feeling that their resolution was not 'well considered,' while the *British Weekly* thought that Christians, apart from Manning, should have done more than 'whispering in apprehensive tones "Socialism," wondering what Burns would do next, and in the mean time finding bread and collecting money for the workers . . . Even now when the Bishop of London has come forward we ask, where was Mr Spurgeon?' On the settlement of the strike there was enthusiasm for Manning and a marked lack of it for Free Church leaders, including John Clifford, while the *Nonconformist* thought they had been wise to leave it all to Manning, because he was the best-qualified man for the task, adding a glowing tribute. But Nonconformists had done useful work too. The *British Weekly* printed an interview with Burns and Tillett, attacking the Nonconformists and praising Manning.[2]

---

[1] *Church Times*, September 6th and September 13th, 1889.

[2] *Nonconformist*, August 29th, September 12th and September 19th, 1889; *British Weekly*, August 30th, September 6th, September 13th, September 20th, September 27th, 1889.

It was indeed the dock strike which more than anything else brought the aged Cardinal prominently before the public at large as a social reformer, a character Protestants had never associated with a Church they were inclined to dismiss as thoroughly reactionary. Indeed Manning's views seemed odd even to his co-religionists, who, to his regret, continued to display very little interest in social questions. Manning recognized the ideals of the working classes, and perhaps because the religious tradition into which he had entered still seemed to be eccentric to English life he had a ready sympathy for trade union agitators. In the dock strike he was able to address the directors with some authority, as the brother of a former dock chairman, and he warned them that revolution was imminent, though he also 'confided to the strikers that he had never "preached to so impenitent a congregation"!' Lord Buxton described how Manning 'day after day from ten in the morning till seven or eight at night' busied himself 'interviewing, discussing, negotiating, sometimes waiting hour after hour patiently at the Mansion House. He never appeared disheartened or cast down.' Compared to leaders of other Churches Tillett found him 'more human and subtle, his diplomacy that of the ages and of the Church.' On one occasion the dockers refused to accept a settlement negotiated by Burns and Tillett. Bishop Temple 'withdrew in disgust' and 'Manning drove down alone to Poplar' for a three-hour conference in Wade Street school. When the men refused to accept the increase in wages as from November 4th, demanding that it should date from October 1st, Manning threatened to appeal to Irish Catholic labourers who would pay attention to him. The directors agreed to consider the terms 'if they came through Cardinal Manning,' and it was by this means that the strike was settled. His reward was in the influence he gained over the working classes. Tom Mann said of him:

> I shall ever remember him as the finest example of genuine devotion to the down-trodden. He was never too busy to be consulted, or too occupied with Church affairs to admit of his giving detailed attention to any group of men, whom kindly influence could help, and he was equally keen to understand any plans of ours to improve the lot of these men.

And Tillett added even more enthusiastically, of Manning's character: 'How it burned and singed my nature and called out of the depths the primitive courage . . .!' After the strike the workers collected £160 for Manning, which he used to endow a bed at

8—TCATLM

the London hospital. In an address they thanked him for his labours and said that in him they seemed to see 'a father in the midst of a loving and well-loved family rather than the ordinary mediator or benefactor in the thick of a trade dispute.' He gained an ascendancy over Tillett which he used in telling him not to make any wild speeches for a time.[1]

Manning's active and friendly interest in union affairs was not limited only to the dock strike and agricultural unionism, nor even to one country. In 1886 he lent warm support to the American Cardinal Gibbons in a campaign which succeeded in averting a Papal condemnation of the Knights of Labour, a body with considerable Roman Catholic support. Some comments reveal his underlying attitude to the questions uppermost in the minds of the workers' leaders at this time. In 1874, addressing mechanics at Leeds, he said: 'I claim for Labour, and for the skill which is always acquired by Labour, the rights of Capital. It is Capital in its truest sense.'[2] Again, in 1887 he urged that wages ought to be related to profits, and said that the refusal of employers to accept such a suggestion showed that their profits were excessive.

The reaction of the *Universe* to Manning's intervention in the dock strike was predictable. It rejoiced at the victory of the men, whose 'conduct throughout was exemplary,' and it had 'no sympathy to waste' on the owners, whose views were 'a fraudulent and selfish perversion of political economy.' It was eager to make its position crystal-clear:

> In this war of labour against capital we make no bones about it—we are thoroughly with labour, as long as it is honest and assiduous . . . The man who rises at the dawn, like those brawny fellows by the riverside, who drudges at hazardous jobs which would tax the strength and courage of a Hercules, who endures all vicissitudes of weather, and is content with his pipe and well-earned pot of beer when the sun sets, is the genuinely valuable member of the commonwealth, the wage-earner, the indispensable factor in the greatness of the country . . . The toilers deserve better treatment, and proud and delighted we are that one important section of them has succeeded in forcing it from reluctant task-masters. Doubly proud and delighted that the almost complete success which has been achieved—and we must be satisfied with that, for ours is a world of compromises—is due to the mediation of the Cardinal Archbishop of Westminster . . .

[1] Leslie, op. cit., 158ff.
[2] Ibid., 149.

He took no partisan attitude, but if he inclined to any side it was that of the hewers of wood and drawers of water. And they will henceforth regard His Eminence as their *decus et tutamen*—their glory and shield.[1]

The article goes on to draw a contrast with other ecclesiastical leaders. The picture of the typical English working man bears little resemblance to the real representatives of that class, least of all to those active in trade unions, who even in mid-Victorian times were far from satisfied with a pipe and a pot of beer; but it is possibly not so very remote from the picture many working men would have drawn of themselves, and no doubt any class is easily persuaded that it is the 'genuinely valuable' element in the community. The *Universe* was able to take such a forthright line because the Roman Catholic Church in England was so largely a working-class body, and it is evident that it was not attempting to be impartial, as Manning at least claimed to be. It was perhaps a fair if unconscious portrayal of his attitude of mind that the *Universe* described him as impartial but inclining to one side in the dispute.

7   *Christian Influence on Trade Unions in the Closing Years of the Nineteenth Century*

After the dock strike of 1889 a change came over trade unionism and the relations between the unions and the Church. The days when middle-class assistance was needed in the formation and maintenance of unions had passed, and the workers had learned the lesson of self-help, though not perhaps in quite the way their numerous mentors had intended. The unions were no longer social clubs providing for a whole range of interests for their members, but more consciously the organized force of Labour directed against Capital. Middle-class Christians no longer felt the same sympathy, and some of the union leaders were hostile to the Church. Yet most of the prominent spokesmen of the unions were Christians of some sort, and tended to talk in the kind of religious language which came so readily to their lips, as for example when Tom Mann said: 'We will, above all things, endeavour to be true to ourselves, and we call upon all who will respond to the call of duty as a religious work.'[2]

There was less scope than formerly for Church leaders to

---

[1] *Universe*, September 21st, 1889.

[2] H. M. Lynd, *England in the Eighteen-Eighties* (1945), 242.

intervene in trade disputes. In the dock strike many clergy, especially those in the East End, had been sympathetic, but Bishop Temple had given an unfortunate impression of indifference, and now the contrast between him and Cardinal Manning was sometimes unjustifiably quoted as the contrast between their respective Churches. Bishop Creighton of Peterborough intervened in a boot trade lock-out in 1895 and by this means helped to secure peace. At Durham Bishop Westcott maintained regular relations with Labour and invited trade union leaders among others to his palace. In the coal strike of 1892 he arranged a truce, and his action, which was loudly praised in many quarters, led to the setting-up of conciliation boards. Such actions were noted: indeed they perhaps received more publicity than they merited, for the intervention of Westcott was rather isolated in its deliberate and prompt nature, and in general the clergy acted only after a good deal of persuasion. But such publicity perhaps balanced the bad press given to Temple and revealed a genuine concern on the part of at least some clergy in the industrial disputes of the time.[1]

There was not much inclination to form Christian trade unions, a triumph for the Nonconformists who had so much influence in the existing unions. Had they not played so large a part it is likely that hostility to religion would have become a mark of English trade unions as much as of those on the Continent, and Christian trade unions would have come into being, as there, in reaction. At a later date Roman Catholic unions were formed in the textile industries, chiefly as pressure groups opposed to secular education, but they remained a minor force and did not extend to other trades. The majority of the Roman Catholics, being members of the working classes, were able to exert a considerable influence within the existing unions, especially among the cotton operatives. There were also Jewish unions, such as the Amalgamated Jewish Tailors, Machinists and Pressers (1893), but these were not so much religious unions, nor even racial, as small unions confined to trades which happened to be predominantly Jewish.[2]

Among individuals prominent at this time in the trade union movement every variety of religious conviction can be found, but the well-established Nonconformist leaders continued to take

[1] Wagner, op. cit., 257ff.
[2] S. and B. Webb, *History of Trade Unionism* (revised edition, 1920), 478f.

an important place, though they were increasingly losing touch
with the new trends. Such a man was William Abraham (1842–
1922).[1] He was born at Cwmavon in South Wales and worked
underground for twenty years from the age of nine, receiving a
'scanty education.' He was brought up in a Calvinistic Methodist
Chapel, and once said: 'What I am today, whatever that may be, I
owe to the Sunday School, the Band of Hope, and to the Eis-
teddfod.'[2] He was a pioneer of trade unionism among the Welsh
miners and a well-known Nonconformist leader, becoming the
first Welsh miners' M.P. He remained always on the Right wing
of the Labour movement, and sat as a Radical, though a member of
the 'Labour' group formed after the 1885 election. He did not
formally join the Labour Party till the affiliation of the miners in
1909. He was described as not an 'ardent advocate' of the Labour
Party's 'socialistic policy'; a leader of the 'most moderate' section
of the Welsh miners; and a 'restraining influence.' He began his
union career in 1871 and was prominent in the mining disputes of
the 'seventies, defending the sliding scale of wages against the
demands for a minimum wage. He was out of sympathy with the
militant policy of the years before 1914, and his influence declined,
especially with the trend towards Syndicalist ideas. He sat in
Parliament for Rhondda, where he ran the Band of Hope and the
choir at the chapel he attended: 'It was generally admitted that
the singing was more fervent and inspired when under his leadership.' It was indeed his custom to lead community hymn-singing
at trade union gatherings, preparing the way for his fervent
oratory. He was a popular lay-preacher, and it was his characteristic saying that Jesus of Nazareth was the miners' best friend,
though religious influence over the miners was decreasing, despite
the Welsh revival of 1904. Abraham's biographer traces some
aspects of his policy to his religious background: 'It is fair to say
that this denomination[3] was more uncompromising in its hostility
towards labour organizations than any other, and he must have
been conscious of this antagonism during his early years. Perhaps
it was for this reason that he always opposed an aggressive trade
union policy and advocated peaceful settlement.'[4]

[1] E. W. Evans, *Mabon* (*William Abraham, 1842–1922*): *A Study in
Trade Union Leadership* (1959).
[2] Ibid., 2.
[3] Calvinistic Methodist.
[4] Evans, op. cit., 101.

Ben Pickard (1842–1904)[1] was also a miner. He was a Wesleyan and a local preacher, who in 1888 became first President of the Miners' Federation. He too was a Liberal and sat as M.P. for Normanton from 1885 to 1904.

A very different type of trade union leader was coming to the fore, sometimes a Roman Catholic, often indifferent to religion, occasionally experimental in his attitude. In the new sphere of women's trade unionism Emilia Dilke (1840–1904)[2] represented the third alternative. She was interested in art, and study of Dante and Thomas à Kempis developed in her a 'mystical sense of religion.' She married Mark Pattison. She was a close friend of George Eliot, and the Pattisons were alleged, rightly or wrongly, to be the originals of Dorothea and Casaubon in *Middlemarch*, a suggestion flattering to Mrs Pattison but decidedly unflattering to her husband. She became interested in social reform, and especially in the position of women, and in 1876 she joined the 'Women's Provident and Protective League,' later the Women's Trade Union League, urging the provision of technical education for women and also their enfranchisement. After the death of Pattison she married Sir Charles Dilke, at the time of the notorious divorce case. She had a great influence over the W.T.U.L., from 1889 to 1894 representing it in the T.U.C., and she had many contacts with Labour leaders and spoke at meetings on Labour questions affecting women. She also wrote books expressing her personal religious convictions, of a mystical nature. Her second husband wrote a memoir of her in her *Book of the Spiritual Life* after her death.

8   Trade Disputes of the 'Nineties

If the participation of Church leaders in trade disputes decreased at this time the interest shown by the religious press did not. At first London was the focus of attention. Both the *Guardian* and the *Nonconformist* disapproved of Will Thorne's gasworkers' strike on the grounds that it was directed against profit-sharing, making light of the conditions attached to the scheme.[3] The *Nonconformist* dismissed a crop of strikes in the capital as the

---

[1] *Dict. Nat. Biog.* (second supplement), s.v. Pickard.
[2] Ibid., s.v. Dilke.
[3] *Guardian*, December 11th, 1889; *Nonconformist*, December 12th, 1889.

'Strike Mania,'[1] while the *British Weekly*, which was by now a much more effective voice for the Free Churches than the older journal, was alarmed at a police union, and at strikes by police and postmen, wishing that instead 'the voice of the poor, half-starved match-box makers of the East-end could be heard.' Then attention turned to Scotland, with a railway strike supported by the *British Weekly*, which praised railway workers for their 'steadiness, courtesy, patience, and sobriety,' believed that the public sympathized with them, and attributed their defeat to the proportion of railwaymen outside the union.[2] The *Universe* also favoured the strike, and quoted Manning against the evils of long hours, adding a rhetorical question with a positively Socialist flavour: 'Who dares to deny that productive labour is the sole author of wealth?'[3] The *Guardian* was delighted at Westcott's intervention in the Durham coal strike of 1892, calling it epoch-making, and his technique of mediation was compared favourably with that of Manning in the dock strike—indeed the chief delight was at finding an Anglican name to answer that of Manning.[4]

This was only a prelude to the great coal strike of 1893. On this the *Guardian* shifted its position. At first it expected the strike to fail, but then it began to demand a compromise solution, thought that the men should have been consulted before the acceptance of contracts at lower prices, and criticized the 'old political economy,' in the person of Sir William Houldsworth, for not realizing that a strike was simply part of that 'higgling of the market' he thought should determine the price of Labour. By late October it was accepted that the strike, which was now bound to succeed, was for a 'living wage,' and that if the interpretation of this standard was raised with each generation, that would have to be accepted—a complete break with classical economics. A minimum wage would have to be allowed, and no disaster would follow. The settlement was a victory for the men, which the owners would have to recognize.[5] The *Church Times* merely criticized both sides for their failure to seek a compromise, and welcomed Government intervention, while a letter from a coal-

---

[1] *Nonconformist*, July 10th, 1890.

[2] *British Weekly*, June 27th, July 11th, 1890; January 1st, January 15th, February 5th, 1891.

[3] *Universe*, February 7th, 1891.

[4] *Guardian*, June 8th, 1892.

[5] Ibid., July 26th, August 30th, September 20th, October 11th, October 25th, November 8th, November 22nd, 1893.

owner explained that the strike was part of a Fabian Society plot
to set up a Labour Government.[1] The *Nonconformist* (by now the
Independent) had an article by an author who said he could not
apportion the blame, but would continue his 'small efforts' on
behalf of the miners. Relief at the end of the strike was increased
by the setting up of machinery for negotiation.[2] The *British
Weekly* also sympathized with the men, and when they were
accused of disorder commented: 'It is not the miners merely that
need to be kept in order. The mine owners need control, perhaps
even more.' It regretted the continuance of the strike, blaming the
intransigence of the owners, thought the men's demands just,
and criticized Asquith for an unsympathetic speech. At first it
thought the Government right not to intervene, but after sixteen
weeks of the strike it was glad there was such an intervention. A
clerical meeting on the subject was 'a sad fiasco.' Lord Rosebery's
settlement, regarded as a victory for the strikers, was satisfactory.[3]

Other strikes of this period concerned transport and communi-
cations. The *Guardian* opposed the Hull dockers' strike because
its objects were not clear,[4] while the *British Weekly* supported it,
though critical of London dockers who struck in sympathy.[5] The
Guardian[6] and the *Church Family Newspaper*[7] were both alarmed
at the violence of the American railway strike, led by Eugene
Debs; the *British Weekly* condemned the violence, but also
blamed the company for its immoderate attitude.[8] The same
three papers were concerned at the 'sympathetic' extension to
Glasgow of a Belfast shipbuilding strike in 1895,[9] the *Church
Family Newspaper* suggesting that the 'solidarity of labour' would
provoke a 'solidarity of Capital' which would prove much more
effective, and warning that this 'barbarous method of settling the
matter' could only benefit foreign competitors. There was a sharp
divergence on the North Wales quarry dispute in 1897. According

---

[1] *Church Times*, November 17th, 1893.

[2] *Independent*, November 9th and November 23rd, 1893.

[3] *British Weekly*, September 28th, October 5th, October 26th, November 9th, November 16th, November 23rd, 1893.

[4] *Guardian*, April 26th and May 24th, 1893.

[5] *British Weekly*, May 4th, 1893.   [6] *Guardian*, July 18th, 1894.

[7] *Church Family Newspaper*, July 13th, 1894.

[8] *British Weekly*, July 12th and July 19th, 1894.

[9] *Guardian*, December 18th, 1895; *Church Family Newspaper*, November
15th and November 29th, 1895; *British Weekly*, November 14th, and
December 19th, 1895.

to the *Church Family Newspaper* Lord Penrhyn was quite within his rights in refusing conciliation, though it was 'a pity,'[1] but for the *British Weekly* there was a political moral:

> Surely the working classes must at length be asking themselves what they have to gain by putting the Conservatives in office. Every day it becomes more apparent that they have given themselves over, bound hand and foot, to their deadly foes. All the dazzling talk about a social programme has vanished into air. The majority of the House of Commons hates working-class legislation, and delights to support the worst class of employer . . . The men who cheered for Lord Penrhyn would welcome any chance of destroying the workmen's charter of liberties.[2]

In the case of the South Wales coal strike of 1898 the *Guardian* and the *Church Family Newspaper*[3] were agreed that a minimum wage was impossible because of foreign competition, though the *Guardian* added that the owners were foolish in saying they would never agree to accept arbitration.[4]

But the most important dispute in the closing years of the century was the engineering strike. Once again there was a marked division in the religious press, with the High Church *Guardian* and the Nonconformist *British Weekly* much more friendly to the strikers than the Low Church *Church Family Newspaper*. In the *Guardian* the employers were strongly criticized for spreading the area of the dispute and for refusing to take part in a Board of Trade conference. The union won little public support because of its past intransigence, but it was the employers who were to blame for the failure of efforts at arbitration, and their proposals, until modified, struck at the root of collective bargaining.[5] The *British Weekly*, while insisting that 'our sympathies in such disputes are naturally with the workers,' emphasized the difficulties of foreign competition. The employers were foolishly hostile to trade unions, and even if they won the struggle, there was likely to be a war of Capital and Labour, with the Liberal Party irrelevantly thinking only of Home Rule. As in the case of Lord

---

[1] *Church Family Newspaper*, February 5th, 1897.

[2] *British Weekly*, February 4th, 1897. See also August 26th, 1897.

[3] *Guardian*, April 13th, 1898; *Church Family Newspaper*, April 29th, 1898.

[4] Ibid., September 7th, 1898.

[5] Ibid., July 14th, July 28th, October 13th, October 20th, November 3rd, December 15th, December 22nd, 1897.

Penrhyn, the political solution was obvious: 'It is astonishing that
thinking men should fail to see that whenever the working men
really combine they can return a Parliament which may change
other things than the hours of labour.' As the crisis approached it
was admitted that the employers would have had a good case, if
they had not refused to accept a public enquiry, and extreme
speeches on both sides were condemned. As in the case of the
Guardian the extravagant claims of the employers were criticized,
and their amendment welcomed. The strike, even if it failed,
might lead to 'militant socialism.' In the New Year, politics
became seriously involved, with the issue of a manifesto by John
Burns, directed against Sir Christopher Furness, Liberal candidate at the York by-election, who was an engineering employer,
urging the workers to vote Conservative if Furness did not accept
union demands. It is difficult to imagine anything calculated more
to infuriate the *British Weekly*, which always regarded the proletariat as a Liberal preserve, though part of the blame was put on
the Liberal Party for choosing such a candidate at such a time.
When Hardie and Burns gave their support to the Conservatives,
the Socialists were written off as hopeless, but the all-important
matter was to attract the workers to the Liberal Party, and the
party leaders were blamed for not taking sides firmly with trade
unions. The *British Weekly* took its revenge by blaming the
Socialist leadership for the collapse of the strike.[1]

The *Church Family Newspaper* was wholly negative. A reduction of hours from fifty-four to forty-eight a week would impossibly
weaken the industry in face of competition. Gifts from German workmen were not surprising, for they hoped to 'keep the strike going in
England until all the work had left these shores for Germany.'
The conflict was a 'death struggle for Trades Unionism,' in which
there was no doubt that the employers would win. The vote to
continue the strike was mad, and the employers were perfectly
right to refuse to employ 1,125 men instead of 1,000 (i.e. by
reducing hours from nine to eight) and in refusing to allow the
unions to lay down conditions for the employment of non-
unionists. There was no value in the suggestion that a body of
churchmen should arbitrate, nor that there should be compulsory
arbitration—how could strikers be forced back to work, or the

[1] *British Weekly*, September 2nd, September 16th, October 14th,
October 28th, November 4th, November 18th, December 9th, December
16th, 1897; January 6th, January 13th, January 20th, January 27th, 1898.

employer be forced to reopen his mill? Many contracts were going abroad because of the strike, and gifts from other unions and Mann's talk of 'unity and solidarity' would not bring victory. Sir Christopher Furness was right to refuse to withdraw from the Federation at the demand of Burns, with the reply that he would not be a 'blackleg.' Throughout the strike there was a marked contrast not only with the *British Weekly*, but also with the *Guardian*, and when the strike failed the *Church Family Newspaper* was inclined to exaggerate the significance of the defeat for the A.S.E., calling it 'a disaster unequalled in the melancholy history of strikes. For many a long year the Amalgamated Society of Engineers will be powerless as a trade society, though as a friendly society it will doubtless continue.' Heavy as the defeat was, it did not quite reduce the union to impotence. Another retreat from reality was the insistence, so familiar in the history of revolutionary movements, that all the trouble was caused by a small minority: 'A handful of agitators and labour leaders undertook to lead a crusade for an eight-hours day. They entrapped the Union into a costly struggle, and have been badly beaten. The whole campaign, in fact, was the result of unscrupulous leadership.'[1]

A strike, especially one on so large a scale and so bitterly fought as the engineering strike, was a dramatic event demanding close public attention, but in many ways strikes were not the most important feature of labour history at this time. The very frequency of strikes led to increased attention to means of averting them. The *British Weekly* welcomed a warning by Burns that it was foolish to strike without a good prospect of success,[2] and the following year it quoted Havelock Wilson to the effect that the answer to strikes was the complete unionization of employees and employers alike.[3] Perhaps the T.U.C. could devise machinery to do away with strikes.[4] Earlier than this the *Nonconformist* had praised the London Chamber of Commerce for favouring conciliation, without seeming very optimistic about the prospects.[5] The

---

[1] *Church Family Newspaper*, October 15th, November 26th, December 10th, December 17th, December 31st, 1897; January 7th, January 14th, January 21st, January 28th, 1898.

[2] *British Weekly*, November 5th, 1891.

[3] Ibid., September 1st, 1892.

[4] Ibid., September 7th, 1893.

[5] *Nonconformist*, December 27th, 1889.

Guardian saw no value in passing an Act setting up conciliation boards if there was no obligation to use them,[1] though the idea of compulsory arbitration, with decisions enforceable by law, was impracticable.[2]

9   Conditions of Work in the 'Nineties

Meanwhile the unions were carrying on two campaigns, one for a standard working day of eight hours, and the other for a minimum wage. These have been mentioned in connexion with some of the disputes of the period, but strikes were only one method by which pressure was being applied. The *Guardian* had no sympathy with the demand for legislation for the reduction of hours, objecting that the unions could achieve their object themselves, or that it was impracticable to make such a reduction at once over the whole of industry; the implication of the former point, that if necessary a strike for the eight-hour day was justified, was accepted. On the other hand Bernard Shaw's assumption that the case for the eight-hour day was too obvious to need arguing was found rather irritating. A review of John Rae's book *Eight Hours for Work* was sympathetic, though Rae was in favour of legislation if necessary.[3] The *Church Family Newspaper* opposed the idea of an eight-hours Bill for miners on the grounds that they could well look after themselves and that they were not unanimous about it.[4] As for the *Church Times*, it was at its silliest on this question. An eight-hour law could not be applied to all—for example to shepherds, grooms, gardeners, (an obscure inclusion relating to the need to attend to hothouse fires) and domestic servants: a somewhat medieval list instructive concerning the Anglo-Catholic clergyman's contacts with the working classes. For employers 'social and industrial life would become not only intolerable, but practically impossible.' By an extraordinary piece of reasoning the professional classes were brought into the discussion, and their ruin envisaged, and indeed the whole campaign was seen as a Socialist plot: 'As a matter of fact the whole fight now going on is with the intention of getting rid of masters, and of making em-

[1] *Guardian*, March 13th, 1895.
[2] Ibid., January 4th, 1899.
[3] Ibid., September 11th, 1889; August 27th, 1890; January 21st, 1891; May 18th, June 22nd, 1892; August 22nd, September 5th, 1894; January 16th, 1895.
[4] *Church Family Newspaper*, August 17th, 1894.

ployers servants of the Trades' Unions. The idea is purely
Socialistic, and it is Socialism in its most extended and aggressive
form.' The workers ought to realize that their enemies were not the
Capitalists, 'but the evil-minded men who spend their time in
arousing the bad passions of their fellows.'[1] A complete contrast is
provided by the *Nonconformist*, which thought a demonstration in
Hyde Park on this subject something 'for Englishmen to be
proud of,' because of its peaceful nature. There were difficulties
in a reduction of hours, as Bradlaugh had pointed out, but in any
case the Church ought to be involved in the question: 'We believe
that the Christian Church is, without knowing the fact, depriving
itself of opportunities of usefulness by its terror of the discussions
classed as "Socialistic" . . . From a true Socialism we have much
to hope . . .'[2] The *British Weekly* thought it right that ministers
should preach about politics, and by way of example printed a
sermon in favour of the eight-hour day, by R. F. Horton. It
congratulated a Sunderland firm and the War Office on the introduction of the eight-hour day, and approved a recommendation
that the Board of Trade should be given power to stop excessive
hours on the railways. On the other hand the defeat of Broadhurst
in the General Election of 1892, attributed to his opposition to the
eight-hour demand, was deplored, and on the plea that the res-
triction should be universal there was the usual point about the
difficulty with home-workers. But with current hours and wages
there could be no doubt that the campaign was justified. Trade
unionists would do well to give more attention to the long hours of
women and children.[3] Thus the Nonconformist press noticed the
difficulties, but still warmly supported the demand, while the
Anglican tended to see in every obstacle an impossibility.

The *Universe* objected to the Hyde Park demonstration on two
grounds: because it was held on a Sunday, and because of 'the
introduction of the Anarchist and Socialist element into what
purports to be a labour demonstration.' The demand for legislation was 'artificial' and 'utterly preposterous,' for the law should
intervene only in such exceptional cases as women and children
and workers in dangerous occupations. But like the *Nonconformist*

---

[1] *Church Times*, August 29th, 1890.
[2] *Nonconformist*, May 9th and July 31st, 1890.
[3] *British Weekly*, November 5th, December 17th, 1891; June 9th, June
23rd, July 7th, 1892; May 11th, 1893, January 11th, August 2nd,
1894.

the *Universe* was impressed with the orderliness of the demonstration, and praised speeches by Mann and Davitt.[1]

The other campaign, for the establishment of minimum wages, with which was coupled the continuing battle against 'sweating,' received less notice. The *Guardian* drew a distinction between the idea of a minimum wage, which was no concern of the state, and the regulation of conditions, which was, but it realized that the two were closely related, and that they also involved the question of unemployment. Sweating should be dealt with at once, even if thereby unemployment was increased: 'Sweating can go on *ad infinitum*, dragging down the whole scale of remuneration and of living throughout the country, while complete absence of employment for certain classes at least calls attention, and eventually works its own cure.' It was not yet realized that unemployment was to be the great social evil of the next generation. The demand for a 'living wage' was approved, but not the term itself, because it was misleading; the claim meant that wages should be regarded as a factor in determining cost, not a residual element when costs had been deducted. But this was not a subject for state intervention, but for the action of trade unions. True, this would increase unemployment, 'but, as Canon Scott Holland truly said, let us settle one thing at a time.' However, this position was not maintained consistently, for later the unions were criticized for fixing minimum wages and thereby causing the dismissal of older men who would have stayed on for lower wages.[2]

The *Church Times* and the *Church Family Newspaper* had little to say on this issue, though the former had one very typical comment: 'Before a living wage can even be thought of, several things must first be assured. There must, first of all, be profits, regular profits,' a comment constituting a perfect gift for Marxist critics of the Church, though it is fair to remember that the 'living wage' was a technical (though ambiguous) term, and that the Anglo-Catholic party was not literally in favour of starving the workers. The *Manchester Guardian* was criticized for its claim that every man ought to be able to afford to educate 'four or five children.'[3]

The *British Weekly* gave full support to this campaign, for example by quoting, with approving comment, a sermon by

[1] *Universe*, May 3rd and May 10th, 1890.
[2] *Guardian*, November 29th, December 6th, 1893; February 17th, 1897.
[3] *Church Times*, March 30th, 1894.

Stopford Brooke, and by welcoming enthusiastically support from prominent Church leaders.[1]

The *Universe*, while always sure that the Roman Catholic Church represented the interests of the working classes, had not much to say, though it did express the hope that a Labour conference at Berlin would 'break down the cast-iron rules of an obsolete political economy, which, under its too limited principle of "supply and demand," took no count of the rights of labour, no heed of the moral claims of the working population.' 'Every nerve ought to be strained' to improve the condition of the workers. 'The day is happily past when capital could dictate its own terms to labour ... The men are no longer driven like dumb cattle.'[2] These were broad terms, but the only clear and uninhibited support for the workers' claims was once again from the Nonconformist side.

Other social changes were initiated by the Government rather than by the trade unions, and these were noticed much more by the Anglican press than by the Nonconformist or Roman Catholic, especially when it was a Conservative Government. The *Guardian* warmly welcomed the Workmen's Compensation Bill, which became law in July 1898, greatly extending the scope of employers' liability, and supported Lord Salisbury's dismissal of the cry of 'Socialism' raised by Lord Wemyss. The only doubt was whether it would not be better to make the state, rather than the employer, liable—the Webbs' suggestion; this even if the idea 'smacks very much of Socialism.'[3] The *Church Family Newspaper* took a similar line. There was criticism of the previous Liberal Government for refusing to accept amendments on 'contracting out' agreed by the Lords, and a warm welcome for the Conservative social legislation—favourably contrasted with the Liberals' absorption with Home Rule. The compensation bill was very good, and by no means contrary to Conservative principles, as alleged by Lord Londonderry. Other measures welcomed were new factory legislation (by the Liberals), and a private member's Bill raising the age for factory work to twelve.[4]

---

[1] *British Weekly*, November 2nd and December 7th, 1893.

[2] *Universe*, March 22nd, 1890.

[3] *Guardian*, January 6th, June 2nd, July 21st, August 4th, 1897; July 27th; 1898.

[4] *Church Family Newspaper*, February 23rd, 1894; April 26th, 1895; July 31st, 1896; May 14th, July 23rd, 1897; March 3rd, 1899.

For the *British Weekly* opposition in the House of Lords to the principle of employers' liability kindled indignation, and there was enthusiasm for a protest meeting in Hyde Park, addressed by Burns. The Government Bill of 1897 received praise, albeit grudging, and there was even a work of commendation for Chamberlain, the minister chiefly responsible, a concession indeed for a Radical journal. The revolt of some northern Conservative members allowed the *British Weekly* to return to a more normal standpoint, and the group's attack on Chamberlain gave satisfaction as a sign of dissension on the Government benches. How far the Radical wing of the Liberals had moved from *laissez-faire* is indicated by the welcome this paper gave to a Bill providing for the regulation of laundries: 'It is full of the spirit of wise collectivism, which is becoming more and more the policy of the Labour Party.'[1]

On the great new social problem of the age, unemployment, these newspapers had nothing to contribute. The *Guardian* thought the L.C.C. on the wrong lines in forbidding its employees to take additional employment in their spare time, and brought up the old idea that many people were voluntarily unemployed: 'Incurable idleness is one cause of the complex phenomenon of the unemployed.' Industry was in a bad way, but the *Guardian* admitted it did not know the reason, and if the question was asked on what principles the problem should be approached, no answer was given, though the trade unions should realize the part played by foreign competition. The report of the Select Committee on Unemployment in 1896 was 'rather colourless and disappointing' and had no remedy to offer.[2] The *British Weekly* ridiculed Baroness Burdett-Coutts for her 'furious and orotund' reply to the suggestion that she should employ unemployed men rather than painters working in their spare time, and the I.L.P. for demanding that local authorities should be compelled to provide work for the unemployed at 24/- a week. It advocated increased powers for the Poor-Law Guardians.[3]

---

[1] *British Weekly*, March 22nd, May 3rd, 1894; May 6th, October 21st, 1897.

[2] *Guardian*, November 28th, 1894; January 9th, February 13th, March 20th, 1895; September 9th, September 30th, 1896.

[3] *British Weekly*, September 27th, 1894; April 18th, July 18th, 1895.

10 *Attitudes to the T.U.C. down to 1900*

In the eighteen-eighties the religious press suddenly began to pay a good deal of attention to the T.U.C. In 1880 the *Nonconformist* commented that the political activities of the T.U.C. were approved by 'advanced Liberals' as 'one of the best instruments of progress.' Trade unionists elected to Parliament, like Broadhurst, became very moderate, and the more such men were elected the better. The next year this paper was full of enthusiasm for trade union leaders, who showed a 'breadth and elevation of thought such as are rarely heard in Parliament'—except from one or two Liberals, of course. Other points for praise were their moderation and their ruthless suppression of troublesome delegates. In 1882 the T.U.C. was defended against the accusation that it arrogantly spoke for the nation; in any case it had a better right to do so than the House of Lords.[1] In 1883 the same newspaper heaped praise on 'the common sense, the practical wisdom, and the moderation, which distinguish meetings of this kind in England from analogous assemblies in foreign lands,' while the *Guardian* spoke in similar terms and was delighted at the failure of the Congress to give official support to Chamberlain's plan for the payment of M.P.s.[2] The next three years brought little comment, except for more praise for 'moderation' from the *Guardian*.[3] In 1887 the moderation was not so evident, and the *Nonconformist* ate its own words in saying: 'We are not quite sure that unionists act wisely in determining to give their movement a marked political character,' with demands for widespread state interference. The speech of the President was 'nonsense—infantile nonsense,' better disregarded, had it not come from an important public figure. The limit of state action had been reached when Free Trade was established—a claim revealing the gap between Radical and working-class ideals and posing great problems for the future co-operation of Nonconformist Radicalism and the working-class movement.[4] The *British Weekly* thought the demands made at the Congress would bankrupt employers and increase unemployment.[5]

---

[1] *Nonconformist*, September 23rd, 1880; September 22nd, 1881; September 28th, 1882.

[2] Ibid., September 20th, 1883; *Guardian*, September 19th, 1883.

[3] *Guardian*, September 23rd, 1885.

[4] *Nonconformist*, September 15th, 1887.

[5] *British Weekly*, September 16th, 1887.

In 1888 the *Guardian* praised the unions, while rejecting their specific demands—for land nationalization and the eight-hour day,[1] while the *Nonconformist* noted at rather tedious length the decline of the wages-fund doctrine.[2] The 1889 Congress, at Dundee, fell during the dock strike, and the *Nonconformist* said very broadly of the wage-earners: 'Our sympathies are with them . . .' It was easy to say this, but the feeling of sympathy was not strong enough to bring with it support for the chief union demands. There was a call for a legislative eight-hour day, 'but happiness, ease, and prosperity' could not be conferred by Act of Parliament. The President (Ritchie) quoted the success of the Ten Hours' Act, 'but surely the case of women and children is very different from that of the able-bodied men whom he would make the subjects of grandmotherly legislation.'[3]

In the early 'nineties attention was concentrated on the arrival of the 'New Unionists.' The *Church Times* was alarmed that their triumph would ruin the country by driving Capital abroad, though Capitalists who refused to make reasonable concessions, such as those demanded by Plimsoll, were equally at fault. Hostile references to the clergy by Burns were regretted.[4] The *Nonconformist* thought the 1890 Congress critical, and the *British Weekly* described it as without doubt 'the most important assembly of working men ever held in this country.' It was not true to say that moderation had prevailed, and indeed there was every sign of a stand-up fight with Capital.[5] The Congress of 1891 was again 'perhaps the most important that the Labour Parliament has ever held,' for the unskilled workers were at last making their voice heard.[6] In 1892 the *British Weekly* was pleased with the Congress, but the report dealt mainly with the discussion of the Sunday opening of museums and art galleries and of temperance, and the *Independent*, as it now was, despite the broad title: 'The Harmonization of Capital and Labour,' had not much more to add, except a plea for more working-class J.P.s. The *Guardian* too once again found the Congress satisfactorily moderate, and had little to say about Keir Hardie's resolution in favour of

[1] *Guardian*, September 12th, 1888.
[2] *Nonconformist*, September 13th, 1888.
[3] Ibid., September 5th, 1889.
[4] *Church Times*, September 12th, 1890.
[5] *Nonconformist*, September 11th, 1890; *British Weekly*, September 12th, 1890.
[6] *British Weekly*, September 17th, 1891.

'independent Labour representation.'[1] The next year the *Guardian* noticed and criticized a trend towards Socialism,[2] and in 1894 this trend was much more marked and attracted the attention of all the press.[3] The *Guardian* was moved to ridicule by the carrying without discussion, of Hardie's Socialist resolution in favour of general nationalization, as an amendment to a proposal relating only to the mines, and regretted the under-representation of the big unions. The *Church Family Newspaper* was worried that this should happen at a time when industry already had enough troubles, while the *British Weekly* commented shrewdly that the best safeguard against nationalization was the property owned by the working classes, and that the greatest danger was that such resolutions might frighten some Liberals into reaction. All three papers rejoiced in 1895 that Hardie's challenge had been met by the institution of the block vote, though the *Guardian* did notice something rather autocratic about the procedure followed.[4] The two Anglican papers were also well satisfied with the next Congress, which did not interest the *British Weekly*, for in the words of the *Church Family Newspaper*: 'Altogether better influences are, we believe, at work, and the political agitator is rather at a discount.' The desire for Labour representation in Parliament was 'very natural,' but it was 'scarcely fair' to expect it for nothing.[5] The *Church Family Newspaper* also dismissed as a mere dream talk in 1897 about a general Labour federation and the 'solidarity of Labour,' and the *British Weekly* thought that the continuing Socialist influence was to the advantage of the Tories.[6] In 1898 the *Church Family Newspaper* was as usual convinced that the political ambitions of Socialists such as the President, O'Grady, were absurd, and that the unions would 'sign their own death warrant if they turn their societies into mere political organizations,' but the

[1] *British Weekly*, September 15th, 1892; *Independent*, September 16th, 1892; *Guardian*, September 14th, 1892.

[2] *Guardian*, September 13th, 1893.

[3] Ibid., September 19th, 1894; *Church Family Newspaper*, September 7th, 1894; *British Weekly*, September 13th, 1894.

[4] *Guardian*, September 11th, 1895; *Church Family Newspaper*, August 30th, 1895 (see also August 2nd and September 6th, 1895); *British Weekly*, September 5th, and September 12th, 1895.

[5] *Guardian*, September 16th, 1896; *Church Family Newspaper*, September 11th, 1896.

[6] *Church Family Newspaper*, September 17th, 1897; *British Weekly*, September 16th, 1897.

Guardian was quite alarmed that for the first time the President was a thoroughgoing Socialist.[1] In 1900, after a quiet year, the *Guardian* lamented the increasing control exercised by the Parliamentary Committee, and the *British Weekly* pointed out that resolutions condemning the Boer War and the Government's education policy were probably very unrepresentative of the working classes as a whole.[2]

This concern with the political aspects of the unions was reflected also, from an opposite point of view, in the *Church Family Newspaper*, which had hopes that they would be converted to Imperialism and abandon the Liberals, and a little later showed interest in a statement by Pickard, as President of the Miners' Federation, apparently despairing of the Liberal Party. The basis for a breakaway of the unions was the payment of M.P.s, but this newspaper failed to see this implication, and was hostile to the idea that the country should pay over £200,000 a year 'in order that a few Labour members, possibly three or four, may enjoy the privilege of being members of Parliament at the country's expense.' An article on the agricultural labourers dwelt with satisfaction on the fact that their votes were usually a source of disappointment to Radicals.[3]

11 *Scope and Character of Trade Unionism at the End of the Nineteenth Century*

The most fundamental topic of discussion at this period was the scope of trade unionism. The continued existence of the unions was no longer in doubt, but there was still room for debate how far their influence should extend. The *Guardian* rejected Scott Holland's advocacy of the complete unionization of Labour, on the grounds that it would enable unions to fix wages, whereas workers ought to be paid 'what their labour is worth' and what is 'morally fair'—the method of calculation was not given.[4] It was strongly critical of the Labour Commission Report of 1895, to which it devoted five leaders. The Minority Report (signed by Tom Mann and others) was more precise than the Majority, but

[1] *Church Family Newspaper*, September 2nd, 1898; *Guardian*, September 7th, 1898.

[2] *Guardian*, September 12th, 1900; *British Weekly*, September 13th, 1900.

[3] *Church Family Newspaper*, April 6th, September 14th, November 23rd, 1894; January 13th, 1899.

[4] *Guardian*, September 24th, 1890.

neither had much to say. The conclusions on unemployment were no use. So far as scope was concerned, the *Guardian* approved the recommendation of this largely Conservative Commission that unions should be extended to trades at present lacking them, and it attributed the lower standards experienced by women workers to lack of organization.[1] The *British Weekly* welcomed the formation of the Women's Trade Association in the East End,[2] and the *Nonconformist* ridiculed the suggestion that women's unions were an impossibility, while admitting that there were difficulties.[3] The former paper welcomed the Labour Commission's recommendation of an investigation into women's work, and hoped to see a union of domestic servants. The London County Council was congratulated on the announcement that in future no contracts would be given where trade union conditions were not observed. The position of the unions in the eyes of the Nonconformist press was summed up in an article in 1891 claiming that they had 'distinctly conquered public opinion' and that they were the main barriers against Socialism. Keeping up wages was 'at least as important as keeping up dividends, and those concerned in the one are as much entitled to take steps to attain their object as are those concerned in the other.' The progress of trade unions would create moral problems, but the state's function was merely to see fair play.[4]

Completely divergent attitudes to the working classes and their organizations were revealed in two articles on the agricultural workers. The *Church Times* protested loudly at unfair references to the clergy, who could not be expected to do the whole work of social reform themselves. It was a 'mysterious fact' that the working classes did not respond to the love of the clergy, the explanation being that they were tired of 'charity.' The need was for more allotments and closer co-operation between the clergy and the workers.[5] The *Universe* was conscious that its own convictions were on the incoming tide, and spoke with more vigour and confidence:

[1] *Guardian*, April 25th, June 27th, July 18th, July 25th, August 15th, 1894.
[2] *British Weekly*, October 18th, October 25th, 1889.
[3] *Nonconformist*, June 5th, 1890.
[4] *British Weekly*, January 22nd, 1891; February 18th, June 2nd, 1892; January 18th, 1894.
[5] *Church Times*, January 8th, 1891.

Squire and parson still hold sway in the depleted agricultural districts, and the poverty-stricken sons of the soil are still as ready to acclaim the squire and his relations, and to make dutiful profession of the lowness of their station, and to vote Tory as their squire-and-parson-venerating, lowly-souled, Tory-voting ancestors. One Joseph Arch does not make an agricultural revolution, and it is through the want of men of his stamp to fight the battle of the English tiller and delver that rural England presents the hopeless picture it does today.[1]

Thus the same period in which the Nonconformist press was full of enthusiasm for a Roman Cardinal was noteworthy for Roman Catholic enthusiasm for a Methodist local preacher; and this last quotation could very well be from the *Nonconformist* save for one thing: in the latter newspaper such liveliness of style did not survive Edward Miall.

12 *The New Challenge to the Unions*

In the early years of the twentieth century four main topics relating to trade unions were discussed in the religious press: firstly, the uncertainty of the legal position of the unions, and the consequent entry of the union leadership into large-scale political activity; secondly, what may generally be described as the 'social problem'—wages, hours, conditions, and the demand for legislation on all these; thirdly, industrial disputes; and fourthly, the general position of trade unionism, its possible future, and the relationship of the Church and the unions.

For some years discussion centred round the Taff Vale judgement and what action ought to follow it. The decision that a union might be liable for damages after a strike, even if it had not in any way broken the law, provoked a demand for legislation, and many trade unionists who had been indifferent to politics suddenly began to engage in political activity with this end in view. Nothing did more to create the Labour Party as a major force in British public life than this apparently minor dispute. The middle-class public did not at first realize the significance of this issue, and were pleased at the judgement, dwelling on abstract justice, with no regard to the implications. Thus the *Guardian* thought the judgement sound, though admitting that the law needed clarifying, and the *Church Family Newspaper* thought it would help to avert great strikes such as those occurring in America, for now the unions would find themselves in the same position as 'any other

[1] *Universe*, May 12th, 1900.

corporation.' Even the *British Weekly* stressed the advantage of a likely reduction of strikes, though the *Universe*, now busy catching up with Manning, supported demands for the legal protection of funds. At the same time it deprecated the attitude of a speaker at the T.U.C. who urged an effort to unseat every sitting M.P.[1] As the unions' campaign got under way, the *Guardian* came out in support of legal protection for peaceful picketing, but not for union funds (against litigation) unless fighting and benevolent funds were separated. It watched 'with interest' the move for increased Labour representation, but was sorry to see the T.U.C. attacking Conservative policy.[2] The *Church Family Newspaper* also thought unions would be more useful if their agents were to be held 'strictly responsible for any financial losses inflicted by illegal action on their part,' and approved the Government's refusal to accept a trade union Bill, though no doubt it would be used as propaganda against them at the next election. An account of the 1902 Congress started with high praise for trade unions which had been 'of very considerable benefit to our working-men,' but immediately went on to attack them for 'very serious mistakes.' The President's speech was 'like an ultra-Radical's electioneering address,' especially on the Taff Vale issue: 'Why, for example, should Trade Unions, any more than individuals, or companies, or societies, not be held responsible for the acts of those they employ as their representatives?' The decision was 'as sound in equity as in law.' In 1904 the President's speech was again 'a Radical manifesto,' despite the fact that 'the Conservative party has done quite as much for labour, if not more than the Liberal.' It would be unfair to reverse Taff Vale, and the T.U.C. would be more effective 'if it kept itself as clear of party politics as possible and ceased to strive for what is evidently unattainable.' In 1905 the T.U.C. was 'more political than usual,' and the *Church Family Newspaper* spoke in pained tones: 'The Government were certainly not very successful in their efforts last Session to legislate for labour, but it is foolish to describe all their efforts as "Tory shams".' The interests of Capital and Labour were 'identical.' On one issue the T.U.C. had spoken unequivocally: 1,253,000 votes were cast for Free Trade against 26,000 for Protection, and this

[1] *Guardian*, September 11th, 1901; *Church Family Newspaper*, July 26th, 1901; *British Weekly*, September 5th, 1901; *Universe*, September 6th and 13th, 1901.
[2] *Guardian*, September 10th, 1902.

newspaper commented, with some understatement: 'Obviously the principle of Protection has made very little progress with skilled and organized labour.'[1] The *British Weekly* was more conscious of the gap between the resolutions of the Congress and the real political convictions of the working classes—indicated by the T.U.C.'s opposition to the Boer War.[2] The Liberal Government's Trades Disputes Bill of 1906 gave general dissatisfaction, on various grounds. The *Guardian* asserted roundly: 'The history of industrial disputes warrants the generalization that picketing means intimidation, and the forcible prevention of that which a man has a perfect right to do.' If it were fully legalized 'no employer would ever again be victorious in a strike.' If the Government weakly continued to make concessions to Labour employers would 'take measures for their own protection which may be neither agreeable to their adversaries, nor conducive to the quiet prosperity of the country.'[3] The *Church Family Newspaper* was dismayed at the spectacle of a huge majority for the Bill, 'some of the strong Chamberlainites actually voting with the Government.' Such desertion was the last straw: 'Plainly the Opposition is not in working order, and it will never be in working order till it chooses a leader and follows him. It will not add to its real strength in the country, or to the hopefulness of its prospects, by trifling with the Socialists.' The passing of this 'iniquitous' Bill would be 'the prelude to embittered labour struggles in this country on a scale hitherto unknown.'[4] In sharp contrast the *British Weekly*, under the heading 'The Blunder of the Government,' condemned the Bill as inadequate, as alleged by Labour, and the criticism was extended to hostile remarks by the Attorney-General on trade unions in introducing it. The Liberal leaders were losing touch with their followers—only a few weeks after coming to power.[5]

The Osborne judgement, which ruled that trade union funds could not be used for political purposes, renewed the discussion on the political character of trade unions. The *Church Family Newspaper* thought it 'extremely important and clearly equitable,' for it was not right that trade unions 'formed for purely benevolent

[1] *Church Family Newspaper*, September 5th, December 26th, 1902; September 9th, 1904; May 12th, September 8th, 1905.
[2] *British Weekly*, September 14th, 1905.
[3] *Guardian*, April 4th, 1906.
[4] *Church Family Newspaper*, April 6th, September 14th, 1906.
[5] *British Weekly*, April 5th, 1906.

and trade purposes' should interfere in politics. Labour would demand legislation 'so that trade unions may be enabled to do what now they cannot and ought not to do,' and union protests were reported ironically. Labour wanted to reverse the decision, but to that 'odious tyranny the Unionist Party will never consent,' though the Liberal Government might well give in to 'Mr Ramsay Macdonald and his friends.'[1] The *Guardian* regarded the judgement as a blow not at the unions but at the Socialists who controlled them. There was no need to introduce payment of M.P.s, since the Labour M.P.s (who were threatened with the loss of their income if the unions could not engage in politics) did not represent the British workers. There was strong criticism of the Labour campaign against the judgement, and it was asserted that 'for several years the Labour politicians have been losing grip of labour,' by which it was meant that rank and file trade union members would not keep agreements negotiated by their leaders.[2] The *British Weekly* thought the judgement would increase rather than reduce the power of trade unions, and urged changes in the law, including payment of M.P.s, though there should also be protection for non-Socialist union members.[3] Towards the end of this period the *Church Family Newspaper* commented that even the Unionists had become reconciled to the political activities of trade unions: 'Mr Bonar Law did well to show that his party does not stand in the way of Trade Unions' exercising their due political influence in the life of the nation,' and the compromise of contracting-out had been accepted generally. But the continued alliance with the Liberals was a disappointment, and trade unions would do better 'by keeping aloof from party denunciation' and not favouring one party and condemning the other.[4]

13   Conditions of Work in Edwardian England

The discussion of the continuing demand for a 'living wage' was now mainly concerned with what the Church's attitude should be, and on this issue the *Church Family Newspaper* and the *British Weekly* had an unusual measure of agreement. The latter appealed

[1] *Church Family Newspaper*, December 4th, 1908; August 12th, October 14th, 1910.
[2] *Guardian*, August 26th, September 23rd, 1910.
[3] *British Weekly*, December 3rd, 1908; August 25th, September 15th, 1910.
[4] *Church Family Newspaper*, February 7th, September 5th, 1913.

for full Church support, and quoted the warning example of such Liberals as Bright, Cobden, and Gladstone, who had opposed Lord Shaftesbury's reforms. It was very pleased at the lead given by Gore and other leading churchmen,[1] as was the *Church Family Newspaper*, which assured employers that trade unions did good to their employees without harming themselves. Speakers in the York Convocation were right to demand that wages should rank before profits, and that they should be a 'first charge upon the estate.' The Church had too long tolerated poverty, and should set an example by paying poor clergy more.[2]

Perhaps on wages, and certainly on conditions of work, Government intervention was now welcomed, and the same two newspapers provide examples of this new attitude. At the beginning of the century the *Church Family Newspaper* thought an amendment increasing the Saturday half-holiday would be disastrous, but soon it welcomed a Conservative defeat on the refusal to give statistics of railwaymen working excessive hours, and by 1908 the Sweated Industries Bill was approved, despite economic arguments against it: '. . . Political economy is not everything, and men who have hearts to be moved are resolved that in some way sweating must come to an end.' Fear of public intervention was decreasing, and Churchill's Bill on shop hours was also welcomed, since legislation was evidently necessary. But such intervention should be cautious.[3] In the *British Weekly* Lord Milner's demands for a legal minimum wage were supported, and the Trade Boards Bill, directed against sweating, was welcomed, as was an eight-hours Bill for miners.[4] A rather different piece of legislation supported by the *Church Family Newspaper* was the creation of an Industrial Council of employers and union leaders, though a union leader showing signs of 'responsibility and moderation' was apt to lose support.[5]

Unemployment was as big a mystery as ever. In the early years of the century the *Church Times* was still eager with advice. The Church should try to find remedies, although many of those

[1] *British Weekly*, September 21st, 1911; November 27th, 1913.

[2] *Church Family Newspaper*, November 28th, 1913; April 24th, May 15th, 1914.

[3] Ibid., August 16th, 1901; February 28th, 1902; February 28th, 1908; July 8th, 1910; April 18th, 1912.

[4] *British Weekly*, December 12th, 1907; July 9th, 1908; September 2nd, 1909.

[5] *Church Family Newspaper*, October 13th, 1911.

who marched to London were undeserving: 'The number of those who are out of work undoubtedly includes a proportion whose profession is looking for work—and not finding it.' The solution to the problem was to attract men back to the land—a good specimen of the impracticable advice generally offered on this topic. The paper expressed some sympathy with thirteen M.P.s who made a last-ditch stand against the Unemployed Workmen Bill, though they ignored facts, like the defenders of Free Trade—an extraordinarily inapposite comparison, at least in terms of strength. The remedy for unemployment was 'some kind of special work'—undefined.[1] The *Church Family Newspaper* seemed inclined to despair:

> According to the theories of political economists, the problem of the unemployed ought to solve itself automatically. If there are more men in a trade than there is work for the surplus labour will turn to other sources of employment. Unfortunately all the home sources of employment seem to be in the same boat just now.

A reference to an article in the *Economic Review* suggested no remedy, though it mentioned the amount spent on drink. After a clash of police and unemployed at Manchester sympathy was with the former, and the invocation of 'the spirit of Peterloo' by 'Mr Keir Hardy' (sic) was dismissed.[2] The *British Weekly* praised a demonstration led by Crooks and Lansbury, and rejected the idea that the cure lay in Protection.[3]

A year or two later there was another wave of discussion and the *Guardian* showed itself disappointingly negative. The great difficulty was to distinguish the genuinely unemployed from 'loafers and parasites' attracted by the 'spirit of lawlessness' raised by Victor Grayson. Unemployment was inevitable because it was 'in the nature of trade to fluctuate' and it was driven abroad by strikes. The state should intervene to enforce apprenticeship and reduce casual unskilled labour. The working classes were unthrifty and provided for the old age only of the publicans. The Labour Party looked for a 'radical cure,' but this was hopeless: 'Palliatives are all that is possible in the circumstances of the moment.' The Labour Party exaggerated the distress, but John Burns had learned

---

[1] *Church Times*, December 2nd, 1904; June 16th, June 23rd, 1905.
[2] *Church Family Newspaper*, February 10th, July 28th, August 4th, 1905.
[3] *British Weekly*, November 9th, November 23rd, 1905.

responsibility, as was shown by his attacks on the party and on the working classes in general. A leader headed 'Unemployment' was very critical of W. H. Beveridge's book of that name.[1] In all this the *Guardian* reveals how far the Anglican middle classes were from understanding the seriousness of the problem and the strength of the workers' bitterness about it. The *British Weekly* at first praised Burns's administration of unemployment relief, but later supported Labour hostility to him, and especially to his assertion that many undeserving received relief. Churchill was praised for his emphasis on this question, and the principle of a 'Right-to-Work' Bill (unsatisfactory in detail) was supported. The Government's measures, though only palliatives, were useful, as was the action of the Methodist jam-manufacturer, William P. Hartley, in finding work for 150 men in making a recreation ground. But a Labour motion in 1911 on the right to work was impracticable.[2]

14   Trade Disputes after 1900

The first few years of the century were quiet. The most revealing issue was the continuing trouble at the Bethesda slate quarries of Lord Penrhyn. Both the *Universe* and the *British Weekly* supported Opposition criticism of the Government for not intervening, and the latter blamed the working classes for submitting to a Government 'that tramples on their rights.'[3] But the *Church Family Newspaper* thought such interference 'likely to do much more harm than good,' and that Asquith, the Government's critic, would act in the same way if he were in power.[4]

From 1907 to the early years of the reign of George V there was a crescendo of strikes. In 1907 the railway dispute brought condemnation for the strikers from the *Guardian*,[5] while in the *Church Times* the regular correspondent 'Lancastrian' thought the solution was state regulation of wages.[6] The *Church Family Newspaper* thought the companies wrong to refuse at least temporary recognition to the union, but its attitude was mainly one of simple alarm at 'the almost inconceivably serious disaster, a

[1] *Guardian*, October 21st, October 28th, 1908; March 3rd, 1909.

[2] *British Weekly*, July 26th, 1906; February 6th, February 13th, March 19th, September 10th, October 29th, 1908; February 25th, September 9th, 1909; February 16th, 1911.

[3] *Universe*, October 4th, 1901; *British Weekly*, April 30th, 1903.

[4] *Church Family Newspaper*, April 9th, May 1st, 1903.

[5] *Guardian*, November 6th, 1907.

[6] *Church Times*, October 18th, 1907.

railway strike,' and relief at its settlement.[1] The *British Weekly* condemned the companies and praised the union leader, Bell, claiming that public opinion was with the men and that the strike was justified. Credit for the settlement was given to Bell and Lloyd George.[2]

The climax of the unrest came in the years 1910–1912. The *Guardian*, in the former year, accused the Boilermakers' Union of having struck irresponsibly, and wanted to see the Trade Disputes Act repealed,[3] while the *British Weekly* was also concerned for the maintenance of discipline in the unions.[4] The big strike of that year was in the coal industry—'a strike of a desperate and lawless character,' the *Church Family Newspaper* called it. The failure of the union leaders to control the men was blamed partly on 'the renewed incitements which Mr Lloyd George has just given to the passions of class warfare', though it was grudgingly admitted that the Government was 'showing no failure' in suppressing the violence.[5] The *British Weekly*, which was quite alarmed at the wave of strikes, did not blame Lloyd George, but, reflecting a different political creed, it did blame the House of Lords, and demanded a 'steady policy of reform.' The 'general confederation of Labour' of which Socialists dreamed—with the object of the General Strike—was a weapon 'too formidable for handling.' Churchill was right to send troops to Tonypandy, for there was a revolutionary element among the trade unions.[6]

In 1911 strikes affected the seamen and dockers, miners, railwaymen, carmen, cotton workers, and others. The *Guardian*, on the 'Labour Unrest,' was not unsympathetic to the strikers: behaviour was on the whole good and riots the work of a minority of hooligans, and Christians should realize the need for sympathy as well as justice.[7] The *Church Family Newspaper* was likewise sympathetic to the shipping strike, emphasizing the bad conditions, and thought the carmen who had just gained a week of

[1] *Church Family Newspaper*, September 20th, November 1st, November 8th, 1907.

[2] *British Weekly*, September 19th, September 26th, October 24th, October 31st, November 7th, November 14th, 1907.

[3] *Guardian*, September 9th, 1910.

[4] *British Weekly*, September 8th, 1910.

[5] *Church Family Newspaper*, November 11th, 1910.

[6] *British Weekly*, September 15th, September 22nd, November 17th, 1910.

[7] *Guardian*, August 25th, 1911.

seventy-two hours for twenty-seven shillings 'had plenty of
reason to be discontented with their previous lot,' but in other
cases there was criticism of the indiscipline of the strikers, and
especially of Keir Hardie's 'disgraceful outburst,' in which he
accused Asquith of having said that he would keep the mines open
even if he 'had to shoot down every striker.' Compulsory arbitration would not solve the problem, but something definite ought to
be done to stop the Socialists 'stealing the hearts of the people.'
As a fundamental cure of contemporary violence only religion
would suffice. The union leaders had lost control through 'lack of
moral courage' and instead of denouncing violence they blamed
the Government and the troops. The Irish railway strikers made
'anarchistic' demands, and the public would no longer consider
the directors 'a little high-handed' for refusing to recognize the
unions, while another Irish strike prompted the comment that
these disorders were 'an imperative summons for the application
and vindication of Christian morality.' The settlement of the
railway dispute offered an occasion for union leaders to 'assert
their position' and restore discipline; yet the year ended with
more strikes and more evidence of 'the tyranny of trade unions.'[1]
The *British Weekly* was especially concerned about the railway
disputes. An article by Sir Joseph Compton-Rickett advocated a
limitation to the right to strike, and an interview with the Baptist
leader F. B. Meyer urged the Church to act more decisively,
though impartially, in industrial disputes. The settlement was
credited to Lloyd George, and the bitter struggle of the summer
partly blamed on the hot weather.[2]

1912 brought three significant strikes, the first two on a very
large scale and the third interesting though of minor importance.
The great coal strike interested all the press. The *Guardian*
thought it better to nationalize the mines rather than continue to
run 'the present risks'. The Syndicalists wanted to ruin the
mines so they could easily be appropriated—just like the Government's attitude to landed property. The right to strike should be
limited. Disorder and violence were the result of the 'insane
tolerance' of peaceful picketing, and all picketing should be
banned as an infringement of a 'fundamental liberty,' and if trade

---

[1] *Church Family Newspaper*, June 30th, August 18th, August 25th,
September 8th, September 22nd, October 6th, December 15th, December
29th, 1911.

[2] *British Weekly*, August 24th, August 31st, 1911.

unionism 'stands in the way of it the claws of Trade Unionism must be cut.' For once Lloyd George and Asquith found Conservative defenders, against Radical and Labour attacks. The strike was 'this crime against society' and the Syndicalist theories preached were 'collective robbery.' The right to strike should be 'strictly controlled by the State,' with compulsory arbitration. There should be authority for the seizure of union funds and the imprisonment of individuals who broke the law. An article published during the strike was about miners at Heanor, to show that they were good fellows and that the Church of England was doing better among them than Nonconformity, while another traced the strike to the decline of religion and recommended a great mission as the cure. Both these articles were rather silly.[1] The *Church Family Newspaper* thought the strike would prove 'the greatest disaster of modern times.' Both sides were acting conscientiously, but in South Wales especially the workers had abandoned their 'wise and trusted leaders' for revolutionary theorists. There should be prayers in face of 'the greatest industrial and social disaster the nation has ever been called to face.' The miners refused arbitration and insisted on being 'judge and jury in their own case,' so forfeiting public sympathy. Despite the catastrophic nature of this strike, it might be the prelude to 'upheavals' which would make it seem trivial. Trade unions did some good work, but sometimes developed into a tyranny 'which must be resisted at all costs,' associated with Syndicalism, 'a great menace to our nation and Empire,' and a 'diabolical system' aiming at a 'Socialistic Republic.' The *Church Family Newspaper* joined its rather immoderate criticisms with an appeal for moderation, pointing to the 'noble example of public service' set by Parliament in setting aside party feeling; the Christian should try to make peace in industry and avert recriminations: 'It is absurd to speak of the miners as predatory anarchists, or the masters as grasping plutocrats.' It was also the duty of the Church to 'break down the barrier' between rich and poor, and to 'gather both together into the Christian society, where all souls are equal . . .' A proper balance was attained when the Unionists accepted the Government's minimum wage Bill and a Syndicalist author and printer were sent to prison for sedition—a combination of the moderation and firmness recommended. With their defeat in the

[1] *Guardian*, March 1st, March 8th, March 15th, March 22nd, 1912.

strike it was hoped the miners had learned the dangers of Socialist leadership, and there was praise for the Government.[1]

The *British Weekly* was more inclined to emphasize public sympathy for the miners, but was just as alarmed as the other papers, calling for public services 'to plead with Almighty God for peace and reconciliation.' The state should take strong action, and must not allow 'men like Mr D. A. Thomas' (the owners' spokesman) to 'lay their hands on the throat of the nation.' The rights of property should be ignored in the crisis. Another article traced the rise of the power of the masses, and ridiculed the suggestion that trade unions should be suppressed. The Government was considered to have done well, and was defended against Ramsay Macdonald, and it was noted that the effects of the strike had not been as bad as had been expected. But next week the gloom returned, with forecasts of great disasters, including starvation, soon. This was the fault of the Government, for not writing the minimum wages into the Bill, as demanded by Labour. Such a course would be disastrous for the Liberals. The criticism was repeated, with a condemnation of Conservative demands for strong action against the strike. When the strike ended it was remarked that on another occasion the nation might indeed collapse. But there was no justification for abuse of the miners. When the miners were awarded less than expected it was said that it would be better to accept their full demands rather than face another strike.[2]

The other major strike of 1912 was the London dock strike, for which the *Church Family Newspaper* was inclined to blame both sides. Public sympathy was with the employers, but 'the hour has come for the injured to extend forgiveness, and by a generous overlooking of faults to make such terms with the men as will enable them to resume work.' It was unreasonable of Ben Tillett to lead the strikers in the prayer: 'O, God, strike Lord Devonport dead,' and the newspaper was content to appeal to Devonport and his colleagues to be generous. The strike ended, like so many, with fond hopes of better relations in the future.[3] The *British Weekly*

[1] *Church Family Newspaper*, February 23rd, March 1st, March 8th, March 22nd, March 29th, April 4th, April 11th, 1912.

[2] *British Weekly*, January 18th, February 22nd, February 29th, March 7th, March 14th, March 21st, March 28th, April 4th, April 11th, May 16th, 1912.

[3] *Church Family Newspaper*, May 24th, May 31st, June 7th, June 14th, July 5th, July 19th, July 26th, August 2nd, 1912.

was as usual more definite in its sympathy with the strikers. Their grievances were genuine, and if they had acted hastily the employers had alienated public sympathy. The latter were responsible for the prolongation of the strike: 'The employers have made a disastrous blunder, and must be held responsible for the present deadlock.' The Government should act more decisively: 'What is Sir George Askwith doing?' The ultimate effect of the defeat of the workers would only be to embitter and so unite them.[1]

Both these papers were completely out of sympathy with the minor strike at the end of the year—over the dismissal of Driver Knox for being drunk off duty. The *Church Family Newspaper* thought that: 'No general rule can be laid down as to the right of an employee to act as he wishes during his off duty hours,' while the *British Weekly* criticized the men for striking without negotiating.[2]

The most notable strike in 1913 was at Dublin, led by the colourful Jim Larkin, and once more these two papers were in sharp disagreement. The *Church Family Newspaper*, 'without expressing an opinion on the details of the Dublin lock-out,' thought that business would have become impossible if no action had been taken 'to end the tyranny that prevailed in every department of trade.' But by this time even papers which normally opposed trade union activities were learning to pass more balanced judgements, and this paper soon went on to criticize the formation of an Employers' Defence Union, registered as a trade union:

> Whether they have acted wisely or not is another matter. The solidarity of the trade unions grows every year, and they are learning to stand together and to help one another in Labour war . . . The formation of this new Union enables agitators to point to the giant resources that are ranged in opposition to them and to rouse discontent.

Another reference was even more ready to follow Bishop Gore in seeing genuine grievances behind the disorders:

> . . . If the Church does not lead, others will. This is quite obvious from Mr Larkin's campaign. It is easy to write down these men as revolutionary agitators, but it behoves Churchmen to look at facts as

---

[1] *British Weekly*, May 30th, June 6th, June 13th, July 11th, July 18th, August 1st, 1912.

[2] *Church Family Newspaper*, December 13th, 1912; *British Weekly*, December 12th and December 19th, 1912.

they are, and then we believe there will be more practical sympathy with the oppressed and sweated.[1]

The *British Weekly* was extremely radical on this strike. The imprisonment of Larkin for sedition offered an obvious opportunity for a blow at the Carsonites: 'There have been other voices in Ireland during recent months than those of James Larkin. If the fire-eaters must have their meal of fire there must be no leavings.' This paper joined wholeheartedly in Labour criticisms of the Government, and attributed to its policy poor by-election results:

> There is the crowning grievance of Mr James Larkin's imprisonment. As we have said from the first, this is a matter to make workingmen think furiously. The whole business was beyond excuse and beyond explanation. Such stupendous crassitude defies all analysis. It has been one of the costliest blunders which any Government has ever made, and the price is not yet paid. Even if James Larkin were out tomorrow there would be no present peace. We firmly believe that reconciliation can be effected if only the Liberals will recognize the just claims of the Labourists, and if social measures are resolutely advanced.

Larkin's trial was said to be unjust, and if he had said some wild things, he had also said some thought-provoking things.[2]

1914 was comparatively quiet, though the *British Weekly* supported the London building workers in their refusal to sign a 'document' to keep the peace with non-union men.[3]

Little has been said in this section about the attitude of the *Universe*. Its comments on industrial disputes were usually very general. The troubled events of 1911 were described in a leader entitled 'The Labour War'. Some sympathy was due to the strikers, but their motives were mixed and a spirit of mere destructiveness was at work. 'Sympathetic' strikes were wrong, and the great need was for a return to religion. It was important to investigate the real causes of the trouble: 'No language can be too strong to denounce the blatant vapourings of so-called leaders who find street oratory, incitement to mob-law, and falsehoods calculated to rouse the passions of the crowd, more lucrative than honest labour.' The belief in equality was unsound, and what was

[1] *Church Family Newspaper*, September 19th, October 3rd, November 21st, 1913.
[2] *British Weekly*, October 30th, November 13th, November 20th, 1913.
[3] Ibid., January 29th, 1914.

really wanted was a return to the Church: 'The Church of Christ stands as the peacemaker between warring classes; affirming the moral responsibilities of the master and the duty of the men.' Labour made excessive claims, as for example when Ben Tillett said that the workers should keep asking for more. The expression 'living wage' was ambiguous, and it was not realized that there must be dividends if Capital was to be found, though the Church should take care to protect the interests of the workers. The Labour disturbances throughout Europe were a revolution, and agitators, such as Tillett and Mann, should be suppressed, though the means of suppression were left conveniently vague: 'It is the amputation of sedition-mongers from society with their fellow-citizens that is primarily needed.' The coal strike should not be allowed, though the Socialist movement was a protest against Protestant Individualism and hence Catholics should not raise a cry of 'Behold the Enemy' but oppose the Socialists with sympathy. The Government was tamely submitting to demands which came not from the miners but from 'a small band of revolutionaries who have gained control of the miners' organization.' Trade unions had 'become a positive curse to the British workman' and were worse tyrants than the employers, and the Trade Disputes Act which had legalized the tyranny ought to be repealed.

The *Universe* seemed to have gone back a whole generation, and forgotten all it had learned from Manning, in face of the disturbances of these years. The trade unions had been 'captured and engineered by a political caucus and made subservient to political ends,' and this caucus itself—the I.L.P.—had been captured by the Socialists and 'made an instrument of propaganda for the Social Revolution.' Unions were useful, but compulsory membership and compulsory strikes were unjustified, 'but the very last word of insensate folly and moral turpitude is the syndicalist strike, and the greatest traitors to the working man are the Tilletts and the Larkins.' Unions had no right 'to override the rights of the community and dislocate society at large.' Recent strikes abroad 'have been engineered by subversive politicians . . . to further the ends of the social revolution . . . Syndicalist strikes have been one long orgy of barbarism.' But rather belatedly a more sympathetic note was struck, and some of the blame placed on the Capitalists. The two sides in industry were not equal, for the Capitalist could do what he wished with his Capital, but the workers had no such choice. The bad Capitalist 'opens the gates of peace and invokes the evil spirits of hatred and disorder.'[1]

15 Position and Prospects of Trade Unionism in the Edwardian Period

The *Church Times* has received, and merited, little attention in the foregoing survey, for its contact with the world in which trade unionists lived, never very close, weakened still further in the early twentieth century. In 1901 it noted that most of the diocesan conferences had dealt with the relationship of the Church to social problems, and it feared that, having been too unfavourable to unions in the past, the Church was now in danger of showing too much favour to them. The unions had a political character and sought to change society, but the Church had no social standpoint, and made no promise of a Utopia. A rebuke to the Church of England for taking little interest in the Preston Guild seemed to hold out the hope that guilds, centred on the Church, might replace trade unions.[2]

The *Church Family Newspaper*, in principle at least, was friendly to the unions, and emphasized their moderation; only 19% of their expenditure was for strike pay, compared with 61% for friendly society benefits, so that the unions were turning from 'mere organizations for fostering discord between capital and labour' into 'benefit societies in the ordinary sense,' a change due partly to greater respect for them on the part of the employers, but also to their own increasing responsibility. Years later the T.U.C. was still regarded as a force for moderation, though the movement as a whole was not what it had been, and there was need for the recovery of 'some of that discipline and self-respect which the propagation of Socialistic teaching has done so much to obliterate.' Even after the period of the great strikes the mood was friendly; the increasing membership of trade unions was an impressive sign of the progress of the working classes, to whom the unions had been 'an inestimable boon,' bringing about many gains, including moral gains. The unions had many friends in the Church, though they must not alienate them with excessive demands. It was quite true that the workers' share in the national wealth was less than

---

[1] *Universe*, August 18th, August 25th, September 15th, September 22nd, 1911; February 23rd, March 22nd, 1912; September 5th, 1913; January 30th, February 6th, 1914.

[2] *Church Times*, November 22nd, 1901; February 5th, 1902.

ever: 'A fairer distribution of wealth is the great problem before the country at the present time.'[1]

There were of course some general criticisms of trade unions. There were restrictive practices—though the *Times* had exaggerated them;[2] there was the tyranny of the 'closed shop';[3] and, to the great indignation even of the *British Weekly*, there was the policy of 'ca' canny.'[4] But when they were least specific these papers were most friendly to the unions.

For the Roman Catholic Church none of these things was the main issue, but as is natural with a minority—and this Church was still very conscious of being a minority—the most important point was how the trend of events affected the position of its own adherents. The 1905 T.U.C. was 'unique' in having a Catholic President, James Sexton, for whom the *Universe* showed great enthusiasm. An article on 'Catholic Citizenship' asserted that industrial relations which acted unfairly on the workers were 'against the spirit of Catholic civilization'. Other references concerned the position of Catholics as union members. Those in Lancashire did well to protest against T.U.C. support for secular education. A threat by Catholics to leave the unions on this issue need not be carried out, because they were strong enough to make their wishes effective. Socialist delegates did not really represent the workers, but the right course for Catholics was to fight them from within the unions. Catholics would not be dictated to on education policy by Socialists, even if the Government would, and even though secular education was supported by an overwhelming vote at the 1910 T.U.C. A Catholic trade union group which had issued a manifesto had shown how to reconcile Catholic and democratic principles, but any political ideal must be subordinate to religion.[5]

16 *Conclusion*

The preceding survey sufficiently proves at least one fact on the relations of Church and trade unions: the religious press was

[1] *Church Family Newspaper*, December 19th, 1902; September 16th, 1910; September 6th, 1912.

[2] *Guardian*, January 8th, 1902.

[3] *Church Family Newspaper*, September 15th, 1911.

[4] *British Weekly*, November 21st, 1901.

[5] *Universe*, September 9th, November 4th, 1905; September 14th, September 21st, 1906; January 31st, 1908; September 10th, 1909; September 23rd, 1910; April 11th, 1913.

consistently interested in trade unionism, even if the nature of its interest fluctuated widely. In the early period the churches made two quite distinct but important contributions to the growth of trade unionism at a critical stage in its history, when it was struggling for recognition. The Christian Socialists were acting as friends and advisers to the unions, fighting for their legal security, and urging their virtues in clerical circles. In contrast the Methodists were beginning to take the lead in the local organization of the miners. Both contributions were valuable, but if a choice must be made between them it must be said that the future of the Labour movement lay with the leaders thrown up by the workers themselves, rather than with the paternal encouragement of the wealthy middle classes, so that in this respect the Methodist aspect was more significant for the future.

Once the future of trade unionism was secure, and it was plain that it was not a form of revolutionary subversion, a period of close and friendly relations began. The clergy took an active interest in forming and guiding unions, and the religious press, of all parties, was at least prepared to admit that even if political economy had proved conclusively that the working classes could not possibly gain from trade unions, some gains had in fact been achieved. The Nonconformist press, and now, at first sight surprisingly, the Roman Catholic too, was enthusiastic for the trade union movement, and the more intelligent elements in the Church of England, represented for example by the *Guardian* on the High Church side and by Fraser on the Low, were strongly inclined to friendliness. Thus the 'seventies and 'eighties were a golden age in the relations of religion and the unions. A partial exception, it is true, was the agricultural movement, for the enthusiasm of Nonconformist and Roman Catholic supporters of Joseph Arch was in some sense the measure of his hostility, readily shared by them, to the Church of England. But even Arch did not provoke the leaders of Anglican opinion to outright opposition, and many were prepared to learn penitence from his denunciations.

Much of the new support was due to the recognition of the social service performed by trade unions in their capacity of friendly societies, and in so far as this is regarded as a byway of Labour history the support of the Churches may be discounted. It is certainly true that the religious press was sometimes inclined to praise the unions most when they behaved least like trade unions. With this criticism may be linked the gross failure to appreciate the

seriousness of social problems. It was only in the middle 'eighties—
the cynic might say only with the revival of militant Socialism—
that the 'condition of England' began to shock the pious middle
classes, although the condition of England was much what it had
been for generations. The problem of poverty it was hoped to
solve by exhortations to Christian charity, and unemployment was
spoken of in puzzled accents as something which could not really
exist in Capitalist society, though no one could deny that it did.

This happy period was ended not so much by the dock strike
and the growth of the more militant 'New Unionism,' for there
was a widespread feeling that the latter represented the really
needy classes of society much better than the well-established and
prosperous craft unions, as by the changing relative importance in
British life of religion and organized Labour. By the 'nineties
fewer people cared what the religious press thought about trade
unions, or anything else, and there was less and less inclination to
ask clergy to arbitrate in disputes. Both the Nonconformist and the
Roman Catholic press still insisted on proclaiming support for the
unions, and the *Guardian* strove to be fair to them, but the *Church
Times* and the *Church Family Newspaper*, in their intervals from
attacking each other, still had little of any value to contribute. It
was just at the time when the religious world as a whole had been
fully converted to the kind of trade unionism typified by the
'Junta'—cautious, pragmatic, concerned with the piecemeal
advancement of the workers' share of the national wealth—that
the new kind represented by Tillett and Mann drove the Anglican,
and then the Roman Catholic, press back into hostility. But it was
not so much the change in trade unionism as the decline in
religion which influenced the character of comments on this
theme towards the end of the century.

In the Edwardian period two features of the attitude of the
religious press to the trade unions stand out. Firstly, there was in
general little understanding of the aims and outlook of the unions,
and even though tributes to their achievements were frequent,
almost all their specific purposes and demands were found to be
inopportune or unsound. Demands for legislation were apt to be
answered by the assertion that the unions were asking to be
treated as a special case, and it did not occur to the authors of such
comments that they were in fact a special case. When significant
strikes occurred the policy frequently advocated was that commonplace of the Right, 'firmness,' though the precise meaning of the

term was not usually made clear. In fact lengthy leading articles often amounted to no more than a demand that the Government should do something about it—a tribute to the progress of the conviction that the state was necessarily deeply involved in economic life. Party politics were always a relevant factor, and the scoring of party points explains much that was said in both the Liberal and the Conservative press.

The other feature is that there was a marked difference of approach according to religious denomination. To put it simply, the Anglican press was Conservative and quite out of touch with the world of trade unions, despite the long efforts of the Christian Socialists, and it did not now make a great deal of difference whether it was High Church or Low Church. Among the Roman Catholics the *Universe* was not really interested at all except in so far as the position of the Church was affected, and it approached specific issues empirically from this standpoint, giving a quite erroneous impression of inconsistency. Radical at times, grossly reactionary at others, it was in its way the most consistent of all these newspapers, seeking always the good of the Catholic Church. The *British Weekly* steadily supported the trade unions, always on the assumption that their activities were part of the traditional Radical movement. These differences of approach can be seen in the case of some of the major issues of this period. On the Taff Vale decision the only one of these papers which supported the unions was the *Universe*, though the *Guardian* thought that some amendment ought to be made to the law. On the Trade Disputes Act of 1906 the Anglican and Roman Catholic papers were hostile, the *Church Family Newspaper* calling the Act 'iniquitous,' while the *British Weekly* in contrast thought it did not go far enough to meet the union demands. On the Osborne judgement there was general approval, but the *British Weekly* alone advocated the payment of M.P.s, which of course met the main union demand. Unemployment was hardly noticed by the *Universe*. The Anglican press thought that nothing could be done about it, since it was all due to a failure of demand, largely for exports, though the *Church Times* favoured public works. These papers were also concerned to point out from time to time that some of the unemployed—perhaps many—were idle people who had no wish to find work, precisely the kind of imputation which most offended the working classes. The *British Weekly* rejected Protection as a remedy, but wanted more action from the Government. It denied that many undeserving were receiving help and criticized Burns's administration of relief on the same lines as the Labour Party. It accepted the principle of a 'right to work,' but weakened the effect of such acceptance by rejecting as impracticable the Labour Party's proposals without suggesting alternatives.

On the greatest of the strikes of the period, the coal strike of 1912, the *Universe* was critical in its usual violent terms. The *Guardian* wanted the strike to be put down and thought the Government slow to act. The right to strike should be limited. The *Church Family Newspaper* blamed the Syndicalists and wanted 'firmness,' but also moderation, and deprecated abuse of the miners. The *British Weekly* also wanted strong action, but it wanted it against the owners—'men like Mr D. A. Thomas.' It envisaged the possibility of the state taking over the mines, or perhaps fixing wages by law.

The effect of years of such comments was that the Anglican and Roman Catholic papers seemed irrevocably hostile to the unions—for party reasons; and the *British Weekly* seemed consistently friendly—for party reasons. In their formative years trade unions received much sympathy from all denominations, but once they were established as a new estate of the realm the religious press naturally split along party lines, and it happened that to the Nonconformists it seemed that trade unionists counted among their friends. Any trade unionists who were interested to know the attitude of religious newspapers were likely to remember that one group were biased Tories, and the other honest Radicals friendly to Labour. Prejudice is only noticeable in one's opponents.

CHAPTER 3

SOME OTHER FORMS OF WORKING-CLASS ORGANIZATION

1 *The Co-operative Movement*

THE EARLY AND MIDDLE YEARS of the reign of Queen Victoria were as important in the history of co-operation as in that of trade unionism. A few years earlier the word had been associated with the revolutionary and impracticable schemes of Robert Owen. The Christian Socialists had barely succeeded in making the word respectable; to many people they were well-meaning but misguided philanthropists, prepared to lose their own and other people's money in setting up co-operative workshops inevitably destined to fail. They did however provoke discussion on the theme, even if the conclusions reached were not wholly what the devoted band of Maurice's disciples wished. In the *Guardian*, for example, there was an article in 1850 on 'Co-operative Associations,'[1] which maintained Adam Smith's view that except where the unit of production was very large, an individual business would prove more efficient than a large company. The project of organizing a large-scale tailoring co-operative was therefore questioned, because it would share the disadvantages of a joint-stock company. However, since the shareholders in such an enterprise would have a direct interest in the work, the *Guardian* thought that perhaps a producers' co-operative would do better than a joint-stock capitalist company, and was content to suspend judgement.

After the Christian Socialist episode producers' co-operation slowly fell out of public attention, and consumers' co-operation took its place, and the *Guardian* spared a brief word of praise for the Rochdale society, as well as advocating 'co-operative kitchens' for workers' meals, a forward glance to the works canteen.[2]

The Roman Catholic press was not interested in co-operation, but the *Nonconformist* naturally gave some attention to what was

[1] *Guardian*, March 6th, 1850.
[2] Ibid., October 31st, 1860.

increasingly a Dissenting movement. In quoting statistics to show the improved social condition of the working classes, it laid special emphasis on co-operation, commenting: 'The advantages resulting from this new element in the social life of our working population are immense.' But it added the reactionary conclusion that state assistance for education was no longer required, since everyone could afford to pay for it. The co-operative movement was 'one of the most remarkable and hopeful signs of the times.' It contained great promise, though so far it was small in relation to the total paid out in wages, or even to the drink bill. New attempts at co-operative production, this time in the cotton industry, were attended by many difficulties; if one such co-operative succeeded it would be 'an important era in the history of our industrial enterprise.' Profit-sharing might be a useful stage on the way. There was support for Holyoake in advocating profit-sharing and co-partnership.[1]

Thus even the *Nonconformist* was still chiefly interested in the productive side of co-operation, and the consumers' movement made remarkably little impact on the religious press as a whole. But the emergence of the Rochdale society marked a radical departure, in two respects. For the first time the emphasis shifted to the combination of consumers, and for the first time the working classes themselves took the lead. The gradual but extraordinary progress of the consumers' movement showed that this form of co-operation was neither the instrument of civil war nor the day-dream of benevolent clergymen, but the creation of hard-headed men pursuing their own rational self-interest. But it shared in the atmosphere of the time, and the Rochdale group was a mutual improvement society as well as a new form of commercial enterprise. Its objects were declared to be 'the moral and intellectual advancement of its members.'[2] The religious and moral basis of co-operation had not been abandoned. Among this group Nonconformists were dominant. John Thomas Whitehead Mitchell (1828–1895), the leading member, and President of the C.W.S. from 1874 till his death, in 1846 joined Providence Congregational Sunday School; in 1854 he became a teacher, and he was later Superintendent till his death. In 1847 he took the pledge of total abstinence. He was also in middle life Superintendent of the

---

[1] *Nonconformist*, December 5th, 1860, September 23rd, 1863; January 18th, October 18th, 1865.

[2] Young, op. cit., 7.

Sunday School at Milton Congregational Church. He joined the Pioneers in 1853, was elected to the committee in 1856, and in 1857 became part-time secretary. His life was divided between his religious work and the co-operative movement—if indeed this should be counted as a division, for he served and defended consumers' co-operation on the most elevated grounds and with truly religious enthusiasm. A number of the Pioneers belonged to Clover Street Chapel, which was known as the 'Co-operative Chapel.' It belonged to the Methodist Unitarian movement.[1]

The Unitarian contribution to co-operation in general was much greater than to trade unionism. Holyoake found the Unitarians 'at all times more liberal than any other English sect, often opening their chapels and schoolrooms to lectures and even discussions.'[2] A number of Unitarian ministers helped to establish societies—William Mitchell at Hinckley, Henry Solly at Lancaster, and William Blazeby at Dewsbury. Other ministers actively working for local societies were John Wilson and S. A. Steinthal at Liverpool, Isaac Wrigley at Lye and Robert Elliot in Durham. J. C. Farn was an early editor of the *Co-operative News*, and E. O. Greening was a founder of the National Co-operative Conference, whose foundation meeting was attended by J. P. Hopps and Professor W. S. Jevons, all these being Unitarians. Greening pioneered the Co-operative Federation, Co-operative Festivals, the International Co-operative Alliance, and the first co-operative candidate for Parliament. A different kind of Nonconformist influence was felt at Manchester, where the local co-operative society, destined to become the largest in England, grew out of the Roby Brotherhood, connected with Roby Chapel in Piccadilly, a Congregational foundation. At Rochdale itself an Anglican clergyman, the Rev W. N. Molesworth, gave support to the Pioneers and made the first suggestion that they should obtain legal protection.[3]

Besides the Anglican and Nonconformist elements there emerged a third school which dispensed with religion or became actively hostile to it. The Christian Socialist tradition was mediated to this school largely through Lloyd Jones (1811–1886).[4] He was

[1] See Margaret Cole, *Makers of the Labour Movement* (1948); P. Redfern, *The New History of the C.W.S.* (1938); and Holt, op. cit.
[2] G. J. Holyoake, *The History of Co-operation in England* (1906), I, 244.
[3] Ibid., I, 289, note 1, and II, 626.
[4] *Dict. Nat. Biog.*, s.v. Jones. See also biographical sketch by his son William Cairns Jones, prefaced to Lloyd Jones's *The Life, Times and Labours of Robert Owen* (2nd edition 1895).

an Owenite and an advocate of Owen's type of communistic communities. Such plans were strongly opposed by the clergy, because of the element of immorality supposed to be involved in them, but Jones himself was closely associated with the Christian Socialists. With J. M. Ludlow he wrote *Progress of the Working Classes* (1867). The entry on Jones in the *Dictionary of National Biography*, by Holyoake, is unsatisfactory, as are others by the same author, in minimizing or ignoring religious affiliations, such as Jones's connexions with the Maurice group. Jones was of more than doubtful orthodoxy in religious belief, but he belonged to the Christian rather than the Secularist side of the movement.

William King (1786–1865)[1] was another Christian advocate of co-operation. He was the son of the Rev John King, master of Ipswich Grammar School, and had intended to take Orders, but found that he could not accept the Thirty-Nine Articles, becoming a physician instead. His literary efforts included medical works, the editorship of the *Co-operator* from 1828 to 1830, and *Thoughts on the Teaching of Christ*, published posthumously in 1872. He fostered co-operation in Brighton, and was an example of those who supported the movement on broad grounds of principle:

> In his ideal, the objects of a Co-operative Society should be (1) the mutual protection of the members against poverty, (2) the attainment of a greater share of the comforts of life, and (3) the attainment of independence by means of a common capital. As the means of attaining these objects, he advocated a weekly subscription for accumulating common capital to be used first in trading, then in manufacturing for the Society, and finally in the purchase of land for the purpose of living upon it in community.

King influenced the Rochdale Pioneers and inspired a Christian Co-operative movement in York. He was convinced that co-operation was a natural expression of the Christian faith.[2]

John Alfred Langford (1823–1903)[3] was active from an early age in the work of the Birmingham Co-operative Society, becoming secretary on its foundation in 1846. The following year he joined a new Unitarian body known as the 'Church of the Saviour,' founded by George Dawson.

W. H. Ashurst (1792–1855) was still further from orthodoxy. He was a solicitor and a friend of Owen, who refused to pay taxes

[1] *Dict. Nat. Biog.*, s.v. King.
[2] Binyon, op. cit., 46f.
[3] *Dict. Nat. Biog.*, (second supplement), s.v. Langford.

until the Reform Bill was passed, and also refused to pay Church rates. He supported various Radical causes and defended Holyoake on his imprisonment in 1842. For a time he belonged to a small sect called 'Free-thinking Christians,' but later broke these rather loose bonds and belonged to no religious body, though retaining some flavour of Christianity: '. . . He regarded his political principles as the logical outcome of the doctrine of human brotherhood.' He was a 'warm supporter of co-operation.'[1]

J. G. Barmby (1820–1881) was an active Radical from an early age, and claimed to have invented the word 'Communism.' He represents an extreme of Owenite idealism, and his activities included a visit to France in 1848 as a messenger of the 'Communistic Church,' but he was also an advocate of his own version of Christian Socialism, joining the Unitarians and becoming a minister in various places, especially Wakefield. He belongs chiefly to the history of Socialism, but he advocated co-operation in Owen's sense.[2]

Minor figures among Christian advocates of co-operation were C. B. Dunn, curate of Cumberworth, near Wakefield, who helped to start co-operative societies and wrote verse; John Rabone of Birmingham who urged that co-operation rested on a Christian basis, and may possibly have originated the term 'Christian Socialist'; and the Rev Joseph Marriott of Warrington, a chairman of the first Co-operative Congress in 1831.[3]

At the Left-wing extreme, from the religious point of view, stood Holyoake and his Secularism. He was a dominant figure in all co-operative assemblies from about 1840 to the end of the century, and the co-operative movement presents the interesting spectacle of such men as Neale and Ludlow, whose whole motive was theological, sitting down in committees not only with the Nonconformist Mitchell, but also with the Secularist Holyoake.

Thus in these years there were three strands in the co-operative movement, from a religious standpoint:

(a) The surviving exponents of Owenism, for whom 'co-operation' was the name of one aspect of a profoundly revolutionary attempt to transform civilization. Despite the rationalism of Owen

---

[1] *Dict. Nat. Biog.*, s.v. Ashurst.

[2] Ibid., s.v. Barmby. See also Richard K. P. Pankhurst, *The Saint Simonians Mill and Carlyle* (no date), 141f.

[3] Binyon, op. cit., 48f.

himself, many of these were tinged with religion, mostly more or less unorthodox.

(*b*) The Christian Socialist tradition, influenced by Owenism and in some ways as revolutionary in intention, but with an orthodox theological basis, for Maurice was fundamentally orthodox, despite all appearance to the contrary. This movement was basically Anglican. Through Lloyd Jones it had links with the Owenite tradition, and even with its anti-religious element, represented by Holyoake.

(*c*) The northern consumers' movement, which rose and flourished as the other traditions declined. This was chiefly Nonconformist, but whereas the trade union Nonconformists were chiefly Methodists, these were more generally Congregationalists and Unitarians.

These three traditions were all characteristic of the Labour movement as a whole during the nineteenth century.

2   *Friendly Societies*[1]

A comparatively little-noticed form of working-class organization during this period was the friendly society, of which the most important group was the Odd Fellows, dating from the first half of the eighteenth century. The 'branches' which survived were in fact entirely separate societies, the oldest being the Independent Order of Oddfellows (Manchester Unity) (1822). The Foresters, dating from 1745, were reorganized in 1834 as the Ancient Order of Foresters. The Order of Druids dated from 1858, the Loyal Order of Shepherds (Ashton Unity) from 1826, the National Independent Order of Oddfellows from 1844, the National United Order of Free Gardeners from 1820. Such societies were at once insurance agencies and social organizations, and even to some extent religious bodies, supplying a need which the active leaders of the workers did not find answered in the established Churches. In the past friendly societies had laid stress on elaborate and secret rituals, and this had brought down on them the hostility of Church leaders. A select committee of the House of Lords in 1848 had been alarmed at the growth of the Odd Fellows, and objected to 'the employment of secret signs, the circulation of lectures, and the introduction of funeral orations after the burial service.' But later the emphasis on ritual passed into the

[1] See Joseph Maria Baernreither: *English Associations of Working Men.* English edition, translated by Alice Taylor (1893).

background. Three features of the movement were prominent in the middle of the nineteenth century: the growth of 'Working Men's Orders'; connexion with the temperance movement; and the predominance of Lancashire, many of the leading societies being based on the Manchester district.

The growing relationship to the temperance movement was especially significant. Formerly friendly societies had often met in public houses and heavy drinking had been common, but now some societies introduced fines for drunkenness. The railway societies sponsored friendly societies at Crewe and Swindon, and these were abstinence bodies. Friendly societies specifically for total abstainers were formed: the Order of Rechabites (Salford Unity), and the Sons of Temperance; while other societies introduced rules forbidding the spending of society funds on drink and the holding of meetings in public houses. Branches of the abstinence societies often met on church premises, and devoted laymen with the ambition to organize found an outlet for their energies as local officials. These tendencies brought the societies into close contact with the strong temperance movement in the Churches, and especially in Nonconformity. Through them, and through temperance societies of other kinds, many prominent figures in the Labour movement in later years first learned to speak in public. At an enormous demonstration in Hyde Park in 1890, called by all the temperance organizations to protest against the Conservative Government's licensing Bill, the speakers included Tom Mann, Ben Tillett, and John Burns—the very latest generation of Labour leaders.

The large societies were strictly neutral on religion:

> No member, no lodge, no district of an Order is allowed, as such, to issue any religious or political circular. All conversation on these subjects is forbidden at the meetings. Accordingly, men of the most different religious and political opinions work harmoniously side by side.[1]

But the clergy became increasingly sympathetic as the old rituals fell into the background. The general assemblies of the two great Orders, the Foresters and the Odd Fellows, started with a service and 'a sermon suited to the occasion.' Clergymen therefore came to see the value of friendly societies, and along with landlords and employers assisted in forming them. Their services consisted in

[1] Baernreither, op. cit., 397.

the making of subscriptions, giving advice, and acting as trustees. For example the Hitchin Friendly Institute was originally managed by gentry and clergy, but when in the 'seventies control was handed over to the ordinary members all the former officials and trustees were unanimously re-elected. Religious motives were sometimes at work in the encouragement given by large employers to the formation of friendly societies in their factories, the outstanding case being that of Sir Titus Salt. In many cases there were still close personal relations between the employer and his men, fostered by common membership of Nonconformist churches. Class conflict could not easily arise when the employer sat with his employees every Sunday in church, 'and, as happens among Presbyterian bodies, administers with them, on a footing of perfect equality, the spiritual and ecclesiastical functions peculiar to the same denomination.'[1] ('Presbyterian' here is an obvious simplification into Continental terms of the curious phenomenon of English Nonconformity. Strictly speaking hardly any English working men were Presbyterians. The Methodists had, broadly speaking, a Presbyterian organization.)

Among clergy who supported friendly societies two names are outstanding. John Thomas Becher (1770–1848) belongs to the immediately preceding period.[2] He was Vicar-General of the Collegiate Church at Southwell and helped to form a friendly society there in 1823, described as 'a pattern of its kind.'[3] In 1824 he published a book on friendly societies and in 1825 tables for their use. He also wrote other works on actuarial matters.

Samuel Best was a regular advocate of friendly societies. In 1871 he spoke at the Friendly Societies Association urging the clergy to pay attention to the 'promotion of the temporal welfare and social improvement of the people.'[4] He was the inventor of deposit friendly societies, which combined the techniques of the friendly society and the savings bank.

At Birmingham the Christ Church Provident Institute had as President and Vice-President two of the local clergy *ex officio*.[5]

The development of trustee savings banks was parallel to the growth of friendly societies. A name worth mentioning here is

---

[1] Baernreither, op. cit., 204f.
[2] *Dict. Nat. Biog.*, s.v. Becher.
[3] Baernreither, op. cit., 246.
[4] Ibid., 278.   [5] Ibid., 180.

that of Hugh S. Brown (1823–1886),[1] son of an Evangelical
clergyman in the Isle of Man. Brown worked on the railway and
studied for the Church, but as he neared the time of his ordination
he changed his views and became a Baptist minister in Liverpool
from 1847 to his death. He opened a workmen's savings bank in
which deposits rose to £80,000. He also delivered lectures to
working men on Sunday afternoons, drawing on his early experience. He was President of the Baptist Union in 1878.

3 *Mechanics' Institutes, Clubs, and Other Forms of Working-class Organization*

Brown's Sunday afternoon lectures were a form of education for
the workers. The national system of education was still in a
rudimentary state at the beginning of this period, and very largely, especially in the rural areas, in the hands of the clergy. This
system had been supplemented for a long time by the mechanics'
institutes, in which, in theory, the workers could gain 'useful
knowledge' to enable them to 'better themselves.' A typical
institute of this kind was the one at Manchester, founded chiefly by
Sir Benjamin Heywood (1793–1865), a banker and a member of
the great Lancashire Dissenting family whose Nonconformity
dated back to 1662.[2] He was President from the foundation of the
Institute to 1840, a period of fifteen years, and also a Whig M.P.
for a short time in 1831–1832. But the institutes in general had
gone into decline, and in many cases they had failed to provide
much education of any kind for the class for which they were
originally intended.

On the whole the Church of England was indifferent or hostile
to the mechanics' institutes, regarding them as subversive. The
Guardian was rather scornful, and tended to dismiss them as
having fallen into the hands of the middle classes. It attributed
their partial failure to the fact that they were organized by one
class on behalf of another, 'at all times a dangerous plan,' and to
their attempt to 'elevate, educate, and improve the working man,
instead of merely interesting and amusing him,' a rather surprising
blow at Victorian earnestness. Instead of 'the eternal lecturing' it
recommended classes and also 'amusements, *purs et simples*'; the
examples given were music, and cricket, frivolities apparently
necessitating a lapse into French to introduce them. Straight-

[1] *Dict. Nat. Biog.* (supplement), s.v. Brown.
[2] Ibid., s.v. Heywood.

forward clubs were recommended too, primarily as 'associations for amusement and instruction,' and it was urged that if upper-class assistance was given in starting them it ought to be with-drawn as soon as possible, to avoid the dangers of patronage. This was a valuable point to which the paper returned a number of times. Lord Brougham was quoted approvingly on the virtues of leaving the management of mechanics' institutes to 'the class for which they are designed,' and the *Guardian* found it true of other types of 'institutions for the benefit of working men' that 'they are popular with them in proportion as the active inter-ference of their superiors is reduced to a minimum.' The Working Men's Club and Institute Union was recommended on a number of occasions, and also the holding of 'working-men's industrial exhibitions,' which offered opportunities for co-operation between classes without 'meddlesome dictation or ostentatious patronage.' Other organizations of, or for, the working classes were frequently referred to in the correspondence columns, largely because of the extent of clerical interest in them; such were 'Penny Banks,' and of course friendly societies. The *Guardian* lost no opportunity of commending the latter, while mentioning the disadvantages which still sometimes occurred in the shape of financial insecurity and excessive drinking.[1]

The working men's clubs were something of an alternative to the mechanics' institutes. They began to appear from about 1860, chiefly owing to the enthusiastic advocacy of Henry Solly,[2] a Unitarian minister who has been mentioned above, in connex-ion with the co-operative movement. He was also sympathetic to the Chartists. He intended his clubs to rival the public houses, but as he left control in the hands of the members they gradually began to sell alcoholic drinks. In 1862 Solly united the clubs in the Working Men's Club and Institute Union, and in 1870 he became editor of the *Beehive*. He tried to link the Union with the London Trades Council, and although he failed in this there were 'friendly relations' between the two bodies; for example the Council used the Club Union hall in Clerkenwell. The transition from mech-anics' institute to working men's club can be illustrated from the

[1] *Guardian*, June 15th, 1853; March 10th, September 22nd, 1858; October 19th, 1859; April 15th, 1863; April 19th, September 6th, 1865.
[2] G. D. H. Cole, *A Short History of the British Working Class Movement* (Vol. II, 1926), 46, 112. See also Holt, op. cit., 141, and *London Trades Council, 1860–1950* (1950), 12.

career of H. W. Crosskey, another Unitarian. He tried to bring working men back into the Derby Mechanics' Institute Library, which by 1850 had become middle class, and, failing in this, he founded a working men's institute.[1] The *Nonconformist* was very pleased at the promise of trade union support for Solly, and urged support by its readers, supplying his address, and describing with great enthusiasm the work of the clubs.[2] The *Universe* too was highly favourable, and echoed the *Guardian's* insistence that too much interference by the prosperous would harm them. So far the main initiative had come from the working men themselves:

> This is how it should be; on no other basis would we wish to see working men's clubs established—to be permanent and prosperous they should be self-reliant and self-supporting, depending on the regular subscriptions of their members and not on the casual donations of this or that wealthy philanthropist.

They did valuable work, but had one shortcoming: they were all 'sectarian'; that is to say, Catholics were not very welcome. The cure for their sectarianism was to form Catholic working men's clubs, such as Manning had established in his parish.[3]

Besides Solly and Crosskey another Unitarian active in the same cause was Peter Alfred Taylor (1819–1891).[4] Taylor was Radical—and later Liberal Unionist—M.P. for Leicester, active in promoting the rights of Nonconformists and the education and leisure-time activities of the working classes.

Another outstanding servant of working-class interests in Victorian times was the Evangelical clergyman William Weldon Champneys (1807–1875).[5] The son of the Rev William Betton Champneys, in 1837 he became Rector of St Mary's, Whitechapel. There he founded schools, including the first ragged school in London. He engaged in a great variety of philanthropic enterprises:

> He founded a provident society, assisted in the commencement of a shoeblack brigade, with a refuge and an industrial home for the boys, and co-operated with others in the work of building the Whitechapel Foundation Commercial School. He was the originator of a

[1] Holt, op. cit., 269.
[2] *Nonconformist*, April 29th, October 28th, 1863.
[3] *Universe*, April 22nd, 1865.
[4] *Dict. Nat. Biog.*, s.v. Taylor.
[5] Ibid., s.v. Champneys.

local association for the promotion, health and comfort of the industrial classes, and also of the Church of England Young Men's Society, the first association of young men for religious purposes and mutual improvement which was seen in Whitechapel. The London coal-whippers were indebted to him for the establishment of an office, under an act of parliament in 1843, where alone they could be legally hired, instead of as before being obliged to wait in public houses . . . His sermons attracted working men by plain appeals to their good sense and right feeling.

In 1860 he became Vicar of St Pancras, and in 1868 Dean of Lichfield.

On the Nonconformist side John Ashton Nicholls (1823–1859),[1] a Manchester manufacturer, devoted himself to the education of the workers. He organized classes in Ancoats and made tours to study the condition of the people. He was one of the first secretaries of the Unitarian Home Missionary Board, formed in 1854. Lectures he gave on the subject of strikes, during a period of industrial conflict, led to correspondence with Kingsley, who was surprised to find that he was a Capitalist. Nicholls advocated libraries, museums, and bands on Sundays, and on his death he was commemorated not only by a tablet in Cross Street Chapel, but also by an obelisk erected by the working men of Manchester. The Nicholls hospital was established by his parents in his memory.

Benjamin Scott (1814–1892),[2] who served as Chamberlain of London and later became a banker, devoted much time to lectures to the working classes, and in 1851 he was a chief promoter of the Working Men's Educational Union. He was a 'staunch Nonconformist, temperance advocate, and social reformer.' He gave £2,000 to the (Congregationalist) Pilgrim Church in Southwark.

Scott's namesake, Alexander John Scott (1805–1866),[3] was the son of a minister at Greenock, and became a minister himself, serving as assistant to Edward Irving, the founder of the Catholic Apostolic Church, though without sharing his views. He did however run into trouble with the ecclesiastical authorities, in that in 1831 he was charged with heresy for rejecting Calvinism and denying the identity of Sunday with the Sabbath. In 1851 he became the first Principal of Owens College, Manchester, and

---

[1] *Dict. Nat. Biog.*, s.v. Nicholls.
[2] Ibid., s.v. Scott.   [3] Ibid., s.v. Scott.

with William Gaskell he started the Manchester Working Men's College, which later merged with it. Gaskell was a Unitarian and the husband of Elizabeth Gaskell, the novelist. He was minister at Cross Street Chapel. Elizabeth Gaskell herself wrote *Mary Barton* in 1848, expressing sympathy with the Manchester workers in their struggle against the employers, who complained that she had drawn an unfair picture of them.[1] With Scott and Gaskell there was associated Joseph Gouge Greenwood (1821–1894),[2] the son of a Congregational minister at Petersfield, Huntingdonshire. In 1850 he became Professor of Classics at Owens College, and in 1857 Principal. 'His private opinions were through life those of an orthodox but liberal churchman.' He became honorary secretary of the working men's college referred to above and in 1861 was responsible for its amalgamation with Owens.

Most of the forms of working-class organization referred to in this chapter received the warm and friendly support of religious leaders of all denominations. They did not arouse the fears which efforts at the political organization of the workers awakened, and which were stirred even by trade union activities. They aimed to raise the status of the working man, through forms of insurance and saving for the future, through education, through forms of entertainment, through 'self-help,' through informal social contacts. In so far as they tended to make him more contented, they operated against those forms of organization, such as Chartism, which cherished a more-or-less revolutionary programme. But they contributed to building up a powerful and well-led Labour movement, and since a revolution is not necessarily less thorough because the ultimate sanctions of physical force are not required, they proved in the long run to be a revolutionary development themselves. In the creation of a working class united enough and informed enough both to demand and to secure recognition as worthy of full citizenship—upon which rested in turn the hope of obtaining a wider measure of social justice—the Churches played an extensive part through their support of such activities.

[1] *Dict. Nat. Biog.*, s.v. Elizabeth Gaskell.
[2] Ibid. (supplement), s.v. Greenwood.

CHAPTER 4

CHRISTIAN SOCIALISM

1 *The Decline of the Original Christian Socialist Group*

IN THE EIGHTEEN-FIFTIES the original Christian Socialist movement was in decline. According to Karl Marx this movement arose from the guilty conscience of the upper classes: 'Christian Socialism is but the holy water with which the priest consecrates the heart-burnings of the aristocrat.'[1] There is a good deal of obvious truth in this, for the reaction of F. D. Maurice to the Chartist protest was clearly and indeed consciously a sense of sin, because the Church of which he was a representative had been so remote from the needs and ambitions of the working classes. But this does not mean that the place of the movement in the history of the English working classes is small. On the contrary many pages in this book are largely concerned with tracing the remote consequences which flowed from these limited origins. It is possible to see Maurice himself, so often portrayed as the conservative of the group, as the real revolutionary. So he seemed to his opponents; a revolutionary all the more dangerous because he subverted the established order both in theology and in society: 'Maurice's social reform advocated the rising of the poor against their masters, while at the same time his theological eccentricities removed the only guarantee of the morality of the poor which is provided by the fear of the here-after.'[2] For he rejected both the existing class system and the doctrine of eternal punishment. He was opposed to competition, on metaphysical and therefore uncompromising grounds, and so far as he was able he carried this prejudice into practice. He abolished the system of prizes at Queen's College, and aimed to do the same at the Working Men's College. The other members of the group started from similar fundamental principles; Ludlow gave a philosophical reason for the concern with producers' co-operation:

---

[1] Quoted by John Saville in *The Christian Socialists of 1848* (in *Democracy and the Labour Movement*, edited by Saville, 1954).

[2] C. F. G. Masterman, *Frederick Denison Maurice* (1907), 127.

'Consumption . . . is the merely human element in life; production, the divine. God is the Eternal Producer.' For Neale co-operation was an attempt to realize on earth 'the Kingdom of God and his righteousness.' Even the issuing of 'Tracts,' under that name, was provocative, for it would immediately remind the public, and especially the clerical public, of those other tracts which a few years earlier had abruptly terminated at number ninety; the choice of the term, like the use of the name 'Christian Socialism' itself, was intended to shock the world with the expectation of revolution.[1]

It is neither possible nor necessary here to retrace the frequently-told story of the enterprises and hopes of the group in the years following the 1848 revolutions. The immediately important aspect is the long-term effect of their efforts. It must be admitted that the first experience was discouraging, in view of the large-scale ideals they cherished. Starting with the vague intention of bringing Christianity and Socialism together, they chose to attack the pressing economic problems of the day by an inappropriate method, for they believed that the solution to those problems lay in co-operative production. It is true that they did not have in mind only small self-governing workshops; it was hoped to bring in the trade unions to take over control, and Ludlow favoured action by the state. But in one form or another producers' co-operation was the weapon with which they chose to fight the main battle. The source of their inspiration was not, directly, the native Owenite tradition, but the *ateliers nationaux* organized in France by Louis Blanc, which J. M. Ludlow, the driving force of the group, as Maurice was its intellectual leader, had studied at first hand, returning with enthusiastic plans for imitating them in London. Yet Ludlow was also in touch with the followers of Owen, for among his friends were John Minter Morgan, Lloyd Jones, Walter Cooper, and Gerald Massey, all Owenites. But whatever the source of the idea, it was not a fortunate choice. It has been objected, as it was widely objected at the time, that human nature lacks a moral incentive high enough to make success possible where men are their own masters; but there is also a more precise objection which can be made. The whole conception of producers' co-operation, as the Christian Socialists envisaged it, belonged essentially to a vanished era of small-scale industry. A more recent revival of similar ideas adopted the word 'Guild'

[1] Binyon, op. cit., 75, 78, 93.

(more properly perhaps 'Gild') to describe the self-governing industries it was hoped to create. Such expressions look back to the past. The Christian Socialists were anti-Capitalist, but their hostility to Capitalism lies open to the objection that it was doctrinaire, in that they held that co-operation, not competition, was the natural state for the Christian. If the competitive spirit and the profit motive so important to the new middle classes could be abolished, the objects of the movement would be achieved. They were more troubled by the spirit of the age—of the rich and poor alike—than by the conditions of the age. They hoped that their experiments in co-operative production would gradually extend until they permeated and transformed the whole economic order; before Sidney Webb they were believers in gradualism. Such a programme could not succeed, for it took no account of contemporary trends, except such of them as it consciously opposed. The Marxists in contrast sought to analyse the tendencies of the time and encourage those they approved.

No one except the Christian Socialists themselves expected them to achieve much success. On the Socialist side Ernest Jones, in debate with Lloyd Jones, attacked them on both theoretical and practical grounds; fundamentally his argument was that society could not be transformed merely by creating little islands of co-operation, which would only collapse in face of Capitalist hostility, as the experiments of Owen had collapsed. The Chartists were on sounder lines in maintaining that Capitalism could only be abolished when its enemies, the working classes, captured *political* power. On the other hand the adherents of the current economic faith naturally believed that competitive Capitalism was the law of nature in the economic world. For this reason they did not attack very severely the Christian Socialists, since they believed that in any case their schemes were bound to fail. Not only would there be no harmful result; positive good would be done, since the workers would realize the futility of opposing the system, and by their failure would learn to accept its standards. This was in fact a fairly sound appraisal of the career of the 'New Model' trade unionism. The opposite possibility was overlooked: that if the workers became convinced that the system could not be changed by a process of leavening they might attempt to destroy it altogether.

The prophets proved right; the producers' associations gradually disappeared, though the hope that some day similar schemes would meet with success long remained. It is a mistake to think

that only a few prosperous men, remote from the world of working people, believed in this kind of co-operation. On the contrary,
many trade unionists showed great interest, especially the leaders
of the Amalgamated Society of Engineers, which passed a resolution in favour of co-operative production. In the same union, in
1856, there was a majority in favour of setting aside £10,000 for a
producers' co-operative, though the scheme came to nothing. The
two chief leaders of the Left wing of Chartism, Harney and Ernest
Jones, split on this issue, since Harney, influenced by Gerald
Massey, continued to advocate co-operation, while Jones continued to oppose it.

The Christian Socialists advocated producers' co-operation
'with an almost apostolic fervour,'[1] and were thus associated with a
form of working-class activity which held no great promise for the
future. It has been said that this co-operative endeavour was a
rival movement to trade unionism; certainly it is true that there
was hardly room for both to develop. The trade union movement
itself had an ambiguous relationship to the Capitalist order: it
might, as in the 'sixties and 'seventies, be a device for ensuring
that the workers got a reasonable share of the produce of the
system; or it might provide the basis for a political movement to
overthrow it; but in either case the movement for producers'
co-operation was a sideline.

Thus one reason for the decline of the Christian Socialist
movement was that it tried the wrong method of benefiting the
workers. The conditions of working-class life began to improve as
the century passed its half-way mark, and with increased prosperity the bitterness of class warfare decreased, the immediate
occasion of the movement's rise being thereby removed. A further
reason for the decline was the feeling that it had in part achieved
its objects; it had certainly called attention to the gulf separating
the clergy and the prosperous middle classes from the masses of
the urban population, though in this respect its success was
limited by the fact that the interest of the Christian Socialists was
chiefly confined to London, and they had little knowledge of the
conditions in other areas. This limitation coloured all their
thinking; their plans for producers' co-operation were more
appropriate to the small firms, for example in tailoring and building, which made up the bulk of industry in London, than to
mining, textiles, or heavy industry generally. Nor were the Chris-

[1] S. and B. Webb, *History of Trade Unionism*, 225.

tian Socialists at first conscious of the importance for the future of the new type of co-operation developing in the north. A particular example of the degree to which Christian Socialism was successful in achieving its objects was the Industrial and Provident Societies' Act of 1852 (15 and 16 Vict. c. 31). The passing of the Act was preceded by a Select Committee on Investments for the Savings of the Middle and Working Classes, in 1850, and a Select Committee on the Law of Partnerships, in 1851. R. A. Slaney was chairman of both committees, so that the Act was popularly known as Slaney's Act. The friendship of Slaney with Thomas Hughes, both being Lincoln's Inn men, was an important source of this legal reform.[1] The Christian Socialists played a prominent part in giving evidence before both committees, and in securing the passing of the Act, which provided a legal security for producers' co-operation. To secure such an Act had been a prominent aim of the movement, so that, with the legal obstacles to co-operation cleared away, some members began to lose interest.

Apart from the unhappy emphasis on producers' co-operation and the partial achievement of some of the movement's objects, another cause of decline was one which is always liable to affect societies built upon a body of belief: disagreement on the question how far the assistance of those whose beliefs are unsound is to be welcomed. The crisis arose through the adherence of E. V. Neale, the richest of all the group, who sacrificed his fortune for the cause. Neale sought a less specifically Christian basis than had seemed appropriate for a body originally half-devotional in character, aiming to win the support of non-Christians. The founder of the group, Ludlow, opposed Neale, as indeed he usually did. Maurice, the effective leader, gave his support to Neale, not because he thought little of the theological basis, as his opponents always alleged, but because he could always find a place in his theology for the services, which he would regard as Christian, of those who considered themselves non-Christian. He accepted gladly the heterodox Neale and the still more heterodox Lloyd Jones. Ludlow was distressed to find Maurice's judgement opposed to his own, and something of a permanent breach appeared in the group, though without injury to personal relationships. In the event Maurice still continued to find himself closely associated with Ludlow, while Neale and Lloyd Jones devoted themselves to

[1] Edward C. Mack and W. H. G. Armytage, *Thomas Hughes: The Life of the Author of 'Tom Brown's Schooldays,'* 1952, 68f.

the co-operative movement, in the company of many who were non-Christian to the point of being actively hostile to religion.

For these and other causes the original impulse was lost. The co-operatives with something approaching unanimity began to close down or change their character. The Mile End Ironworks, supported by the wealth of Vansittart, Neale's cousin, had to be wound up in 1853. The members of the co-operative, and the A.S.E., which had promised support, alike failed to attempt any repayment of the money advanced. The Atlas works, another ironworks, soon ran into difficulties, and the A.S.E., crippled by the failure of its strike, again failed to give promised support. Neale struggled on for some years, and lost heavily. The Amalgamated Shoemakers' Association survived into the 'sixties, and was then taken over by Thomas Christmas, the manager, as a private firm. In 1852 Isham, the manager of the printers' co-operative, similarly turned it into a Capitalist enterprise. The Pimlico Builders' Association was wound up in 1853, though its financial position was not serious. The North London Builders carried on till 1860, when they too were taken over by the manager, Pickard. The Castle Street Tailors, the first of the associations, also lasted till 1860, when Walter Cooper, the manager, was found guilty of frauds, and the business broke up. The Central Co-operative Agency, a forerunner of the Co-operative Wholesale Society, was wound up in 1857, Neale finding that he was no longer able to keep it going through a difficult spell. Already at the second conference of the co-operative movement in 1853 the influence of the Christian Socialists was declining. A split began to appear in the movement, between the original group of four, Maurice, Ludlow, Kingsley, and Mansfield, who were increasingly turning their attention to educational work, and those who were predominantly interested in the co-operative movement. In 1854 therefore the Society of Promoters handed over its functions to the executive committee of the co-operative conference. Neale, Hughes and other Christian Socialists were prominent on this body.

The *Guardian* gives some revealing insights into the attitude of enlightened churchmen to the Christian Socialist movement in the early 'fifties. In these early days it was remarkably well-informed on world affairs in general, and it had given a fair amount of attention to Socialism, meaning by this term chiefly the theories of Fourier, Owen and Blanc, but it was startled by the epithet 'Christian.' In three articles the motives of the Christian Socialists, and the idea of co-operative associations, were praised, but it was suspected that there was unsound theology at work. The associations were in no way Socialist, and though useful against low pay they could not affect unemployment, which was a matter of demand. The 'laws' of supply and demand were compared with such 'laws' as that fire burns or water drowns. The Christian Socialists' antipathy to competition was something of a shock, and some obscure passages in their writings were taken to mean that a co-operative association was equivalent to a Church even if all its members were non-Christians. The theology of Maurice and his associates was not quite so extraordinary as that; they meant rather that the Church must learn to express itself through the aspirations of the working classes, such as the search for an effective form of co-operation, and that the ideals of Socialism necessitated a spiritual foundation which could only be provided by Christianity. Kingsley wrote very politely to correct this misapprehension, and there was a ludicrous appendix to the discussion a few weeks later when an unfriendly review of Kingsley's novel *Yeast* led to a bitter exchange in which the novelist called the reviewer a liar (in Latin, of course) and the editor of the *Guardian* denounced the Christian Socialists as 'our opponents.' Maurice intervened to pour oil on troubled waters,[1] and thereafter the *Guardian* gave little attention to the group.

Christian Socialism was very much an Anglican movement, and practically no notice was taken of it in the Nonconformist and Roman Catholic press. The *Nonconformist* did once or twice comment favourably on the associations, the College, and Maurice,[2] but the Roman Catholic press showed no interest.

Perhaps the most important question to ask about the Christian Socialists is the extent of their later influence. An unfriendly critic considers that they distracted the working classes from the all-important task of securing political power and that 'those who helped to destroy their belief in independent political action were guilty, in objective terms, of prolonging and extending the poverty of the labouring millions.'[3] A more sympathetic historian credits them with inspiring many reforming activities:

[1] *Guardian*, February 19th, February 26th, March 5th, March 22nd, May 21st, June 25th, 1851.
[2] *Nonconformist*, June 5th, 1850; November 1st, 1854.
[3] Saville, op. cit., 159.

In every field of social service the influence of their adventure was felt. Ludlow's unobtrusive labours for the Friendly Societies, Maurice's devotion to the education of the workers, Kingsley's enthusiasm for sanitary reform, Octavia Hill's crusade for the better housing of the poor—each of these, and many another half-forgotten heroism, owed its inspiration to Christian Socialism. And all this has been neglected or mentioned with sneers, because 'the Associations failed'.[1]

There is no necessary contradiction between these estimates. On the one hand the movement may well have turned working-class attention from revolutionary activity to self-improvement within the existing form of society, while on the other it may have encouraged measures of amelioration. But the number of prominent figures in the Labour movement later in the century who were inspired wholly or in part by the group around Maurice suggests that the attempt to organize the working classes benefited rather than suffered through its activities.

2   The Working Men's College

One may look with some suspicion on an account of Christian Socialism, however brief, which does not make any mention of the Working Men's College, yet this is in fact what Saville's essay, referred to above, provides. It may be claimed with some reason that the College was the chief permanent memorial to the work of the Christian Socialists. It was Mansfield who suggested the creation of a college, before he left for Paraguay in May 1852. Courses of lectures were begun in December of that year, and a great stimulus was given to the group's educational enterprise by the expulsion of Maurice, on theological grounds, from his position at King's College. An address by 967 working men, including the trade union leaders Newton and Allen, was presented to Maurice in December 1853 in favour of the establishment of a college. Neale wrote to Sheffield for details of a working men's college which had been started there in 1842 and revived in 1848, though the ultimate form of the Christian Socialist college was less democratic than that of the Sheffield People's College, 'where the initiative had come from below, from the students themselves.'[2] The Sheffield college was the work of R. S. Bayley, a Congrega-

---

[1] C. E. Raven, *Christian Socialism 1848–1854*, 143.

[2] J. F. C. Harrison, *A History of the Working Men's College, 1854–1954* (1954), 28.

tional minister, who died in 1859. In 1846 Bayley had founded the *People's College Journal*.[1]

The historian of the Working Men's College lists eight men as founders, these being those named as such on the occasion of the Jubilee in 1904. These were:

F. D. Maurice, the dominating influence.

J. M. Ludlow.

Thomas Hughes, who was less interested in the strictly intellectual aspects of the College's life than in its sporting and recreational activities.

F. J. Furnivall, who might be called the leader of the opposition. He was at odds with Maurice, at various times, over the degree of student control, the admission of women, Sunday excursions (he was a fervent anti-Sabbatarian), and dancing.

The above four belonged to the original group of Christian Socialists.

J. Llewelyn Davies, an early and important adherent of the movement. Davies had a friend, David James Vaughan, who in 1860 became Vicar of St Martin's, Leicester, and in 1862 Vaughan founded a working men's college in Leicester, later known as Vaughan College.

John Westlake, who had been at Cambridge with Davies. Westlake was even younger than most of the group: he was born in 1828 and called to the Bar in 1854. From 1888 he was for twenty years Whewell Professor of International Law at Cambridge. He taught mathematics at the College for many years.

Richard Buckley Litchfield, who had been at Trinity College, Cambridge, like Davies and Westlake. He had been born only in 1832 and at this stage was an unsuccessful barrister. Later he was in the employment of the Ecclesiastical Commission, but his life was devoted to the College. From 1854 to 1901 he was a member of the Council and Bursar, and in the difficult days of the early 'seventies, after the death of Maurice, he was given dictatorial powers.

G. Lowes Dickinson, the Pre-Raphaelite artist, who had been introduced to the group by Archibald Campbell, an early supporter.[2]

The committee of teaching and publication which launched the College included Lord Goderich, William Johnson, Kingsley,

[1] See W. H. G. Armytage, 'The Sheffield People's College', in *Sheffield University Gazette*, vii, 2-3.

[2] Harrison, op. cit., 32ff.

Alexander Macmillan, Mansfield, Neale, and the Rev C. Kegan Paul. Some of these will receive special mention below. Among others associated with the effort were Septimus Hansard, John Sherren Brewer, Richard Chenevix Trench, and Henry J. Hose. All these were clergy, mostly with strong High Church leanings. Hansard, Curate of St Mary's, Marylebone, and later Rector of Bethnal Green, brought in George Grove, the great musical scholar. Brewer, 'a High Churchman and a Tory', became Vice-Principal in 1869. Trench became Archbishop of Dublin in 1864. This list shows how completely the College was the child of the Christian Socialist movement. But from early days other elements were present. The most useful of all the early supporters, because of his eminence, was Ruskin. He was deeply interested in the work of the College, and it was from his association with it that he received his first impulse to social thought, which came to have so great an influence. Ruskin brought in artists, including Rossetti and other Pre-Raphaelites. There was also a group of Positivists, with whom the Christian Socialists had been associated in connexion with trade union questions. Frederic Harrison taught from 1857, and the Lushington twins, Godfrey and Vernon, were also associated with the College. Llewelyn Davies, though himself a clergyman, was related through his wife to Henry Crompton and E. S. Beesly, both leading Positivists, and he was on friendly terms with the group. There were close connexions with Chartism, and among Chartists interested were Thomas Shorter, the first secretary of the College, Joseph Millbank, John Roebuck, and Walter Cooper. The Christian Socialist tradition was thus diluted from an early date, and as an Anglican movement it was further diluted by the number of Nonconformist students in the early days, some of them followers of the Congregational hymn-writer, Thomas Toke Lynch.

The Christian Socialists had created the College, but in its later years it tended to become secularized. The struggles between Maurice and Furnivall helped in this process. In 1858 Maurice attempted to resign the Principalship in protest against Furnivall's Sunday excursions and especially his sympathies with the Sunday League. College prayers lapsed, until they were revived in 1859 by Hughes. By 1863 few students attended the Bible Class, although for Maurice the Bible study group had been the core of the Christian Socialist movement. In the later nineteenth century the College was dominated by George Tansley, whose whole life was given to its service. Tansley was an agnostic, a parallel to Huxley in combining a rigid morality with freethinking. But at least the initial impulse came from the Christian Socialists, and they set the pattern for the future of the College. Raven emphasizes the work of the College in bringing together various classes and in educating the future leaders of the Labour movement, and considers that some of the credit given to later pioneers of such work, such as Toynbee and Barnett, should properly be given to Maurice and his associates.

3 *Services of the Christian Socialists to the Co-operative Movement and Trade Unionism*

Another sphere in which the Christian Socialists and their disciples continued to give excellent service for many years was in the development of consumers' co-operation. Holyoake, who had no bias in favour of Christians, Socialist or otherwise, paid tribute to their services and their 'patient and laborious attentiveness.'[1] It is a mistake to suppose that they were only interested in co-operative production. Of Ludlow and Hughes it would be true to say that this was their primary interest, but even this would not be true of Neale. In the case of Ludlow it is necessary to remember that his upbringing had been in France, and that he had at one time intended to become a French citizen. He was the father of the original Christian Socialist co-operative associations, and almost a lifetime later, not long before his death in 1911 at the age of ninety, he emerged as an advocate of co-partnership, still seeking an expression of the co-operative ideal. Hughes too was chiefly concerned with production as the principal sphere of co-operation, and increasingly as time went by he would denounce the desertion of the true co-operative principle by those who were interested only in the stores, and who did not give the employees of the consumer co-operatives any share in control. Hughes was the most active and ardent of all the advocates of producers' co-operation, travelling on missionary tours and never giving way to despair. In 1869 as first chairman of the co-operative conference, he denounced the tendency to forget all about the productive side. His attitude involved him in a continuous struggle with J. T. W. Mitchell, leader of the Rochdale Pioneers, and the staunchest advocate of the consumers' movement, and he made a final rather desperate effort to win the movement back to what he considered

[1] G. J. Holyoake, *The History of Co-operation in England* (1906), II, 543.
12—TCATLM

the true road after Mitchell's death. It was partly due to this vigorous advocacy that the idea of co-operative production survived in the Labour movement into the twentieth century, and as remote successors of Hughes in this respect his biographers mention the names of A. J. Penty, A. R. Orage, G. D. H. Cole, R. H. Tawney, and M. B. Reckitt.

But others among the Christian Socialists were interested in consumers' co-operation and were responsible for its extension to the south of England by opening a store in London. It is important to remember that the distinction of the two—one might almost say the rival—types of co-operation was not clear in the public mind, and while the Rochdale experiment was being made the very word 'co-operation' had a sinister ring in the ears of the respectable classes of the south because of its connexion with Owenism. The support of the Christian Socialists was largely responsible for making co-operation an acceptable part of the social order, at least in London.

In 1869 the first co-operative congress was held. Kingsley served on the responsible committee; as mentioned above Hughes was President; Ludlow wrote the first report, and he and Neale were elected to the central board. Hughes and Neale wrote a *Manual for Co-operators* containing a good deal about Christianity —so much indeed that Holyoake raised objection at the congress of 1881; but despite his protest the congress adopted the manual as official. But in the main the Christian Socialists used their influence with the consumers' movement in trying to encourage productive co-operation, and periodically the congress passed resolutions in its favour, but at no stage was much progress made. The Christian Socialists urged the formation of separate societies for production, and quite logically they were hostile when the Co-operative Wholesale Society began manufacturing. Hughes's absorption with the productive side was so complete that he insisted on regarding the profit-sharing scheme operated by Archibald Briggs at his colliery as co-operative production, although it was obviously no such thing, nor even of much practical benefit to the employees. Ludlow in contrast was a strong critic of a scheme which 'ran exactly counter to the most vital points of co-operation,'[1] explaining that the bonus for the employees was inadequate and that they were given no share in management.

[1] Wagner, op. cit., 128f.

The considerable services which the Christian Socialists gave to consumers' co-operation were therefore given half-unwillingly, by men who would much rather have continued the great experiment they had once unsuccessfully tried. Nevertheless the services were given. The limitation was perhaps that the Christian Socialists did not themselves really understand the nature of co-operation. They believed that the conflict of the two kinds of co-operative effort was the conflict of the ideal and the practical; hence their conviction that the co-operators were choosing the second-best. They failed to realize that consumers' co-operation might be idealistic, or that producers' co-operation might be purely selfish and materialistic. Ludlow feared a new class war, between the producer and the consumer, perhaps fiercer than the conflict of Capital and Labour.

Another way in which the Christian Socialists continued for many years to serve the workers' cause was in the help which they gave to trade unions. They were able to render this service more effectively in the third quarter of the nineteenth century than they could have done at any other time, since it was at this period that their own outlook was most closely shared by union leaders. After the failure of Owen's ambitious plans a mood of conservatism settled on the unions, which accorded well with the ideals of Maurice and his associates. The revolutionary unionism of the 'thirties and 'forties and the 'New Unionism' of the 'nineties would have offered a much less fruitful field for co-operation. While the movement was still in its prime there was a lock-out in the engineering industry, in 1852, when the Christian Socialists supported the A.S.E. with subscriptions, letters to the press, and lectures to the public. Lord Goderich gave the union executive £500 towards strike pay. When the strike failed the men who refused to submit and sign the employers' 'document' were advanced £1,030 by Neale, which was all repaid. Similar firm support led to a more successful conclusion in 1861, when the London builders proposed to pay their employees by the hour. The workers 'failed to make clear their objection to the Hour System, or even to obtain a hearing of their case. Their position was, for the first time, intelligibly explained in two brilliant letters addressed to the newspapers by eight Positivists and Christian Socialists, which did much to bring about the tacit compromise in which the struggle ended.'[1]

[1] S. and B. Webb, *History of Trade Unionism*, 245f.

The greatest crisis in the history of English trade unionism in the latter part of the nineteenth century arose over the Sheffield outrages in 1867 and the Queen's Bench judgement that trade unions were in restraint of trade and so could not enjoy legal protection for their funds. Public feeling was very hostile to the unions, tending to believe that Broadhead, who was responsible for the outrages on non-union members, was a typical specimen of a trade union leader, and that the crimes committed at Sheffield were common. At first the only 'friend of the Unions' on the Royal Commission which was set up was Hughes, though his influence was later reinforced by the arrival of the Positivist Frederic Harrison. Other Christian Socialists supplied the unions with help and advice in presenting their case to the Commission, and when its report was published a minority report also appeared, signed by Hughes, Harrison, and the Earl of Lichfield. This demanded that no action should become an illegality merely because it was performed by a person in the position of an employee, and that no action legal if committed by one man should become illegal merely because it was committed by a combination of men. In 1869 there was a demonstration at Exeter Hall addressed by Mundella and Hughes as part of a campaign in favour of these proposals. But Hughes was losing touch with the union leadership, and when the Royal Commission of 1875 presented its report Hughes was with the majority in recommending only slight changes in the law apart from the repeal of the penal clauses of the Master and Servant Act. The minority report advocated the complete repeal of the Criminal Law Amendment Act, and in the main the union demands were accepted by the Conservative Government, which thus showed itself more accommodating than Gladstone had done. Hughes had taken up an ambiguous attitude to the majority report, criticizing it and yet signing it. Such vacillation ended his popularity and influence with the unions, which considered that he had let them down.

4 *Later Careers of Maurice and his Associates*

Enough has been said to show that much of the most valuable work of the Christian Socialists was done after the original group broke up, though this has not been emphasized by historians. This brief outline may be supplemented by a glance at the later careers of some of the figures involved.

Frederick Denison Maurice (1805–1872) did not contribute very greatly in a direct way to working-class activity except in connexion with the College. Although a quiet and scholarly man, averse to public prominence, he seemed destined throughout his life to be a figure of controversy, a fact which distressed and saddened him. At the time of the Christian Socialist movement he was already a mature man, approaching middle age, while Ludlow, Kingsley, Mansfield and Hughes were all under thirty. He stood in the position of a latter-day Socrates, without the satirical wit, and his rewards were similar, allowing for the gentler and subtler means which advancing civilization had devised for silencing inconvenient criticism. At the time of the Christian Socialist movement he was already in trouble over his Chair at King's College, because of his association with the co-operative movement, which aroused in the minds of the middle classes instinctive fears of republicanism, atheism and subversion. In 1853 he was driven out of his Chair because of his rejection of the doctrine of everlasting punishment, and the stimulus thereby given to the creation of the Working Men's College has been mentioned. By 1860 the general ostracism he had faced had weakened enough for him to be appointed to the chapel of St Peter, Vere Street. There were further protests at this appointment, but by now there was also a strong body of support. Further difficulties befell him in the early 'sixties as a result of his friendship with Bishop Colenso, though Maurice was far from sharing all Colenso's opinions on the Pentateuch. In 1866 he was appointed to the Chair of Moral Philosophy at Cambridge. Throughout this time he remained Principal of the Working Men's College, though attending rarely. At his death in 1872 he was still misunderstood, though increasingly regarded as a prophetic figure.

The second of Lord Altrincham's *Two Anglican Essays* (1958) deals with 'F. D. Maurice and Christian Socialism,' and emphasizes the conservative aspects of Maurice's views, for example his preference for a stratified rather than an egalitarian society, and the defensive character of the Christian Socialist movement itself: 'Maurice's mind prescribed Christian Socialism as the prophylactic for revolution.'[1] His economic views are dismissed out of hand: 'Technically they do not deserve to be classed as economics at all, since they in fact represent a laudable attempt on the part of a complete amateur to kill economics with kindness.'[2]

[1] Lord Altrincham, *Two Anglican Essays* (1958), 101.
[2] Ibid., 104.

This comment is just, as is also the dismissal of the idea that the Christian Socialists prevented the emergence in England of the gulf between Church and workers characteristic of some European countries: 'Nonconformity, and not the Established Church, can claim the credit.'[1] But it is misleading to deny all connexion between Maurice and the more extreme Christian Socialists of the later nineteenth century and to suggest that he would have been opposed to them. This is to ignore the different circumstances of the times. In his day Maurice was regarded as a shocking revolutionary, just as Stewart Headlam was in his, and in challenging both the theological and the social presuppositions of his generation he opened the way for more radical challenges later. At any rate all the Christian Socialists of that later time were convinced that their inspiration came from Maurice, and it can be dangerous, if tempting, to speculate what outstanding figures of one age would have said about another.

J. M. F. Ludlow (1821–1911), as well as serving the College and the co-operative movement, became, in 1875, Chief Registrar of Friendly Societies, and after retiring in 1891 lived for twenty years longer.

Charles Kingsley (1819–1875) is accused of deserting the movement, but in reality he was never wholly of it. His fame as a writer and his personality made him appear more prominent and more extreme than he really was. He hated Liberalism and the 'Manchester School,' and his 'Socialism' was really directed against them. He was more a Tory than a Radical, and attacked political economy and the individualism it encouraged, as well as the ideal of equality. His fundamental views did not change greatly, though he became somewhat disillusioned with the working classes for not living up to his ideals for them, and he became increasingly absorbed in his parish work and in the question of sanitary reform.

C. B. Mansfield (1819–1855) had no chance to do more for the workers' movement, as he was fatally injured in a fire while engaged in scientific work.

Thomas Hughes (1822–1896), apart from his services to co-operation, was actively interested in the College. It was he who moved the resolution 'that it be referred to the committee of teaching and publications to frame and, so far as they think fit, to carry out a plan for the establishment of a people's college in

[1] Altrincham, op. cit., 110.

connexion with the metropolitan associations.' Hughes did little teaching, but he was active in the social life of the College, he commanded its volunteer corps, and he was Principal from 1872 to 1883. In Parliament he furthered working-class interests, and he also carried out a somewhat Owenite experiment in founding a model community in America, in 1879, under the name of Rugby.[1] It was no more successful than the general run of such schemes. In the latter part of his life Hughes was a County Court judge at Chester.

Edward Vansittart Neale (1810–1892) was primarily interested in co-operation, and in 1851 he established the Central Co-operative Agency without authority from the rest of the group, which led to an attempt to expel him and Hughes. In 1852 he tried to reorganize the Atlas ironworks in Southwark, which he had bought, as a co-operative, but this was a total failure. Neale was reputed to have spent £40,000 on the advancement of co-operation. He was closely associated with the growth of consumers' co-operation in the north, often acting as legal adviser, and many Acts of Parliament concerning co-operation were largely his work. Among his many interests in this field was the Co-operative Wholesale Society (1863), for which he drafted the rules, and in 1875 he became the general secretary of the Central Board, receiving a salary of £250, later increased to £350. He gradually dissipated the suspicion surrounding a middle-class employee of the working classes, and visited Europe and America on co-operative work. He also took a class on political economy at the College, and at the end of his life he joined the Christian Social Union. He was the main link between the Christian Socialists and the consumers' movement, and tried, unsuccessfully, to persuade the C.W.S. to introduce profit-sharing.

F. J. Furnivall (1825–1910) was joint treasurer to the Council of Promoters, having been brought into the group by Ludlow, and his unrealized ambition was to bring together Maurice and Ruskin. He was one of the chief organizers of the College and a pillar of its social life, coming into sharp conflict with Maurice through his anti-Sabbatarianism. His religious views changed, and he became a bitter critic of religion, provoking Maurice to attempts to resign the Principalship of the College. He opposed Maurice not only on religious grounds, but because of the refusal to admit

---

[1] Thomas Hughes, *Rugby, Tennessee* . . . (1881). Part III, Chapter 4, pp. 136ff, is a report on farming prospects, less than enthusiastic, by Colonel F. W. Killibrew, Commissioner of Agriculture for Tennessee.

working men to the College Council, but he continued his support, as well as achieving fame in literary work.[1]

Daniel Macmillan (1813–1857), founder of the publishing firm and grandfather of the Prime Minister, introduced a number of important members to the group and prospered well from his Christian Socialist connexions—the reverse of Neale's experience —by publishing *Westward Ho!* and *Tom Brown's Schooldays.* In his early days in London, from 1837 to 1842, Macmillan attended King's Weigh House Congregational Church, during the ministry of Thomas Binney, and Thomas Hughes, in his memoir, prints an interesting letter to Binney explaining his reasons for transferring to the Church of England, a rambling apology beginning with the difficulty of finding a seat in the body of the church. But Hughes thinks the evasion is simply to avoid hurting Binney's feelings, and that the truth is rather that Macmillan had fallen under the influence of Maurice. Another reason given in the letter is that no one had spoken to the young Highlander in all his visits—but Hughes dismisses this on the curious grounds that it would have been much the same in the Church of England. Writing to his brother Macmillan gave his judgement on Maurice: 'He is a grand man, and must endure like other prophets. The good people of the next age will build his tomb.'[2]

Daniel Macmillan's brother Alexander (1818–1896) was the author of an unpublished Socratic-type tract defending Socialism, in or about 1849. He blamed the religious infidelity of Socialists on the unsatisfactory lives of Christians. He was associated with the Working Men's College, and also with the Working Women's College (1874), becoming treasurer of the latter for twelve years. His early political radicalism was always subject to severe limitations:

> In his early days he had strong leanings towards Socialism, but it was the Christian Socialism of Maurice which discouraged political agitation and sought to teach the working men that 'Law and Christianity are the only protectors of all classes from the selfishness, which is the destruction of all.' He strongly disapproved of attempts to stir up class prejudice . . .[3]

Not surprisingly he ended as a Liberal Unionist.

[1] See *Frederick James Furnivall: A Volume of Personal Record* (1911), containing a biography by John Munro and memoirs by many people.
[2] Thomas Hughes, *Memoir of Daniel Macmillan* (1883), 251.
[3] Charles L. Graves, *Life and Letters of Alexander Macmillan* (1910), 407.

J. Llewelyn Davies (1826–1916) was an interpreter of Maurice to the many who found him obscure. For thirty-three years from 1856 he held the living of Christ Church, Marylebone, doing much for the education of women and strongly supporting Gladstone (except on Home Rule). He gave valuable assistance in 1872 to the new agricultural trade unionism, and was responsible for a revival of the 'Broad Church' party in the Church of England.

George Frederick Samuel Robinson, first Marquess of Ripon (1827–1909) was born at 10, Downing Street, while his father, Lord Goderich, was briefly Prime Minister. By 1848 he had developed violently Radical views. He disliked the Manchester School, and 'in spite of certain tendencies of his own towards medievalism, especially in religion and art, he was equally un-attracted by the romanticist solicitude of Disraeli and the Young England party for the working man,' while the Socialists 'grated on him by their lack of an elevating, and more particularly a religious, inspiration.'[1] He was much more attracted by the teachings of Christian Socialism, becoming a lifelong friend of Hughes. But he soon began to drift away from others of the group, finding that they, and especially Kingsley, were Tories at heart, while he was 'a Revolutionary Radical as well as a Christian Socialist...'[2] In 1852 he sent £500 to the engineers on strike, joining Hughes and Ludlow in giving enthusiastic support, despite the lukewarmness of Maurice and Kingsley. He lectured at the College and wrote a plea for democracy, read and approved by Hughes, Kingsley and Ludlow, which tried to expand Christian Socialism into Christian Democracy and put forward, as divinely authorized, an extreme democratic programme. Maurice sup-pressed this tract as being too Radical and violently attacked its author. The latter became a Liberal M.P. and in time a Cabinet minister, resigning in 1873 for religious reasons, the next year becoming a Roman Catholic, presumably being the first convert to have held the position of Grand Master of the Freemasons of England. Re-entering politics, he became Governor-General of India, being accused of advancing too rapidly the position of the native population, and on his retirement in 1908 he proclaimed that he was still, as at the beginning, a Radical. It was char-acteristic that he called his son Oliver, after the Lord Protector, who was both his ancestor and his great hero. His Radicalism

[1] Lucien Wolf, *Life of the First Marquess of Ripon* (1921), I, 23.
[2] Ibid., I, 27.

survived right to the end of his long life, and in his last days had a Lloyd Georgian flavour, inclining to Socialistic measures.

Charles Kegan Paul (1828–1902) was another publisher. At his ordination he belonged to the Broad Church school, meeting the Christian Socialists through his friendship with Kingsley, though he never became a Maurician: 'I saw much of Maurice, but while loving him personally, as did all who came in contact with him, I am free to confess that I never could make head or tail of what he taught or what he meant.'[1] Meanwhile he became a High Churchman, a Ritualist, and a Radical. He adopted Republican and Socialist views, and showed a political fixity which contrasted with the fluidity of his religious convictions: 'In politics, at least, my creed has never changed since I became able to formulate it, while it has, on the religious side, passed through Positivism and landed me in the one true home of Faith, the Roman church.'[2] In 1870 he joined a Unitarian society, without leaving the Church of England, and in 1872 he was prominent in support of Joseph Arch. While teaching at Eton he fell foul of the school authorities and the Bishop (Wilberforce) on account of a Christian Socialist tract of theologically heterodox tendency which he wrote. In 1874 he resigned his living and became a publisher, and in 1890 he completed a strange spiritual pilgrimage by joining the Roman Catholic Church.

Something of the change wrought by the Christian Socialist movement is shown in a review of a volume of Kingsley's letters edited by his widow, when the *Guardian* said that the term 'Christian Socialism' belonged to a time when 'unchecked individualism —the gospel of mere Free Trade, with its sacred laws of supply and demand'—had failed; and that Chartism and the 1848 revolutions had taught England a lesson 'which has never been forgotten.'[3] This comment may be regarded as a summing-up of the Christian Socialist movement. It had not succeeded in transforming the industrial system, nor even in penetrating very deeply the trade union movement or the political organs of the working classes; but it had begun a trend in the Church of England which never afterwards completely ceased. All later Anglican social thought was strongly affected by Maurice and his followers until

---

[1] C. Kegan Paul, *Memories* (1899), 165.
[2] Ibid., 166.
[3] *Guardian*, January 10th, 1877.

well into the next century. They were also one of the factors operating to weaken the influence over men's minds of *laissez-faire*, joining with the more humanitarian economics of the later Victorian period to eliminate the idea that the existing condition of society was prescribed by external laws and for ever unalterable by man. In this latter capacity the influence of the group was wider, though more difficult to trace, than in the former.

5 Academic and Ecclesiastical Leaders influenced by Maurice

By 1867 the original Christian Socialist movement was largely a spent force. A new age was beginning, with the enfranchisement of the working classes, and the men who had given a lead in 1848 were being replaced by others. Maurice was nearing the end of his life, still a controversial figure; Kingsley had ceased to count for much; Ludlow, Neale and Hughes were active in specialized directions. To a certain extent intellectual leadership had passed to Llewelyn Davies, and through him, despite the fact that he was sharply at variance with some of the theological tendencies of the age, the tradition of Maurice was handed on to a new generation. Prominent among the younger men were the famous trio of Cambridge scholars, Lightfoot, Westcott, and Hort. Their reputation rests primarily upon their great achievements as Biblical scholars, in respect of which it is perhaps not too much to say that they provided the answer of orthodox Christianity—albeit theirs was a liberal orthodoxy—to the rationalistic scholarship of the German Higher Critics. Lightfoot and Westcott both turned from academic work to become successive Bishops of Durham, Lightfoot serving from 1879 to 1889, being followed in 1890 by Westcott.

J. B. Lightfoot (1828–1889) is the least important of the three from the present point of view, though he established a tradition in which he was followed by Westcott of concerning himself with the social problems of his diocese and of the nation, and like Fraser he was popular with the workers, though temperamentally he was less a man of the people.

B. F. Westcott (1825–1901), though older, belongs as Bishop of Durham to a later generation. But he was already an elderly and famous man when he went there. Despite his dedication to scholarship he had taken a wide interest in social questions, influenced by his friendship with Llewelyn Davies. To some of his contemporaries he appeared almost another Maurice, though more successful in winning general and official support for his teachings. But Westcott had arrived at his convictions by his own efforts, and in order to safeguard his independence of thought he deliberately refrained from reading the works of Maurice until he had decided the relevant questions for himself. After reading Maurice's *Life and Letters* he wrote to Davies expressing his surprise at the closeness of his own judgements to Maurice's. It is interesting that Westcott was also a friend of Alfred Marshall.

F. J. A. Hort (1828–1892) did not become a bishop, and he lacked the popular reputation of Lightfoot and Westcott, though in scholarship he was in no way inferior. He came of an Evangelical family, but his outlook was remodelled by his education at Rugby, where his thinking took on the imprint of Thomas Arnold. This prepared him for Cambridge in the early 'fifties, where he made friends with Maurice, and through him met the rest of the group of Christian Socialists. He seemed to find in Maurice something lacking both from the old Evangelicalism and also from the more recently fashionable Oxford Movement. But he saw moral problems which the Christian Socialists too easily passed over, and he describes a conversation with Ludlow, in which he asked how, if competition was the enemy to be driven out, competition between the associations—which might be worse than that between individuals—was to be averted. Ludlow had no satisfactory answer.[1]

Westcott and Hort represented a reaction against Evangelical individualism, and indeed Westcott was influenced by the Tractarians. He belonged to the early stages of a new movement in Anglican theology, which a few years earlier would have seemed a monstrous absurdity: the synthesis of Tractarianism and Broad Church doctrines. Maurice himself laid the foundations of such a fusion, despite the bitter antipathy between him and the Anglo-Catholic party. Llewelyn Davies continued in the Maurician Broad Church tradition and was a forerunner of twentieth-century Liberal Modernism; but Westcott was in some ways a High Churchman, and in the seemingly impossible conjunction of apparently opposite attitudes he foreshadowed the powerful Liberal Catholic movement which can be fairly precisely dated from the book *Lux Mundi* of 1889. There was one feature which Llewelyn Davies's Liberalism and the doctrines of Anglo-Catho-

[1] Arthur Fenton Hort, *Life and Letters of Fenton John Anthony Hort* (1896), I, 162.

lics had in common—both alike emphasized the social aspects of Christianity against Evangelical atomism, and it was this tendency towards a 'social Christianity' which was beginning to bring Mauricians and Ritualists together. Landmarks in the process were Westcott's *Essay on Comtism* of 1864, Hort's Hulsean Lectures of 1871 on 'The Way, the Truth, and the Life', and Llewelyn Davies's emphasis on the social significance of the Sacraments.

6 Stewart Headlam and the Revival of Christian Socialism

Another Maurician was William Johnson, better known as W. J. Cory, and famous as the author of one short poem, *Heraclitus*. Johnson was a Christian Socialist in the unpromising situation of a master at Eton, and among his pupils there were two key figures of the next generation, Stewart Headlam and Scott Holland. Headlam represents a new beginning in Christian Socialism. So far exponents of a social version of Christianity had started from Maurice, though many were also influenced by Anglo-Catholicism. Headlam was a thoroughgoing Anglo-Catholic associated with the slum Ritualists, though he too built on the foundations laid by Maurice. He was born in 1847 and educated at Eton, where, according to his biographer, his latent interest in politics was awakened by Johnson. From there he went to Cambridge, which 'as he recalled it, meant Maurice and little more'.[1] Amongst other effects his discipleship to Maurice liberated him from a dread of the popular idea of Hell. As curate at Drury Lane he was influenced by 'a real saint,' the Rev Thomas Wodehouse, Chaplain at the Savoy, who was the author of a work called *The Grammar of Socialism*, and the provider of dinners for poor children. From 1873 to 1878 Headlam was curate at Bethnal Green, where his rector was the Christian Socialist Septimus Hansard, who was described as 'at once a Radical and an autocrat,' a not wholly unfamiliar combination.[2] He was on friendly terms with trade union leaders, and he gave full support to his curate in a campaign to have museums and art galleries opened on Sundays. Headlam went to live in the workers' tenements, took part in the effort to form women's trade unions, again with the support of Hansard, and joined the Commonwealth Club, the local Radical club, where Arthur Stanton lectured on 'Liberty, Equality, and Fraternity.' But in 1878 Hansard's patience was suddenly

[1] F. G. Bettany, *Stewart Headlam* (1926), 19.
[2] Ibid., 35.

exhausted by an article Headlam wrote in defence of music-halls, and he dismissed him from the curacy, though they remained on friendly terms. Thereafter Headlam's life was uncertain and his income insecure. In 1882 he lost the chance of a curacy by speaking (along with Michael Davitt) at a meeting in Hyde Park in favour of the abolition of the House of Lords.

The Guild of St Matthew, which made Headlam famous, arose out of his Anglo-Catholicism rather than his Socialism. For many years guilds had been founded in parishes for various religious objects, and in the Anglo-Catholic parishes they had become commonplace as a means of advancing the purposes of the movement. As curate at St Matthew's, Bethnal Green, it was quite natural that Headlam should form a guild with similar objects, called by the name of the patron saint. The guild was formed on St Peter's Day, 1877, with Headlam bearing the usual title of 'Warden.' Its objects were an interesting compound of Maurice and the Oxford Movement:

(1) To get rid, by every possible means, of the existing prejudices, especially on the part of Secularists, against the Church, her sacraments and doctrines, and to endeavour to 'justify God to the people.'

(2) To promote frequent and reverent worship in the Holy Communion and a better observance of the teaching of the Church of England, as set forth in the Book of Common Prayer.

(3) To promote the study of social and political questions in the light of the Incarnation.[1]

The immediate occasion of the formation of the Guild was nothing more than the introduction of an early morning celebration of Holy Communion, a regular aim of Anglo-Catholics, and the desire to guarantee a supply of communicants. The following year Headlam's curacy was terminated, and he took the opportunity to make the Guild a nation-wide, if small, organization. The original forty members increased in thirteen years to 200, including seventy in Orders; thereafter the figures were: 1893, 285 (77 in Orders); 1894, 333 (93 ordained); 1895, 364 (99 ordained). Then came decline. By 1906 the membership was about 200. Most of the leading figures in the Christian Socialist movement belonged to the Guild, among them H. C. Shuttleworth, T. Hancock, C. W. Stubbs (later Bishop of Truro), Conrad Noel, Percy Dearmer, and J. G. Adderley.

[1] Binyon, op. cit., 119f.

The Guild is sometimes claimed to have been a thoroughly Socialist organization. If this were true it would deserve a very important place in the history of British Socialism, since it antedated by three years the foundation of the Democratic Federation (later Social Democratic Federation) in 1880, which marked the beginning of the revival of organized Socialism in Britain. But it is not true. Apart from the Tractarians and Maurice there was a third influence on Headlam, and this was Henry George. George was one of the many social reformers who learned to speak in the accents of the Bible and Evangelical religion: 'In support of his claims, George used to quote extensively from the Old Testament. He . . . linked social problems to religion and used the Bible as a textbook.'[1] The teaching of George had for a time a great vogue in England, and Headlam was thoroughly converted. According to his biographer: 'If Maurice was the first big inspiring influence of his life, Henry George was certainly the second.'[2] Headlam's Socialism was therefore very much concerned with the question of land values. Although later a member of the Fabian Society he remained all his life more of a Georgite than a Socialist. As in all other matters he knew nothing of moderation: '. . . By easy transitions, he connected prostitution and drunkenness with the absence of a tax on land values.'[3]

Headlam's career was a continual revolt against contemporary conventions. In 1879 he founded another guild, the 'Church and Stage' Guild, whose very name was a conjunction of incompatibles in the eyes of many Church people. Indeed Headlam's friendship with theatrical personalities, especially with female ballet-dancers, gave even more offence than his alleged Socialism. In the Church and Stage Guild the names were much the same as in the Guild of St Matthew—Arthur Stanton, whom Headlam himself described as a 'bulwark' of the second guild, J. E. Symes, and H. C. Shuttleworth. The following year Headlam was in the news again, on the occasion of the Church Congress at Leicester, when, with his closest associates, Symes and G. Sarson, he prepared unofficial papers, largely on social questions, with a protest at the failure to invite a trade union leader to speak, and handed them out to delegates. On Maundy Thursday 1881 he preached a sermon in Westminster Abbey on 'The Service of Humanity,' in which he

[1] K. Hutchinson, *The Decline and Fall of British Capitalism* (1951), 33.
[2] Bettany, op. cit., 84.
[3] Wagner, op. cit., 193.

proclaimed that the work of Jesus Christ and his Church was 'secular' work. The Church overlooked

> the Christian communism of the Church of the Carpenter . . .
> They think it more religious to have mystic sweet communion with
> those whose work is done, than to have real genuine fellowship
> though equally mystic and sweet with those whose work is still going
> on.[1]

In another address he said that the Church was 'distinctly and essentially democratic,' and Jesus Christ 'a carpenter, who became a radical reformer both in social and religious matters.' The Church was opposed to aristocracy of any kind, and to 'plutocracy —that curse which has led so many descendants of the grand old outcast Nonconformists to become rich, respectable persecutors of poor Jesuits, Secularists, Socialists, and Ritualists . . .'[2] One notes the surprising collection of dissident groups here referred to—an indication that the true identification of Headlam is with the well-established tradition of English Radicalism, not to say eccentricity.

Besides the Guild of St Matthew there was another Christian Socialist group, associated with the Land Reform Union, which had been influenced by Headlam as well as by George, and had become the English Land Restoration League. The leaders of this group, H. H. Champion and J. L. Joynes, in 1883 started the *Christian Socialist*. James Leigh Joynes was like Johnson a master at Eton, resigning his post there to lead this work. His father, also J. L. Joynes, had been Headlam's housemaster at Eton. The second Joynes was the author of *The Socialist Catechism* (1884) and *Socialist Rhymes* (1885). Headlam gave his support to this venture, and through the group came into contact with Olivier and the founders of the Fabian Society. Champion himself was associated with Davidson, the founder of the Fellowship of the New Life, from which the Fabian Society was an offshoot, and Shaw had taken part in meetings of the Guild of St Matthew. It was therefore not altogether surprising that Headlam was an early member of the Fabian Society, joining it in December 1886. He was a member of the Executive in 1890–1891, 1901–1902, and 1910–1911, and he was also a member of the committee of fifteen which drew up the basis of the society in 1887 and, according to Sidney Webb he was responsible for some of the most extreme items.

[1] Binyon, op. cit., 120.
[2] Ibid., 120f.

He was a member of the society for 38 years and often presided over its meetings. He accepted collectivist views, especially with regard to municipal enterprises, but according to Shaw he had little influence on the society: 'Politically he was a Liberal plus a Land Nationalizer.'[1] In a lecture he gave in 1908 he insisted that land nationalization was the very essence of Socialism, and satirized Socialists for other interests. He worked in friendly co-operation with another member inclined to chronic dissidence, H. G. Wells. Along with other Fabians he took a strong interest in the education question, and in 1888 he was elected to the London School Board as an Independent Progressive. On the Board he joined with Annie Besant in insisting on the payment of trade union rates to employees. But although he was for so long a faithful if argumentative member of the Fabian Society, Headlam was never altogether enthusiastic about it. He and its effective leaders seemed to have little in common. He joined it 'in default of anything better of its kind,'[2] but he was

> never at home in it. Both Mr Webb and Mr Shaw understood that the Fabian atmosphere was uncongenial to him, and that he was one of those whose sympathies are starved on that plane. Fabianism was distasteful to him. But if he was to join any Socialist Society it had to be the Fabian Society, for the Socialist League and the Social Democratic Federation did not admit, or did not welcome, professing Christians into their ranks. Yet either of these societies might perhaps in some ways have suited Headlam better.[3]

He found in the Fabian Society a rather arid intellectualism, and, much worse in Headlam's eyes, a sort of 'ascetic Puritanism.' 'Socialism' turned out to mean very different things to different people: 'Socialism meant for him the men with grimed clothes and horny hands he met in Bethnal Green over against "carriage folk" whose luxury made so striking a contrast to their lack of the social amenities.'[4] He was more interested in principles than in detailed programmes, and he lacked a Fabian conception of scientific—or pseudo-scientific—history. He used past teachings as propaganda, but either thought that past conditions could be revived or subjected them to drastic reinterpretation. Despite Shaw's description of him as a Liberal, he was not, like the Fabian leaders themselves,

[1] Bettany, op. cit., 139.
[2] Ibid., 133.
[3] Binyon, op. cit., 147.
[4] Bettany, op. cit., 134.

a Progressivist, and his nature did not accord well with 'gradual-ism.'

A much more congenial spirit than the Fabians was a fellow-clergyman, Thomas Hancock, with Headlam's own gift for indis-cretion. In 1884, at a time of a sudden revival of interest in Socialism, Hancock preached a sermon entitled 'The Social Democratic Pentecost,' in which he claimed that however material-istic it might appear Socialism was 'born of the Spirit.' Headlam and Hancock were associated with Champion's group in the troubled times of the middle 'eighties. On the occasion of the West End disturbances of February 1886 the *Christian Socialist* rejoiced at this demonstration of the urgency of the situation and condemned a sermon of the Bishop of London advocating as a remedy for the troubles 'morally elevating the masses.' Hancock described the events as a judgement of God, while in similar vein Headlam claimed that God was speaking through Champion and John Burns. Hancock also preached a sermon on a favourite Biblical passage of Christian Socialists, the *Magnificat*, which he described as the 'Hymn of the Universal Social Revolution.' One method of protest used by the unemployed was to march to promi-nent churches, a method which Headlam defended. This provided the occasion for the most famous of Radical sermons since the days of John Ball, that which Hancock preached under the title of 'The Banner of Christ in the Hands of the Socialists,' starting from the observation that the parades of unemployed inscribed on their banners quotations not from Babeuf or Proudhon, Lassalle or Marx, but from Christ. Champion even went so far as to consider armed rebellion, rejecting it as a hopeless venture. After 'Bloody Sunday' (November 13th, 1887) Linnell, the workman who had been killed in the disturbance, was buried by Headlam. The Golden Jubilee of 1887 was another occasion stirring the Christian Socialists to protest, Headlam claiming that the prayer issued for the celebrations, taking satisfaction in the state of the country, was blasphemous. Champion, speaking at the Church Congress,

observed that England had spent £17,000 in fitting up Westminster Abbey in order to return thanks to the God who dwells in temples not made with hands that one woman had been allowed to live fifty years. This was greeted with hisses and cries of 'Shame' and 'Withdraw'. Champion suggested that the money might have been better spent in the cause of the unemployed.[1]

[1] Binyon, op. cit., 137.

Despite the cries of protest the Congress was not unmoved by his case, and his speech received 'general approval on the whole'; none of the speakers made any serious effort to rebut his arguments or to deny that the Church was bound, in some degree at any rate, to be Socialistic. At the same congress Bishop Alexander of Derry contributed a paper arguing that the aspirations of Socialism were Christian and urging the need for a Christian sociology.

The Guild of St Matthew remained in existence for many years. Headlam's policy for it was embodied in the demand for measures:

(a) To restore to the people the value which they give to the land;
(b) To bring about a better distribution of the wealth created by labour;
(c) To give to the whole body of the people a voice in their own government;
(d) To abolish false standards of worth and dignity.[1]

He defended the Guild against those who criticized it for going so far beyond the position of F. D. Maurice, arguing that this policy was the result of applying in different circumstances the same principles. In practical terms he demanded land nationalization, a progressive income tax, universal suffrage, and the abolition of the House of Lords.

In 1884 the Guild held a rally in Trafalgar Square, calling upon Church people to give their support to this policy. For eleven years the Guild ran a newspaper, the *Church Reformer* (1884–1895), which was not particularly successful, and cost Headlam no less than £1,200. Much of it he wrote himself, while Verinder, the secretary of the Guild, contributed reports, and also served as sub-editor, championing the views of Henry George. The failure of the journal was attributed to the fact that those who liked its Socialism disliked its Anglo-Catholicism, and vice versa, so that only the supporters of the Guild itself were likely to welcome both. In other ways the name of Stewart Headlam remained before the public. The Church and Stage Guild, though criticized, attracted the interest of some prominent men; Ruskin gave his support, and Shaw attended and lectured, though Bishop Fraser was among the critics. Shuttleworth, Headlam's close associate in both guilds, was as controversial a figure as himself, and is described as a

[1] Binyon, op. cit., 143.

'red-hot "ritualist." '[1] In 1890 Dolling of Landport got into
trouble over indiscreet expressions used by Headlam while lecturing at Dolling's Church on land nationalization. But the Guild
of St Matthew and its warden throve on public hostility. More
serious was the growth of rival societies. The *Christian Socialist*
group has been mentioned, and in 1886 the 'Christian Socialist
Society' was founded, taking over the *Christian Socialist* as its
official organ, edited by W. H. P. Campbell and Alfred Howard.
It differed from the Guild of St Matthew in having no theological
standpoint, and its Socialism too was very vague. Howard argued
that current Christianity was a perversion of the teaching of Christ
and that no theology was needed. The Society was thus an expression of the rising theological liberalism, as the Guild was a social
expression of the Anglo-Catholic movement. But the Society was
short-lived and of little influence. The most effective rival was the
Christian Social Union, founded in 1889, and there was from the
start a good deal of hostility between the two bodies. Scott Holland
of the C.S.U. characteristically referred to Headlam and Shuttleworth as 'Headlong' and 'Shuttlecock.' In 1909 Headlam formally
dissolved the Guild, though it had been of little influence for a long
time previously. Many of the Guild members joined the Church
Socialist League, but Headlam was unenthusiastic about a body
which lacked the Guild's precise theological position. During the
lifetime of the Guild two of Headlam's closest associates were
George Sarson and Thomas Hancock. Sarson, who died in 1902,
worked from 1871 to 1878 in the London slums. In 1877 he and
Hancock wrote for the Church Congress 'The Church's Mission
to the Upper Classes'—'a noteworthy reversal of conventional
ideas.' Sarson also wrote 'a Maurician commentary on, or companion to, the Anglican Liturgy, entitled "The Holy Communion
and Common Life" . . .'[2] Hancock was ordained in 1861 and died
in 1903, and was personally acquainted with Maurice. In 1875 he
published a volume of sermons entitled *Christ and the People*.
He was 'the theologian of the Christian Socialist Movement,' but
he was not appreciated and found it difficult to secure a living until
through the influence of Shuttleworth he became lecturer at St
Nicholas, Cole Abbey.

There were other, more isolated, protagonists of Christian
Socialist views at this time. The Rev R. W. Corbet, who was of a

[1] Binyon, op. cit., 150.
[2] Ibid., 113.

mystical turn of mind, founded in 1869 the Society of the Holy
Spirit to study the questions of the day. Similarly the Rev J. W.
Farquhar (died 1898) wrote *The Gospel of the Divine Humanity* in
1884, and similar views were expressed by John Pulsford. Some of
the most outspoken Secularists started from a Christian standpoint
and despite themselves retained traces of Christian Socialist views
later. Such were G. J. Holyoake, George Odger, of whom very
typically Headlam said that the Church should be grateful to him
for making the phrase 'dearly beloved brethren' a reality, Edward
Carpenter, once Maurice's curate, who leant towards Eastern
philosophy, and even H. M. Hyndman, who was 'brought up in
the strictest Simeonite Evangelical tradition, and, reacting against
it, had become a Secularist.'[1] Hyndman's highly formal dress,
including a silk hat, when addressing street-corner crowds, might
be thought to betray this kind of background. Arnold Toynbee
made a reverse pilgrimage, from Secularism to the Church of
England, and advocated 'a form of Christianity in harmony with
progress, liberty, and knowledge.'[2] The Rev William Tuckwell
wrote *Reminiscences of a Radical Parson*, and upheld hopes of a
classless Utopia.

In this period the Christian Socialist movement revived vigorously after its period of eclipse. There were many differences from
the original Christian Socialist group. There was no longer the
same intellectual eminence, though Westcott, Lightfoot and Hort
were at least 'fellow-travellers' of the Christian Socialists and from
this point of view were inferior to no one in the Church of England.
The movement was more emotional and denunciatory, centred less
in scholarly circles and more in slum parishes, and above all, and
ironically enough, the leadership had passed to the successors of
the Tractarians, who had been the bitterest opponents of the
original Christian Socialists. The influence of Headlam was small
compared with that of Maurice, a man who won much more
respect from his opponents, but he kept the issues before the public and stimulated others to think about them. He helped to establish the High Church party in the minds of a section of the public
as the party of the poor and outcast elements in society. But as
with the slum Ritualists one must conclude that his participation
in the working-class movement was rendered less effective because
of the paternalism, not to say the autocracy, of his manner, and

[1] Binyon, op. cit., 112.
[2] Ibid., 118f.

because of the hostility he aroused on ecclesiastical grounds in the minds of some who might on political and social issues have been more friendly to him. The effective leadership of the workers, even so far as it was Christian, continued to be unattracted by Anglo-Catholicism.

7 Scott Holland and the Christian Social Union

One of the most important events in the religious history of England in the closing decade of the nineteenth century was the conversion of a large proportion of the clergy of the Church of England, if not to Christian Socialism, at least to a lively concern with social matters. It became a marked feature of the time that Anglican clerics, for example in the Convocations of Canterbury and York, were more socially aware than the laity.

The year 1889, the year of the London dock strike and of *Fabian Essays*, was also, not less significantly, the year of the founding of the Christian Social Union, and of the publication of *Lux Mundi*. This volume, the work of a group of Anglican scholars, marked an epoch in the history of the Church of England,[1] revealing, to the dismay of many, that progressive Anglican thought, quite apart from the rebellious elements who years if not decades before had already been given up as inveterate heretics, was ready to accept wholeheartedly the findings of Biblical scholarship. But throughout the book it was the implications and assumptions as much as the overt arguments which occasioned alarm in some quarters—and gave delight in others. Not the least important was the recognition that Christianity implied some social consequences.

The social concern expressed in *Lux Mundi* was not great, but several of the contributors, especially Gore, the editor, were influenced by the Christian Socialists and themselves interested in social reform. There was little inclination towards Socialism, but it was recognized that there was no absolute right of property. Some new ground was broken by the type of subject covered, in that whereas previous volumes of essays, such as *Essays and Reviews*, which, nearly a generation earlier, had provoked great controversy, were concerned with theological or liturgical matters, *Lux Mundi* contained an essay on 'Christianity and Politics' by W. J. H. Campion, in which discussion of the relationship of the

[1] Note, for example, the dating of Carpenter's work—*Church and People, 1789–1889.*

Church and state was revived after having lapsed for many years. Amongst other things Campion emphasized the Church's care for the poor before the Reformation. In another essay, on Christian ethics, R. L. Ottley stressed the place of personality in the sphere of economics, and wanted to see abstract terms, such as Capital and Labour, replaced by personal.[1]

The expression of a Christian interest in political and social affairs by the *Lux Mundi* group was closely bound up with the foundation of the Christian Social Union later the same year, and behind both lay the pronouncement by the Lambeth Conference on Socialism in 1888, which encouraged discussion of the attitude which the Church ought to take to such a movement. The C.S.U. was founded by the same group of people which had taken the lead in producing *Lux Mundi*, prominent among them Gore and Scott Holland, and its objects were clearly stated as follows:

(1) To claim for the Christian Law the ultimate authority to rule social practice.

(2) To study in common how to apply the moral truths and principles of Christianity to the social and economic difficulties of the present time.

(3) To present Christ in practical life as the living Master and King, the enemy of wrong and selfishness, the power of righteousness and love.[2]

For the C.S.U. the word 'Socialism' meant not a political or economic system, but the ideal of brotherhood.

At this date the Guild of St Matthew was still very active, and the C.S.U. came into being in some measure of conscious rivalry with Headlam's group. It was designed to give more attention to research into social problems and less to agitation, and also to create a group which could be 'Christian Socialist' in a broad way without having to live with Stewart Headlam himself. It aimed, successfully, to attract some who might have joined the Guild of St Matthew 'had it not been for its ecclesiastical and other peculiarities.'[3] It lacked the Anglo-Catholic bias, and whereas the Guild was very much Headlam's own personal group, the C.S.U. made a wider appeal and won the support of distinguished Church leaders such as Westcott, who was the first President. He was an outstanding figure of the age:

[1] Some relevant passages from *Lux Mundi* are quoted, Appendix I.
[2] Binyon, op. cit., 158.
[3] Ibid., 160.

His position as Christian Socialist is not to be estimated by his action as mediator in the coal-strike of 1892, nor even by his occasional utterances about methods of social organization. Like Maurice he was a prophet, a seer, a theologian—and we do not always see him at his best when dealing with the practical application of his ideals. His greatness is to be found in the largeness of his spiritual vision.[1]

He was in fact regarded as the legitimate successor of Maurice: 'The succession, Coleridge-Maurice-Westcott, represents the true line of Christian Social Theology.'[2] He addressed the Church Congress on Socialism in 1890, treating it as the antithesis of individualism. Such a man as Westcott could never have belonged to the Guild of St Matthew; but there was, nevertheless, some overlap of membership, Percy Dearmer, for example, being a prominent member of both groups. The C.S.U. was milder than the Guild, being content to assert general principles and leave their application to the conscience of individuals. It did not produce plans for reform, but imagined that all social problems would be well on the way to solution if all persons became Christians. It objected to some features of Socialism—to what it considered 'levelling-down,' and to the emphasis on the state. It was consciously modest in its aims: its object was to investigate social problems in the light of Christian morality, while leaving the remedies to others, including its own members in their private capacity. It indulged in a good deal of publication, including the *Economic Review* (1891–1914), and it was a much larger body than the Guild. In 1897 there were 27 branches with 2,600 members, a large proportion of them clergy. Of the London group 42% were clergy, 32% women, and 26% laymen; of the Oxford group the percentages were clergy 50, women 23, laymen 27. There was an American organization founded in 1892 which rose to 1,000 members, and in 1897 there were branches in Australia and South Africa.

To the public the C.S.U. meant Scott Holland, who stood on the Left of this very moderate movement: 'As a Socialist he was far more "advanced" and definite than Westcott . . . His Socialism has been called Christian Fabianism . . .'[3] Westcott was followed as President by Gore, from 1902 to 1911. He was 'far more ecclesiastical than his predecessor,' and perhaps the dominant leader of the High Church party in the Church of England in the

[1] Binyon, op. cit., 160   [2] Ibid., 162.   [3] Ibid., 164.

early decades of the twentieth century. Gore was followed by Dr Kempthorne, from 1911 to 1920. He was at the time Bishop of Hull, and later Bishop of Lichfield. The C.S.U. represented all parties in the Church of England, and study remained the main activity, poor working conditions being attacked by means of 'white lists,' that is, lists of workshops where the employees were fairly treated. In 1904 Lewis Donaldson, the Vicar of St Mark's, Leicester, led a march of unemployed from Leicester to London. The influence of the C.S.U. was shown 'by the advance in the declarations on social matters made by the assembled Bishops in successive Lambeth Conferences.'[1] The first and second conferences, in 1867 and 1878, made no mention of social matters, but in 1888 the Encyclical thought that the clergy ought to show 'how much of what is good and true in Socialism is to be found in the precepts of Christ.' In 1897 the Conference emphasized the four principles of Brotherhood, Labour, Justice, and Public Responsibility. In an official statement by a committee of the Convocation of Canterbury in 1907 on 'The Moral Witness of the Church on Economic Subjects' it was admitted that the Church had 'allowed itself to be silenced by the terrors of supposed inexorable laws.' The principle that 'the first charge upon any industry must be the proper maintenance of the labourer' was recognized, and the demand for a change in society was based on a plea for justice. The high-water mark of C.S.U. influence came with the Pan-Anglican and Lambeth Conferences of 1908, when Ludlow, now in his eighties, spoke, and asserted that everybody present was a Christian Socialist. This was not exactly true, but it was true that the influence of Christian Socialism had spread very widely, though the real progress was much less than the original Christian Socialists would have wished. For by now, after two decades of Fabian penetration of the Church at large, 'the stream of Christian Socialism, deep and strong when the Christian Social Union was founded in 1889, had . . . come to have far more width than depth.'[2] Many had joined the C.S.U. as an interesting society, without having any very strong convictions, so that it became increasingly remote from the main stream of the Labour movement: 'The Christian Social Union exerted a great permeating influence on the Church; it reached the Bishops, but it never reached the working men.' Perhaps it was something to have

[1] Binyon, op. cit., 176.
[2] Ibid., 177.

reached the Bishops, but it was not enough, and the more progressive clergy lost patience with it.[1]

Taken together the Guild and the Union did a number of useful jobs at this time. They diffused Christian Socialist ideas through tracts, journals, the C.S.U. Lenten lectures, and even through works of fiction, especially Adderley's influential novel *Stephen Remarx* (1893). They explored the social teaching of the Bible and of the Church. This was an aspect of the matter neglected by the Union, but not by the Guild, for whom the lead was taken by C. L. Marson, an Evangelical turned Anglo-Catholic, given to satire, especially caustic in the case of the clergy. A landmark was A. J. Carlyle's *History of Political Thought in the Middle Ages*, of which the first volume appeared in 1903, and there were also some Biblical commentaries. These societies also began a social interpretation of the Creeds and Sacraments, Adderley, Dearmer, and Gore being prominent in this work. Collectively the Guild again did more than the Union, perhaps helped by having a less comprehensive membership, for it did not have the almost semi-official status of the C.S.U. and was freer to make imaginative explorations.

At the centre of all these activities was Henry Scott Holland (1847–1918). At Eton his tutor was Johnson Cory, the Christian Socialist, but Holland called him a 'Whig' and said that he was hostile to 'popular forces.'[2] Holland quickly associated himself with Radicalism, and in a letter of 1878 revealed that he was thinking of attacking the Society for the Propagation of Christian Knowledge for 'its one-sided Political Economy publications— condemning so strongly all Trade Unions and giving nothing but the masters' view.'[3] On Whit Sunday 1882 he preached at St Paul's to the Co-operative Congress, and in his sermon emphasized the claims of the community as against individualism, sending a copy of the sermon to Ruskin, who wrote approving it. In 1888 he wrote: 'We live in economic blindness down here, of the blackest kind. The world seems to have reacted into the mind of forty years ago. You would think it had never talked democratic language.'[4] He was already associated with Oxford House and with the Christ Church mission in Poplar, 'and he was already studying the bearing

[1] Binyon, op. cit., 178f.

[2] Stephen Paget (ed.), *Henry Scott Holland: Memoir and Letters* (1921), 10 (note).

[3] Ibid., 97.   [4] Ibid., 169.

of Christian principles upon economic questions . . .'[1] When the C.S.U. was formed and Westcott became President, Holland became the first Chairman of the committee, the secretaries being G. C. Fletcher and Cyril Bickersteth, who were followed by John Carter. It was Bickersteth who went to Dolgelley during the 1889 dock strike, to persuade Bishop Temple to return to London. The C.S.U. began with the statement of objects quoted above, adding the comment: 'Members are expected to pray for the well-being of the Union at Holy Communion, more particularly on or about the following days—the Feast of the Epiphany, the Feast of the Ascension, the Feast of St Michael and all Angels.' Holland wrote a pamphlet explaining the various points. In 1894 Holland and Adderley started *Goodwill* to propagate their views, and from 1895 to 1912 Holland edited the *Commonwealth*, 'a paper devoted to the study of the various elements in social life in the light of Christianity . . .'[2] It was intended to have a wider appeal than *Goodwill*. In 1898 Holland played a prominent part in the founding of the Maurice Hostel in Hoxton as a C.S.U. settlement, and when Donaldson led his march of the unemployed to London Holland wrote expressing his sympathy and sending £10. Like other 'Christian Socialists' of the period Holland was a Radical rather than a Socialist in any strict sense. He was alarmed at the Tory victory in the 1895 election, and complained that the I.L.P.

> have wiped out both themselves and all the Labour Party: they have ceased to exist. They have handed England over to the strongest Government of property and capital and individualism which has been seen for a century. They have annihilated all the sympathetic Radicalism that could mitigate the roaring individualism of property . . . Labour, now, is without a vote in the House that is worth a Whip's counting. Its voice will be outside: and that spells violence.[3]

A little later he asserted that the Liberal Party must concentrate on social policy or it would die: 'Yet it is with Labour that official Liberalism appears to us to be most out of touch; the very growth of the I.L.P. is a symptom of it. The rich Liberal capitalist is not necessarily more in sympathy with the workers than the rich Tory capitalist.'[4] In 1907 he was furious at the victory of the Moderates in the L.C.C. elections, accusing them of unfairness and dishonesty.

[1] *Dict. Nat. Biog.* (1912–1921), s.v. Holland.
[2] Ibid. [3] Paget, op. cit., 205. [4] Ibid., 212.

In the biography of Holland by Stephen Paget there is a chapter contributed by Gore under the title of 'Holland and the Christian Social Union,' which has interesting comments both on Holland and on the Union itself. Gore refers to the influences behind the C.S.U., among them a new view of Church history, the change in economic theory away from Ricardo, the influence of the Christian Socialists, the effect of Seeley's *Ecce Homo*, and the settlement movement. Holland, like Maurice or Westcott, was primarily a theologian, and he was always orthodox in his theology. He was a brilliant orator and wit, and replied to references to 'grandmotherly legislation' with the politically effective phrase: 'Every man his own grandmother.' Asking the question, 'Was the C.S.U. a success?' Gore replies:

> In one sense I should claim that it was. Its output in the way of writings of various kinds, and its preaching and speaking—especially through the weight of Westcott's and Holland's names—did contribute very largely to the change in the whole attitude of society and the Church towards the social question. In particular, within the Church, I think the quite new tone in its more or less official utterances—in the 'Reports' of its Lambeth Conference Committees, in its Convocation and Church Congress debates, in the Report of the Archbishops' Committees on industrial questions—has been very largely due to the efforts of the C.S.U. That is perhaps the main thing. But two things it has not done. It has not succeeded in stirring up what it believes to be the right spirit in the mass of those who preach in the pulpits or sit in the pews of the Anglican churches. Whatever may be said of the central or official church, the Church as represented locally, whether in town or country, whether clerical or lay, remains, I fear, a body which as a whole the social reformer or the Labour man regards as something which is alien to his ends and aims, and which he finds irresponsive and dull. Also the C.S.U. entirely failed to raise up in the ranks of the church a sufficient body of Trade Unionists who were also Churchmen to make any effective impression on the Labour movement as a whole.[1]

Apart from Holland and Gore himself (who will be noticed later), the outstanding name among the founders of the C.S.U. was that of Hastings Rashdall (1858–1924), one of the dominant intellectual leaders of the religious life of his time, a philosopher, a theologian, and an historian. He was a member of the C.S.U. from the start, and from 1892 to 1910 one of the editors of the *Economic Review*,

[1] Paget., op. cit., 249f. The erratic capitalization of 'Church' is as in the original.

the organ of the Oxford branch. He had strong political convictions, which, in contrast to Holland's, were on the side of Liberal Unionism.

As before there were several minor Christian Socialist bodies at this period. A 'Free Church Socialist League' 'intermittently existed,' and John Clifford was 'president at one time of a League which continued or revived the Christian Socialist Society.' This League made a declaration of principle in the following terms:

> Believing that the principle of Brotherhood as taught by Jesus Christ cannot adequately be wrought out under existing industrial and commercial conditions, and that the faithful and commonplace application of this principle must result in the Socialization of all natural resources, as well as the instruments of production, distribution and exchange, the League exists to assist in the work of eliminating the former by building the latter Social Order.

The League was open to all Free Churchmen 'in sympathy with and ready to promote its expressed objects, by all means consistent with conscience and loyalty to Jesus Christ.'[1]

There was a considerable degree of overlapping of membership in the various Christian Socialist societies. Adderley and Ingham the heads of Oxford House, belonged to the C.S.U., and Adderley also belonged to the Guild of St Matthew. Headlam and Verinder of the Guild helped to start the Land Reform Union, which became the Land Restoration League. Even the Fabian Society included Headlam, Dearmer, Charles Marson, Adderley, and Joseph Clayton.

8 *Christian Socialism in the Fabian Society*

The Fabian Society was indeed for some time quite a centre for Christian Socialist discussion. Some of the religious aspects of the society will be noted later, but the Fabian Tracts, which appeared from 1884, besides carrying a variety of more-or-less subtle religious implications, also offered a platform for the direct exposition of Christian Socialism. *Tract 79*, dated about the end of the century, was a reprint of John Woolman's *A Word of Remembrance and Caution to the Rich*, originally published in 1773, the author being described as 'the John the Baptist of the Gospel of Socialism.' Two other Tracts of the period give contemporary statements of Christian Socialist principles. *Tract 42: Christian*

[1] Binyon, op. cit., 182.

Socialism, published in 1892, was the work of Stewart Headlam, who begins by saying that he learned his Christian Socialism from Maurice and Kingsley. Christ, far from being 'other-worldly,' talked about 'the Kingdom of Heaven, or the righteous society to be established on earth.' His miracles were all 'distinctly secular, socialistic works,' aiming at human happiness, and the parables picture the future 'righteous society.' When the unemployed paraded at St Paul's their banners were inscribed with words taken not from Karl Marx, or Lassalle, or Hyndman, or Morris, or Annie Besant, or Champion, from but Christ and his Apostles, so inspiring Hancock's sermon 'The Banner of Christ in the Hands of the Socialists.' The main purpose of the Church was to do 'on a large scale, throughout the world those secular, socialistic works which Christ did on a small scale in Palestine.' St Paul taught that the labourer should get the first share of the fruits of his labour, and that 'if a man is not working for his own living he is preying on the living of others,' while St James's 'little pamphlet . . . is full of burning words on the labour question.' Headlam turns next to the Sacraments. Baptism is 'the great sacrament of equality, teaching that every child 'is equally an inheritor of the Kingdom of Heaven,' and Holy Communion is 'the great sacrament of brotherhood.' The Catechism of the Church says that one has a duty to work, and the Magnificat 'holds up to the scorn of the ages, as pests of society, three sets of people, the proud, the mighty and the rich.' The hostility of the Church to social reform is the result of undemocratic organization, and it should be disestablished and reformed. The author then passes on to practical points, 'because many Christians are somewhat vague in their Socialism.' There should be 'liberal expenditure' to improve schools, especially with regard to music and swimming, while classes should be smaller, and no money should be given to private schools. Christian Socialists should remind the public of its duty to its own employees, and the land should be restored to the people, for the land question was the basis of poverty. The land belonged 'of natural and inalienable right' to each generation, and the landlords should be dispossessed, not by expropriation or purchase, but by 'taxing them out.' There is no conflict of spiritual and material reform, for the latter is part of the former, and the aim of Socialists is 'by degrees to establish the Kingdom of Heaven upon earth.'

There are two comments one might make upon this tract: firstly, that Headlam's interpretation of the Scriptures and the worship of the Church resembled Newman's interpretation of the Thirty-Nine Articles; each was remarkable as an example of how by the exercise of sufficient ingenuity a man might find precisely what he wanted to find, even though no one else could see it was there. And secondly, how extraordinary it seems that an extreme Anglo-Catholic should arrive at a conception of the Kingdom of Heaven closely similar to that held at the same time at the extreme of Liberal Protestantism, a conception which most people in the Churches, Protestant and Catholic alike, would have rejected as too remote from the traditionally accepted idea. Once again it seems that extremes meet.

The other Christian Socialist tract of this period came in fact from a highly vocal exponent of militant Nonconformity, John Clifford, whose *Socialism and the Teaching of Christ* appeared as *Tract 78* in 1897. He begins by denouncing the idea that Christianity is concerned only with the other-worldly, and he takes up the challenge of Professor Flint's recent book on Socialism, describing it as 'one of the largest and least discriminating and most unsatisfactory books I have read on Socialism.' Flint's assertion that Christianity had no direct political or economic programme 'is flat paganism, and as anti-Christian as it is misleading and delusive.' Most Christians recognize the idea of stewardship and work for individual reforms, but disagree about industrial organization. Socialism aims at collective ownership and working of the economic system, and at equality, and 'seeks to build a far better body for the soul of Christ's teaching, and the spirit of his life and death, than this fiercely competitive system, through which he now struggles almost in vain to make his voice heard and his power felt.' From a Christian standpoint collectivism has many advantages. It provides work for all and reduces stealing, lying and the degradation of women. It raises struggle from the lower levels of life to the 'worthiest spheres,' and moral struggle replaces industrial. It creates a more equitable environment, and changes charity from the hobby of the few into the very basis of society. It follows the Greek ideal of 'ordered liberty' and unites the community.

Clifford's tract is essentially the work of a platform orator, unaccustomed to being interrupted for definitions, and it is a veritable storehouse of begged questions. The useful word 'collectivism' is given no clear content, and the point at issue—the consonance of Socialism with the teaching of Christ—is almost taken for granted, so that the speaker can hasten on into the vigorous assertion of doubtful platitudes, such as that the abolition of poverty was a worthy ideal for Christians, or that the effect of collectivism would be to translate the element of struggle from the sordid business of earning a living into the moral realm. Clifford himself was an outstanding figure in the religious life of these years. He lived from 1836 to 1923 and was the son of a Derbyshire factory worker. His mother's family were Baptists and three of his uncles preachers. He began work in a lace factory at the age of eleven, and at 22 he entered the Baptist ministry. He himself regarded his industrial experience as formative:

> I began life in a factory, and I have never forgotten the cruel impressions I received there of men and work. Ebenezer Elliott's prayer was on our lips daily—'When wilt Thou save the people?' Chartists were alive and eloquent. Feargus O'Connor, Thomas Cooper, Henry Vincent, William Lovett were fighting. Holyoake later was going to prison . . . So I came to have sympathy with the working classes, of which I was one . . . and I have it still and I have never lost it after eighty years, and I feel it stronger today than ever.[1]

Clifford was active in the aggressive propaganda of the Free Churches, especially in connexion with the Education Act of 1902, and can be regarded as a successor of such determined Nonconformists as Miall in his antipathy to the existing system both in the Church and in social life.

9 *Discussion of Christian Socialism in the Religious Press in the 'Nineties*

In the press interest was growing. The *Guardian* reported that at the Cardiff Church Congress of 1889 the most loudly-applauded speeches were those with a 'strong Socialistic tone' and was pleased at clerical interest in the subject. Bishop Magee of Peterborough was severely rebuked for attacking Christian Socialism, and was said to have misunderstood the nature of Socialism, which was not 'an attempt to compel men to feel love and compassion,' but 'a question of machinery' and 'simply a question of expediency.' There were favourable articles on the C.S.U. and a welcome for the revival of Christian Socialism in general.[2]

---

[1] Sir James Marchant, *Dr. John Clifford, C.H.: Life, Letters and Reminiscences* (1924), 1.

[2] *Guardian*, October 9th, November 13th, 1889; February 24th, 1892; April 26th, 1893; February 27th, 1895.

But far more space was devoted to Christian Socialism in the *Church Times*. In an historical account of the co-operative movement, in 1889, the work of the Christian Socialists was mentioned, and two years later the chief credit for the Church's growing social concern was given to Maurice. Churchmen of all political opinions were urged to support the C.S.U., with the 'spirit and aims of Lord Shaftesbury.'[1] There was a discussion in the correspondence columns from June to August 1893, with about a score of letters appearing. The debate began with a disagreement over the merits of clerical intervention in industrial disputes, with special reference to Manning in the dock strike, and broadened out into an argument over the alleged 'other-worldliness' of Christianity. A simultaneous discussion centred round a protest by Percy Dearmer that he had been prevented from lecturing on Christian Socialism in a Church school.[2] At the end of the year there was a disagreement between Hensley Henson and J. G. Adderley as to whether it was part of Christianity to seek improvements in social conditions.[3] The next year there was a protest about the C.S.U. policy of inquiring into working conditions, and a debate about the C.S.U. attitude to the education question. A leader praised the C.S.U. in rather lukewarm terms, while reminding its readers that 'the spiritual and the material are distinct spheres.'[4] There followed a tremendous correspondence lasting from the beginning of August 1894 to the middle of October, resumed in the New Year and not finally ending till late in April 1895, in which more than 150 letters appeared, with Henson again a central figure. There was the usual argument over the meaning of the word 'Socialism,' and whether Christian Socialists were real Socialists, and the usual variation in assertions about the implications of political economy, a science still at this time in that fairly early stage of development when even the totally ignorant feel able to air their views. Dearmer and Adderley were as usual far too skilful in debate for most of their opponents, but not necessarily any more convincing, and not always in agreement. Towards the end the discussion turned back again to another familiar theme— the absence of the working classes from the churches; and there

[1] *Church Times*, December 6th, 1889; October 9th, 1891.
[2] Correspondence extended from June 30th, 1893 to August 25th, 1893.
[3] Ibid., December 8th, 1893 to January 26th, 1894.
[4] Ibid., May 18th, July 27th, 1894.

was sharp disagreement whether Christian Socialism could be regarded as a remedy.[1] At the end of the 'nineties there was a further controversy occasioned by the C.S.U. policy of investigating working conditions and publishing their findings.[2]

The *Church Family Newspaper* practically ignored the Christian Socialist movement, except for occasional notices about the C.S.U. On the death of Thomas Hughes his efforts for co-operation were praised, though his true claim to fame was considered to be *Tom Brown's Schooldays*. In 1897 there was a letter published by a group of churchmen of Liberal politics demanding more attention to the needs of Labour. A familiar line of argument was used:

> The rich Liberal capitalist is not necessarily more in sympathy with the workers than the rich Tory capitalist. Parliament is still made up for the most part of wealthy men: nor does official Liberalism show much readiness to concede a fair share of representation to Labour men. This is suicidal and unjust.

The letter 'is not written in haste; it represents many whose names are not at its foot; and it means what it says.' The letter was signed by the names that might be expected of its tone and lively expression: among them those of Holland, Gore, C. W. Stubbs, at this time Dean of Ely, Adderley, and Shuttleworth. The *Church Family Newspaper* commented on the letter, and especially on a reference to the I.L.P.: 'We do not know that the I.L.P. is anything more than a lusty youngster yet, but at the same time its significance lies in the fact that it should exist at all.'[3]

On the Nonconformist side the *Independent* rejoiced at the appointment of a C.S.U. member—Stubbs—as Dean of Ely, while claiming that his views would be approved by Congregationalists rather than by Anglicans.[4] The comments on Christian Socialism by the *British Weekly* at this time were closely linked with the more general discussion of Socialism noted later.

For the Roman Catholics the *Universe* had nothing to say. It did have an article headed 'Christian Socialism,' but it was con-

[1] *Church Times*, August 3rd, 1894 to October 12th, 1894 and January 4th, 1895 to April 11th, 1895.

[2] Ibid., March 3rd, 1899 to April 21st, 1899, followed by two articles on the system of 'preferential dealing' (the source of the dispute), by John Carter, on June 2nd and June 9th, 1899.

[3] *Church Family Newspaper*, April 6th, May 25th, 1894; April 2nd, 1896; January 15th, 1897.

[4] *Independent*, March 1st, 1894.

fined to generalities, such as that while opposing Socialism 'we cannot attempt to disguise from ourselves that there is much in our social system utterly unsound, absolutely gangrened,' and then went on to attack the contrast between the enormous wealth recently left by the Duke of Bedford and the poverty of the East End. Perhaps a Christian Socialist note may be detected in a leader approving University extension work: 'As Cardinal Manning says, the coming century, now so close at hand, will belong not to Kings, not to mere politicians, but to the people.'[1]

By about 1900 the Christian Socialist movement had become fashionable, and it suffered all the penalties of a fashionable movement, of which the worst was that its language and much of its atmosphere had become the commonplace property of everyone who wanted to be up-to-date. The name 'Christian Social Union' gave a strong impetus to this tendency, since to the ill-informed and unthinking it conveyed the suggestion that 'Christian Socialist' was an adjectival phrase pertaining exclusively to the C.S.U., so that there emerged the absurdity of a correspondent who wrote to the press to complain that the C.S.U. was too friendly to the trade unions and hence drifting away from true Christian Socialism. A variety of Socialism which rejected any alliance with working-class organizations was remarkable indeed.

10 The Spirit of Edwardian Christian Socialism

The Christian Socialist movement, if in the early years of the twentieth century it became even more diffuse and vague than in the preceding decade, showed no sign of coming to an end. Some of the leading figures of late Victorian times were still prominent, and younger men were coming forward to succeed them. Among the Nonconformists John Clifford was at the height of his influence, and in 1908 another address given by him appeared as a Fabian tract, under the heading Socialism and the Churches.[2] The tendency of the era to delight in obscure but uplifting terminology, which was typified by the 'New Theology' of R. J. Campbell, had been at work on Clifford since his previous tract of a decade earlier. Socialism he now described as 'a movement, a tendency, a pushing forward of the inner soul of humanity towards its predestined goal.' Again, 'Socialism is a spirit of justice and charity, of broad sympathies and general good will, of universal amity and benevolence,

[1] Universe, January 24th, March 14th, 1891.
[2] Fabian Tract 139 (1908).

of service to others and not of getting for self.' He rejected
the whole outlook which thought of Socialism as essentially a
matter of social engineering, an outlook for which the Fabian
Society itself was noted. Thus he quoted Wells's description (in
New Worlds for Old) of Socialism as 'a project for the re-shaping
of human society upon new and better lines,' but he insisted that
it was more than this:

> It is an ethical and religious effort, proceeding from within the
> soul of the human race, for pulling down principalities and powers,
> and spiritual wickedness in high places, and bringing every thought
> of man into captivity to the obedience of the teaching and spirit of
> Jesus Christ the Savior and Leader of men.[1]

It comes as something of an anti-climax to learn that an example of
Socialism in practice was the Post Office. Socialism sought the
conscious and constructive control of the economic system in the
general interest. Doctrinaire and revolutionary brands had now
been replaced by moderation: 'Few would now expect a sudden
revolution; most work to hasten a natural and orderly evolution of
the Socialistic State. The historic sense is begetting the feeling that
tomorrow must grow out of today, just as whatever elements we
have of order and progress, of liberty and good legislation, have
grown out of yesterday.' In fact the trend of the age was towards
Socialism. A section entitled 'The Divinity of Socialism' went on
to argue that this trend was

> the plan of God. Socialism, in the soul of it, is divine. It is of
> God . . . God has His plan in every generation, and I cannot hesitate
> to believe that 'the plan of God in this generation connects itself with
> that irresistible social tide which rises higher and higher against the
> dry strands of our time . . .'

(Clifford does not give the source of this internal quotation, which
continues for considerably longer in similar vein. Its style sounds
as if he was quoting from himself, but others talked the same
language at this time.) Socialism, he continues, if not necessarily
the final stage of society, was certainly the next stage. It was 'a
thing incredible that any of the churches of Jesus Christ should be
fiercely antagonistic to it, or coldly critical, or haughtily sceptical,
or superciliously indifferent.' Such moods were passing, and a
change was taking place in the views of the Church comparable

---

[1] The spelling is that favoured by the Fabian Society, the syntax of the
sentence perhaps peculiar to Clifford.

with the Reformation or the Evangelical Revival. Unfortunately the Church's response to the situation was slow, so that it was in the rear rather than in the van. It considered political and social questions 'unspiritual things,' not recognizing God's authority over them. There follows a lengthy comparison of the attitude of the Church with that of St Peter at the time of his vision in the *Acts of the Apostles*. The Free Churches had for long been sympathetic to social action, but

> the most welcome sign of change is in the Pan-Anglican Congress, for it has devoted, apparently, about three-fourths of its time, and more of its interest, to these vital problems of the world—gambling and intemperance, opium and alcohol, sweating and housing, low wages and unemployment—tracing their wide ramifications in the social organism, their destructive effects on young and old, indicating the means by which these evils may be abolished.

The Churches must not compromise on their own 'truths and ideals.' They must not allow Socialism to be narrowed down to mere economics:

> It is for the Church to insist upon and secure the *spiritual* quality of Socialism. Owen and Marx have affirmed the economic element. The Fabian Society has illuminated and enforced the historical, and made clear that we cannot bury the old order and start as from creation's dawn. H. G. Wells and others have contended for the rational and ethical element; the Churches must add the most important of all, the spiritual.

Socialism demands a higher morality than individualism, and this the Churches must supply. They must not accept social divisions. Young Christians must be trained and instructed on social conditions and remedies. The Churches ought to secure the election to public office of men pledged to serve the community, and to abolish or reform anti-social institutions, 'such as the House of Lords, the rule of the land by the few, the swollen tyranny of the drink trade, and the like.'

This tract is a curious amalgam of discordant elements. A Fabian insistence that Socialism was the inevitable next stage of social evolution went hand in hand with the demand that Socialism should be looked upon as a moral and religious force, which one would not have expected to triumph by mere economic pressures. There is something perverse in the repeated Christian Socialist argument, originating with Maurice and Kingsley themselves, that the vast bulk of Socialists were quite mistaken in what they believed about Socialism, and that only their own minute company truly appreciated that it was the intervention of God in human affairs.[1] It was a claim equally irritating to Socialists who thought they were opposed to religion, or more commonly indifferent to it, and to good churchpeople who could not understand why Robert Blatchford should be cast in the role of John the Baptist. There is something peculiarly perverse too about the more vocal representatives of the Christian Socialist movement who promulgated a typical programme of traditional Radicalism and insisted that it was really Socialism. Clifford's demands were an extension of the class-conscious Nonconformist Radicalism of figures of the past like Miall. But perhaps the appeal of Socialism to many of its adherents at this time was similarly the appeal of a quite traditional form of Radicalism.

On the Anglican side, which after all was the main stream of Christian Socialism, Percy Dearmer also contributed a Fabian tract.[2] The peculiar perversity of Anglican Christian Socialists was to insist that the Church of England was already fundamentally a Socialist body, except that it did not know it. Thus Dearmer claimed that the Lambeth Conference of 1888 had favoured Socialism, for it said that the clergy ought to show 'how much of what is good and true in Socialism is to be found in the precepts of Christ,' so that in writing his tract he was 'but obeying the instructions of my Fathers in God,' a very characteristic expression of the Anglo-Catholic interpretation of episcopal authority. He would refuse to pick out isolated texts, but would confine himself to the 'central features' of Christianity. In the Incarnation God the Son chose to be not a Prince but a Workman and engaged in 'secular works of mercy'—in contrast with the Greek society based on slavery and despising manual work. In the Incarnation, 'not only was labor given its true position, but the unity of the whole human race was proclaimed.' The Magnificat and John the Baptist's teaching were Socialist in character, and the first public utterance of Christ ('The Spirit of the Lord is upon me, because he hath appointed men to preach the Gospel to the poor,' etc.), was social, if not Socialist. Dearmer then went on to consider the four

[1] Similarly in the mid-twentieth century some theologians, followers of Paul Tillich, not infrequently assured writers who thought themselves atheists, that they were really no such thing.

[2] *Fabian Tract 133: Socialism and Christianity* (1907).

'most prominent' forms of Christ's teaching, i.e. signs, parables, the Sermon on the Mount, and prayer, in order.

1. Signs (i.e. miracles). Christ saved life and healed sickness, the very aims of Socialism. He increased comfort, by feeding the multitude, and even merriment, by turning water into wine.

2. Parables. Many of these attacked money-making, and one of them was the inspiration of Ruskin's *Unto this Last*. The parable of the Good Samaritan preached the internationalization and universalization of love. There were also the parables of the Kingdom, relating to the Church. Christ 'came thus on a social mission to bind men together in love, as well as to purify their individual souls.' And the parable of the Judgement: 'We shall be saved or condemned according to our acts of social service, Christ tells us, saying nothing about churchgoing, or conversion, or orthodoxy . . .'

3. The Sermon on the Mount. The 'clinching passage' was Matthew 7. 16–23, and the keynote:

> Ye shall know them by their fruits . . . Not every one that saith unto me, Lord, Lord, shall enter into the kingdom of heaven; but he that doeth the will of my Father which is in heaven.

The Sermon contradicted modern individualism with its self-righteousness, its parade of so-called charity, and its love of cant. The Beatitudes were secular. The commands of Christ were said to be impracticable, and this was true in modern society, but advance towards them was also advance towards Socialism, though 'as man develops from his present rudimentary condition to the glorious future which evolution and the Gospel foretell, he may pass beyond the ideal of present-day Socialism to something vaster and more sublime.'

4. The Lord's Prayer. This was not individualist or other-worldly, for its opening was social: 'Our Father.' 'And no one can say "Our Father which art in heaven" unless he has first said "Our brethren which are on the earth." ' The opening is followed by three petitions all referring to the earth. To hallow God's Name on earth means 'to make the world a mirror of his love and beauty and justice.' The prayer for the Kingdom to come demands co-operation with God in establishing 'a perfect social state,' a 'heaven on earth.' The prayer for daily bread is likewise social, and the rich man who so prays is bound to distribute to the necessity of others. The prayer for forgiveness might seem irrelevant to

Socialism, but Christ linked it to forgiveness of our neighbour, and it is judged by social tests:

> Therefore it was only to be expected that modern heresy should have raised a cry directly the opposite of Christ's principles. 'No man shall come between me and my God,' is that cry—as if they would make private property even of the Almighty! But the teaching of the Lord's Prayer is that *every man* shall come between me and God.

So far it might seem that nothing had been adduced in favour of 'Economic Socialism, of State Collectivism,' which is true. Christ's teaching was for all time, and collectivism a strictly temporary matter, but the petition 'Lead us not into temptation' in the Lord's Prayer 'teaches us to be Collectivists at the present stage of the evolution of society.' The individualist system, with its emphasis on making money, constituted the great temptation, and indeed this thought Dearmer regarded as the inspiration of his Socialism. 'Deliver us from evil': on this clause the comment was that unsocial Christians must learn that much evil is social, while materialistic Socialists must learn that evil is real, and that social disorder is not merely the result of bad machinery, so that moral and social improvement must go side by side.

After these four sections the tract becomes more general. In the understanding of brotherhood true charity must be distinguished from false; justice, the equivalent of the Biblical concept of 'righteousness,' was also needed. The Bible condemned idleness. It was not true to say that St Paul justified slavery, but on the contrary the slaves were emancipated by Christianity. Christ denounced riches, but this fact was largely ignored in the present-day world, and in the present-day Church. In the parable of Dives and Lazarus Dives is not the 'bad rich man' but simply the 'rich man,' who falls into the temptation of ignoring the need of the poor man. It is a Christian duty to try to remove this temptation from the rich, so that a social revolution would be a blessing for the rich. Dearmer goes on to quote part of the Epistle for May 1st, i.e. Labour Day, from the Epistle of James: 'Let the brother of low degree rejoice in that he is exalted: But the rich, in that he is made low: because as the flower of the grass he shall pass away.' (James 1. 9f.) On this he comments: 'Outside, the Socialist procession may be singing the reactionary Marseillaise, but in church the reactionary vicar is reading to his people the Socialist message of St James! It is a wonderful world we live in.' In the Apostolic age

Christians lived as Communists, and the communal tradition survived in the Church, Dearmer taking an extraordinarily evolutionary and progressivist view of it:

> ... All along, the leaven has been working, and the Kingdom growing nearer and clearer—aye, even amid the deluge of modern avarice. Nor can anyone who has studied the slow processes of evolution in man and nature approve for one moment the ignorant objection that nineteen hundred years is a long time to have taken. It is a short period in the world's history.

The communal tradition survived still in the religious orders. In the past the Church rightly maintained that usury was evil and that there was a 'just price.' Baptism is the sacrament of brotherhood. The Holy Communion maintains 'the communal character of the highest form of worship,' and if Christians share in this, they must also share in 'perishable things.' It was just this thought that 'so shocked people when Mr Stewart Headlam said that those who come to Holy Communion must be holy communists.' But Christians had broken the unity of the Church, 'and have made an apotheosis of selfish individualism by the Calvinistic heresies of justification by faith without works, the impossibility of falling from grace, and the still more hideous doctrine of predestination.' Some people misunderstood the true nature of the religion they professed: 'Christianity is not Individualism. Neither is it Socialism and water. It is Socialism and fire . . .' And so the tract concludes with an appeal to Christians to be Socialists and to Socialists to be Christians.

It is not difficult to understand from such a work why many people grew irritated with Dearmer and the whole group of Anglo-Catholic Christian Socialists, for the interpretation given to the teaching of Christ, more ingenious than convincing, added to the impression created by the leaders of the Oxford Movement themselves, that Anglo-Catholics were irrevocably inclined to casuistry. The other most striking feature of Dearmer's tract is the extent to which, despite its dogmatic basis, it resembled Clifford's in outlook, and the extent to which, with its emphasis on evolution and the slow but inevitable progress of sound ideas over nineteen centuries, it even resembled the current teachings of extreme Liberal Protestantism. It seems that a certain type of High Anglicanism and a certain type of Liberal Nonconformity were

not as far apart as might have been expected. No one more than the
conscious rebel is the child of his generation.

11   *Charles Gore*

The politically radical High Anglican was by now a quite
familiar figure, and indeed he could now be found in eminent
positions. A year or two after Dearmer wrote this tract the influential deanery of Lincoln was given to Thomas Charles Fry
(1846–1930),[1] who had been for twenty-three years Headmaster of
Berkhamsted School, and was described as 'a radical in politics
and a liberal High Churchman.' He was a pioneer in the C.S.U.
and Chairman of the Church Reform League, and at Lincoln he
was active in the W.E.A.

But by far the most important figure was Charles Gore (1853–
1932).[2] At Harrow he came under the influence of H. M. Butler,
the famous Headmaster, and Westcott, who was a master there—
both important figures in the history of Christian Socialism.
Already at Balliol his future course seemed marked out. He spoke
in debates, and in small minorities often found himself in alliance
with Asquith. He defended trade unions and supported the Liberal
Government, from a strongly Radical point of view:

> At Oxford, the first political event that came to operate on his
> mind with overwhelming force was the heroic effort of Joseph Arch,
> the Warwickshire peasant, to organize and improve the lot of agricul-
> tural labourers, in 1872. Gore never forgot Joseph Arch. Circum-
> stances and the obtuseness of Victorian squires and the country clergy
> combined to make Arch critical of the Church. Gore reckoned this
> a tragedy. The Church ought to have thrown all its weight into the
> scale on behalf of Arch's campaign . . . After Arch, the under-
> graduate Radical became conscious of F. D. Maurice, though he
> states that he did not read him very thoroughly. Later still, on turning
> to the Fathers, he began to discover some of the extremely critical
> sentiments upon wealth that are expressed in the Christian tradition,
> and reflected more and more on the implications of our Lord's
> teaching on the subject.[3]

From childhood he was a close friend of Scott Holland, and
they were associated in all their work. In due course Gore became
Principal of Pusey House, and at once invited Stewart Headlam to

[1] *Dict. Nat. Biog.* (1922–1930), s.v. Fry.
[2] G. L. Prestige, *The Life of Charles Gore* (1935).
[3] Ibid., 16f.

address the Oxford Branch of the Guild of St Matthew. Gore and
Headlam shared 'a righteous indignation for every kind of social,
industrial and economic injustice.'[1] On the occasion of the
Trafalgar Square riot of 1887 Holland blamed the Government:
'I have seldom felt so sad, or so mad, at a political wickedness';
and similarly Gore himself remarked: 'It's a pity they did not loot
the West End.'[2] In 1888 the Lambeth Conference called upon
churchmen to study social problems, and the next year Wilfred
Richmond, a friend of Gore, delivered lectures at Sion College,
London, on economic morals. It was decided to unite for practical
action, and the Guild of St Matthew was adjudged unsatisfactory,
since it displayed a 'rather flamboyant type of Christian Socialism,
to which Holland and Richmond, whose object was rather research
and education than political propaganda, did not wish to commit
themselves.' So the C.S.U. was formed, with Gore and Holland
as Vice-Presidents, Gore becoming President on Westcott's death
in 1901. Gore was very hostile to *laissez-faire*, and approved the
epigram with which Holland dismissed it: 'Each for himself and
God for us all, as the elephant said when he danced among the
chickens.'[3] Gore was reckoned an Anglo-Catholic, but the revered
leader of the party, Liddon, was increasingly distressed at his
protégé's tendencies. What he deemed to be the rationalistic
tendencies of *Lux Mundi*, edited by Gore, worried him, but so did
invitations to Tillett and Burns to speak at Pusey House—invitations given by L. T. Hobhouse with Gore's approval—though he
felt that Gore must have some idea of doing good to trade union
leaders. Gore urged on moral grounds adherence to 'socialistic
thought,' though at the same time he denied that he could be
called a Socialist, and always maintained this denial, describing a
paragraph in the *Manchester Guardian* so describing him as
containing 'as many untruths as lines.' He congratulated Manning
for his attitude during the dock strike, and ran into trouble with the
Bishop of Oxford by presiding at a meeting in 1893 addressed by
Tom Mann. He was a close friend of Samuel Barnett, and shared
his social concern:

> He once became a shareholder in a large London store, solely in
> order to attend the shareholders' meeting and to protest against the
> oppressive treatment of employees. He was keenly interested in the
> Co-operative movement, and purchased everything he could from
> shops of that type.

[1] Prestige, op. cit., 74.   [2] Ibid., 79.   [3] Ibid., 92f.

But their goods were not always perfect: he once complained of a pair of co-operative boots: 'The wicked shops are best.'[1] He often spoke at Co-operative Congresses.

Although Gore was a founder of the C.S.U., 'which took no sides, but concentrated on investigation,' he was not typical of its impartiality. During a protest about dangerous trades (in particular about the use of lead glaze) he preached a sermon for the Women's Trade Union League and took the collection himself, and he also gave school prize medals to assist the W.T.U.L. He took an active part, with Talbot and Holland, in Parliamentary conferences preceding the 1901 Factory Act. Among his heroes was Bishop Latimer, whom he regarded as a Christian Socialist. In 1902 he was appointed Bishop of Worcester, and there too he took an active interest in the Co-operative Society, becoming a 'purchasing member' and in his first week there speaking at a co-operative meeting. On a visit to Birmingham in 1903 he insisted on staying at the home of a bricklayer, which caused something of a sensation. In 1905 his diocese was divided in two, and he became the first Bishop of Birmingham. He tended to become more Radical, and in 1906, addressing the C.S.U., 'he took the opportunity of urging on the new Liberal Government the needs of social legislation.'[2] He was in fact drifting away from the C.S.U. tradition:

> He had definitely turned from mere inquiry into social problems to active advocacy of particular reforms. His new attitude caused some friction in the Christian Social Union. He thought the limits set on the Society's operations to be cramping and weak . . .[3]

In this protest he was supported by Holland, but he was conscious of some constraint in his position of President, and thought that perhaps there should be someone of more moderate views in this position, especially as he had become a politically controversial figure: 'Gore himself adhered to no political party, but most of the measures which he advocated on grounds of justice happened also to be included in the political programmes of Liberal or Labour representatives.'[4] He wanted both Church and state 'to be more frankly democratic,' and he followed the tradition of Westcott of concerning himself with the settlement of industrial disputes:

> When industrial disputes broke out, Gore followed events closely and sometimes intervened to bring the parties together. He took the

[1] Prestige, op. cit., 179.
[2] Ibid., 267.   [3] Ibid., 274.   [4] Ibid.

chair at a conference between master bakers and representatives of their workmen, and laboured indefatigably in the interests of the chain-makers. But he had to make a rule to confine his efforts at conciliation to his own diocese. He was asked to interest himself in an important dispute not far from Birmingham but lying outside his jurisdiction. In reply he sent a letter of sympathy and understanding and enclosed a donation for the strike fund, to be given anonymously; but there were so many difficulties for the solution of which he felt a measure of responsibility that he could not exceed his own special sphere of influence. The railway strike of 1907, however, affected all citizens. Gore was shocked that the railway directors refused to treat with the representatives of the men, and suggested that if the union would appeal direct to the shareholders, they would find a great measure of sympathy, as public opinion was with the men. He wrote to several friends, in an attempt to collect the names of shareholders who might be prepared to join in an appeal to the directors in favour of allowing the principle of collective bargaining. 'There is nothing,' his chaplain wrote to Holland, 'about which he feels more keen than about Trade Unions and collective bargaining.'[1]

He called attention to sweating and other evils, and urged the Church not to be content to 'follow with the ambulance waggon' to collect the casualties, but to take an active lead on such social problems. He supported the Trade Boards Bill of 1909. In 1906 a joint committee of the Convocation and the House of Laymen was appointed to report on economic questions, and Gore as convener wrote the report in the main, claiming in it that the support of the worker should be the first charge upon industry, and that the Church should recognize that economic justice was an urgent moral problem. The growing demand for political action at last split the C.S.U. in 1910, and in the next year Gore resigned from the Presidency. He was always an active supporter of the Workers' Educational Association, for the origin of which indeed his sermons were a source of inspiration, and he often spoke for it.

In 1911 Gore was translated to the diocese of Oxford, where his social interests were no less. In a dispute at a Reading works he intervened in support of the workers and sent a subscription, and he was responsible for a survey of the unusually low wages at Reading, made by Professor Bowley. On the other hand he opposed a tramway strike at Oxford in 1913 and recommended arbitration. His later career continued to manifest social and political convictions on the Liberal-Labour borderline. In 1918 he

[1] Prestige, op. cit., 277f.

congratulated the Labour Party on leaving the Coalition and hoped it would be strongly represented in the next Parliament. In the General Strike he sympathized with the workers but urged a negotiated settlement, commenting on the Government that it 'represents everything that I most distrust.' In 1931 he supported Macdonald but warned the working classes to keep a careful watch on their own interests.

Gore was rather a new type of Christian Socialist, for he was not a mere rebel with little influence on the Church at large, such as Stewart Headlam had been, or even Percy Dearmer, though the latter was widely influential on matters of religious art and music. Gore was bishop of three dioceses in turn, ending with the great and historic diocese of Oxford; he was perhaps the outstanding theologian of his generation, and as a writer he had an unusually wide popular appeal. But his 'Socialism' was still very mild, and more a variant form of the old Radical tradition than anything else: 'Although never a socialist in any strict sense of that term, he was profoundly convinced that socialist ideals could find countenance in the Gospel and he hoped to win the Church and the labour movement to share his conviction.'[1]

Even more elevated in the hierarchy of the Church than Gore was Randall Thomas Davidson (1848–1930),[2] who not only served as Archbishop of Canterbury from 1903 to 1928, but is adjudged to have been one of the outstanding modern holders of that office. He was one of the many of his generation whose thinking had taken on a strongly social character ultimately traceable to Maurice, and if he was not a Christian Socialist, he leaned in that direction: 'In connexion with the coal strike of 1893 he was prominent in pleading for the maintenance of a decent standard of living as an essential condition in the settlement of labour disputes.'[3] It should not perhaps have been as surprising as it actually seemed, therefore, when in the General Strike he proposed a compromise settlement, which the B.B.C. refused to broadcast and the official *Gazette* to publish. He and his fellow-Archbishop, Lang of York, who was a long-standing Christian Socialist, were much criticized, but they won much influence with the working classes by their sympathy.

[1] *Dict. Nat. Biog.* (1931–1940), s.v. Gore.
[2] G. K. A. Bell, *Randall Davidson, Archbishop of Canterbury* (2 vols., 1935).
[3] *Dict. Nat. Biog.* (1922–1930), s.v. Davidson.

12 *Christian Socialist Permeation of the Church of England*

Two decades of Christian Socialism had made a great difference to the Church of England. Not only were social questions recognized to be part of the parson's reading, but the old alliance with Conservatism was no longer so complete. On one of the most bitterly-fought political issues of modern British history, the 1909 Budget, the Bishops were divided. Some, like the Bishop of Bristol, echoed the most embittered sentiments of the Opposition; but Davidson adopted an 'Olympian' aloofness, while Gore, Percival of Hereford, and Lang were all among the Budget's supporters, the last-named describing it as a protection against 'extreme and bitter Socialism' and ridiculing the 'thin-end-of-the-wedge' argument. On the Parliament Bill of 1911 the Bishops voted with the Government in the proportion of 13 to 2: had they all voted against, the Bill would have been defeated. If the 1888 Lambeth Conference had given a stimulus to social thought, the next conference, in 1897, spoke on this theme with much greater familiarity. The emphasis on self-help was less. The Church was not to commit itself to any particular social theory, but it ought to support reforms. The report of the committee concerned with this issue was described as being like a C.S.U. pamphlet, and in a way that is just what it was, for the chairman and at least four of the committee were C.S.U. members. Between 1889 and 1913, of fifty-three Bishops appointed, fourteen were members of the C.S.U., and most of these, curiously, were Conservative appointments. Among others who had some connexion was Randall Davidson himself, his wife being a member. The three episcopal spokesmen for the 1909 Budget belonged to the C.S.U. A milestone was reached in 1905 with the setting up of the committee on moral questions, under pressure from Gore, all five Bishops on it belonging to the C.S.U.: Gore (Birmingham); Talbot (Southwark); Percival (Hereford); Hoskyns (Southwell); and Harmer (Rochester). In the 1907 report of this committee, mentioned above in the account of Gore, there was a revolutionary change of tone, in the clear note of self-criticism. Idleness whether of the poor or the rich was condemned. Property was a trust and the living wage a Christian principle; employers must be prepared for sacrifices; and drastic alterations must be made in society. The traditional idea of the Christian duty to the poor was insufficient, and more fundamental measures were needed. There was no opposition to the report in the House of Bishops, but in the Lower House of Convocation 'the debate resembled a museum of antiquities,' and many old arguments were given a new airing. Hensley Henson, as ever the most formidable opponent of Christian Socialist tendencies, called the report 'an extremely able and clever Christian Social Union pamphlet,' which ought not to have the authority of Convocation, and he proposed an amendment condemning the partisan use of the pulpit, which the Bishops struck out. The committee subsequently presented a second report in 1909 dealing with investments, and a third in 1911 on work in the dioceses.[1]

A further example of the degree to which the C.S.U. approach had permeated the Church is William Cunningham's book *Christianity and Social Questions*.[2] It was one of a series of *Studies in Theology*, along with W. R. Inge's *Faith and its Psychology*, which was likewise indicative of new stirrings in the thought of the Church of England, though Inge was as unsympathetic as Henson to the Christian Socialist movement. Cunningham was a significant figure in the development of the study of economic history. Like Marshall, he rejected the attempt to treat economic questions as though they were a branch of mathematics or physics, and always bore in mind their immediate human implications. Thus in discussing 'the criteria of healthy economic life' he comments: 'The sufficiency or insufficiency of employment is the test which shows most clearly whether the economic life of a country is in a healthy condition or not.' It was not satisfactory to measure economic health by 'money measurement,' though 'money measurement' was not to be rejected altogether. Thus a reduction in the hours of labour might diminish the national product, and while it might be said that this was a fair price to pay, it ought not simply to be taken for granted that it could be afforded. Increased state expenditure, implying decreased private wealth—Cunningham was no Keynes—might make for unemployment, which the author evidently regarded as the great social evil. Trade Unions falsely supposed that it was possible to raise prices and wages by restrictive methods, but they were being forced out of this belief by the necessity of considering an industry as a whole, in face of foreign competition. Union action to increase wages might also increase unemployment, and it was not possible to tell in advance whether this would actually occur. On 'sweating' Cunningham pointed out that very often the immediate small-scale employer could not be

[1] Wagner, op. cit., 239ff.
[2] W. Cunningham, *Christianity and Social Questions* (1910).

blamed: it was 'a standing warning against the dangers which are inherent in unregulated competition.' One section of the book deals with 'avowedly Christian Socialism', to which he makes the unusual objection that a reform of society was not necessarily the object only of Christians, so that courtesy to non-Christian reformers invalidated the term. Improving the conditions of the masses must not be put beside the salvation of souls as 'another form of specifically Christian work.' The author referred to the new emphasis on the corporate character of Christianity, for example the idea that the reconstruction of society is part of Christ's mission, but without really coming to grips with it. His book does not fulfil the expectations raised by its title and remains on rather a superficial level.

13   *Conrad Noel and the Church Socialist League*

In the middle of the first decade of the new century the moderate and rather non-committal attitude exemplified by Cunningham's book began to make the more radical Christian Socialists somewhat disillusioned with the C.S.U. Such prominent leaders as Gore and Holland began to feel that the basis was too wide and vague. A similar disillusionment was spreading too in the Guild of St Matthew, and younger men were no longer content always to follow the lead of the dynamic but ageing Headlam. A new group was emerging: W. E. Moll, G. Algernon West, T. C. Gobat, Conrad Noel, P. E. T. Widdrington, Claude Stuart Smith, and N. E. Egerton Swann. There was also F. L. Donaldson, who was fully committed to support for the Labour movement and believed that it represented a new moral ideal for society and that the Church was apostate from its duty. An obviously dominant figure of the future was William Temple, who attacked competition and urged full Christian support for Labour, to the alarm of Hastings Rashdall, who was concerned about the growth of Socialism in the Church. Apart from such intellectual leaders interested in Socialism, in the tradition of Maurice, there were working clergy, especially in the north of England, who were in daily contact with the rank and file of the Labour movement, including local leaders of the I.L.P. The political excitement of the time gave a stimulus:

> Following on the General Election of 1906, there was, all over the country, something approximating to a brief revival of the spirit of the 'eighties. A Church and Labour Conference was held at Mirfield; Churchmen took part in Unemployed Demonstrations; George

Lansbury endeavoured to commit the London Diocesan Conference to the support of Socialism. Just after the election the Rev G. Algernon West, knowing that there were many clergy in sympathy with the Labour point of view and that they were isolated from one another, and feeling that an organization would encourage them and strengthen their position and enable them to represent the Labour point of view in the Church, sent a letter to the *Labour Leader*, signed 'Durham Priest,' in which he put forward this idea. In his original intention the projected society was to be mainly, if not exclusively, for clergy; the matter was talked over with the Rev W. E. Moll and in June a Conference was held at Morecambe. The clergy who attended the Morecambe Conference agreed that the Guild of St Matthew did not meet their needs; it was, for one thing, too limited ecclesiastically. And they felt that the Christian Social Union, while it did valuable work in awakening a social conscience among Church people, was too indefinite, and that the work which attracted them was difficult and unsatisfactory within the limits of its printed objects and official policy; a new society was needed.[1]

But the Conference itself owed much to the C.S.U., for half the speakers were members. Conrad Noel tried to persuade those present to commit themselves to support for the Guild of St Matthew, while Stewart Headlam wanted any new society to have a similar Catholic and sacramental basis, and Percy Widdrington wanted it to deal with a Christian sociology; but all these proposals were lost, and the rejection of the last two later disrupted the new society.

Thus the Church Socialist League came into being, the first Anglican society definitely committed to Socialism. Its principles were:

(1) To cultivate the life of brotherhood by the use of prayer and sacrament and to make manifest the social implications of our faith and worship.

(2) To give practical effect to the sex equality proclaimed by the sacraments of the Church.

(3) To help the advance of Socialism by every just means.

(4) To convert Churchpeople to the principles of Socialism and to promote a better understanding between Churchpeople who are not Socialist and Socialists who are not Churchpeople.

The definite commitment of the C.S.L. to Socialism brought congratulation from Ramsay Macdonald and Keir Hardie, and there was a move to affiliate to the Labour Party, but this was not

[1] Binyon, op. cit., 190f.

done. A paid organizer was appointed, the first being Conrad Noel, and members addressed various Socialist and Labour meetings and helped to organize demonstrations in times of distress. The C.S.L. was more forward-looking than the Guild of St Matthew, but it resembled it much more than the C.S.U. in having a fervent sense of mission. The Guild and the League both drew up statements for the Lambeth Conference of 1908, the Guild saying that real Socialism as well as mere benevolent activities and charity was needed, and that the Church should help to advance it, and the League adding an appeal to the Bishops to give a lead. After the Conference the League welcomed the Encyclical, but regretted that it avoided using the word Socialism. In 1912 it called on the Convocation of Canterbury to secure the application of the principle that the support of the worker should be the first charge upon industry.

One effect of the founding of the C.S.L. was to deal the last blow at the Guild, which closed down in 1909, by which date the League had thirty-five branches and 1,200 members. Among well-known figures who at one time or another belonged to the League were George Lansbury, Henry Slessor, R. H. Tawney, A. J. Penty, the two Chestertons, Maurice Reckitt and the Countess of Warwick, and among clergy were Conrad Noel, Percy Widdrington, Paul Bull, and G. C. Binyon, the historian of Christian Socialism. The only Bishop to belong was W. H. Frere, who became Bishop of Truro in 1923, having previously been Superior of the Community of the Resurrection. This Community, at Mirfield, was an important influence. It had been founded as a religious order and a training college for clergy by Gore in 1892, and many of its members had social interests, some belonging to the C.S.L., and one, Bull, becoming Chairman. He promoted conferences of Labour leaders and clergy at Mirfield, under the chairmanship of Frere. Also at Mirfield was J. N. Figgis, a genuinely original thinker, and an important influence in the history of English political theory, who, though not a member of the League, was a powerful force at work among its members and influenced it towards Guild Socialism. In discussions the spiritual and moral value of the Guild system was stressed, and its advantages for the individual, as against Capitalism and Collectivism. Figgis envisaged a state composed of guilds, analogous to the Catholic Church, with its provinces and dioceses, a comparison made by Donaldson. In the inclination towards Guild Socialism the League was in a way

returning to the original Christian Socialist object of producers'
co-operation, but it was also deviating into what was to prove a
rather unprofitable sideline in Labour politics.

The fissiparous tendencies of small and enthusiastic bodies soon
made themselves felt in the C.S.L. It was limited to Anglicans,
but in order to win converts this was interpreted to include all the
baptized who were not members of any other denomination.
There was not the same emphasis on theology as in the Guild of
St Matthew, but the membership was predominantly High
Church, yet even this did not make for unity. The Anglo-Catholic
movement itself had lost coherence and diverged into two main
streams, the 'Tractarians,' some with Roman Catholic inclinations,
and a Liberal Catholic group ultimately traceable to Maurice,
despite his own hostility to the Oxford Movement. The C.S.L.
had the disadvantage of compounding this disagreement with the
usual variant forms of Socialism, so that its history is one of
schism. In 1918 Noel broke away to form the 'Catholic Crusade,'
which was fully committed both to Socialism and to the Liberal
kind of Anglo-Catholicism. Later there were the 'League of the
Kingdom of God,' whose aim was to produce a Christian sociology,
and a 'League of Socialist Christians,' working within the Labour
movement. Much less fully committed to a theological position
than some of these groups was the older-established 'Fellowship
of Followers,' which began in 1897 at the Browning Settlement
and whose members signed a declaration promising to follow
Jesus. By 1922 it included twenty-five Labour M.P.s. An
influential figure in the Labour movement was the Rev J. Stitt
Wilson, who was brought up in America as a Methodist, was
ordained and converted to Socialism. In 1907 he visited England
and caused something of a sensation by his addresses, such as
'Moses: the Greatest of Labour Leaders,' 'Hebrew Prophets and
the Social Revolution,' and 'Messiah cometh, riding upon the Ass
of Economics.' He called on the clergy to give a lead in the
transforming of society.

A measure of the impression made on the Anglican Church by
the Christian Socialist movement was the atmosphere at the
Pan-Anglican Conference of 1908, when 'The Church and Human
Society' was given an important place in the programme, and a
remarkable report was issued:

To read it is to realize with rather a shock of surprise that the many, and chronically fissiparous, Anglican Societies which had laboured to urge upon the Church the social implications of her Gospel—the Guild of St Matthew, the Christian Social Union, the Church Socialist League, and all the other organized children of Kingsley and Maurice—had done a far more effective work than anybody supposed or even than they themselves dreamed. They had beyond question put the idea of Christian Socialism on the map of the Anglican consciousness, and the debate showed that they had stamped it deep into this apparently unpromising material. The question which all speakers absolutely insisted on discussing was, 'Does Christianity point towards a Socialist Society, and if so, ought the Church to be in alliance with the Labour Party?' Speaker after speaker answered yes to both questions. Lord William Cecil, indeed, complained that he felt 'almost out of place in speaking as a person with no belief in socialism,' whereupon the Rev F. L. Donaldson . . . at once rejoined that Lord William's speech had made 'a good foil to the splendid socialism of the Congress.' By the end of the day, capitalism had been agreed to be immoral or unmoral, or both; the foolish aphorism about the impossibility of making people moral by Act of Parliament had been entombed and sealed by Scott Holland; and Dr William Temple of Queen's, Oxford, had declared for nationalization, and said that 'the Christian is called on to assent to great steps in the direction of collectivism.' That in fact none of this happened until 1940[1] and that nobody could then possibly trace this legislation back to the Pan-Anglican Congress, does not alter the fact that the day of this debate was historic, and that in heaven the spirits of Maurice and Kingsley must have been singing the *Nunc Dimittis* with the heavenly choir.[2]

Whatever the condition of things in celestial spheres, in the terrestrial it was at once obvious to everyone that the Congress was absurdly unrepresentative of the Anglican Church at large on this subject, and a tribute only to the gift for organization and propaganda of the Christian Socialists. The movement had, it is true, convinced many churchmen of the need to consider the relationship of Christianity and the social order, but those who read their religious journals, in particular the *Guardian*, had for more than a generation been kept informed on this matter. The impression that the Church of England had gone Socialist was an illusion, though a fair number of individuals, especially of the rising generation, had indeed become convinced that the Socialist remedy was what the ills of society demanded.

Outstanding among these younger men was Conrad Noel,

[1] Sic.   [2] Lloyd, op. cit., I, 201.

who was born in 1869.[1] His father, although he held for four years
the appointment of Groom of the Privy Chamber, was a Radical,
and wrote a poem called 'The Red Flag.' Noel trained for the
Church and was pleased to discover the radical social views of
some of the most venerable Church Fathers, including Ambrose,
Cyprian, and Gregory the Great. Before his ordination he went to
Portsmouth to assist Father Dolling. Bishop Ryle of Exeter
refused to ordain him to a curacy at Plymouth on the grounds that
he combined the heresies of Romanism and Pantheism, and in
London he stayed in 'doss-houses' to learn about the poor. He
visited Percy Dearmer, who was assistant priest to W. A. Morris,
the Vicar of St Anne's, Lambeth, who was described as 'a vigorous
Socialist with a tremendous voice, a burly black beard, and remarkable eyes.' Noel went as assistant to T. M. Tozer, Vicar of Flowery-
field, near Dukinfield, Cheshire, a district whose character
entirely belied its name, and there he started a 'series of lectures
on Sunday afternoons on Catholic Socialism, which were boycotted
by the ordinary congregation, but thronged by men and women
who had never previously come to church.' But Bishop Jayne of
Chester refused to ordain him priest and cancelled his appointment
for quarrelling with the congregation, and without any appointment he travelled about lecturing on Catholic Socialism, for
example at Hyde and in Yorkshire, and working in Labour
churches at Bradford: 'We began our meetings with hymns and
often said the "Our Father" and other prayers. There was a red-
brick church in the city where Father Redhead was vicar. He was a
Socialist as well as a Catholic and bravely took the chair at the
Labour meetings.' Noel also spoke in Manchester, but the 'difficulty was that in Manchester there was no church preaching
Catholic Socialism.' (St Benedict's, Ardwick, was Catholic
enough, but not Socialist.) He lived in very straitened circumstances in Chorlton-cum-Hardy, but after a time became assistant
to Canon Hicks of St Philip's, Salford, later Bishop of Lincoln,
whose great enthusiasm was for total abstinence. More trouble
awaited him, for he was prosecuted, along with Mrs Pankhurst, for
holding Sunday Socialist meetings in Boggart Hole Clough, and
two other speakers, Leonard Hall and Fred Brocklehurst, were
actually imprisoned for continuing to speak there after warnings.
Next Noel went as assistant to W. E. Moll, the Christian Socialist,
at Newcastle, and with Moll and Widdrington he was responsible

[1] C. Noel, *Autobiography* (ed. Sidney Dark), (1945).

for calling the Morecambe conference which founded the C.S.L., of which society he claims: 'It was much more Socialist than the older Guild of St Matthew, founded by the London educationist, Stewart Headlam.' His comment on the Guild was that it was dominated by the ideas of Henry George, and on Headlam: 'He was, as I thought, more valuable as a theologian writing on behalf of social justice, than as a politician writing under the influence of the land reformers.' And on the C.S.L. he added:

> Its basis was the belief that the Catholic faith, as held and taught by the Church of England, finds its expression and application on the economic side in a Christian Socialism, which is not, as some appear to think, a particular variety of Socialism, milder than the secular brand, but economic Socialism come to by the road of the Christian faith and inspired by the ideas of the Gospel.

From Newcastle Noel went to Paddington to work for A. L. Lilley, a Catholic Modernist, and became friendly with the Chestertons. Frances 'tried to form a local branch of that mild and watery society for social reform, the Christian Social Union,' and there was a meeting at which G. K. Chesterton was chairman and Noel speaker, but there was no result. He also debated with Hilaire Belloc on 'Socialism versus Distributivism.' While living at Coggeshall, Essex, he tried to propagate Socialism in the villages, and then for a time he assisted Dearmer at St Mary's, Primrose Hill, where he preached Socialism and sent a rude reply to a churchwarden who raised objections. He spoke at a Trafalgar Square rally on February 13th, 1900, against sweated labour, and had the experience, unusual for curates so inclined, of delighting his vicar. He took part in various activities; Headlam tried to interest him in ballet, and he conducted a mission at St. Mary the Virgin, Charing Cross Road, directed against evangelical missions. At last his life entered a settled phase when Lady Warwick gave him a living at Thaxted, an appointment which was most unpopular with the parishioners. He began by launching a campaign against pew-rents, suggesting that all seats should be considered free three minutes before the service, a plan which was not accepted. Lady Warwick provided a curate, and also a lay secretary, Charles Jenkinson. It was her hope that Noel would travel as a Socialist lecturer, leaving the parish to these assistants, but he would not do this, and unexpectedly developed into a diligent parish priest, remaining at Thaxted for the rest of his life, down to the second world war. But he continued to be active in Socialist movements, founding the Catholic Crusade, to the end of his days offending many by his views and perhaps more by his violent expression of them.

Charles Jenkinson, Noel's assistant, became equally well known.[1] He was born in a poor home in Poplar in 1887, and attended St Stephen's, Poplar, and then St James the Less, Bethnal Green, where he led a successful agitation against pew-rents, and also supported the C.S.L., helping to organize a week's mission in its support, at which the speakers included Noel and Ramsay Macdonald. He became a friend of Noel and in 1912 joined him at Thaxted as lay secretary. Soon after this there was a campaign organized by N.A.L.U. for better wages and conditions, one of the leaders being the Rev E. G. Maxted, Vicar of Tilty, and Jenkinson assisted him, becoming secretary of the North West Essex Federation of the Union and helping to form branches. In a dispute at Helions Bumpstead in March 1914, when farmers dismissed union members, he helped to organize relief work, and a large strike was successful. He again helped Maxted in his campaign when he stood unsuccessfully as a Socialist candidate for the Essex County Council. In March 1914 he left Noel, and later took Orders, being one of the many strongly influenced by Maurice. His life's work, which brought him fame on a nation-wide scale, was his service to the Leeds City Council as the force behind the great slum clearance and housing schemes of the 'thirties. He died in 1949.

A third member of the Noel group was William Corbett Roberts.[2] His mother's family, the Corbetts, were strict Evangelicals, while his father was interested in theatres and music-halls, but was also, rather curiously, perhaps, a deacon at Union Chapel, Islington, which was more or less a Congregational Church. The son became interested in Anglo-Catholicism, but avoided joining the Church of England till he was 22 in order not to offend his father. At Oxford he came under the influence of Gore and Holland, and especially of his tutor, Sidney Ball, and when he went from there to work at Oxford House he was a 'convinced socialist.' He became a curate at Stratford, London, where in 1902 he met George Lansbury, and they became close friends. When Lansbury left an ethical society to which he belonged and rejoined the

---

[1] H. J. Hammerton, *This Turbulent Priest* (1952).
[2] Susan Miles, *Portrait of a Parson* (1955).

Church of England Roberts organized a meeting at which the future Archbishop Lang, then Bishop of Stepney, took the chair, and Lansbury made 'his public apologia for his renewed Christian faith.' Lansbury's children joined Roberts's Sunday School. After moving to Crick, Northamptonshire, Roberts printed Fabian Tracts in his church magazine. He served on the committee of the C.S.L., which included Noel and Lansbury, and defended the League's policy of not affiliating to the Labour Party, on the grounds that they worked by different means. He was more moderate than Noel and did not follow him into the Catholic Crusade, and he later had trouble with a curate who went even further than Noel, in advocating a thoroughgoing revolution.

14 R. B. Haldane

Christian Socialism always remained closely linked up with Anglo-Catholicism. It would be interesting to speculate on the reasons for this; they might be interpreted as psychological rather than theological. Men like Headlam, Dearmer, and Noel were rebels against many features of their age, and they linked together Capitalism and Protestantism as part of the established order and also as historically associated with each other. Perhaps in another generation they would have found other forms of Radicalism through which to express their dissidence. From an entirely different ecclesiastical standpoint, and in much closer accord with the existing order of things, Richard Burdon Haldane, Viscount Haldane (1856–1928), was an important if rather anomalous figure in the history of the Labour Party. His grandfather, J. A. Haldane, and his great-uncle, Richard Haldane, gave up naval careers to devote themselves to evangelical propaganda in Scotland. His grandfather on his mother's side, Richard Burdon-Sanderson, gave up his profession as a barrister to retire to the countryside and religious contemplation. There was a tradition of evangelical religion on both sides of Haldane's ancestry. His parents proposed to send him to Oxford, but gave up the idea out of suspicion of the unsound religious views his grandfather had encountered there many years before. But Haldane himself abandoned the religious tradition of his parents:

> Haldane never returned to the religious beliefs of his early youth, nor indeed did he subscribe to any orthodox creed thereafter. Perhaps Professor Seth Pringle-Pattison best described his friend's position when he wrote: 'He philosophized to satisfy a religious need,

and the philosophic conclusions in which he rested were held by him with all the intensity which religious convictions possess for the ordinary man.' He always retained, however, a deep respect for the religious beliefs of others and was eager to discuss the ultimate nature of things with his friends. In later years he found particular delight in his friendships with the two Archbishops, Randall Davidson and Cosmo Lang, and, perhaps most of all, with W. R. Inge, Dean of St Paul's.[1]

Haldane is rather an unsympathetic figure today, and his religion, compounded of Neo-Hegelianism and a fondness for Archbishops, does not help.

After the Scottish Church union of 1900, of the Free Church with the United Presbyterians as the United Free Church, he defended the new Church against the claims of the dissident minority to the whole of its property, in a case involving long doctrinal arguments, and when the case was lost, he offered £1,000 to the United Free Church, but a Bill was passed to meet the case. As a young man Haldane lectured at the Working Men's College, and he was associated with the Webbs in founding the London School of Economics, serving also as President of Birkbeck College. He enthusiastically supported the Workers' Educational Association, and it was because he felt that the Labour Party was more interested in his own favourite topic of education than the Liberals that he changed his allegiance to Labour and served as Lord Chancellor in the first Labour Government and subsequently as leader of the Labour peers until his death.

15 *Discussion of Christian Socialism in the Religious Press in the Edwardian Period*

The *Guardian* has little to say about Christian Socialism in this period, but the *Church Times* a great deal. From the beginning of 1906 an intermittent debate went on for years, ranging over Socialism in general, Christian Socialism, Christianity and Socialism (not quite the same thing) and the Labour Party. Much of this is relevant to the next chapter, but it is not possible to disentangle the various threads and it is all dealt with here.

The initial inspiration was the election result of 1906. The *Church Times* was frankly amazed at it, and attributed it mainly to the working-class vote, with special reference to the so-called

[1] Dudley Sommer, *Haldane of Cloan: His Life and Times, 1856–1928* (1960).

'Chinese slavery' issue, that is the campaign against Chinese
indentured labour in South Africa, for which the Conservative
Government was blamed. It anticipated that Labour would
swing away from the Liberals, since the latter would now see no
need to placate Labour by making concessions—and perhaps
Labour and the Irish would even come to an agreement with the
Conservatives. There was an interview with a Labour M.P., who
thought that the Church showed little sympathy with the working
classes, but was more concerned about the schools question—
that is, with safeguarding its own property.[1] This brought letters
from two leading Christian Socialists, Adderley and Donaldson,
who appealed to the Church to join in the working-class movement
before it was too late, and there followed a correspondence which
extended from early February to the middle of May. Adderley,
Donaldson, and Paul Bull, all leading Christian Socialists, came in
for much criticism, and there was a recurrence, once more without
definite conclusions, of the familiar debate on whether Socialism
was essentially Christian or incurably anti-Christian, or in some
less precise relationship to religion. Like newspaper correspondents in every age, some of these writers were more inclined to
satire or denunciation than to serious discussion, but as compared
with similar debates in the correspondence columns of the *Church
Times* in the 'nineties there were more letters friendly to Socialism,
and the emergence of the I.L.P. made the definition of the word
Socialism a little more precise.[2]

After this discussion there was a slight lull, but interest remained
strong. The regular writer 'Lancastrian' described the formation
of the C.S.L., which he considered superfluous, while a peculiar
article in favour of Socialism interpreted it as the restoration of a
lost agrarian paradise of a hierarchical character.[3] Late in 1906
more letters dealt with the attitude of the I.L.P. to denominational
schools, and the enthusiasm of Stewart Headlam and the Guild of
St Matthew for Bernard Shaw,[4] while articles by 'Lancastrian'
in this period were concerned with the C.S.U., Labour Party
policy, and the Socialism of R. J. Campbell's 'New Theology.'[5]

[1] *Church Times*, January 19th, January 26th, 1906.
[2] The letters from Adderley and Donaldson were printed on February
2nd, 1906, pp. 128f. Correspondence continued till May 11th.
[3] *Church Times*, July 6th, August 3rd, 1906.
[4] Ibid., September 28th to October 19th, and December 7th and 14th,
1906.
[5] Ibid., December 7th, 1906; January 11th, March 28th, 1907.

In May 1907 a leader rejoiced at the fall of '*Manchesterismus*' which treated Labour as a commodity, and pointed out that the C.S.U. campaigned for state action, which was really a Conservative principle, while the defenders of 'Conservatism' were actually using traditional Radical arguments. If reform of the individual conscience rather than state Socialism was the aim there would have to be 'an economic casuistry,' for the final consumer could not know the results of his choices. Christian Socialists had committed themselves to the Labour movement, but they ought not to scold churchmen who hesitated to ally themselves with avowed Secularists. It was difficult for the clergy to give judgements on economic matters. Sometimes there was unreasonable partisanship for Labour: for example the 'poor man' of the Bible was identified with the 'modern powerful trades-unionist' and the clergy urged to take his side. There was a danger of secularizing Christianity and preaching only a social Gospel.[1] From late June 1907 there was a further period of fourteen weeks when social issues were continuously discussed in the correspondence columns. This time the controversy began with the C.S.L., not the C.S.U., and quickly widened into a disagreement on the theme: 'What is Socialism?' A variety of interpretations was offered, varying from the mere application of Christian morality, or even a morality so general as not to be specifically Christian, to Arcadian anarchism, by way of a Fabian advocacy of detailed reforms. Socialism had made progress in recent years, and the question most insistently demanded now was not so much: 'Can a Christian be a Socialist?' as: 'Can a Christian not be a Socialist?' Comments by the *Church Times* itself during this discussion, as well as by many of the critics of Socialism, were defensive. The names of Adderley, Dearmer, and Donaldson were once more prominent.[2]

In 1908 Adderley provoked another flood of correspondence, lasting from January to April. Many of the old arguments were repeated now in a wearisome manner, the only new point stressed being the extent of possible co-operation between Christian and secular Socialists, and as the editor commented at the end there was much special pleading on both sides. The Christian Socialists perhaps had rather the better of things, not so much because of their own persuasiveness as because their opponents insisted on pursuing the *non sequitur* that agreement with the Socialist con-

[1] *Church Times*, May 17th, May 24th, 1907.
[2] Correspondence extended from June 21st to September 20th, 1907.

victions of a Blatchford implied agreement with his assaults on religion. The genuine dangers and limitations of Socialism as such tended to be overlooked by critics with so keen an eye for religious heterodoxy.[1] Indeed nothing in the pre-1914 discussion of Socialism seems odder to a later reader than the complete failure of both parties to realize that a Socialist system might be a serious threat to liberty, and that its defects, as evidenced in the history of the Soviet Union, would be those of the traditional extreme Right.

Signs of flagging interest disappeared when the Pan-Anglican Conference was held, with its apparent revelation that the Church of England had been converted to Socialism, and there was a more leisurely correspondence from July to October in which several readers dissociated themselves from the attitude so surprisingly revealed at the conference, while Noel and Adderley were among those on the other side.[2] A couple of leading articles were also thrown in. The first, in August, was somewhat defensive, maintaining only that the new emphasis on social Christianity was not the whole truth. Christ was not the leader of a social revolution, nor was the main task of the Church social, but religious, and if it performed this task satisfactorily 'external improvement will follow in due course.' There followed a remarkable attack on the working classes: 'Indeed, the working classes require much plain and courageous speaking from the Church today. Their greed, their self-indulgence, their dislike of obedience call for stern rebuke.' The other leader pointed out the prevalence of Socialist views at the conference, but added: 'Our conviction is that the great majority of the members of the Congress, after cheering Mr Dearmer and Mr Conrad Noel, will go home and steadily vote for Conservative and Unionist candidates.' A more serious worry, in fact, was the continued identification of the Church and Dissent with the Tory and Liberal parties respectively, but the only remedy suggested was that the Liberals should cease to be hostile to the Church of England so that Anglicans might be free to vote Liberal if they wished.[3]

In 1910 about forty letters went over all the old ground again,

---

[1] Correspondence extended from January 31st to April 10th, 1908. This last issue contained a leading article summing it up.

[2] Letters appeared on July 10th, July 17th, July 24th, July 31st, August 21st, August 28th, September 18th, and October 16th.

[3] *Church Times*, August 14th, October 16th, 1908.

with Donaldson and Adderley once more the spokesmen of
Christian Socialism and another crop of quotations from Blatchford, Hyndman, and other leading Socialists, designed to prove
that because some Socialists were not Christians no Christian
could be a Socialist.[1] In 1911 correspondence on the C.S.U.
during the summer merged into a general discussion of the Labour
unrest and the correct attitude for the Christian, running to about
eighty letters, many of them favourable to the Labour movement
and Christian Socialism.[2] A leader in August condemned existing
social conditions, but had no solution to offer beyond 'a Christian
and a lowly, and withal a generous, spirit . . .' Another in December attacked clergy for 'lackeying of the Labour movement.' The
paper's own position remained obscure. Thus it twice quoted
Gore's demand that the support of the worker should be the first
charge upon industry, but while on one occasion it seemed to see
no particular consequences to follow from this, on the second the
emphasis was all on the duty—and the right—of the clergy to
intervene in industrial affairs. Similarly of two leaders on Socialism,
one dismissed it as 'the most muddle-headed thing of all,' and a
mere revival of medieval absurdities, while the other denied that
the paper was anti-Socialist, and, asking whether there could be
such a thing as Christian Socialism, answered: 'There not only
can, but there must. The interregnum of Individualism is over.'
Anglo-Catholics should welcome corporate tendencies and not be
afraid of state intervention, while still remembering that worldly
improvement was not everything.[3] In all this the *Church Times*
seemed to be trying to reap the benefits of the close association of
Christian Socialism and Anglo-Catholicism without accepting the
disadvantages. Thus it continued to maintain what was by now a
well-established position, that the ritualist clergy were the best
friends of the working classes, and it obviously wished to share the
kudos attaching to the names of Adderley, Dearmer, Donaldson
and Noel, but it was not willing to share their Socialist convictions.
It was small wonder that a movement with so uncertain a voice
did not win the genuine trust of the working classes.

Because Christian Socialism was mainly a High Church movement the *Church Family Newspaper* did not give it so much space,

[1] Correspondence extended from January 14th to February 25th, 1910.
[2] Correspondence extended from June 21st to October 27th, 1911.
[3] *Church Times*, August 18th, December 8th, 1911; April 12th, May
17th, September 27th, 1912; November 21st, 1913.

though it had a series of articles in the spring of 1907 on the Church and Socialism, which dealt with the subject as follows:

1. On the beginnings of Socialism in the Church of England. After pointing out the vagueness of the term 'Socialism' this described the rise of Maurice's group.

2. On the Socialism of Maurice and Kingsley. This tended to emphasize the conservative aims and outlook of the group.

3. Practical Results of the Socialism of Maurice and Kingsley. This continued to stress their divergence from Marxist ideas and their emphasis on individual reformation. Their chief service had been in bringing social classes together.

4. This dealt with the C.S.U. and came to the conclusion that it had nothing to do with Socialism and would do well to say so.

5. Extremer Forms of Socialism in the Church of England. This dealt, critically, with Headlam and the Guild of St Matthew, rejecting his 'secular' interpretation of the teaching of Jesus. The conclusion was that the Guild did not count for much.

6. Prominent Socialists were quoted against Christianity and against the Christian Socialists.

7. New Testament texts apparently favourable to Socialism were alleged to be misunderstood.

8. Socialism and the Family. Hostility to Christian marriage was considered to be sufficiently characteristic of Socialism to serve as a warning to Christians.

9. The same, continued. The Christian idea of marriage was defended against criticisms, and other Socialist ideas condemned were the taking of children from their parents and the 'perilous doctrine' of contraception.

10. Socialism, the Church and the Wage-Earners. This rejected the Marxist doctrine of wages and argued that Socialism would fail for lack of incentives. It then rather curiously turned to patriotism, which Socialists rejected, and ended with a sentimental peroration about 'the village lad who died for England.'

11. The final article advocated social reform as the antidote for Socialism.

Perhaps more useful than any of the articles was a bibliography preceding them, running to well over 100 works.[1]

During the period when the articles were being published another example of an attitude of mind which was disposed to make concessions but withdraw them almost as they were made was an

[1] *Church Family Newspaper*, March 15th to May 31st, 1907.

item praising the C.S.U. demand for a 'living wage' while at the same time questioning the idea of legislation because of the difficulty of defining a fair wage and because of the danger of driving trade overseas. The regulation of wages was not necessarily impossible, but it had always proved very difficult. Again, the Church had a duty to the employed, but it seemed, to judge by this article, to be largely the duty of pointing out their vices.[1]

The series had an interesting aftermath in that it was attacked by the *Liberty Review*, the organ of the 'Liberty and Property Defence League,' for advocating plunder of the rich for the purpose of social reform, just as Philip Snowden advocated it in the interests of Socialism. The *Church Family Newspaper* thought the article 'curious and amusing,' and that only a 'microscopic minority' of the Conservative Party disapproved of graduated taxation.[2]

Contrary to the suspicions of the Liberty and Property Defence League, the *Church Family Newspaper* was not converted to Socialism, even by a statement issued by 100 clergy and ministers in its favour, and considered that nationalization was impracticable and would need a revolution, for if there was to be compensation, there would be an enormous burden of debt. The Pan-Anglican Congress attracted surprisingly little attention beyond the comment: 'The capture of the Pan-Anglican Conference by the Socialists has been keenly and justly resented.' An article contributed by Cunningham early in 1909 represented what may be called the view of the Right wing of the C.S.U. Socialism had high ideals, and if it could 'be brought to accept the leadership of Christ, it seems that enormous progress might be made for the ennobling of man and the service of God.' But the analogy between Socialism and Christianity was misleading:

> Whatever superficial resemblances there may be between Christian philanthropy and Socialistic schemes, I hold that Christianity is quite inconsistent with Socialism as a doctrine of life, and that those Christians who dally with Socialism are in danger of losing their hold on the very essentials of Christianity.

Socialism aimed at increasing enjoyment on earth, while Christianity was essentially spiritual and looked to another world. There was a disagreement on means as well as ends: 'Both aim at

[1] *Church Family Newspaper*, May 17th, 1907.
[2] Ibid., February 21st, 1908.

an improvement in society, but Socialists try to attain it by compelling other people to do their duty, Christianity by inducing every man to do his own.' In compulsion lay the danger of tyranny and of a deterioration of character because of the lessened scope for enterprise. Christians, it was insisted rather surprisingly, could not even co-operate with Socialists in denouncing the evils of society, since 'it is not specially incumbent on the Christian, as a Christian, to denounce what is evil,' and Christians should beware of 'undue haste.' Thus once again a friendly beginning led only to a hostile conclusion.[1]

Apart from the 1908 Pan-Anglican Congress, even the annual Church Congress showed an undue leaning to Socialism, according to the *Church Family Newspaper:* 'The "Socialism" Meeting has of late years been a somewhat startling feature of the Church Congress, and no fair expression of the views of the mass of Churchmen.' Fortunately 1909 saw an improvement, in that the opposite case had also been clearly put. After the autumn of 1909 there was nothing for nearly three years, and then J. E. C. Welldon, the Dean of Manchester, contributed an article on 'The Church and Democracy,' expressing sympathy not only with Christian Socialism, but even with the non-Christian type, because it contained Christian elements, and 'after all, the founder of Christianity was a working man. The first Christians were voluntary Socialists.' Nationalization might be difficult, but it was not anti-Christian, though Socialism was evil if it implied confiscation, violation of personal liberty, or destruction of family life. There could be a trade union tyranny, and strikes were inherently evil. The Church must point men away from selfish ambitions. There was a well-reasoned reply by Vernon Hartshorn, who found this article full of 'that kindly inconclusiveness with which so many representatives of the Christian Church deal with the labour problem.' The conflict was clear enough to demand that one should make a definite choice, not sit on the fence. The Church would lose her remaining influence with the working classes if she would not make up her mind 'upon definite schemes of social reform'. She did not believe that moral influence alone was sufficient in every sphere of life: why should it be the only means of progress in the economic? After several weeks Welldon made a rejoinder, repeating his admiration for the workers, and basing his case on the

[1] *Church Family Newspaper*, January 24th, January 31st, July 3rd, 1908; February 5th, 1909.

danger that Capital would be driven abroad. He claimed not to be
neutral, but to be on the side of the people, but strikes tended to
hurt the poor rather than the rich, and should be kept as a last
resort. The Church must not, like the House of Lords, separate
itself from the people, but there was much more scope for arbitration than Hartshorn admitted. At the end of the next year this
newspaper noted an appeal by Ramsay Macdonald to the Church
to show sympathy to the workers, commenting: 'This warning is
not unneeded ... We appeal to the Churchmen to do all in their
power to bring about a better understanding between employers
and employees.'[1]

The *British Weekly* showed little interest in the Christian
Socialist movement. It criticized Gore for combining Socialism
of a sort with Catholicism of a sort and not seeing the incompatibility between the democracy of the one and the autocracy of
the priesthood in the other. A little later there was an account of a
visit to the Guild of St Matthew, and the correspondent found
the enthusiasm of an Anglican guild for Shaw amusing. A year
later there was reference to the manifesto of Socialist clergy and
ministers, the *British Weekly* dwelling on the disputed question of
compensation.[2] Otherwise it was more interested in Socialism in a
general way than specifically in the Christian Socialist tradition.

The *Universe* was not really interested at all in Christian
Socialism. It welcomed a condemnation by the Bishop of Salford
of a Catholic Socialist Society in his diocese, and much later noted
with mixed feelings increasing interest on the part of Catholics in
social problems:

> Catholic social policy is in danger of becoming nothing more than
> a dilution of Shavian, Webbian and Fabian theories and doctrines,
> with the protecting word 'Catholic' prefixed to their undigested
> nostrums and their thin compound of quack specifics for the
> rehabilitation of the diseased members of the sick body politic.

A true social policy must start from a religious basis and not
merely repeat phrases such as 'the redistribution of wealth,' and
Catholics should favour a middle course between 'reaction and

[1] *Church Family Newspaper*, October 8th, 1909; June 7th, June 21st,
August 9th, 1912; December 12th, 1913.
[2] *British Weekly*, October 11th, December 27th, 1906; January 23rd,
1908.

upheaval.'[1] Otherwise there was practically no notice of the movement.

In the last decade before the first world war the Christian Socialist tradition showed no signs of coming to an end. It is true that the Socialism which was so described was becoming increasingly vague and indefinite, but on the other hand several developments were making some kind of Christian Socialism more important than ever in the life of the Church. For one thing the movement was no longer so closely associated with Anglo-Catholicism as it had been for some years previously, though Ritualism and Socialism often still went together. There was even a kind of Nonconformist Christian Socialism, better represented perhaps by Clifford's Fabian Tract, which with all its airiness obviously owed something to the old tradition of popular oratory beloved by Dissenters, than by Campbell's 'New Theology.' In the Church of England Christian Socialism was no longer the prerogative of people otherwise eccentric, but began to count among its adherents members of the hierarchy. The Roman Catholic Church lagged, but otherwise it is probably true to say that in 1914 Christian Socialism was stronger than it had ever been before. But it remained very much a minority movement; a minority movement so well-entrenched, especially in influential places, that it might sometimes give the completely false impression that it commanded the allegiance of a majority. To such an impression the Anglican press is a useful corrective; even in this sphere there was one achievement to the credit of the Christian Socialists: they could not be ignored, and the press was forced to devote a great deal of space to their refutation. But the attitude of the press was always a matter of too little and too late: it was always ready to concede the claims of the working classes of a generation ago, but never enthusiastic for those of the present day.

[1] *Universe*, December 25th, 1908; August 16th, 1912.

CHAPTER 5

RELATIONSHIPS OF THE CHURCHES AND THE SECULAR SOCIALIST MOVEMENT

U NSYMPATHETIC CONTEMPORARIES were inclined to protest that the Christian Socialists were not Christian, while historians are more of the opinion that they were not Socialists. It is worth-while therefore to turn to the main stream of the history of English Socialism and trace out the changing relationships between the secular Socialist movement and the Churches.

1 *The Catholic Revival and the Young England Movement*
The 'fifties and 'sixties were not especially important in the development of English Socialism, constituting a relatively peaceful era between the Chartist and Owenite phase and the emergence of new forms of Socialist theory in the 'seventies and 'eighties. But there were one or two features of present interest.
This was the time of the second phase of the Catholic revival. The Roman Catholic hierarchy was restored in 1850, but for many years the Roman Catholic Church was a less important influence in England, despite the conversions of Newman and Manning, than the Tractarian or Anglo-Catholic tradition. The work of social reform had for some decades been largely associated with the Evangelical school, and the Tractarians were at first theological and ecclesiastical in interest and had little concern with social problems. But by their emphasis on the corporate life of the Church against Evangelical individualism, and by their emphasis on the Middle Ages against the Capitalist philosophy of their own times, they opened a way for a possible *rapprochement* between religion and Socialism. They did not like Socialism, but neither did they like the prevailing Liberalism. Even Newman himself, though he is often regarded as an arch-reactionary, could be represented as a progressive thinker, for his *Essay on Development* (1845) brought a radical historicism into the whole theology of the Church, and in his writings on natural law he taught that scien-

242

tific laws were to be regarded only as approximations. This teaching might by analogy be extended to the social order. The Church, which recognizes the fact of development in its theology, is not necessarily averse to quite sweeping changes in the form of society, so long as they are of the right kind; and the extension of the concept of scientific law into the economic and social field, so fashionable at the time, and so useful an argument against those who protested on ethical grounds against aspects of contemporary society, would lose much of its force if scientific law as a whole was vaguer and less binding than Newtonian physics had held. There were thus features of Newman's teaching which ran counter to some of his main convictions, and despite his emphasis on authority it is possible to call him—with a little hyperbole—'a free and adventurous soul, a romantic ally of the liberal spirit he distrusted.'[1] But the Catholic reformers were far from being Socialists, and they had no doubts about the lawfulness of private property.

A political expression of the spirit represented by the Catholic revival was the Young England movement. The members of this group were a heterogeneous collection, and for the dominant member, Disraeli, there was perhaps more opportunism—a stick to beat Peel—than principle. The inspiration of the past, the sense of corporate life which the group found, or thought it found, in the Middle Ages, the attempt to unite the gentleman and the workman against the tradesman whose philosophy was increasingly dominant—all this could have a Socialist aspect. It was from here that William Morris started, and his early career is indicative of the atmosphere of the early 'fifties. Born in 1834, he was brought up in a family whose religion was 'of the normal type of a somewhat sterile Evangelicalism.'[2] He soon developed an interest in old Gothic churches, and was educated at Marlborough, a school with a High Church tradition which Morris left 'a pronounced Anglo-Catholic.' Partly under the influence of his sister, who married a High Church clergyman, he decided to enter the ministry. In 1854 he was on the point of joining the Roman Catholic Church, but changed his mind. The following year, influenced by Carlyle, Ruskin, and Kingsley, he planned a monastery to combine an ascetic life with the production of religious art, but the same year he and Burne-Jones, on holiday together in France, abandoned their idea of taking Orders. Such was the early spiritual struggle of

[1] Brinton, op. cit., 164.
[2] J. W. Mackail, *The Life of William Morris* (1899), I, 10.

the most prominent of later nineteenth-century English Socialists. Until he was approaching his fiftieth year Morris remained a Liberal, but how greatly his outlook differed from the predominant ethos of the Liberal Party can easily be seen.

The Young England group themselves were of course Tories. The most representative member of the group was John James Robert Manners (1818–1906), later the seventh Duke of Rutland. He helped to bring the group together about 1843, with the aim of leading the aristocracy to engage in the work of social reform and of opposing the Liberal philosophy. In 1843 he supported a motion by Lord Howick for an inquiry into the condition of England and the disaffection of the working classes. He urged national holidays, and the following year associated with Ashley in the campaign for a ten-hour day. He advocated the allocation of waste land for the use of agricultural workers. The group broke up largely over religious differences. Manners was sympathetic to the Tractarians and a close friend of Frederick William Faber, and although he never considered joining the Roman Catholic Church he shared with other Anglo-Catholics a desire to see better relations with the Vatican, and a fairer treatment for the Irish Catholics. The grant by the British Government to Maynooth College in 1845 and the repeal of the Corn Laws in 1846 were in line with this policy, but also provided too good an opportunity for Disraeli to ignore for attacking Peel on unpopular measures. The group therefore broke up. Manners lived right on into the next century, and great as was the pressure of the prevailing economic doctrine of the Manchester school the ideas of Tory democracy never completely succumbed.[1]

2 *The Owenite Tradition*

The Catholic revival and the Young England movement represent an island of resistance to the full tide of Radical and individualist ideas. A more definitely Socialist philosophy was still in the main confined to the followers of Robert Owen. Owen himself had little time for religion until his later years, and then it was in spiritualism and various unorthodox beliefs that he became interested, but some of his followers were Christians and even ministers of various creeds. James Elimalet Smith (1801–1857),[2] known as 'Shepherd' Smith, made a spiritual pilgrimage all his own. Start-

[1] For Manners see Charles Whibley, *Lord John Manners and his Friends* (2 vols., 1925).   [2] *Dict. Nat. Biog.*, s.v. Smith.

ing from the Church of Scotland, he became a 'Southcottian' and opened a chapel in London. He was converted to the views of Owen and travelled as an Owenite lecturer. Next he came to hold pantheistic views, and then became a follower of Fourier. Finally he achieved fame writing for the *Family Herald*, answering letters from correspondents, many of which he wrote himself. He has been described as vaguely 'Catholic' in outlook.[1] He looked for a 'general restoration of human society,' which he held would be equivalent to the Second Advent of Christ.[2]

Dr Arthur S. Wade, Vicar of Warwick, was 'a prop and pillar of militant Owenism,' and remarked that he would rather sink with the poor than rise with the rich.[3]

John Minter Morgan was an Anglican layman, influenced by Owen and also by the communistic society created by the Jesuits in Paraguay. Unlike most of the other supporters of Owen he saw a theological significance in Owenism, and quoted the Bible and Church history to show the strength of communal trends in Christianity. He demanded that economics should be subordinated to ethics.

Dr William King of Brighton, who has been mentioned previously as an advocate of co-operation, was also a follower of Owen, who distinguished the social and religious views of Owen and argued that a useful social innovation should not be rejected because of the religious outlook of its creator.

These Christian disciples of Owen had mostly flourished earlier than the period covered by this book, but their influence was not yet at an end.

The secularist tradition in Owenism was represented by Robert Buchanan (1813–1866), who lectured and wrote on Socialism and attacked the Church of England. He lectured in an Owenite 'Hall of Science' in Manchester and was prosecuted for charging for admission to lectures on Sundays, contrary to statute.

The hall was registered as a meeting-house for a society of

[1] Binyon, op. cit., 43.
[2] Ibid. Smith translated Henri de St Simon's *New Christianity*. There is a good deal about him in Richard K. P. Pankhurst's book *The Saint Simonians Mill and Carlyle* (N.D.), where however he is always referred to as Elishama Smith. The book deals chiefly with Saint Simonian contacts with Mill and Carlyle, but has a chapter on the 'New Christianity' which was an integral part of St Simon's teaching and foreshadowed the Comtian religion. (See Pankhurst, op. cit., 113ff.)
[3] Binyon, op. cit., 43.

dissenters called 'Rational Religionists,' the name used by Owenites, and Buchanan was fined for refusing to take the oaths demanded of dissenting ministers. As a religious society the Owenites were of course a legal fiction.

Charles Bray (1811–1884), an important figure in the history of English Socialism, promoted unsectarian schools, opposed to those belonging to the Church of England. Bray's sister-in-law Mary Hennell (1802–1843) who came of a Manchester Unitarian family, wrote an appendix to his *Philosophy of Necessity* in 1841, entitled *An Outline of the Various Social Systems and Communities which have been founded on the Principle of Co-operation.* Her brother Charles Christian Hennell wrote against Bray's anti-religious views.

3   Chartism

There was a close if not always happy link between Owenism and the Chartist movement, to which most of the leaders of the Church were unsympathetic. It has been said that: 'In the Ten Hour Movement and the Anti-Corn Law League the workers learned in the company of their middle and upper class champions how to campaign. In the Chartist movement they learned how to act alone: the Chartists having no friends higher than the rank of Baptists and Primitive Methodists.'[1] The Christian Socialists were more sympathetic than most clergy, but even they felt that Chartism was a misdirection of revolutionary fervour which ought to have been subordinated to the control of the Church. Among the Unitarians there were as usual sympathizers: James Stansfeld, John Fielden, John Bowring, J. W. Morris, Henry Solly, William Wrigley, and Ebenezer Elliott.[2] A curious and rather obscure movement was that known as 'Christian Chartism,' of which the founder was a very young man by the name of Arthur O'Neill. It was 'a protest against the exclusiveness and the Toryism of the Established Church, and against the repellent narrowness of some of the Dissenting bodies, notably of the Wesleyan Methodists.'[3] The most famous Chartist church was at Birmingham, run by O'Neill and John Collins, with occasional visits from Henry Vincent and others:

[1] C. R. Fay, *Great Britain from Adam Smith to the Present Day* (1928), 388.

[2] Holt, op. cit., 141.

[3] M. Hovell, *The Chartist Movement*, (Second edition, 1925), 200.

It consisted of a political association which studied democratic thought as laid down in the works of Cobbett, Hunt, Paine, and Cartwright, and a Church whose purpose was to further temperance, morality and knowledge. It had schools for children and for young men, and a sick club. O'Neill seems to have had no little success in the Birmingham area. He was on good terms with the working people and even with their employers. An iron-master in the district allowed him the use of a large room 'which was crowded to suffocation every Sabbath afternoon from half-past two till a quarter past four . . .'[1]

O'Neill's procedure was described by a Wesleyan minister who, like most of his fellows, 'was no friend to Chartism':

> O'Neill called himself a Christian Chartist and always began his discourse with a text, after the manner of a sermon; and some of our people went to hear him just to observe the proceedings and were shocked beyond description: there was unmeasured abuse of Her Majesty and the Constitution, about the public expenditure and radical doctrines of all kinds. They have a hymn-book of their own and affect to be a denomination of Christians. This is the way they gained converts here, by the name. There were very few political chartists here, but Christian Chartist was a name that took. It is almost blasphemy to prostitute the name of Christian to such purposes.[2]

But this account is no doubt biased.

During the strike of 1842 a Government commissioner attended a 'Christian Chartist Tea Party' at Birmingham, at which O'Neill spoke. The commissioner reported that it caused him 'pain' to attend, but his review of the 'sermon' quotes O'Neill only as urging his hearers to form a new Church, 'free from the principles of Mammon and active in support of the struggles of the people.' O'Neill was in fact a moderate. Henry Vincent preached regularly at a Chartist church at Bath, and, having abandoned his earlier violent opinions, fervently commended temperance: 'In fact "temperance Chartism" was in the way of becoming a regular cult, until, along with Christian Chartism and "Knowledge Chartism," it came under the ban of O'Connor, to whom knowledge and temperance were alike alien.' Christian Chartism also flourished in Scotland, notably at Paisley and Partick.[3]

The connexion with the temperance movement is again a

---

[1] Hovell, op. cit., 200f. Source of quotation not given.
[2] Ibid., 201, quoting *Parl. Papers 1843*, xiii, p. cxxxii.
[3] Ibid., 201ff.

feature of the Labour movement at this time, showing how far
the reforming spirit associated with the churches, and especially
with the Nonconformist churches, was shared with working-class
movements not predominantly religious.

Yet in a wider sense Chartism itself could be considered a
religious movement. A

> strain of exalted mysticism gave force and fervour to many
> Chartists . . . Even among the doubters there were elements of
> spiritual emotion, sometimes extinguished by environment, but at
> other times kindled into flame by favourable conditions. Thomas
> Cooper, a Methodist preacher in his youth, the missionary of free-
> thought in his mid-career, the unwearied vindicator of the Christian
> faith in his old age, belonged at one time or another to all the chief
> religious types of Chartism.[1]

The Chartist churches 'never comprehended all the religious
fervour of the Chartist fold.'

Besides some support from the established denominations, and
the rather inchoate religious aspirations of the Chartists themselves
the movement attracted the sympathy of some members of the
traditionally radical Society of Friends. Henry Vincent, mentioned above, lived from 1813 to 1878. He was an active leader in
the Chartist movement, whose sympathies belonged primarily to
the Society of Friends, though he was not formally a member and
on Sundays he was often occupied in preaching in Nonconformist
churches. Joseph Sturge (1793–1859),[2] a well-known figure among
the Quakers, had played an important part in the anti-Corn Law
and anti-slavery campaigns. He came out in support of Chartism
and stood for Parliament in 1842. His aim was to win middle-class
support for the movement, but he gradually withdrew owing to the
dominance of the more violent elements, and devoted himself to
philanthropy. Even W. E. Forster (1818–1886),[3] later regarded as a
very conservative Gladstonian, started as a Radical. He was
acquainted with Owen, Thomas Cooper, and Maurice, and was
broadly sympathetic to Chartism. In 1848 he addressed a meeting
at Bradford on behalf of the 'moral force' element. He too was a
Quaker by upbringing.

Other Chartist supporters represented a curious assortment of
religious viewpoints. Capell Lofft (1806–1873), a scholar and

---

[1] Hovell, op. cit., 308f.

[2] Henry Richard, *Memoirs of Joseph Sturge*, (1864).

[3] Sir T. W. Reid, *Life of the Rt. Hon. William Edward Forster*, (1888).

versifier who portrayed the history and future of Chartism dramatically in an epic called *Ernest* (1839), was brought to a realization of the importance of religion while travelling and studying the Bible in Devonshire, and like John Wesley he was influenced towards his conversion by William Law's *Serious Call.* William Sharman Crawford (1781–1861), an Irish Protestant landlord, advocated Roman Catholic emancipation and legal reforms. In 1835 he was elected to Parliament as an advanced Radical, supporting the Chartists and helping to draft Chartist bills. He was bitterly hostile to O'Connell, but a consistent advocate of Roman Catholic rights, although he voted for the Ecclesiastical Titles Bill in 1850. Thomas Cooper, who has already been mentioned, lived from 1805 to 1892. He came from Leicester and was a Methodist local preacher as well as a prominent and extreme Chartist. But he deviated into the freethought movement and was active in it till 1856. Then, when he was due to lecture on the characteristic Victorian theme of 'Sweden and the Swedes,' he found he could not begin his lecture but gave instead a personal testimony:

> I told them my great feeling of error was that while I had perpetually been insisting on the observance of a moral life, in all my public teachings for some years, I had neglected to teach the right foundation of morals—the existence of the Divine Moral Governor, and the fact that we should have to give up our account to him, and receive his sentence, in a future state.[1]

But he is emphatic that at this stage he taught only Theism, and his conversion was only completed in 1858 when he escaped uninjured in a railway accident near Nuneaton. After contemplating a return to the Methodists he became instead a Baptist, and spent the remainder of his life lecturing on Christian evidences.

Most of the above were active in one way or another after 1850, but in most cases their main contribution to the Socialist movement was made earlier.

4 *Comment on Socialism in the Religious Press down to the Period of the Second Reform Act*

After the decline of Chartism a period of quiescence set in, and the religious press reflects the general lack of interest in Socialism. In the *Guardian* there was very little. In 1858 there was a review of

[1] *The Life of Thomas Cooper, written by himself* (1877 edition), 353.

Louis Blanc's *1848: Historical Revolutions: inscribed to Lord Normanby*.[1] It was surprisingly favourable, explaining that Blanc held 'a theory which a political economist like Mr John Stuart Mill looks on with respect.' His theories had tended to produce disorder, but this was not his intention, and he showed a welcome hostility to Proudhon and Blanqui. In 1862 Ruskin's attempt, in *Unto This Last*, to make a place for personality in economics produced the comment: 'Really, if this is not nonsense, there is no such thing in the world,' and the author was accused of 'utter ignorance' of political economy.[2]

The *Nonconformist* had little to say on this issue, beyond an article in 1856 claiming that much of the criticism of the Chartists was mere bias, though the Chartists were foolish to accept such leaders as Frost and Ernest Jones.[3]

The *Tablet* had some extreme things to say about Socialism, mostly looking to Europe. It was the work of 'demons' against 'the fair and rich edifice of European society.' Its real aim was to destroy the Papacy, the very heart of civilization, and it had made a start—a somewhat limited start, one would think—with the expulsion of the Jesuits from certain Cantons of Switzerland: 'Till Europe is thoroughly freed from this pest, statesmen can neither have adequate leisure nor power to address themselves to meet those very questions of legislation for the labouring classes, of which society requires the solution . . .' Thus social reform was used as an argument against Socialism; but more frequently the argument was purely negative. According to the title of one leader, Socialism had been 'an exploded theory two thousand years ago'—in that Aristotle had disproved it. In France there were 'Socialist atrocities' and 'horrible Socialist dangers.' The *Tablet* supported the Crimean War, but only after some heart-searching arising from reflections on the good services of the Russian Government against Socialism. Britain ought not to give sanctuary to Kossuth, Mazzini and Ledru-Rollin, who were partners in a Socialist conspiracy to murder Louis Napoleon and establish a dictatorship. Later there were some rather different comments. There was a fierce attack on political economy, which was blamed for all the troubles of the age, including defeats in the war, and it was identified with the sin of avarice. It was also closely allied with Protestantism. Disturbances in Hyde Park were

---

[1] *Guardian*, May 26th, 1858.   [2] Ibid., August 27th, 1862.
[3] *Nonconformist*, September 24th, 1856.

due to Protestantism and the greed of Capitalists. There was a surprising attack on the London press for making fun of Chartist demands for Parliamentary reform—but there is an easy explanation of this sudden Radicalism—the importance of reform for Ireland. The Irish question often made the Roman Catholic press quite revolutionary in sentiment.[1]

The Socialist movement of this period, chiefly Owenite and Chartist, was strongly influenced by religion, though much of it was of a highly unorthodox kind. In the Church of England Christian Socialism had some contacts with the secular movement, though not enough to exert much influence over it. Evangelicalism might still appear an alternative dynamic force, as in the case of William Booth, suggesting a different approach to the distresses of the age. Nonconformity, a powerful influence in many working-class endeavours, was rather detached from Socialism, except for a few groups on the extreme of Dissent, such as Unitarians and Quakers. The Roman Catholic Church still regarded Socialism from the Continental standpoint, where it appeared as an aggressively anti-religious, and perhaps especially anti-Papal, movement.

5 The Revival of Interest in Socialism

For most of the mid-Victorian period Socialism was in eclipse. The decline of Chartism and Owenism and the growth of prosperity and the newer type of trade unionism, which was prepared to make terms with Capitalism, made the revolutionary fervour of the previous generation seem altogether outdated. The Commune of Paris gave a more sinister flavour than ever to the term, and the activities of the International and Karl Marx and his colleagues and rivals within it furthered the impression that Socialism was something foreign, and that England's isolation from the instabilities of Europe was appropriate in this sphere also.

The revival of Socialism began with the foundation of the Democratic Federation (later the Social Democratic Federation— the S.D.F.) in 1880. Hyndman was a Marxist, of his own peculiar type, and he shared Marx's hostility to religion, extending his antipathy to the Christian Socialists. His attitude to religion made the S.D.F. even weaker than it might otherwise have been, since most of the active leaders of the working classes were Christians

---

[1] *Tablet*, February 15th, May 10th, December 20th, 1851; February 25th, 1854; May 26th, July 7th, July 14th, October 13th, 1855; May 10th, September 20th, 1856.

of one sort or another, and the disciples of Maurice were generally respected by the workers.

The foundation of the S.D.F. was symptomatic, for in the 'eighties Socialism again became a most prominent topic of public discussion. It was felt that there was a pervasive atmosphere of Socialism, albeit undefined. The science of political economy was changing its character, becoming less sure of the rigid and universal validity of its laws and more ready to admit the significance of ethical criteria.[1] The influence of German historicism suggested that the existing economic system might be changing into a different form; a conception which through Arnold Toynbee came to contribute to the distinctive position of the Fabian Society, which was also guided by the work of Cunningham and Ashley. P. H. Wicksteed, a Unitarian minister, was one of the outstanding economists of the day, and a potent force in this change of outlook. He was Dunkin lecturer in sociology at Manchester College, Oxford, probably the first person to hold any position of this kind in a theological college. He gained in importance from his influence on Shaw.

The prevailing interest in questions on the borderline of ethics and economics as well as the vagueness with which they were conceived is well illustrated by a curious incident recorded in the biography of Bishop Fraser. In December 1879 the *Contemporary Review* printed a letter from Ruskin claiming that he had publicly challenged 'the Bishops of England generally, and by name the Bishop of Manchester, to say whether usury was or was not according to the will of God,' and had received no answer. Fraser replied that he had never heard of the challenge, and that the answer depended upon the meaning of the word. 'Covetousness' meant taking more than one's fair share; in the parable of the talents usury was commended rather than condemned. Fraser went on to quote various types of loans at interest which he considered to be for the common good. Ruskin replied with a very long and

---

[1] Mark Blaug, in his *Ricardian Economics* (1958) considers that the 'last treatise in the classical tradition' was J. E. Cairnes's *Leading Principles of Political Economy Newly Expounded* (1874), a work whose numerous modifications of established doctrines opened the way to 'historism' (sic) (p. 214). Blaug comments: 'The amazing thing is not that Ricardian economics survived but that it lasted down to the 1870s long after it had become palpably incongruent with reality and top-heavy with the infusion of antithetical ideas' (p. 229). The beginning of the end was marked by W. S. Jevons's *Theory of Political Economy* (1871).

bitter rejoinder in a tone of heavy irony, which Fraser thought 'more like the ravings of a lunatic than anything else.' The same vagueness appears in Fraser's address to Convocation in 1880: 'It would be found that every panacea involved some kind of Socialism. But it would be found as surely that Christianity would beat Socialism, and that all that was sound in Socialism was Christian.'[1]

Another leading cleric who was not unsympathetic to the change of mood was Cardinal Manning. In 1885 he met Henry George and discussed with him the significance of property. Manning argued that the law of property was a law of nature and of Christianity, and understood George not to deny this, but to be challenging abuse of the law. He spoke favourably of George and of his book *Social Problems*, not having read *Progress and Poverty*, and George thought mistakenly that he had converted Manning. Such a discussion indeed left much room for interpretations. Manning also expressed his sympathy with Dr McGlynn, an American Catholic priest who had fallen foul of the church authorities for his vigorous support of George, though he could not excuse McGlynn's attacks on the hierarchy. In 1888 Manning and the American Cardinal Gibbons helped to avert the placing of *Progress and Poverty* on the Index. After the dock strike of 1889 Manning wrote to Lord Buxton: 'I have been turning over the strike matters, and the more I think the more I am on the side of labour. Labour and skill are capital as much as gold and silver. Gold and silver are dependent on labour and skill, but labour and skill are independent *in limine*.' Leo XIII's Encyclical *Rerum Novarum* (1891) was produced partly under the influence of Manning and in some measure reflected his views. In it Socialism was condemned, but a sufficient sympathy was shown for the ambitions of the working classes to win the approval of some of their leaders. Ben Tillett wrote to Manning:

> I have just been reading the Pope's letter—a very courageous one indeed, one that will test good Catholics much more effectively than any exhortation to public worship. As you know, some of us would disagree very strongly with many of the strictures laid upon Socialists. These are minor matters. The Catholic sympathy abounds in a generous strength. I hardly think our Protestant prelates would dare utter such wholesome doctrine.[2]

[1] Hughes, *James Fraser*, 250ff., 305, 316.
[2] Leslie, op. cit., 150ff., 156f., 163ff.

6 *The Fabian Society*

In English Socialism one of the most important events of the revival in the 'eighties was the foundation of the Fabian Society in 1884. In the transformation of the dynamic of English society from religious to secular objectives the Fabians played an important part, but the first few years of the society's life were interesting in that it was poised rather uncertainly before several alternatives. It might have been an ethical rather than a political society, since it was an offshoot of the 'Fellowship of the New Life,' which rested upon the principle of 'the subordination of material things to spiritual.'[1] Frank Podmore, one of the founders, was interested in psychical research and spiritualism, and he had a father and a brother in the ranks of the clergy. Podmore and Pease, the historian of the society, came together through what Pease calls a common interest in 'ghost-hunting.'[2] The idealism of the Fellowship overflowed into the society, and for some of its early members 'Christian Socialism opened the way to salvation.'[3] Much of the early support came from the Guild of St Matthew and members of the other similar groups, including Headlam, Olivier, C. L. Marson, and W. E. Moll, and Bernard Shaw later satirized the early mood, commenting that 'in 1883 we were content with nothing less than the prompt "reconstruction of society in accordance with the highest moral possibilities".'[4] At the Fabian Conference of 1886 the National Secular Society was among the bodies represented, but Headlam also 'spoke for Christian Socialism and the Guild of St Matthew.'[5] The first of the Fabian Tracts, dated 1884 and drafted by W. L. Phillips, was 'remarkable as containing a sneer at Christianity, the only one to be found in the publications of the society.'[6] The 'sneer' was rhetorical: 'Teach, preach and pray to all eternity in your schools and churches: it will avail you nothing until you have swept away this blind idol of Competition . . .' Indeed the author was inclined somewhat readily to assume the mantle of a minor prophet and draw denunciations from the Bible:

> You who live dainty and pleasant lives, reflect that your ease and luxury are paid for by the misery and want of others! Your super-fluities are the parents of their poverty. Surely all humanity is not

[1] E. R. Pease, *History of the Fabian Society* (1916), 32.
[2] Ibid., 28.   [3] Ibid., 25.
[4] *Fabian Tract 41: The Fabian Society: Its Early History*, 1892 (by Bernard Shaw), 3.
[5] Ibid., 1of.   [6] Pease, op. cit., 39.

burnt out of you by the gold your fathers left you! Come out from your ease and superfluities and help us![1]

Fortunately or unfortunately the Fabian Society did not for long speak the language of a latter-day, and perhaps not greatly inspired, Amos, and the proportion of sentences ending with exclamation marks rapidly decreased. Sidney Webb and others had discovered a new truth: that it was far more effective in the modern era to convince the prosperous that the time-spirit was active against them than to proclaim that the Lord was angry with them.

It was in the 'nineties that the Fabian Society blossomed forth into full vigour. Shaw considered that Socialism continued to be on the whole divergent from conventional religious belief:

> It must be added that though the tradition that Socialism excludes the established creeds was overthrown by the Fabians, and the claim of the Christian Socialists to rank with the best of us was insisted on faithfully by them, the Fabian leaders did not break the tradition in their own practice.

The contention that 'Socialists are atheists' was ridiculous, but the Fabian essayists did not themselves attend church—they were too busy preaching themselves:

> To describe them as irreligious in view of their work would be silly; but until Hubert Bland towards the end of his life took refuge in the Catholic Church, and Mrs Besant devoted herself to Theosophy, no leading Fabian found a refuge for his soul in the temples of any established denomination.[2]

But this account has a characteristically Shavian bias. Dearmer and Headlam were both members of the executive for part of this period, and even in Shaw's own account Headlam appears as an active and prominent member of the society. The reference quoted above indeed bears the marks of prejudice in itself, a prejudice against religion in general, but especially against 'any established denomination.' While Annie Besant 'devoted herself' to Theosophy, Hubert Bland 'took refuge' in the Catholic Church, which sounds a less creditable procedure.

The Fabian Tracts as a platform for the preaching of Christian Socialism have been considered in the preceding chapter, but there

---

[1] *Fabian Tract 1: Why are the Many Poor?*, 3.
[2] Bernard Shaw, in Pease, op. cit., 264f.

were many more casual references to religion in other tracts. One by Sir Oliver Lodge came back to the question of the land, with something of the same almost mystical approach which seemed to many people appropriate to the topic; the hope for corporate ownership 'feels to me almost like part of the meaning of that great prayer "Thy Kingdom come"; and if so we are again not far away from the atmosphere of Christianity.'[1] In 1906 a tract attacked sectarian disputes over education: 'Socialists have no sympathy with the quaint individualist superstition that it is wicked to make a man pay for public institutions unless he individually approve of everything that is done in them.' The solution to the problem was to make school education purely secular.[2] One tract, called 'The Secret of Rural Depopulation,' was violently anti-clerical. The parsons were said to be a joke in the villages, and it was a common saying that the public-house sign 'The Farmer's Man' ought to be hung outside the parsonage, for the prosperous farmers became churchwardens and were the 'Aaron and Hur who hold up the hands of Moses,' and hence had to be treated deferentially. Everybody went to church in a village, but 'religion, as a rule of conduct or a motive power, is absolutely non-existent.' The Church had missed her opportunity: 'For many, many years the position of Moses lay open to the acceptance of the Church. All she had to do was to qualify by slaying an Egyptian or two, by ranging herself definitely on the side of the oppressed. But the fear of families, as Job says, is too much for her.' The Church had killed the old village band, because it was too independent, and 'the guns of the Church, directed by the landed interest, range unobstructed over a plain of dead and flat submission.' Dissent was useless, because the 'old Puritan spirit' had been 'squeezed out of it.'[3] The author was a lively stylist, but it is evident that he was given to exaggeration, and it is curious to find a Socialist publication which wholly ignores agricultural trade unionism.

Tract 72, on 'The Moral Aspects of Socialism,' by Sidney Ball, looked forward to a Comtian religion based upon the 'solidarity of mankind.'[4] A survey of the Fabian outlook called *Twentieth Century Politics: A Policy of National Efficiency*, by Sidney Webb, appeared at the beginning of the new century. It attacked 'nineteenth century Liberalism' for 'thinking in individuals' and seeing the world as consisting of 'independent Roundheads' pursuing

[1] *Fabian Tract 121*, 6.   [2] Ibid., *127*, 10f.
[3] Ibid., *118*, 14ff.   [4] Ibid., *72*, 23.

abstract rights. Thus it opposed state churches on the basis of an argument which would end all corporate action, that it was wrong to make people support institutions they did not individually approve. Such an attitude was 'part of the characteristically Whig conception of the citizen's contribution to the expenses of the social organization, as a bill paid by a private man for certain specific commodities which he has ordered and purchased for his own use.' This was 'administrative Nihilism,' and its advocates had a 'destructive revolutionary tradition' in their bones: 'They will reform nothing unless it can be done at the expense of their enemies. Moral superiority, virtuous indignation, are necessaries of political life to them: a Liberal reform is never simply a social means to a social end, but a campaign of Good against Evil.'[1]

Such a passage is interesting proof that the Fabians were right in believing that they were more like Tories than old-fashioned Radicals, who were indeed always filled with moral indignation. But two things should be added. On the one hand the Fabians more often found themselves allies than opponents of the very Radicals they mocked. And on the other hand Socialists were often even in principle suspiciously like these very Radicals. Nearly all the criticisms Webb makes of 'Liberalism' were true also of Primitive Methodist trade union leaders, who were building the real Labour Party, and even of Keir Hardie, who was leading it. The subsequent history of the Labour movement has been a synthesis of three things: an economic theory; bread-and-butter empirical demands for better conditions for the working classes; and the highly vocal indignation of moral idealism. Webb knew all about Radicalism, and saw it with clear and disenchanted vision; but did he ever understand the Labour movement he helped to make? There is a certain refreshment in turning from the cant of the immediate past to the cant of the next generation, and Webb was always up-to-date. He scornfully dismissed 'nineteenth-century Liberalism' when the nineteenth century had barely finished, and in rejecting ethical considerations he showed himself to be a true prophet of the new age. It is not after all so surprising that he ended by finding in Stalin's Soviet Union a 'new civilization.' A 'Policy of National Efficiency' was Stalin's aim too.

[1] *Fabian Tract 108*, 4f.

7   *The Religious History of Beatrice Webb*

The religious development of one Socialist, and some interesting illustrations of the decline of a religious outlook on life, can be traced in the biography of Beatrice Webb. Both her grandfathers were Nonconformists, members of Parliament, friends of Cobden and Bright, and supporters of the Anti-Corn Law League. Her paternal grandfather was, 'as a leading Unitarian,' a founder of London University.[1] Her father started as a Unitarian, but 'by middle life he was already attending Anglican services—and being asked to read the lessons!—and disapproving strongly of Disraeli's Reform Act.'[2] In his struggle with sin he had 'two powerful aids—his wife and God,' but he had a very simple faith, expressed even in maturity by the use of childish prayers. Beatrice did not approve of his heroes: '. . . He was a fanatical admirer of Burke and Carlyle and John Henry Newman—an oddly assorted trio, proving, I think that his preferences were inspired by emotional thought rather than pure reason.'[3] Much of Beatrice Webb is in this comment: the vaguely disapproving judgement on her father that he did not choose his enthusiasms by 'pure reason' like herself; and her typically obtuse failure to notice that she was listing a trio of 'reactionaries'—men literally in reaction against the disruptive tendencies of their own age. Her husband and her father shared at least one thing: a distaste for traditional Radicalism. Her mother was pious, and spent much time in religious study and practice, but she held rationalistic and Utilitarian ideas of man inconsistent with her 'mystical cravings.' Another member of the family was Martha Mills, her mother's companion, who held a 'primitive, if not barbaric' creed, that of a Particular Baptist, but only because she was brought up to it. In reality her life was guided by an intense personal devotion to Jesus and a conviction that all that really counted was love. Both the Potter parents went to church, and the girls attended casually, with no pressure on them to do so, and the atmosphere of the home was 'peculiarly free-thinking,' with no restrictions on reading or conversation. Among family friends were Bishop Ellicott and Cardinal Manning —but also Herbert Spencer.

In childhood and youth Beatrice was absorbed with religion. She quotes a writing produced when she was about ten, in which

---

[1] Beatrice Webb, *My Apprenticeship* (1926), 2.

[2] M. Cole, *Beatrice Webb* (1945), 11.

[3] Beatrice Webb, op. cit., 10.

she lamented her great sins and her 'intellectual difficulties of faith,' and a couple of years later she was rejecting authority and 'trying to gain a firm belief' for herself, asserting her determination to 'work, work, until I have.' She was sorry she had ever gone off the path of 'orthodox religion,' but since she had wandered, she had to think out her own faith. She attended a 'fashionable girls' school' in Bournemouth, and sought 'mental security in traditional Christianity,' becoming an earnest, and Low Church, candidate for Confirmation, though troubled by doubts on the Atonement. Perhaps she was wrong, she reflected, to spend all her time studying the Old Testament. She confided her difficulties about the Atonement to her spiritual director, who lent her a book on the subject.

Even in her precocious childhood she sought a possible alternative to Christianity in a religion of science. She read Spencer, Winwood Reade, and Comte, and was friendly with Frederic Harrison, but at this stage she could sum up her conclusion in words her father used to Spencer: 'Won't work, my dear Spencer, won't work.' Indeed this philosopher lost influence over her, and himself lost confidence as he came to realize that natural laws were not always beneficent. Beatrice thought the religion of science less self-centred than Christianity, and gained from Spencer the idea that beauty and mystery could remain when orthodox religion was abandoned, but she found the religion of science inadequate in face of suffering: a happy future was no compensation to past generations. In 1876 she lost her hold on 'orthodox Christianity,' partly merely as a result of growing up, but also because of the discovery, shared with many of her generation, of Oriental religions. Later in life she criticized Christianity for its individualism, but at this stage she simply reacted against the claim of one religion to universal validity as against Buddhism and other great religions. But she retained her faith in prayer and attributed to its practice her survival of mental and spiritual troubles. She was influenced by Brian Houghton Hodgson (1800–1894), a neighbour of the Potters who was interested in Oriental religions, and she found in study of his books that for her Hinduism threw into the shade 'the barbaric Jehovah of the Jews and the mean doings of their kings . . .' Buddha seemed superior to Christ, and his renunciation of the world more complete than that of the Christians, and Buddhist philosophy seemed more in accord with that of modern science—that is, of Herbert Spencer. But she did not become a convert to Indian religion: only away from Christianity. There was something selfish in all the great religions, and none of them recognized the real insignificance of man, or taught that men should simply obey natural laws, without hope of reward. But it was clear to her 'that we are at a very early period of man's existence, and that we have only just arrived at the true basis of knowledge: and that bright and glorious days are in store for our successors on this earth.'[1]

Despite this cheerful conviction, she felt some reaction from her abandonment of Christianity. If human life was to end in 'complete dissolution' it was not worth living. Though she did not follow Annie Besant's course of becoming a convert to Oriental religion, she came within sight of following Hubert Bland's and 'taking refuge' in the Roman Catholic Church. In 1880, watching Mass in St. Peter's at Rome she regretted the loss of her faith, though guiltily convinced that 'there was a great deal of mere emotion in it.' She attempted to preserve something from the wreck, and like Thomas Hardy spent much time wishing that Christianity was after all true: 'I tried afterwards to work out in my mind the theory of the Roman Catholic faith as it might be accepted by the agnostic,' analysing her attitude to 'something above and around us which is worthy of absolute devotion and devout worship,' differing from the Spencerian 'Unknowable' because 'the unknowable has no qualities, and cannot be an object for feeling.' God was worshipped by Protestant and Catholic alike, but Protestantism was too rationalist in spirit and fell into scepticism. In contrast Catholicism, while not rejecting logic, offered the Church as 'the supreme reason ... You do not renounce the authority of reason, but only that of your individual reason; and this only on a question which it has already proved its incompetency to deal with to the satisfaction of the rest of your nature.' The temptation to commit 'this intellectual (and perhaps moral) suicide is strong to one whose life without a religious faith is unbearable,' but in joining the Catholic Church 'you would be obliged to stifle your sense of what was right as well as of what was true.' Such reflections show that at least at this stage of her life Beatrice Potter was a profoundly religious woman, though she found no resting-place in the accepted systems of her day. Spencer compared her to George Eliot, and both are examples of the honest doubt so characteristic of the time. George Eliot sublimated her

[1] Beatrice Webb, op. cit., 97.

religious emotions (and perhaps her guilt at transgressing the moral code she affected to ignore) into the portrayal of impossibly good men and women; Beatrice Webb into doing good to the working classes. It is a matter of personal choice whether one regards Maggie Tulliver and Adam Bede or the Minority Report on the Poor-Law as the greater achievement.

Beatrice faced another crisis on the death of her mother, and though she felt sure there was no future life she also had 'a new and wondrous faith . . . in goodness—in God. I must pray, I do pray and I feel better for it; and more able to put aside all compromise with worldliness and to devote myself with single-heartedness to my duty.' She returned for the moment to the Church, to Communion, seeing the sacrifice of the Body and Blood of Christ as symbols of self-sacrifice, and regarded her six years of absence from Communion as 'years of more or less dreary materialism.' She now returned to a religion which was 'an instinctive faith in a mysterious goodness,' and to prayer, 'communion with an all-pervading spiritual force.' But this was only a temporary reaction, and much of the interest of her life is as an example of the transfer of idealism from religion to social service, one of the outstanding features of the later nineteenth century. It seemed to Beatrice that the most useful social service for her was social investigation, and this launched her on her career. Both the Webbs became less sympathetic to religion, and in the early years of the twentieth century their attitude was one of 'non-militant atheism.' But she continued to regard her work as a mission, and her idealism was sustained, at least for a time, by 'faith in the Great Spirit, before whom all things are equally small.' She tried to defend religion against Eleanor Marx, who dismissed it as 'an immoral illusion' and refused 'to recognize the beauty of the Christian religion,' and during her investigation into sweating in 1888 she found prayer a source of strength and that sitting in St. Paul's Cathedral gave a 'wonderful restfulness.'[1]

She was conscious of the importance of the Christian Socialist tradition, quoting Samuel Barnett to the effect that much social progress resulted from a 'sense of sin'—this being understood of a collective rather than an individual feeling. Such an attitude was on the other hand quite lacking in the Charity Organization Society, which fell short of the Christian ideal of indiscriminate love. She was fascinated by the Barnetts, giving brilliant descriptions

[1] Beatrice Webb, op. cit., 283f., 301.

of them, and adding the curious comment: 'In religious faith
Mr Barnett is an idealistic Christian without dogma, and Mrs
Barnett is an agnostic with idealism; in social faith, the man is a
Christian Socialist, the woman an individualist.'[1]

It is perhaps more unexpected to find a Nonconformist influence
in the development of her ideas, but some of the most interesting
sections of her autobiography describe her contacts with Dissent in
Bacup, which she visited in 1883 as 'Miss Jones,' a farmer's
daughter from South Wales. She wrote to her father:

> I have spent the day in the chapels and schools. After dinner a
> dissenting minister dropped in and I had a long talk with him; he is
> coming for a cigarette this evening after chapel. He told me that in all
> the chapels there was a growing desire among the congregation to have
> political and social subjects treated in the pulpit, and that it was very
> difficult for a minister, now, to please. He also remarked that, in
> districts where co-operation amongst the workmen (in industrial
> enterprise) existed, they were a much more independent and free-
> thinking set . . . Of course, I am just in the centre of the dissenting
> organization, and as our host is the chapel keeper and entertains all
> the ministers who come here, I hear all about the internal manage-
> ment. Each chapel, even of the same denomination, manages its own
> affairs; and there are monthly meetings of all the members (male and
> female) to discuss questions of expenditure, etc. In fact each chapel
> is a self-governing community, regulating not only chapel matters
> but overlooking the private life of its members.
>
> One cannot help feeling what an excellent thing these dissenting
> organizations have been for educating this class in self-government.
> I can't help thinking, too, that one of the best preventives against the
> socialistic tendency of the coming democracy would lie in local
> government; which would force the respectable working man to
> consider political questions as they come up in local administration.

She wanted to ensure that 'when the religious channel is closed
up,' the 'spare energy' of the workers would go into practical
social improvement, not theoretical politics.[2] The absorption of the
Bacup workers with religion reminded her of the single-mindedness of Birmingham Radicals in their politics, and this seemed a
symbol of the transfer of devotion from religion to politics, with
just as much dogmatism among the Radicals, and the Radical
Programme as the equivalent of the Bible. A few years later she
visited Bacup again, and found the town still religious, though less

[1] Beatrice Webb, op. cit., 180, 198ff, 203ff., 213.
[2] Ibid., 160ff.

so. The young men still went to chapel, but no longer taught in the Sunday School or Bible Class, preferring to read books from the free 'Co-op' library. She wrote to her father again about the chapels: 'The religious socialism of the dissenting communities is very remarkable, each circle forming a "law unto itself" to which the individual must submit or be an outcast.' She commented on the peace and contentment of Bacup, and added:

> But one wonders what will happen when the religious feeling of the people is undermined by advancing scientific culture; for though the 'Co-op.' and the chapel at present work together, the secularism of the 'Co-op.' is half unconsciously recognized by earnest chapel-goers as a rival attraction to the prayer-meeting and the Bible class . . . Labouchère seems the principal favourite—a man they would not tolerate as a 'Co-op.' or 'chapel' leader.[1]

There was a new minister at the chapel:

> The minister, one of the 'new college men,' with measured phrases and long words; a poor exchange for the old-fashioned minister 'called of God from among the people,' no more educated than his fellows but rising to leadership by force of character. This man is more of a politician than a preacher—a politician of the shallowest and most unreal type, using endless words and not touching facts.[2]

Summing up her impression of Bacup she wrote in her diary that there she 'felt as if I were living through a page of Puritan history.' She noted the religious devotion of the people: 'And I realized the strength of the motive which enlightened people believe is passing away. I realized the permeating influence, and wondered what would fill the void it would leave, what inspiring motive would take its place?'[3]

For Beatrice Webb the answer to this question was Socialism, but she turned away from religion with nostalgic regret, and though she insisted that social service had taken its place, she took a long time to convince herself that the exchange was profitable. She quoted a comment by Hort that Maurice's idea of a self-governing workshop would not, as its author thought, do away with selfishness, since 'our interest' would simply take the place of 'my interest,' and her awareness of this kind of moral problem made it difficult for her to regard Socialism as a real substitute for the old idealism of religion, however desirable it might be as an economic

[1] Beatrice Webb, op. cit., 167.
[2] Ibid., 169.   [3] Ibid., 171.

arrangement. Her writings about herself take on an unexpected and peculiar charm: it is the charm of period, for she emerges as a splendid representative of a generation which seems extraordinarily remote, the pre-Lytton Strachey generation, which took life seriously, when problems of faith and conduct bulked just as large for those who rejected traditional convictions as for those who defended them. This was the last generation to possess the luxury of a faith to lose, for it had not occurred to any except the few in every age born with a natural irreverence that the religious issue could simply be ignored, or that life could be lived without a cause to serve. In many ways she is typical of her time—the late-Victorian age: in her wrestlings with doubt; in her extremely Protestant flirtation with Catholicism; in her deliberate adoption of a life of social service as a psychological and ethical substitute for religion; in her easy assurance that the world would be a much better place fairly soon; and not least, though perhaps a little paradoxically, in her regret at the passing of beliefs and a way of life she did not herself accept.

8   Some other Interpretations of Socialism

The Socialism of the last decades of the nineteenth century was extremely varied in type, and the personalities involved were equally diverse. Socialism as an emotional revolt against the standards of the age, in the tradition of William Morris, is exemplified by Edward Carpenter (1844–1929).[1] His father, a retired naval officer, was a friend of F. W. Robertson and Maurice. Carpenter became a Fellow of Trinity Hall, Cambridge, took Orders, and served as curate to Maurice, and later told his friends 'how he used to visit the old women and read the Bible to them, and how he liked and admired Maurice.'[2] Coming under the influence of Walt Whitman, he resigned his Orders and became a University extension lecturer. Then he went to live with working-class friends near Sheffield and worked on their farm while writing *Towards Democracy*. He also discovered Hyndman and Morris, set up as a sandal-maker, and in 1885 started a Socialist society in Sheffield. He collected 'Chants of Labour' and wrote on a variety of subjects. His life was a protest against all that is con-

[1] Tom Swann, *Edward Carpenter: The Man and his Message* (revised edition, 1922).
[2] G. Lowes Dickinson in *Edward Carpenter: In Appreciation*, Edited by Gilbert Beith (1931), 38f.

ventionally implied by the epithet 'Victorian,' and he turned away
from his own class as a demonstration against the exploitation of
the poor. His religious views were very much of his own generation, and he was 'firmly convinced that there has been slowly
emerging through the ages a World Religion that is destined to
supersede all other religions; that will break down the barriers
between race and race, and class and class; and free men's souls
from the fetters that have hitherto bound them.'[1] In the case of
Carpenter there was a progress from Christian Socialism to a
more radical though romantic challenge to the ethos of the age.

A much more famous rebel was John Ruskin (1819–1900).
Ruskin was deeply attached to his mother, who was a strict and
narrow Evangelical. They read the whole Bible together repeatedly, reading alternate verses, covering two or three chapters a
day, and beginning again as soon as they reached the end, and he
had to learn by heart the Scottish paraphrases. She intended him
for the Church, and he went up to Oxford, where he was surprisingly untouched by the Anglo-Catholic movement. It was on a
visit to France that he realized for the first time there was an
alternative form of Christianity besides his own Evangelicalism,
and he was attracted to it, though after a little hesitation he
remained faithful to what he had received from his mother: 'He
had been conscious of the seduction of Catholic tradition and Catholic ritual, but had not allowed himself to be seduced . . .'[2] He felt
the attraction again while living at Venice in 1851–1852, when his
Biblicism was suffering from the aggressions of the geologists and
their 'dreadful Hammers.' From quite early in his adult life he
inclined to Socialism, especially in seeking increased State activity in the way of welfare services. In 1851 he wrote *Notes on the
Construction of Sheepfolds*, a tract on Christian unity, which led to
acquaintance with Maurice. He rejected Maurice's theology, and
indeed denied that Maurice was a great man, finding him sentimental and muddled, as well as heretical in his views on the Bible,
but he was filled with enthusiasm for his social work, and took
charge of the drawing classes at the Working Men's College,
attending regularly till 1858 and bringing Rossetti into the work.
He was not a Christian Socialist, though in more recent terminology he might be called a fellow-traveller. Like Kingsley he

[1] Swann, op. cit., 19. Even the biographer's choice of capital letters is
significant.
[2] Joan Evans, *John Ruskin* (1954), 114.

actively discouraged the working-class students at the College from trying to rise out of their own social class. He contemplated a 'Protestant Convent' of craftsmen employed in copying old manuscripts. In his economic writings, which began with *Unto this Last* (1860), he advocated national education, organization of Labour, old age pensions, and better housing. In all these ideas he did reflect the influence of Christian Socialism, but he had a quite different starting-point—art rather than theology or ethics. He achieved immense popularity as a lecturer and established *Fors Clavigera* (1871), a monthly periodical for the working classes. He started the Guild of St George for the establishment of a Utopia (though rejecting the word itself), based on a system of tithing, and contributed £7,000 himself. Among his efforts at reform were model farms, local industries and co-operatives, the encouragement of art education, and above all the exclusion of machinery and railways. In middle life he drifted away from his evangelical upbringing, and adopted more liberal views. For a time he seemed to turn away from Christianity, but after about 1875 he returned to it, and became friendly with Cardinal Manning, so that it was rumoured that he was inclined to Roman Catholicism. After the death of Rose la Touche, whom he had spent much of his life nearly marrying, he became interested in Spiritualism. In Ruskin's case too there was a pilgrimage resembling that of William Morris—from the characteristic Evangelicalism of the early Victorian age to a less definite religious position coloured by 'Catholic' elements. But Ruskin's religious position remained peculiar, reflecting perhaps a schism in his own nature, for to the end he combined an intense devotion to the Bible with a 'religion of Beauty' prevalent at the time but very rarely associated with Evangelicalism. One of his rather numerous biographers has said: 'His fundamental beliefs were two: the existence of God and the divine quality of beauty.'[1] But in some ways the two remained side by side, never reconciled in a unified view of life.

If Ruskin held some views unusual in his age, A. R. Wallace (1823–1913)[2] would perhaps have been eccentric in any, though he is assured of permanent fame as the co-discoverer with Darwin of the principle of natural selection. He was a phrenologist, an anti-vaccinationist, and a Spiritualist, and believed that the soul

[1] Joan Evans, op. cit., 412.
[2] James Marchant, *Alfred Russel Wallace: Letters and Reminiscences*, 1916. For political and social views see pp. 379–400.

was produced by divine intervention. He was also a highly theoretical Socialist, with extreme views on land nationalization. In his case Socialism was associated with the rejection of traditional religion in favour not of agnosticism, but of religious beliefs peculiar to himself.

In contrast to all these rebels John Stuart Mill (1806–1873),[1] who reflected in his economic writings the contemporary drift towards Socialism, lacked the advantage of a religion against which to rebel. The method of his education is well-known, and he himself bore witness to the fact that he had been brought up an agnostic and had simply never had any religious faith, though he went to church in his youth and valued the Bible (along with Homer). His views on religion were set out in posthumous essays, but he had little knowledge of the subject.

9 *Comment on Socialism in the Religious Press from the Second Reform Act to the London Dock Strike of 1889*

In considering the attitude of the religious press to Socialism during these years it is not practicable to separate out comment on Christian Socialism from that on more secular varieties, since they are often mingled together and the relations between these various Socialisms is one of the points at issue. The earlier part of the period was a time of revolutionary Socialism on the Continent. The *Guardian* dismissed the International as un-English, with all its talk of class-war, and contrasted it with the sober realism of the T.U.C. The Commune of Paris was a sensational event attracting much attention. Its rise was attributed to the low morale of the French people, and it was expected to collapse through economic difficulties. It was not based on 'Communist' theory, and its 'Socialist' measures of confiscation were merely a means of paying its army, though it was foolish to refuse the services of Louis Blanc, 'an intelligent leader.' Thiers was a merciful man, anxious to do his duty, but the Commune itself had not been too harsh, for example in sparing its hostages—a very ill-timed comment, dating only three days before the shooting of the Archbishop of Paris and his companions. The savagery of the final collapse shocked the *Guardian*, which drew the conclusion that religion must advance liberty as well as defend authority, but that Democracy as shown in the Commune—and also in English trade unions—was tyrannical. In the months following there was some criticism of undue

[1] Michael St John Packe, *The Life of John Stuart Mill* (1954).

severity in the punishment of the Communards, though as late as
1880 the coincidence of an amnesty for them and suppression of the
Jesuits was regretted.[1] Like the *Guardian*, the *Church Times*
made some attempt at constructive criticism. The possibility
that the Commune might be imitated in London was revealed by
the existence of support for the views of Owen and also those
of Bradlaugh. There were elements of truth in the Commune's
position: the right of the locality against a nation-wide bureaucracy; the right of the intelligent townsman against the unthinking
peasant; the doctrine that government existed to promote individual liberty; and the claim that property was for the benefit
of all. But these points were true only in a Christian context: the
'distinguishing peculiarity of Christianity . . . is its democratic
aspect . . . The Church was the first Revolution . . . In her
declaration that the rich are merely the stewards of God, the
Father of all, a wider Socialism than that of Proudhon and Fourier
is promulgated.'[2]

The *Nonconformist* too was much interested, though in 1869
it had made the rash prophecy that revolutions in Paris were a
thing of the past. The most reassuring feature was the progress of
the moderate Left and the defeats for extremists. The rising of
March 1871 could not last long, and was due to the unsatisfactory
character of the French people—always a popular doctrine in
Victorian England—especially the Emperor, the priests, and the
peasants. The safeguard against similar events at home was social
legislation—and of course disestablishment. Though the Commune had some excuse, many of its ideas were 'not only Utopian,
but wholly inadmissible,' and though its hostility to the religion of
the priests was not surprising the 'utter defeat' of the rebels was
'a matter for rejoicing.' The atrocities were largely the fault of
Thiers and the Versailles army. On the difficult question of whether
Communard refugees in England should be extradited, the
Nonconformist gave a negative answer, and the amnesty of 1880
was welcomed.[3]

In contrast the *Universe* lost all sense of proportion. It had

[1] *Guardian*, September 16th, 1868; September 22nd, 1869; March
22nd, March 29th, April 5th, April 12th, May 10th, May 24th, May 31st,
August 30th, September 27th, December 27th, 1871; July 7th, 1880.
[2] *Church Times*, June 2nd, 1871.
[3] *Nonconformist*, June 16th, November 24th, 1869; March 22nd,
March 29th, April 5th, April 12th, May 24th, May 31st, June 14th, 1871;
July 15th, 1880.

already dismissed French 'Communism' in 1869 with ridicule, but
the French had not heeded, and now it was hoped that the rising
would be quickly suppressed: 'France has prospered, and may
again under a republic of the tricolor, but from the fraternity,
liberty, and equality of the Red Flag, may France be spared.'
There was something worse, it seemed, than mere Radicalism.
The insurrection could not be put down by sheer force:

> A victory achieved by an enormous sacrifice of life in the streets of
> Paris would only earn for the National Assembly that disgrace which
> the Reds have now all to themselves, and would destroy that confi-
> dence which the masses of the nation still place in the representatives
> they have chosen.

But despite this recognition that a conciliatory spirit was needed
on the part of the Government, the *Universe* became progressively
more immoderate. Early in April there was a much premature
celebration of victory:

> The two armies that fought the great battle of Monday last are
> merely the representatives of the two great contending powers of
> Europe—the Church and the Revolution. So far the revolution has
> had its way by the unscrupulous use of force; but we hope the day
> may not be far distant when the party of the Church, in intellect
> and numbers by far the stronger of two, may arouse itself in its
> might, and with the old battle cry of 'God wills it' crush with the
> resistless power of right joined to might the incubus of modern
> liberalism, the enemy of God and man.

There was great rejoicing at the final defeat of the Commune,
since

> these miscreants had attempted to establish a system of government
> which started from the principle of negation of religion as a founda-
> tion . . . They who had never been tired protesting against the
> tyranny of the empire coolly proceeded to establish a worse tyranny
> of their own, because it had not even the sanction of universal
> suffrage.

There was imminent danger that the story would be repeated in
England, as was revealed, for example, by a meeting to express
sympathy with the Communard refugees, and by the description
of the Commune (by Whalley, the violently anti-Catholic M.P. for
North Warwickshire) as 'a model of efficiency, order, and moderation.'

Comment on the execution of Communards was distinctly full-blooded:

> By all human law this vile Ferré forfeited his life—ten lives if he had had them; and instead of being shot, which is generally looked upon as an honourable mode of death, he should have been hanged, drawn, and quartered. We are not sanguinary, but we have no hesitation in saying that no torture could be too great—neither that of the burning brand nor the pitch-cap, the wheel nor the cat-o'-nine tails—to supplement the capital penalty inflicted on this fiend in human shape . . . It is not for man to pronounce on the awful question of a criminal's position in the other world. All we have to do with is the sentence in this; and deliberately we repeat that it was too lenient, in the instance of this miscreant, and that any and every additional pang that was caused him by the length of time the black shadow of the scaffold has been brooding over his dungeon was richly merited.

Even this was not the end. Another article describing the identifying of the bodies of the priests shot by the Communards expressed the hope that 'justice' would 'make its work complete,' and eight years later the *Universe* was naturally in agreement with the *Guardian* in protesting against the amnesty for Communard prisoners, coinciding with the expulsion of the Jesuits. Even eighteen years after the Commune those who celebrated its anniversary were abused. France continued to be unsatisfactory, with intrigues by Blanqui, and lectures against the Jesuits by Blanc. But a note of mildness was creeping in, and a heavy sentence on an insurrectionary writer only suggested the reflection that it would have been unnecessary in England.[1]

Protestants who glanced at the issues of the *Universe* dealing with the Commune must have derived much satisfaction from the reflection that Rome could still summon up the old thunder against the enemies of the Church. The rather hysterical violence of the *Universe's* attitude suggests that fear was the underlying motive, for despite the progress of Roman Catholicism in England, this newspaper was attentive to disasters on the Continent, with the Commune following so closely on the crisis of Italian unification. These comments are an interesting reflection on the under-

---

[1] *Universe*, February 6th, 1869; March 25th, April 1st, April 8th, June 3rd, June 10th, June 24th, December 2nd, 1871; January 27th, 1872; April 26th, June 21st, June 28th, 1879; June 26th, July 10th, 1880; June 30th, 1883; June 1st, 1889.

tone of violence in Victorian England and the nagging fear of revolution. The *Universe* too was aware of the existence of the International, which was 'wearisome, a nuisance, and an injustice.' In control of it were 'the Russian Nihilist, Bokouswine,[1] and the German Jew, Karl Marx. The one is an avowed and self-glorifying atheist; the other a subtle and dangerous night-worker, hating established society as he does the religion founded on the Saviour's life and sacrifices.' Even worse was to find an Irish Catholic active in the International. There was a sad contrast between the Government's stern repression of the Fenians and its easy toleration of the 'infidels and socialists and political disturbers' of the International.[2]

After these turbulent episodes Socialism became once more a domestic matter. Maurice and Kingsley received highly favourable obituaries (in 1872 and 1875 respectively) in both the *Guardian* and the *Church Times*.[3] The *Guardian* was glad to forget the controversies of the past, and even praised their Socialist activities, with the caution that not all their views had proved practicable. The *Church Times* had 'little agreement' with Maurice's theology, but praised his 'exertions for the elevation of the working-classes,' and it showed great enthusiasm for Kingsley, with the exception of his early 'exaggerated socialistic views.' The change of tone from the days when the *Guardian* had talked the language of *laissez-faire* is illustrated by an article in 1874 answering trade unionists who were critical of political economy, for in analysing the use of the term 'economic law' it treated it as a statistical generalization from experience, thus favouring an historical rather than a traditionally *a priori* interpretation of economics. Similarly, in the discussion of co-operation in this period, co-operatives were defended against criticism by retailers, and attributed to the 'vicious system of competition' among the latter.[4] On this issue the *Nonconformist* shared Hughes's fear that making money was now the main aim of the co-operatives. It was hoped that there was still a future for producers' co-operation:

[1] Sic: Bakunin is intended.

[2] *Universe*, October 7th, 1871; January 20th, March 23rd, 1872.

[3] *Guardian*, April 10th, 1872; January 27th, 1875; *Church Times*, April 5th, 1872; January 29th, 1875.

[4] *Guardian*, January 1st, 1873; June 10th, August 19th, 1874; January 29th, 1879.

It is true that societies of the latter class are exceedingly few in number hitherto, and their influence is proportionately limited. But there are those who think that with such societies lies the real future of co-operation, and it must be admitted that if they are found practicable they will be the means of solving problems far profounder and more perplexing than any to which the former kind of co-operation is applicable.

But a year later there was no progress to report, a failure attributed to unwillingness to pay for outstanding business ability. The opposition of French Socialists showed the conflict between the two principles: 'If you wish to discourage communism encourage co-operation.' In the dispute over whether profits made by the consumers' movement by manufacture rightly belonged to the workers or to the consumers the *Nonconformist* supported older leaders like Lord Ripon who thought they belonged to the employees, and was grieved to see co-operation reduced to 'a mere means of money-making.'[1] The *Universe* was also enthusiastic for co-operation as an antidote to Socialism: 'The system of co-operation, freed from the absurdities and destructive errors of Socialism, has done more for the working classes than any other movement undertaken in the present century.' There was no real antagonism of worker and Capitalist, and what was needed was a revival of the 'old Catholic idea that the capitalist is the natural friend of the labourer.'[2]

The conclusion to be drawn from these references to co-operation is that except to idealists in the Christian Socialist tradition productive co-operation was now overshadowed by the Rochdale movement, which had little to do with Socialism. But at least competition was not so securely enthroned as previously.

'Socialism' continued on the whole to mean something foreign, but now not so much French as German, and the *Guardian* found the theories of Socialism well-suited to the Teutonic mind, a verdict unfavourable to both. Not much was to be hoped 'from the preaching of pure individualism, as in the gospel of unlimited free-trade and untempered political economy,' for this doctrine 'is discredited by the actual condition of European society, and . . . does not harmonize with the prevailing tendencies of modern thought,' a somewhat hasty dismissal of *laissez-faire*. The real

[1] *Nonconformist*, June 2nd, 1869; May 24th, 1883; June 4th, 1885; October 7th, 1886; May 31st, 1888.
[2] *Universe*, September 13th, September 20th, November 1st, 1879.

answer to Socialism was Christianity, 'simply because it recognizes the principle which gives life to Socialism and puts it in its right harmony with others,' combining the individual and the social. Perhaps it is fair to say that the *Guardian* had been converted to Christian Socialism, for this was precisely what the first Christian Socialists had said in 1848. The argument that only Christianity could deal with Socialism was repeated when anti-Socialist legislation was passed in Germany.[1]

The *Church Times* too noticed the rise of Prussian Socialism, and compared it—and unfavourably too—with that of the Commune: but this was only the prelude to an attack on Protestantism and state education. It was admitted that 'there is no theoretical incompatibility between Socialism and the Gospel,' but modern Socialism bore no resemblance to the community of goods in the Apostolic Church. Marx and Lassalle were both Jews, and Catholic influence in Germany was slight.[2] The *Nonconformist* interpreted events in Germany in a precisely opposite sense, noting electoral alliances between Socialists and Ultramontane Catholics against the National Liberals, and hoped the anti-Socialist laws would be effective.[3] Bismarck's other campaign, against the Catholics, was itself the reason for Socialist progress, according to the *Universe*. In Russia the growth of Nihilism and Socialism was the result of atheism and Tsarist tyranny, and when the Nihilists assassinated Alexander II the *Universe* came out with the wholly unexpected comment that they were 'in reality nothing like so bad as they are painted,' and that but for the Imperial tyranny they would be harmless Liberals.[4]

In the 'eighties the discussion of Socialism rose to its peak, and the *Guardian* felt called upon to review many books on the subject, of which some of the most important were as follows:

(*a*) *Communism and Socialism in their History and Theory*, by Theodore D. Woolsey, an American.

(*b*) *The Coming Democracy*, by G. Harwood.

(*c*) *The Historical Basis of Socialism in England*, by H. M. Hyndman.

(*d*) *Six Centuries of Work and Wages*, by Thorold Rogers,

[1] *Guardian*, March 27th, October 23rd, 1878.
[2] *Church Times*, March 29th, June 16th, 1878.
[3] *Nonconformist*, August 28th, 1878.
[4] *Universe*, June 8th, 1878; April 19th, June 7th, 1879; March 19th, 1881.

welcomed for its historical approach to economics and its rejection of 'arbitrary *a priori* assumptions.'

(*e*) *Contemporary Socialism*, by John Rae.

(*f*) *A Politician in Trouble about his Soul*, by Auberon Herbert, and *The Limits of Individual Liberty*, by F. C. Montague, a joint review,

(*g*) *Labour, Leisure, and Luxury*, by Alex Wylie.

(*h*) *The Co-operative Commonwealth in its Outline*, by Lawrence Gronlund.

(*i*) *Poverty and the State*, by H. V. Mills.

(*j*) *Labour, Land and Law*, by W. A. Phillips.

(*k*) A review of four books at once, with the comment that it was 'a curious and characteristic feature of our time' that there should be four books on Socialism to review simultaneously. *An Enquiry into Socialism*, by Thomas Kirkup, and a book by the Avelings on the American Labour movement were among them.[1]

In these reviews it was clear that the word Socialism had now completed its transformation from a term of abuse into a vague academic expression and was soon to begin the change back. There were numerous other comments on Socialism. Stewart Headlam was rebuked for associating with Bradlaugh and Annie Besant. The statistics of Robert Giffen were considered to show that the workers had made great gains in half a century, but Alfred Austin, the future Poet Laureate, was regarded as right in saying that the rich had gained far more, and this sense of injustice was the basis of Socialism. Lord Randolph Churchill was condemned (after the *Pall Mall Gazette*) for being a Chartist and Socialist (i.e. a Conservative M.P. who gave trouble to the party leaders), but Frederic Harrison was justified in his appeal: 'Moralize Industry', as was Lord Salisbury, replying to protests about 'Socialistic legislation,' in saying that there was good Socialism and bad, the former being state intervention for the good of the whole community—under which head the *Guardian* included the rehousing of the poor. It was during this phase that the *Guardian* attacked a Church Congress discussion of the relations of rich and poor for having nothing more to offer than 'the old-fashioned plan of inculcating brotherly love upon rich and poor, employers and employed,' instead of proposing specific reforms and analysing the

---

[1] *Guardian*, January 12th, 1881; October 4th, 1882; April 30th, August 20th, September 24th, 1884; April 29th, June 24th, 1885; November 17th, 1886; January 5th, 1887; February 29th, September 26th, 1888.

nature of society. Less constructive was the condemnation of Socialist rioters in the West End as a 'mob of roughs' who deserved their prosecution.[1]

This return of violence to the streets of London seemed to alarm all the press, and the *Nonconformist* and the *Universe* each responded in its accustomed manner: the *Nonconformist* with involved and obscure censures, and the *Universe* aggressively. The former commented on demonstrations in Trafalgar Square:

> The frequency with which a few well-known and irresponsible persons have of late collected large multitudes in London and other great towns, for the avowed purpose of terrorizing the community compels attention to the possibility of tolerating a continued abuse of a liberty which has for a long time proved of the utmost value.

The Socialists had no right to speak for the working classes, and to create work as a cure for unemployment would be charity—a sufficient condemnation for such an idea. The distress in London should be dealt with in a 'comprehensive, far-reaching, and even authoritative manner'—a recommendation apparently considered precise enough without further elucidation. The Socialist parade to St Paul's Cathedral was designed merely to outrage the feelings of 'decent and religious people,' and such mobs did not consist of the real sufferers, but of 'young roughs, loafers and thieves.' If the poor would come to church to worship, so much the better, but such disturbances should be 'sternly suppressed.' But there was no sympathy with the Government's decision to close Trafalgar Square to meetings, and indeed the conclusion to be drawn from these incidents was that the best thing would be to turn the Tories out.[2]

Very typically the *Universe* favoured the heading: 'The Reign of Terror in London' for a somewhat blood-curdling article:

> For hours whole quarters of the West-end were abandoned to the mercies of a howling rabble mostly of professional thieves. The disturbances were got up ostensibly in the name of the unemployed workmen; but we decline to believe that any, or at least many, of the real horny-handed sons of toil shared in the acts of wanton

[1] *Guardian*, August 16th, 1882; December 12th, 1883; December 3rd, 1884; February 4th, August 12th, October 21st, 1885; February 17th, 1886; November 16th, 1887.

[2] *Nonconformist*, November 25th, 1886, March 3rd, November 17th, 1887.

destruction which startled the town from its propriety . . . Where were the police while all this was going on?

If this had been in Ireland there would have been brutal repression but it was different in England: 'The sleek Mr Hyndman and the sect of prating, indolent, gutter-agitators, who never suffer from want of food, not they, and never moisten their brows with the sweat of labour, are still at large.' There ought to be more 'beautiful Christian charity,' but meanwhile 'these apostles of jaw should get a course of practice on the treadmill in our opinion.' They would run away from force: 'The sight of half-a-dozen trotting Life Guards would have sent the ruck of bull-necked ragamuffins to their heels,' though if they obtained arms 'the Commune of Paris at its reddest and worst would be outrivalled.' The Irish must secure their great object, and then 'Ireland may be able to come over and lend John Bull a hand in setting his house in order.'[1]

Towards the end of the 'eighties the theoretical discussion of Socialism reached its climax, for the old fear of state intervention and social action had weakened. The *Guardian* supported the proposal to supply schoolchildren with free dinners, against the opposition of the Charity Organization Society. The shift in emphasis was noticed: 'The old *laissez-faire* view that Governments existed almost exclusively to keep the peace and that all other objects should be accomplished by private effort, has been apparently eradicated from all but a very few minds,' and there was need to draw a new boundary between public affairs suitable for legislative interference and those not suitable. When the Lambeth Conference of 1888 discussed Socialism, the *Guardian* was content to say that the Church should be neutral on this issue, and shortly before the dock strike it appealed for a more discriminating use of the term 'Socialism,' but without much in the way of clarification.[2]

The *Church Times* was absorbed with the question of Christian Socialism. In 1881 a spate of letters argued whether the Guild of St Matthew was republican and revolutionary, while another guild, that of St Alban, in Holborn, came in for criticism for fraternizing with 'infidels and socialists,' a criticism which provoked further correspondence. A leader under the heading 'Socialism, Christian and Otherwise,' said that too much emphasis

[1] *Universe*, February 13th, 1886.
[2] *Guardian*, January 4th, May 23rd, July 11th, 1888; February 20th, 1889.

was being placed on the subject. Some Socialists were 'atheists and blasphemers, and the motive which underlies their schemes is a desire to banish the very idea of a Divine Ruler from the world.' The Christian Socialists were inspired by worthy motives, but misled. The divergence of social classes was not increasing, and the community of goods in the *Acts of the Apostles* contained no approach to Communism. The Capitalist was entitled to his reward, for without him there would be no employment. In 1884 a leader entitled simply 'Socialism' gave a contemptuous account of the English visit of Henry George, describing his doctrines as the 'offspring of the wildest absurdity.' The article then went on to attack and ridicule Hyndman. Better than preaching revolution would be to teach people to live 'according to the good old-fashioned rule of life, which everyone has learned, or should have learned, in his Catechism.' In the *Church Times* hostility to Socialism reached a peak in 1885 with an article putting the blame for subversive tendencies on Joseph Chamberlain, and fearing that an 'assault upon the sanctity of property would . . . bring upon us "Red ruin and the breaking up of laws." ' Marxism was 'a theory of value which no sane person would look at for a single moment,' and Lassalle showed a typically French confusion of mind (despite his being a German). Much poverty could be averted by reforming the character of the poor, and the rest by relief, if only one could clearly distinguish between 'the poverty which is and the poverty which is not culpable.' Parliament could do nothing worth speaking of for the working man, while the success of co-operation seemed merely coincidental. The *Church Times* hoped that in the new Parliament of 1886 Conservative, Liberal, and even Radical members would unite against the 'Jacobin' and 'Communist,' 'for the defence of the Empire, and of all that makes life worth living.' Christian Socialists might be right in representing early Christianity as a Radical force, but the teaching of the Bible clearly implied monarchical government in church and state alike. True, 'some Socialistic action must needs enter into practical Christianity, personal and corporate,' but this seems only to refer to poor-relief. Modern Socialism 'tends to destroy individual effort, and to abolish liberty by abolishing private rights, thereby enfeebling the moral nature, and bringing about a dead level of mediocrity in aims and action . . .' The cure for the miseries of the poor was 'not to run after the will-o'-the-wisp of Socialistic reform still less to plan a Socialistic revolt,' but merely to make the rich realize their duties. If, as Socialists demanded, there were to be guaranteed wages, 'the slave-driver and the stock-whip in some form or other would be unavoidable.' The remedy for social evils was to make all employers Christians.[1]

In 1888 the *Church Times* printed a series of articles under the title of *Christianity and Socialism*. The first drew a distinction between the moral influence of Christianity and the legal compulsion characteristic of Socialism, but went on to admit that the Church had neglected social teaching. *Laissez-faire* was in retreat, and the test of any Socialistic proposal was simply whether it would benefit the people. The second article produced arguments against the demand for the whole product of Labour, and pointed out the difficulties, which it regarded as insuperable, in the way of nationalization. It did not mention Christianity. The third dealt most ineffectively with unemployment, and was overshadowed by the doctrines of Malthus; the only reference to Christianity was rather absurd: if early marriage, a cause of over-population, was discouraged, Christianity would be valuable in countering any increase in immorality. The fourth dealt with rent, and made no mention of Christianity, except to say that there would be no oppression if people were 'actuated by Christian principles.' The fifth and concluding article dealt in generalities, such as that the fault lay not in the system but in the people. If people acted in a brotherly way, Socialism would be unnecessary, while if they did not, it would be slavery. The only way to improve things was by 'the influence of Christian principles operating from within,' and through the Christianization of industry.[2] In the correspondence which followed Sidney Webb took part, as usual to urge that Socialists did not want revolution, but merely the continuance of the inevitable trends of the time.

The *Nonconformist* too had a few further references to Socialism in this period. The principle of state intervention in economic life was now accepted: 'It is altogether too late in the day, and would be quite superfluous, to discuss the policy of legislative interference with industry.' As a remedy for unemployment emigration was to be preferred to public works, in which there was 'always

---

[1] *Church Times*, January 6th to 27th, 1881; December 7th, December 14th, December 21st, 1883; April 4th, 1884; November 20th, 1885; February 5th, March 26th, August 20th, 1886; October 14th, 1887.

[2] Ibid., February 2nd, March 2nd, March 9th, March 16th, March 23rd, 1888.

considerable danger.' References to Henry George showed a marked change of emphasis. In 1884 the 'only reason for giving any attention to Mr Henry George is the fact that he has attracted so large an amount of attention already.' He was 'a mere charlatan, who has never thought out his subject in detail.' But in 1889, though difficult to understand, he was worth listening to. There was no absolute ownership, and no injustice in appropriating increases in land values.[1]

The *British Weekly* was not very sympathetic to Socialism in its first few years. It was critical of a Congregational minister who started a pastorate at Newcastle-on-Tyne by preaching about Kropotkin; it attacked some American Socialists for opposing marriage; it deprecated the interruptions at St Paul's by Socialists; and it considered Stewart Headlam mistaken in believing he could Christianize 'that blend of materialism and discontent known as Socialism.' Holyoake was right in saying that improvements must be made within the existing system, not through its destruction. Christianity had no specific teaching on political and social problems, but worked by changing individuals; yet Lord Aberdeen had been right in calling Liberalism 'the Christianity of politics,' which seems a contradiction. In more approving vein, public libraries were Socialistic but good, and the work of such unbelievers as Annie Besant was praised. The Liberal victory in the Kennington by-election was due to Socialist support, but none the less welcome for that.[2]

The references quoted earlier from the *Universe* showed intense hostility to Socialism, but these were concerned with Continental affairs. On some matters the *Universe*, like Manning, could see merit in state intervention, and on others it was at least Radical, and in an empirical way allied with the Socialists. Of the former kind was the advocacy of compulsory membership of a friendly society, and of the latter were two articles on 'The Undeserving Rich,' finding fault with the prosperous classes. There was also a series of savage attacks on the House of Lords over the 1884 Reform Bill, with Ireland of course the real point. One leader, called 'Lords or Louts?,' opposed abolition of the House only

---

[1] *Nonconformist*, August 7th, 1867; January 6th, 1869; January 17th, 1884; April 25th, 1889.

[2] *British Weekly*, November 19th, December 3rd, December 10th, 1886; February 11th, March 4th, June 17th, September 9th, September 30th, 1887; October 12th, 1888; March 22nd, 1889.

because it was a picturesque survival. Another called it 'the
embodied realization of class selfishness, and the most fatuous
resistance to every measure which is just and progressive,' favourably quoting Morley and Bright. And another ridiculed the
hereditary principle and the Conservative working man, whom
Sala rightly called the 'under-butler type of humanity,' and who
should be 'put under a glass case as a natural curiosity.'[1]

It is difficult to attempt any summing-up of the relationship
of religion to the progress of Socialism during this period, because
of the repeated failure of all parties to the debate to define what
they meant by the term. Changes in the outlook of economists, the
trend towards state intervention in industry, the co-operative
movement—even on the side of consumers' co-operation, which in
some ways was a rival development—the German Social Democrats, the Paris Commune, the Fabian Society and the S.D.F., and
the whole disorganized body of thought and opinion which was
casually associated together under the convenient but inaccurate
title of 'Christian Socialism'—all these diverse elements offered
endless opportunity for inconclusive debate. When the press
argued over whether Christianity and Socialism were compatible
the only possible conclusion was that reached by the correspondent of the *Church Times* who said that it all depended on the
definition given to these two very broad terms; and when Sidney
Webb and his critics disagreed as to whether there was a current
trend towards Socialism, the answer was once again that the
argument was about meanings. The *Universe* meant very much the
same as Marx—proletarian revolution. But every observer
attached his own meaning to the name, and often it was in any
case a meaning which was very vague. In general the Churches
remained very suspicious of Socialism, whatever it meant. Memories of Chartism were reinforced by the Commune, and then
again by fairly harmless but apparently sinister events in Trafalgar
Square, and every informed person knew that whatever Maurice
and Kingsley had said in the 'forties, or Stewart Headlam said in
the 'eighties, their brand of Socialism was flatly disowned by the
most generally accepted spokesmen of the Socialist movement at
large. In that movement there were leaders who were religious
men, even in the more restricted sense of owing allegiance to
one or other of the recognized denominations, and even so worldly

[1] *Universe*, July 19th, July 26th, 1879; January 20th, February 3rd,
1883; July 26th, September 13th, October 4th, December 6th, 1884.

a group of Socialists as the Fabian Society started as an offshoot of the highly idealistic movement of the early 'eighties, which itself was closely allied with Christian Socialism. Well-meaning and philanthropic onlookers like Manning and Fraser, and even more systematic intellectuals like Westcott and Hort, were apt to confuse the issue by periodically announcing the 'real' or 'inner' meaning of Socialism, and discovering something there which was from a Christian standpoint at the very least quite innocuous. In the main the leaders of Christian opinion still opposed Socialism, if not as a dangerous international conspiracy, at least as an attempt to substitute worldly and materialistic aims for 'spiritual.' There was not the same inclination to abandon a critical attitude as in the case of trade unions. The greatest promise for the future was twofold: one aspect was in the changing character of economics itself, which, without giving up anything of its scientific character, was becoming more ready to adopt at least humanistic standards of judgement and to see the importance of questions of human welfare; the other was in the theological development, directly traceable to Maurice himself, which saw a place in God's purposes for a corporate redemptive activity in this world as well as an individual salvation in the next. This was what men like Headlam had in mind when they so repeatedly, and apparently perversely, asserted that Christ's miracles were secular works of mercy, or that various outspoken atheists and agnostics were speaking in the Name of God, though this was not altogether a good way of convincing their critics. But one's main impression is of a chaotic variation in the use of a term, a variation which robs the lively discussion of it in the press and elsewhere of much of its value.

10 Socialist Trends of the 'Nineties

In the 'nineties Socialism was in the air, and surprising people showed a liking for it. Among the Nonconformists the 'municipal Socialism' stemming from Joseph Chamberlain won support. A theological change was involved: Nonconformity was increasingly inclined to pay attention to this world rather than the next, and the 'establishment of the Kingdom of God on earth' was easily identified with change in the social order. The dominant personality among the Nonconformists was the Fabian John Clifford. A. M. Fairbairn of Mansfield College was influenced by Ruskin, and R. F. Horton by Arnold Toynbee and Henry George. J. B. Paton was active in social work at Nottingham and in 1893 founded the

English Land Colonization Society. George Macdonald, the poet, a Congregational minister for three years, was a friend of Maurice, who persuaded him to join the Church of England.[1] Horton, chairman of the Congregational Union in 1903, was a fervent admirer of Robert Blatchford, as is recorded in the biography of Blatchford:

> Dr Horton, a famous Congregational minister, compared Blatchford with Isaiah, Amos, and Micah, and declared that 'if Jesus Christ were a man on earth today, he would read the book not only with interest but with approval, and he would say to any officious disciples who took exception to parts of it, "Forbid him not; he that is not against me is for me".'[2]

The book of which these surprising words were written was *Merrie England*. Later the enthusiasm cooled: when Blatchford wrote his articles in the *Daily Mail* calling attention to the German threat in 1910 Horton found in them 'a proper fruit of infidelity.' Blatchford himself was married in a Congregational church, Zion, Halifax.

Benjamin Kirkman Gray (1862–1907) was the son of a Congregational minister, and became one himself in 1892. From 1894 to 1897 he was a Unitarian minister. He studied economics and became a strong Socialist, joining the I.L.P.[3] Sir Ebenezer Howard (1850–1928),[4] the pioneer of garden cities, was employed for a time as secretary to the Rev Joseph Parker, the leading Congregational preacher of his generation, whose dominant personality made a permanent impression on him. But this employment lasted only three months, and a visit to the United States made him a 'Christian Humanist.' In 1898 he read Bellamy's *Looking Backward*, and his idealism responded warmly, causing him to enlist in the cause of building a new civilization, motivated by altruism. It was this ambition which launched him into his career of advocating garden cities.

[1] Greville Macdonald: *George Macdonald and his Wife* (1924). On the influence of Maurice see pp. 397–406. Macdonald was driven from his Congregational pastorate at Arundel by a heresy hunt on the part of the deacons, who dropped a hint by reducing his stipend (pp. 177–183).

[2] L. Thompson, *Robert Blatchford: Portrait of an Englishman* (1951), 100. Source of quotation not given.

[3] *Dict. Nat. Biog.* (second supplement), s.v. Gray.

[4] Dugald Macfadyen, *Sir Ebenezer Howard and the Town Planning Movement* (1933).

David George Ritchie (1853–1903) represented a philosophical trend. He was the son of George Ritchie, minister at Jedburgh, who rose to be Moderator of the General Assembly of the Church of Scotland, and he was related to Carlyle. David Ritchie received his education at Edinburgh and Oxford, coming under the influence of T. H. Green and Arnold Toynbee, and developed Radical and even Socialist views: 'He was a zealous democrat, although his mode of thought seemed to have little affinity with that of common men. He was a socialist, and had the strongest belief in state action wherever possible. He had, I think, an instinctive antipathy to the English way of regarding political questions.'[1] He had been brought up in 'the orthodox religion of his ancestral creed' and was intended for the ministry, but lost his orthodox beliefs. He shared the conviction of some of his contemporaries that social and political action was the real religion: 'The essence of Christianity is democracy, in the very widest sense. Walt Whitman is more Christian than an archbishop, "ranking next the Prince of Wales," can ever be (though I don't think much of him as a poet).'[2] He insisted that in saying this he was not turning religion into politics, but raising politics to the level of religion.

Somewhat similar views were held by Mary Augusta Ward (1851–1920), better known as Mrs Humphry Ward. She was the grand-daughter of Thomas Arnold, and her father, another Thomas, surpassed some distinguished contemporaries by being converted to the Roman Catholic Church twice. She believed that Christianity could be revitalized by discarding its miraculous elements and concentrating on the social, and these ideas she preached in her novel *Robert Elsmere* (1888), which achieved an extraordinary success—the sort of success which goes with saying what the current generation is thinking rather better than other people. In 1890 she helped to form a settlement at University Hall, Gordon Square, based on a simplified Christianity of social character, which developed into the Passmore Edwards Settlement. Her later career was like that of some other prominent Radicals: she opposed the suffrage movement and supported her son as a Conservative candidate for Parliament.[3]

[1] F. C. Montague, quoted in D. G. Ritchie, *Philosophical Studies*, edited, with a memoir, by Robert Latta (1905), 7.
[2] Ibid., 58.
[3] Janet Penrose Trevelyan, *The Life of Mrs Humphry Ward* (1923).

11   *Comment on Socialism in the Religious Press in the 'Nineties*

In this period the discussion of Socialism was not quite so intense as previously. In the *Guardian* a number of books were reviewed, among those favourable to Socialism being *The Quintessence of Socialism*, by A. Schäffle, *Fabian Essays*, praised for their clarity and gradualism, but not liked much otherwise, Kautsky's *Communism in Central Europe in the Time of the Reformation*, and the Webbs' *Problems of Modern Industry*. Among books hostile to Socialism were *Socialism, Old and New*, by W. Graham, *Socialism*, by Robert Flint, and J. Shield Nicholson's *Historical Progress and Ideal Socialism*. The leader columns showed that the *Guardian's* hostility to Socialism was hardening. Alfred Marshall was quoted to the effect that the new 'humanitarian' economics, while very different from the old system, was still opposed to Socialism. Socialism was shown to be essentially reactionary by reasoning drawn from the works of Herbert Spencer, and Tom Mann was said not to have faced the problem of management. On the other hand 'educated Socialists, such as Marx and Hyndman' were at least more logical than land-nationalizers, and the greater equalization of wealth was a worthy object of public policy. Ruskin, condemned in his lifetime, was praised at his death for his part in restoring 'moral and spiritual elements' to economics and helping to destroy *laissez-faire*.

The 'State Socialism' of Germany the *Guardian* seemed to think contrary to nature. At home Socialism referred to nothing so grandiose, yet the *Guardian* opposed free meals for children as harmful to parental responsibility, a reversal of a previous opinion. The paper also opposed legislation on hours and 'sweating.' Municipal Socialism was a prominent issue in London. The *Guardian* gave space to Webb to present the Progressive case at the 1895 L.C.C. election, but supported the Moderates because their opponents intended 'a series of collectivist experiments' likely to prove expensive. At the 1898 election the Progressives were attacked for acting as agents not of the ratepayers, but of Labour. The *Guardian* claimed to be glad they had secured a large majority, but only so that their failings might be the more clearly demonstrated. Municipal employment of the unemployed was wrong, but municipal trading was defended. Co-operation came in for hearty praise, and Holyoake's autobiography, despite his religious views, brought enthusiasm for both book and author. But the *Guardian's* hopes were turning from co-operation to profit-sharing, though the benefits of the latter were suspected to be illusory.[1]

The *Church Times* had nothing to say at this time about Social-ism, except for the material on Christian Socialism already dealt with, but there was a certain amount in the *Church Family News-paper*, mostly on co-operation. It advocated an extension of agricultural co-operation, and hoped that the development of co-operation would lead to a general betterment of industrial relations, though speaking in so vague a way that perhaps only profit-sharing was intended. Comment on a discussion of co-opera-tion and Socialism at the 1895 Church Congress amounted to a suspension of judgement. It was a great merit in co-operation that it gave men a sense of purpose, and a ring of Scottish butchers against the co-operatives was 'illegal and ought to be quashed.' The revelation that the I.L.P. had a balance in hand of only £224 provoked the comment that

> Socialism has never taken root in England. The plant is an exotic to begin with, and the soil is not suited to its growth and propagation. It is a pity that men like Mr Keir Hardie and Mr Tom Mann cannot or will not recognize this fact. It shows their ignorance of the charac-ter of their own countrymen, and an imperviousness to the facts of our social and political history truly phenomenal.

Another article, made the point, at length, that the investor deserved a reward. The idea that Socialism was a perversity of Continentals persisted, no doubt to the despair of disciples of Robert Owen. The miners who met at Berlin were all Socialists except the English delegates, who proved that the English working man was 'totally different' from foreigners; a French anarchist, speaking in his own defence, showed how he had slipped down the perilous slope from Socialism to Anarchism; and an International Labour Congress at the Queen's Hall ended in violence. Mankind would never derive any benefit from congresses of this kind, which John Burns had wisely learned to treat with contempt. Yet there

---

[1] *Guardian*, July 10th, September 4th, November 13th, 1889; January 8th, February 12th, May 7th, May 21st, September 10th, September 24th, October 29th, November 5th, 1890; January 15th, January 28th, April 1st, 1891; November 23rd, December 14th, 1892; July 5th, 1893; February 13th, February 27th, July 3rd, August 28th, September 25th, 1895; March 2nd, March 9th, April 13th, August 3rd, September 14th, 1898; January 31st, August 1st, 1900.

were some similarities with the Continent after all, for Socialist defeats in elections on both sides of the Channel showed that 'the wave of reaction against the absurdities of Collectivist theories is running as rapidly across the Channel as it is here.'[1]

The *Nonconformist* was more sympathetic to a measure of Socialism. Characteristically it supported school meals, with the pertinent comment that those who were so concerned about parental responsibility said similar things at the time of the 1870 Education Act. Besides profit-sharing this paper advocated producers' co-operation, as late as 1891, and a leader entitled 'Labour's Best Hope' was a plea for co-partnership. Comments on *Fabian Essays* were meant to be moderate and constructive, though the now traditional assertion that Socialism was un-English appeared again. The essayists were said to ignore the possibility of improvements within the existing system, and expropriation would be robbery, however angry the essayists might become at this assertion. On the other hand an article a few years later eagerly accepted the saying 'We are all Socialists now,' though the author's own Socialism was extremely vague. In Germany some Socialists were as militaristic as Bismarck, whose efforts at repression only helped them. A deeper solution was needed: 'Socialism is a symptom of the times, and we cannot expect it to disappear until the times themselves change.' Only a Christian society could end class conflict. The Pope's Encyclical against Socialism would have no effect: 'There is no hope that Roman Catholicism will gain any considerable control of the socialistic movement. If this can be done by any Church it must be by Protestantism.'[2]

The *British Weekly*, too, while not interested in the Christian Socialist movement, showed much interest in Socialism in general. The mood at the beginning of this period was critical. An open letter was printed rebuking W. T. Stead, usually a great hero of the *British Weekly*, for his inclination towards Socialism. An article by Thomas Kirkup took up a moderate position, condemning violent revolution and the extension of the role of the state, but warning that Socialism must be judged on its merits, not on the aberrations

[1] *Church Family Newspaper*, May 4th, May 18th, May 25th, 1894; June 7th, August 9th, October 18th, 1895; April 10th, July 31st, August 7th, 1896; June 11th, 1897; January 21st, June 3rd, 1898.

[2] *Nonconformist* (later *Independent*), November 7th, 1889; January 16th, March 6th, 1890; February 13th, May 1st, July 3rd, November 6th, 1891; April 19th, 1894.

of individuals. *Laissez-faire* had failed, for example in housing, and Capitalism reduced the worker's freedom. Socialism—by which Kirkup meant chiefly producers' co-operation—had economic and moral advantages: 'We believe, then, that Socialism, rightly understood, is in entire harmony with the great factors of human progress, and is indeed the outcome and consummation of them in the social-economic sphere.' The progress of German Socialism aroused mixed feelings. Anti-Socialist legislation was criticized, though 'the German Socialist is a more dangerous person than his British comrade.' Yet a few years later sweeping gains were welcomed: 'The spirit of the Social Democrats is hostile to war, and in their increasing success lies one great hope for the peace of Europe.' In the event the German Socialists proved that they deserved neither the fears nor the hopes expressed of them.

Among miscellaneous references to Socialism in the *British Weekly* were an expression of sympathy with Socialists that their societies attracted such unwelcome supporters as anarchists; a favourable obituary on the old Chartist, Thomas Cooper; a long and glowing account of the Webbs by an interviewer full of enthusiasm for them; and a note supporting an L.C.C. investigation into transport and urging slum clearance.[1]

There were two special periods of vigorous discussion. In 1894 a series of articles on Socialism was published. The first, by Professor Marcus Dods, rejected Socialism on grounds of incentives and liberty, and thought Christian Socialism a matter of altering the spirit of society rather than proposing specific reforms. The second was a reply by Keir Hardie. Socialism, like early Christianity, attracted faddists, but essentially it made a moral appeal, more Christian than the reliance on private profit. Questions asked by Dods were 'trumpery little details,' for 'the Christian must first decide whether Socialism be right or wrong.' The third article was by the Rev Robert A. Watson, who attacked state Socialism as tyranny, and claimed that sufficient reforms were possible within the existing system. The fourth, by the Rev Hugh Black, adopted a mediating position, drawing analogies between Christianity and Socialism. Yet Marxists were anti-religious, and Socialists made an appeal to materialistic motives. The Christian ideal 'surpasses because it includes the Socialist ideal.' The fifth article, by H. H.

[1] *British Weekly*, November 15th, November 22nd, 1889; January 31st, 1890; April 7th, July 21st, 1892; June 22nd, July 29th, November 23rd, 1893.

Champion, found fault with all the preceding, especially that by his fellow-Socialist Hardie, and insisted, with a reference to Engels, that Socialism was a scientific, not a moral, matter. After a gap of two issues another article appeared, by the Rev C. Fleming Williams, who held an extremely optimistic view of the future, and answered Champion by saying that Socialism was not a scientific theory, but an 'affection.'[1] A fair number of letters were attracted by the series, with the emphasis on two disagreements: how far was Socialism a moral issue? And how far did it consist in piecemeal reforms?

A further discussion of Socialism took place nearly two years later, following a leader entitled: 'Should Wealthy Christians be Socialists?'[2] There was a considerable debate in the correspondence columns over whether a Christian could be right in amassing wealth, and over the related question whether a wealthy class was necessary to society.[3]

The *Universe* continued to have no friendly feelings towards Socialism which it still regarded as a matter of international rather than English significance. A reference to anti-Socialist legislation in Germany recognized that there were genuine grievances, but in general Socialism continued to be dismissed out of hand:

> When the advocates of reform talk of working steadily for the *collective ownership* of all the means and instruments of producing wealth by the *whole community* as the only method of emancipation from industrial slavery they talk balderdash, and wander into the realms of Utopia.

Leo XIII did well to show his concern for the real welfare of the workers while condemning Socialism, which was a 'horrible organization' spread throughout the world, related to the Commune, the Nihilists, and atheism. Socialists attacked property, the family, religion, and all the foundations of society.[4]

In the 'nineties as in the preceding years the discussion of Socialism was still confused by the failure to arrive at—or even attempt—a satisfactory definition of the term. At one extreme

---

[1] *British Weekly*, January 4th, January 18th, January 25th, February 1st, February 8th, March 1st, 1894.

[2] Ibid., October 24th, 1895.

[3] Correspondence extended from October 31st, 1895 to December 12th, 1895.

[4] *Universe*, February 15th, May 3rd, 1890; June 13th, 1891; April 16th, April 23rd, 1892.

there was a tendency to describe almost any kind of social reform as the 'right kind' of Socialism, even when the degree of state or municipal intervention or the degree of private corporate activity was quite negligible. At the other some Christians still thought of Socialism as an international conspiracy directed against the Christian religion and Christian morality. But the divergence was showing signs of narrowing a little. The one tendency was decreasing as Socialism became a more organized body of opinion, and the other as it became clear that there was an alternative interpretation of the meaning of the word Socialism, represented in England by both the I.L.P. and the Fabian Society. But by far the most significant development of this period was the secularization of religious enthusiasm, exemplified most clearly by self-conscious (and vocal) converts from Evangelical Christianity to reformist Socialism, like Beatrice Webb. Perhaps the same tendency can be found within the religious world itself, in the increasing inclination of Nonconformists to identify the coming of the Kingdom with the establishment of a just social order; in the deliberately shocking assertion of Anglo-Catholics like Dearmer and Headlam that the work of the Church—and even the work of Christ—was a secular and 'Socialist' work; in the concentration of much Anglican and Nonconformist energy on the Settlement movement, with its gradually declining religious inspiration; and even in the changed methods of William Booth, from purely 'spiritual' evangelism to highly organized methods of social improvement.

12   Socialism in the Period 1900–1914

Socialism continued to be a subject of great interest to the Church, but the discussion of it tended in some ways to become more confused than ever, because while Nonconformity was still in closer contact with the working classes than the Church of England it was less inclined to be attracted by Socialist collectivism, and the Roman Catholic Church still regarded Socialism as an international conspiracy against social order. The attraction of a 'Catholic' type of religion for Beatrice Webb was typical of the experience of other people of a similar cast of mind. The Fabians spent a great deal of effort asserting that the kind of Radicalism associated with Nonconformity had nothing to do with their own Gospel, and Shaw attacked Evangelical religion as hostile to the interests of the workers in *Major Barbara* in 1905. The Webbs were not unhappy about the Education Act of 1902, which so much offended the Nonconformists—above all their fellow-Fabian Clifford. They were not particularly opposed to concessions to Anglican and even Roman Catholic schools, partly because they 'regarded the Catholic type of Christianity as more in harmony with the Socialist ideal than Protestant individualism.'[1] Legislation which could be regarded as Socialist in tendency might now even gain the support of religious forces traditionally regarded as reactionary. Thus in 1905 the Unemployed Workmen Bill, which was opposed by many Conservatives, was carried partly with the aid of the Bishops. An aspect of 'Socialism' in a very broad sense was the campaign for Old Age Pensions, to which the Churches gave strong support, the Nonconformists being active, as were a number of Anglican bishops and Cardinal Vaughan.

With the trend towards Socialism the Roman Catholic Church found itself in a difficult position, for its members were predominantly working class and attracted by the Labour Party, but Socialism was still regarded with hostility by a hierarchy versed in European politics, in which Socialism and Catholicism were often locked in conflict. The remedy was to keep the Labour Party away from Socialism. In the Salford diocese, one of the most important, trade unionists formed a federation to oppose the Liberal Government's education policy, which could also be used against Socialism. It helped to secure the defeat of Winston Churchill in a famous by-election at North-West Manchester in 1908, to the anger of the local Irish leaders, who worked for Churchill. The federation lobbied Labour conferences on the education question, and it led to the formation of the National Conference of Catholic Trade Unionists, which fought to keep the Labour Party non-Socialist, and came to an end in 1918, when the party definitely committed itself to Socialism.

A Roman Catholic view of Socialism just before the war was stated by Bernard Vaughan in his book *Socialism from the Christian Standpoint* (1912), described as consisting of ten 'conferences.' Most of these were sermons preached on a visit to New York, but there is little in them that relates to the American scene. The ten sections were as follows:

1. Socialism and the Papacy. This can be summed up in the quotation: 'The Pope has ever been the champion of the toiler, the

[1] E. Halévy, *Hist. of Eng. People: V. Imperialism and the Rise of Labour* second edition, 1951), 207.

defender of the weak, the advocate of the down-trodden, and the poor man's best friend.'

2. *Socialism and the State.* Socialism and the Catholic Church

both protest against the evils of modern capitalism, of fierce individualism, of iniquitous competition, and of colossal wealth in the hands of the few. Read the Encyclicals of Leo XIII on the great questions of the day, and you will imagine, at times, that you are reading passages from a socialist manifesto.

But in reality there was an 'irreconcilable antagonism' because of the 'materialistic theory of evolution' of Socialism. There was an historical alliance of Socialism with atheism, and even Christians in the Socialist ranks were involved in atheistic ideas: 'They have broken with the Catholic tradition.' There followed quotations from Ramsay Macdonald, drawing analogies between biological phenomena and society, which Vaughan considered materialist.

3. *Socialism and the Individual.* Socialism replaced a false individualism with a false collectivism and sacrificed the present to the future. Only Christianity safeguarded the rights of personality.

4. *Socialism and the Family.* This emphasized the sacredness of family life and quoted some Socialists as hostile to it, while other Socialists made no effective answer.

5. *Socialism and Religion.* Vaughan quoted Marx, Engels, Bebel, Liebknecht and others against religion, and continued:

Let me repeat it: I am not asking whether Socialism, as a bare economic theory, is or is not compatible with Christianity, nor am I asking whether individual Socialists are or are not anti-Christian: I am asking whether the actual movement called Socialism is or is not deeply imbued with an essentially anti-Christian spirit.

He went on to quote extensively from statements of the Socialist Party of Great Britain. In reply to the claim that British Socialism was not anti-religious, he referred to the S.D.F., to the I.L.P., which maintained contacts with Continental atheists and supported Blatchford, and to the Fabian Society, in which the anti-Christians were much more influential than the Christians. There were many quotations from Wells, who at this stage of his career was earnestly seeking to show that religion and Socialism were not incompatible.

6. *Socialism and Christian Socialists.* On this topic Vaughan reached two conclusions:

The first is that the movement stands not the slightest chance of counteracting the predominantly anti-Christian tone of current Socialism. The second is that in so far as it is really socialistic and not merely social, it has cut the ground from under its feet by abandoning what is most characteristic and vital in Christianity.

Real Socialists only tolerated Christians for tactical reasons. There was a criticism of Anglicans—Westcott was named—who used the name Socialism to cover general social reforms. Christian Socialists had abandoned true Christianity: '. . . They have robbed that message of its deepest truth, and deprived it of those very characteristics which have been the secret of its power,' by making it worldly, an allegation illustrated by quotations from the Fabian Tracts written by Stewart Headlam and Percy Dearmer. There was a danger of identifying the Socialist state and the Kingdom of God; hence R. J. Campbell's assertion on Blatchford: 'He has preached the Kingdom of God.' A materialistic interpretation was given to the Bible and to the Church fathers. Vaughan summed it up in an epigram: 'Socialism makes for a Paradise beneath the moon, Christianity leads to a Heaven beyond the stars.'

7. *Socialism and the Rights of Ownership.* Private property was the basis of society. The Socialist and the Catholic might support the same measures, but it would be for different motives.

8. *Socialism and the Duties of Ownership.* This was mainly an exposition of Catholic, i.e. Thomist, philosophy of property.

9. *Socialism and its Problems.* After condemning the chameleon-like propaganda of Socialism, infinitely varied according to audience, Vaughan described some of the problems of a Socialist state, principally relating to incentives.

10. *Socialism and Social Reformation.* Vaughan described the social evils of America and Britain. The remedy was not Socialism, with all its evils, nor 'the Christianity of Christ alone.' The social problem 'demands the positive action of civil authority.' Various factors were required: legislation; private initiative, especially through profit-sharing; and also the action of the Church:

> The Catholic Church protests against current Capitalism with its unmoral or immoral economies,[1] its false boast of freedom, its undisguised utilitarianism. She protests against Socialism, which, in the ultimate analysis, is equally utilitarian.

[1] Sic.

The Church had guidance for both employers and workers. That such criticisms of Socialism from a Christian standpoint were not confined to Catholics is shown by a crop of attacks on it at this time by religious writers of various schools, mostly at a much lower level of polemic than Vaughan's. As an example of these, without date, but obviously belonging to the turn of the century, was a little book entitled The 'Clarion' or the Bible,[1] intended as an answer to the attacks on Christianity by Blatchford, and abusive in style. The working classes were turning from indifference to Christianity to active hostility. In using his Socialism as a cloak in attacking Christianity, Blatchford had 'struck socialism a heavy blow.' The last chapter included Socialism among the substitutes for Christianity. There was a welcome for Christian Socialism and 'what Socialism has borrowed from Christianity,' but the aims and ideals of Socialism were impossible. The Labour theory of value was mistaken, and Socialism was inconsistent because its advocates wore clothes made by sweated labour. It did not take an active part in temperance reform, and it was 'distinctly atheistic' in 'heart and tendency,' as Blatchford had shown, and as was also shown by 'the socialism of France, Italy, and Germany.'

13 *Comment on Socialism in the Religious Press in the Edwardian Period*

The *Guardian* virtually ignored Socialism after the beginning of the new century. Reviewers were not unfriendly to 'Socialistic' trends in Australia and New Zealand, and favoured social legislation in America. But Asquith was criticized for not realizing the danger from Socialism, and his Government for its wildly extravagant old-age pensions scheme.[2]

The *Church Times* had much to say, but what it said was inextricably bound up with comment on Christian Socialism and the Labour Party, and is dealt with elsewhere under these topics. A distinct matter was the Russian revolution of 1905, which it was hoped the Government would defeat by a combination of repression and reform.[3]

The *Church Family Newspaper* offered firm opposition to Socialistic tendencies after the 1906 election:

[1] T. Waugh, *The 'Clarion' or the Bible*. (No date.)
[2] *Guardian*, March 4th, June 3rd, 1902; November 20th, 1907; May 13th, 1908.
[3] *Church Times*, January 27th, 1905.

The Labour members in Parliament are having it all their own way. The Government does not resist them and of the Conservatives it may be said that with very few exceptions they are encouraging them. Principle after principle is being conceded. On Friday the House accepted the principle of a Bill for the feeding of hungry children by the local teaching authority. We are not saying this was done without reason . . . But . . . the difficulties of such legislation are enormous. Parents who do their duty by their children are made to pay for those parents who bring children into the world and refuse to recognize their responsibility. Then the demand never stops. If the children are to be fed they must be medically inspected; then they must be clothed, and after that will come fresh claims.

It is an interesting reflection on how far independent moral principles can become submerged by the atmosphere of an age that here one finds a Christian newspaper solemnly opposing the feeding of hungry children, without realizing that some sort of explanation might be demanded for so radical a departure from Church tradition. Another issue was that of post-office wages: 'Here, again, it is right to give fair consideration to the demands of the post office staff, but the taxpayer has to find the money.' A conclusive argument! Again, a resolution had been carried in favour of the payment of M.P.s. A halt would have to be called: 'The day will come very soon when the man in the street and the great host of middle-class people who are leading a difficult life will make a fierce stand against the excessive taxation. An anti-social-ism party will be quickly formed if a leader can be found.' For this extreme Conservative position, with its emphasis on economical government, based on hungry children and underpaid postmen, the Unionist Opposition was a broken reed. Thus the debates on the Workmen's Compensation Bill, with Labour complaints that it did not go far enough, opened up the possibility of a more radical measure actually supported by the Opposition, and if this hap-pened, 'the responsibility must largely rest upon Unionist shoul-ders.' Chamberlain advocated the inclusion of clerks and domestic servants, and in face of this desertion to Socialistic forces, there was room for a 'Middle-Class Party' to offer sterner resistance. The 'sturdy self-reliance' of the British people was being under-mined, though hope was to be drawn from a meeting of income-tax payers directed against the 'menace of Socialistic legislation of all kinds.' The T.U.C. demands for old-age pensions and a minimum wage could not be achieved without 'the wholesale confiscation of property and the complete destruction of trade.' Catholics were right to oppose Socialism and Asquith to say it would mean despotism. The other parties must take a stand on grounds of principle, especially against old-age pensions, a 'gigantic system of doles in reversal of all the principles of our legislation of the last hundred years, which have been directed to the encouragement of thrift and industry rather than to extravagant plans for bribing the democracy to be thriftless.' Equally bad was the National Insurance scheme, and very strikingly the greatest indignation was reserved for the inclusion of domestic servants, a measure designed to 'bureaucratize the kitchen and interfere between mistress and maids'—and many must have been the nods of approval in Low Church drawing-rooms at this.

It is plain that in all this the *Church Family Newspaper* had abandoned any attempt to exercise specifically Christian judgement, and was simply constituting itself the mouthpiece of the most reactionary and negative elements in society, who found even the Unionist Party tainted with Socialism. Such opposition to all the social legislation of the Liberals was no doubt merely the reaction of a social group which had just suffered a catastrophic defeat. There was also still some, mainly hostile, interest in foreign Socialism, French, German, Russian and Italian, while the teachings of H. G. Wells were considered to show that even domestic Socialists were enemies of the family. The L.C.C. ought not to allow its schools to be used on Sundays for 'an atheistical and Socialistic propaganda.' But Socialism still continued to progress, and 'all the conservative and reasonable elements of the nation' ought to band together 'to open the eyes of those deluded by the Socialist mania.' Socialists regarded the Roman Catholic Church as their 'worst enemy,' but a more effective limitation was their own division into groups centred round Blatchford, the I.L.P., and the S.D.F. Particular difficulties of Socialism were the need for coercion for unpleasant work, harm to employee and consumer if the state was the only employer, and the impossible amount of expenditure involved, for example through the necessary bureaucracy and through compensation to property owners. The progress of Socialism was due not only to the enthusiasm of its supporters, but also to the sympathy and forbearance of the rich towards the poor: 'The moment the true battle is set in array we shall find the Socialist go down helplessly before the privileged . . .' The defection of Blatchford to the Conservatives was a symptom of the loss of the working classes: 'Socialism was loud in this country but never very strong, and it is weaker today than it has been for years.'[1]

The *British Weekly* showed a lively interest in Socialism, as in trade union affairs. A controversial figure of the past, G. J. Holyoake, received a warm obituary when he died in 1906, with special praise for his work for co-operation and a reference to his Congregationalist background.[2] But the antipathy his name had formerly aroused, on account both of his Socialism and his anti-religious views, continued to surround Robert Blatchford, who was still alive and active, and the *British Weekly* went so far as to print seventeen longish articles directed againt his religious views, written by the young Congregational minister, Frank Ballard, entitled 'The "Clarion" and Christianity.'[3] It also noticed a controversy in the *Labour Leader* between Blatchford and Bruce Glasier on religion, the latter arguing that Socialism should be religiously neutral, while the former thought it should be closely linked with rationalism. The *British Weekly* thought the victory of Blatchford would be a disaster for Socialism. The issue became complicated with Blatchford's campaign to warn Britain of the danger of war and to urge strong military preparations, for to Nonconformists, with a traditionally anti-militarist bias, this added to his offences. In a by-election at Croydon in 1909 the Liberals lost the seat to the Conservatives, and the Labour vote declined from 4,007 to 886, a result which the *British Weekly* attributed to the naval scare:

> What has happened is that the Labourists have practically deserted in a body to the Tory. There is nothing wonderful in this. Journalists who ought to know better talk as if Socialism in this country was friendly to peace. No doubt the leaders are, or at least some of them. But the rank and file on the smallest provocation are the fiercest of jingoes. Mr Keir Hardie may speak as he pleases, but his men melt away from him like snow. Mr Robert Blatchford of the *Clarion* is what we should call a thorough jingo, and many of the most influential

[1] *Church Family Newspaper*, July 8th, 1904; November 3rd, 1905; March 9th, March 30th, April 6th, November 16th, 1906; February 2nd, March 15th, March 28th, July 12th, September 13th, October 25th, November 29th, 1907; January 24th, February 7th, March 6th, June 12th, October 2nd, October 23rd, 1908; July 1st, 1910; November 24th, 1911; February 2nd, 1912.

[2] *British Weekly*, January 25th, 1906.

[3] Ibid., July 16th, to November 19th, 1903.

of the Fabians are among the same. Perhaps we should recall the word jingo and say that they are very strongly patriotic, and intent on a strong Army and strong Navy. As we showed in our papers on Socialism, the Continental Socialists are divided in the same way. With the great majority patriotism comes first. Let no one deceive himself into supposing that more than a mere fraction of the German Socialists will fail to side with their country. The Socialists nowadays only make a good show when they stand alone against Protectionists, and secure about two-thirds of the Liberal votes. In other respects they seem to be weakening with Liberalism, and much more rapidly. This Navy scare has scattered their ranks, but when it is over they may conceivably return.

Blatchford's articles in the *Daily Mail* caused great offence: 'Happily Mr Blatchford's action is repudiated by the Socialist party. Whatever their merits or demerits, no one can deny that the Socialists are the friends of peace'—a sentiment in direct contradiction to the article quoted above. On Blatchford's abandonment of the Labour Party and Socialism the *British Weekly* described him as 'merely a second-rate, elderly journalist,' and praised an article against him in the *Labour Leader*.

On Socialism in general a leader entitled 'The Socialist Art of Persuasion' was full of praise for the efficiency and enthusiasm of Socialist propaganda and missionary work, as an example to Christians, and another article called 'The Evangelists of Socialism' proved rather surprisingly to be about the growing number of motor-cars, which revealed too clearly the wealth of the upper classes. The varying attitudes of different Socialists to the drink question were noted, with criticism of those who were neutral. The warm sympathy with Socialism expressed at the 1909 Church Congress caused surprise, and it was contrasted with the Tory cry of 'Socialism' against the Budget. On the Budget itself, the *British Weekly* agreed that it could be called 'Socialist'—but this was the 'right kind' of Socialism. This was in reply to Lord Rosebery, but when Balfour made the same allegation, it was met with a flat denial that the Budget was Socialist in any sense, and Kautsky, Hardie and Snowden were quoted against Liberalism, to show the difference between Liberals and Socialists. Even if the Labour Party supported the Budget, the real Socialists—Grayson and Hyndman—were very hostile to it. The social legislation passed in these years was always championed by this newspaper. The Labour demand for school meals was supported; the

Workmen's Compensation Bill of 1906 did not go far enough; Lord Rosebery was wrong to think old-age pensions would ruin the working classes and the Empire; and the *Daily Mail* was wrong in its campaign for the exclusion of domestic servants from National Insurance. On the other hand the Minority Report on the poor-law made proposals which were too expensive.[1]

In the spring and early summer of 1908 the *British Weekly* published a series of articles on Socialism extending over nineteen issues. A preliminary article rejected merely destructive criticism of Socialism, gave a descriptive bibliography of recent works on the subject, and dismissed the Christian Socialism of Maurice as no longer a live issue. The scope of the remaining articles was as follows:

Part I

1. This dealt with Marxism, a doctrine now largely abandoned, especially by Bernstein. Aspects of Marx's teaching were summarized.

2. On Socialist tendencies of the last ten years. There were different attitudes to social amelioration. Special reference was made to Kautsky. The article was not unsympathetic to the demand that the whole system should be changed, and emphasized the miseries of the present.

3. On expropriation. This sympathized with Socialists who had to face the false criticism that their aim was to socialize all property, including even the most personal, and added a rather learned analysis of recent Socialist discussion of where the boundary should be drawn between social and personal property.

4. On compensation. Most present-day Socialists were in favour, but there was no agreement in detail.

5. On inheritance. This gave the views of various Continental and English writers.

6. On Socialists and small property owners. This showed how modern Socialists, even including so thorough a theorist as Kautsky, had been led to promise to leave small property owners alone, the author considering this the abandonment of a vital principle.

[1] *British Weekly*, March 8th, March 29th, 1906; October 10th, 1907; January 16th, February 6th, July 23rd, 1908; February 25th, April 1st, September 16th, September 30th, October 14th, October 21st, December 16th, December 23rd, 1909; January 6th, 1910; November 23rd, November 30th, 1911; May 14th, 1914.

Part II: Constructive Socialism

1. The Practical Working of the Socialist State. This quoted views on such topics as monarchy, the suffrage, Parliament, and the need for a bureaucracy.

2. The Commandeering of Lives under Socialism. Quoted Socialists for and against individual liberty, especially Karl Pearson. The author considered Socialism inherently unfavourable to liberty, for 'the Socialist State could not afford to tolerate rebels.'

3. The Rewards of Labour under Socialism. Quoted Blatchford on the need for absolute equality, showing that nearly all other Socialists had abandoned this idea.

4. Socialism and the Family. Socialists were not hostile to the family, and indeed they alleged that it was Capitalism that disrupted family life. This was partly true, but not all evils were of social origin. Socialists favoured the emancipation of women and easier divorce. On the treatment of children modern Socialists held the same views as Liberals.

5. Socialism and Religion. English Socialists were not hostile to religion. (There were quotations from Hardie, Macdonald, and Wells.) French, Italian and German Socialists were against religion, and Socialists in general were critical of the Roman Catholic Church and in favour of disestablishment. The question was asked whether there could be a Christian Socialism, and it was answered that Christian Socialist literature revealed that it stood only for 'sober and gradual reform.' A Christian Socialist like Adderley differed little from ordinary social reformers, and the real Socialists did not accept the Christian kind.

6. On the Press. Analysed the difficulties of a free press under Socialism.

7. On Patriotism, Armaments, and Foreign Policy. This described the Socialists' return to patriotism and their desire to replace standing armies with a citizen force, and to moralize diplomacy.

8. 'The Dream of Internationalism.' Described the internationalism of Socialism, traceable back to Marx.

9. 'At the Grave of Karl Marx.' The title was literal, in that the article described a visit to Highgate Cemetery, but also symbolic, in referring to the abandonment of many of Marx's ideas by modern Socialists. Real social progress was being made.[1]

This series of articles was well-informed and penetrating in its

[1] *British Weekly.*, March 5th to July 9th, 1908.

criticisms, for example in its demonstration that Christian Socialism had little in common with Marxism, and in its approach to Marx as a prophetic figure of the past rather than as a contemporary threat. It was not unfriendly to Socialism, and accepted the criticisms of Capitalist society, but it also emphasized the tendency to divergence and disintegration in the contemporary Socialist movement.

The series showed too that the *British Weekly* took notice of the international Socialist movement, and there were numerous other references to events abroad. Unlike the *Church Times*, the *British Weekly* fully supported the Russian Revolution of 1905. Germany was often in the news. There was no regret at the heavy defeat of the Socialists in the General Election of 1907. Among leading personalities in the news from time to time were Liebknecht, Kautsky, and Bebel, for whom there was enthusiasm. Divisions in German Socialist ranks were noted, while big Socialist gains in 1912 were attributed to miseries resulting from tariffs, and regarded as a triumph for the cause of peace. Not so much attention was paid to France. When a Socialist was imprisoned for antipatriotic propaganda it was considered that the Government would be guilty of 'culpable weakness' if it released him early, as on previous occasions, and debates about Socialism and religion involving Jaurès were reported. Other references had a more cosmopolitan character. Comment on an international conference at Stuttgart in 1907 included praise for the moderation of Bernstein and Ramsay Macdonald, and in 1909 Socialist splits in France, England, and Germany were duly reported. In 1910 the *British Weekly* analysed a number of possible spheres of Socialist disagreement.[1]

The *Universe* remained as hostile as ever to Socialism, though there was little comment before the 1906 election, except for an appeal by an American Franciscan to Catholics to oppose it, printed without comment. The main question, as with trade unions, was what attitude Catholics ought to adopt. It was admitted that many Catholics were Socialists, and even read the *Clarion*, thus associating themselves with a Socialism which was

[1] *British Weekly*, January 6th, 1905; January 31st, August 22nd, August 29th, October 17th, 1907; January 2nd, September 17th, September 24th, November 19th, 1908; January 28th, April 15th, September 16th, 1909; February 24th, April 4th, September 1st, 1910; January 18th, January 25th, 1912; August 8th, 1913.

'an open and avowed enemy of Christianity.' Blatchford was
working for a materialistic state, and 'Catholics can have no hand
in playing Frankenstein,[1] and helping to create such a monster
without a soul,' though the word Socialism was 'by itself too wide
a term to be the exclusive possession of anti-Christian propagandists.'

This approach seemed to offer a faint hope of a more moderate
attitude through the distinction of good and bad forms of Socialism, but the impression was illusory. Hardie's declaration of the
hostility of Socialists to all other parties was noted and Catholics
were urged not to support Socialism under any name. An article in
the *Labour Leader* by an ex-Catholic priest, attacking Catholicism,
brought the comment: 'This is Socialism in practice!' The most
shocked response was to the 'threat' of Socialism to the family,
with two articles replying to Macdonald's denial that Socialism
was opposed either to religion or to the family. These articles
quoted Marx, Belfort Bax, Morris, and the inevitable Blatchford.
Momentarily in 1909 a much more sympathetic approach was
adopted, and the attitude so familiar in the Church of England
made its appearance in the title: 'True and False Socialism.' The
Church had condemned 'official Socialism'—again a useful
phrase for those seeking a compromise with some kind of 'unofficial Socialism'—but Socialists were often attacked unjustly, and
many of their criticisms of society were true. There were many
'high-principled social workers' in the movement. Socialism was
a reaction against Protestantism, a surprising conclusion to be
explained by the identification of Protestantism and individualism.
Fortunately Socialists were learning to blame the Reformation for
Capitalism, so they might come to see that the true Socialism was
Catholicism. Again Socialism arose from the privileges of the rich,
and the true 'champion, defender and friend' of Labour was the
Catholic Church, for all the evils of society rose from 'Protestantism, the religion of individualism and self-interest.' But this
more constructive approach was not continued, and when Jowett
and Hardie spoke of the full commitment of the I.L.P. to Socialism
the *Universe* condemned the latter by the odd means of quoting
against it such aggressive Secularists as Spencer, Ingersoll, and
Bradlaugh. Socialism was interfering in moral affairs, and it was
basically Secularist: 'Hence, at all costs Catholics must be taught
that Socialism is fundamentally and radically a false system.' In the

[1] Sic.

disturbed period before the war the hostility to Socialism was once again as fierce as it had ever been, and an article starting out from troubles in Spain but ranging far afield linked together 'Anarchism, Socialism, Suffragism' as works of the Devil: 'Socialism is the catchword of Antichrist to rally round him the forces of destruction . . . The workers are, indeed, nothing more nor less than the conscripts of the social revolution, who are being sedulously drilled by the Lawless One for the universal anarchy.' The three groups mentioned were 'microbes of social disintegration.' Examples of Socialist tyranny were Henry George's plans of expropriation, 'closed shop' trade unionism, and forcing the unwilling to strike. In Australia Socialism had shown itself both a failure and anti-religious. In France it was worse: 'The syndicalist and his compatriot, the true socialist, represent man in his most repulsive guise—without God, without charity, without patriotism.' In England, 'Catholics are, or should be, the natural enemies of Socialism.' Even the co-operative movement had gone astray, for the Co-operative Congress had become a sphere for the advocacy of easier divorce, though Catholic co-operators were protesting.[1]

The conclusion on this chapter must be similar to that on the trade unions. Towards the end of the period the Anglican press was not so interested in Socialism as previously, and it was less sympathetic. The *Guardian* was in any case less concerned now with social issues; the *Church Times* was absorbed with the Christian Socialist movement, which was by now traditionally associated with Anglo-Catholicism; while the *Church Family Newspaper* merely represented the less constructive aspects of the Conservative Party, and was more concerned to use the term 'Socialism' as a stick to beat Lloyd George than anything else. The *Universe*, except for a brief spell of more positive interest, was simply destructive in its criticism, though its approach continually revealed that many of the faithful stubbornly persisted in believing that Catholics could be Socialists. They were in day-to-day touch with the Labour movement in the north, and they must have found many of the more apocalyptic utterances of their newspaper quite irrelevant to the colleagues they knew personally in the

[1] *Universe*, January 24th, 1905; February 23rd, September 28th, 1906; January 10th, January 17th, January 24th, 1908; March 12th, July 9th, 1909; April 1st, 1910; April 18th, June 13th, July 11th, August 22nd, October 31st, 1913; June 26th, 1914.

I.L.P. branch or the trade union lodge. In the future the Roman Catholic contribution to the Labour movement in Britain was to be much larger than one would expect from the attitude at this period of the hierarchy and the press. In the formative period of modern British Socialism the Roman Catholic Church maintained consistently a position of uncompromising hostility—indeed of that particularly adamant hostility which consists in the refusal even to distinguish between the more and less pernicious aspects of a movement. The *Universe* not only attacked Karl Marx and Ramsay Macdonald, but it attacked Ramsay Macdonald as though he were Karl Marx. The *British Weekly* in contrast was consistently friendly to many moderate Socialists, and while it sometimes attacked Socialism, at other times it said that it ought not to be attacked. It was the best-informed of all these newspapers, not only on English Socialism, but even on the ramifications of the movement in France and Germany, and even the most Marxist and Secularist brands were spoken of with respect. Many of the criticisms of English Socialists were not of their Socialism at all; thus there was a bitter antipathy to those who openly preferred to support the Conservative Party rather than the Liberals, the *British Weekly* regarding them not only as sinners, but as unnatural ones too. Blatchford was hated not for his Socialism, nor even so much for his anti-religious views, as for what was regarded as his jingoism. Finally the *British Weekly* was ranged against all the rest of these papers in that much of what these attacked as Socialism was nothing more than the policy of the Liberal Government, enthusiastically supported by Nonconformist Radicalism.

Thus a commonly-accepted view needs some modification. It is often supposed that the collectivist trend of this period was advantageous to the Roman Catholic Church, and especially disadvantageous to Nonconformity, with its strongly individualistic tradition. This may perhaps have been so, but it is a certain fact that of the newspapers here discussed the Roman Catholic paper showed the firmest attachment to the existing economic and social system, while the Free Church paper was the most ready to welcome collectivist trends.

CHAPTER 6

THE CHURCHES AND THE POLITICAL ORGANIZATION OF THE WORKING CLASSES

1 *The Enfranchisement of the Working Classes*

NOWHERE IS THERE a clearer contrast of apparent and real Radicalism than in the debates which so often recurred during the middle decades of the nineteenth century on the franchise issue. Those groups which repeatedly proclaimed their sympathy with the working classes but found abundant reasons why they should not be given the vote were sharply contrasted with others which simply accepted the working-class political spokesmen as natural allies in a struggle against entrenched privilege. While Anglican clerics of Christian Socialist inclinations regarded themselves as the workers' best friends, the more dissident wing of Dissent co-operated easily with some of the workers' leaders for whom the Church of England and the restricted franchise were alike parts of a coherent system of upper-class self-interest.

In the Chartist era the expression of this alliance was the Complete Suffrage movement: 'It was a deliberate overture made by the free-traders and Radicals to the Chartists, but the inspiration of it was as much nonconformist as free-trade or Radical.'[1] Many Nonconformists were still suspicious of political action, but the situation was changing; on the Right wing the Wesleyans were still a rather unpromising field for Radical propaganda, but Baptists, Congregationalists, Unitarians and Quakers all offered considerable promise from this point of view. The dominant economic school was already attacked by Socialists as an instrument of the bourgeoisie, but it was still generally regarded as a Radical force, and it seemed natural to try to establish a link between it and the leadership of the working classes. In the Complete Suffrage movement the Nonconformists were trying to act as 'mediators' between these two forces.

[1] F. E. Gillespie, *Labor and Politics in England: 1850–1867* (1927), 23.

The immediate inspiration of the new movement was a series of articles in the *Nonconformist* by Edward Miall, its editor, in 1841, on the subject of 'The reconciliation between the Middle and Labouring Classes.' Joseph Sturge had the articles published as a pamphlet. It reached a fortieth edition in the course of several years.

The movement found expression in the Complete Suffrage Union, a short-lived society founded in 1842:

> The large religious element in its support is shown by the fact that it had about two hundred ministers among its adherents, and by the general tenor of its petition to parliament in April, 1842, which based its appeal for universal suffrage upon natural right, British constitutional precedent with regard to taxation and representation, and upon 'holy religion.'[1]

The movement attracted the attention of the Chartists: 'Edward Miall's tract, which had inspired the Complete Suffrage Movement, was reprinted and was discussed favourably in Chartist journals.'[2] This movement was quite distinct from Christian Socialism, and there was even an open antagonism between the two, since the Christian Socialists thought political reform of small account compared with new forms of economic organization, under the workers' control—a familiar controversy in Labour history. Some, though not all, of the Christian Socialists were distinctly suspicious of political democracy. Moreover the two groups saw the social conflict in quite different terms; for Kingsley, as for the Tory democrats of the Young England group, the real battle was between the Church, the gentlemen and the workers on the one hand, against the shopkeepers and the Manchester School on the other, and Ludlow at the 1852 election advised the workers to support a Tory who was opposed both to the extension of the franchise and to the reduction of wages rather than the most extreme Radical who lived on cheap labour. They did not realize that the economic emancipation of the working classes was to be found in the use of political power. The People's League, founded by Lovett in 1848, was a renewed attempt at an alliance of the workers and the middle classes, and again 'Edward Miall and a few other middle-class leaders gave their adhesion to the project...'[3] In 1849 the National Parliamentary and Financial Reform Association was founded to promote franchise reform,

---

[1] Gillespie, op. cit., 23f., 25, note 2.
[2] Ibid., 31.   [3] Ibid., 67.

with strong support from Miall and the Rev Thomas Spencer. But if the Christian Socialists were socially remote from the working classes the lower middle-class Nonconformists were alienated from them by some of the most characteristic features of their own tradition, especially their Sabbatarianism. The National Sunday League, formed to advocate the opening of museums and art-galleries on Sundays, received considerable working-class support, but was opposed by Nonconformists. Sir Joshua Walmsley, who was President first of the Parliamentary and Financial Reform Association and then of the National Sunday League, was defeated in the Leicester election of 1857, and this helped to break the alliance of Nonconformists and working-class Radicals.

The *Nonconformist* was naturally a consistent advocate of Miall's policy, since Miall edited it, and it was thus a reliable platform for the demand for a further reform of Parliament. In 1858 it rather ingenuously opposed the idea of 'weighted' franchises, designed to equalize the strength of various social classes, on the grounds that it was 'everywhere admitted' that the interests of Labour and property were 'identical.' Wealth would exercise enough influence even under universal suffrage, and needed no special protection. In any case the reform demanded was only a recognition of the fact that 'real power is already with the people.'[1] Over the same period the *Guardian* fought a prolonged rearguard action, always finding objections to particular proposals for reform, though never forthrightly opposing the principle. Slightly earlier it had taken its stand on the Christian Socialist ground that social, not political, reform was most urgent. In 1852 it was still too early to alter the 1832 Act. In 1853 a wider franchise was opposed because the classes involved were showing their irresponsibility by strikes. In 1854 it was wrong to deal with this issue on the eve of a war. By 1858 the *Guardian* wanted to abolish the property qualification for M.P.s (not for the vote) so as to steal the Chartists' thunder and put real workers into Parliament instead of 'dabbling speculators of a higher class.' The assimilation of county and borough franchises was opposed because it would give predominance to one class. There was no real demand for reform. By 1859 the *Guardian* was in retreat. It would be unfair to enfranchise the town workers but not the rural, but the franchise could be gradually widened. The ballot was a dangerous innovation. The Government's proposals were too extreme, not, as the Radicals said,

[1] *Nonconformist*, December 15th, 1858.

too mild. Russell was guided by self-interest, and Cobden was right to say that education was more important than the vote. Even Bright was praised, for abandoning extreme demands and accepting a compromise. When a borough qualification of £6 was suggested, the *Guardian* proposed £7 instead. A dissident Liberal protest that some constituencies would be controlled by trade unions brought ready illustrations of their tyranny. It was all very well for Bright to say that the new voters would not act in unison: he expected those concerned to act in concert at any rate in the campaign for reform. There might be fifty to 100 trade union M.P.s. A little later the *Guardian* modified its offer for the boroughs to £8, but thought that perhaps no change at all was needed, with the decline in the value of money having brought about a doubling of the £10 householders since 1835. Democracy was the cause of all the troubles of America and Australia. The workers could easily qualify as ten-pounders if they drank less beer. If Gladstone thought that the record of the Rochdale Pioneers proved that the workers deserved the vote the *Guardian* thought that they had shown the way to qualify under the existing law. Indeed many were so qualified, and the change would transfer power to one class, who might then form 'a distinct political party.' When Hughes urged that the workers held different economic doctrines from the middle classes, and ought to have an opportunity of making them known, this was taken as a warning that enfranchisement would lead to a social conflict. But it was grudgingly admitted that America had shown that democracy, whatever its faults, could produce great men.[1]

In the end the issue was decided by what the *Nonconformist* called 'The Hyde Park Mêlée,' and the various newspapers reacted according to their own traditions. The *Guardian* blamed the organizers, and the *Nonconformist* the Government, while the *Universe* contrasted the lenient treatment of the 'rioters' with fierce sentences passed on Fenians. But by now everybody was worried: the *Guardian* thought it perhaps better to pass the Bill than to have more trouble, and when further demonstrations were

[1] *Guardian*, June 14th, 1848; February 11th, 1852; December 7th, 1853; February 15th, 1854; June 9th, July 7th, December 15th, 1858; February 2nd, February 9th, March 2nd, March 9th, March 23rd, August 24th, December 14th, 1859; March 7th, March 28th, April 18th, May 9th, 1860; April 17th, December 18th, 1861; May 10th, 1865; March 14th, March 21st, April 25th, June 6th, 1866.

promised the *Nonconformist* too began to get alarmed, and was glad when they turned out smaller than expected. Both papers were full of praise this time for the demonstrators, and both thought the time for further delay was past, though the *Guardian* still only advocated the enfranchisement of the 'more eligible' workers. The *Nonconformist* warned the workers not to go too far, and to remember 1848.[1]

Thus at the very end of the period terminating with the second Reform Act the well-established middle-class Radicalism of the Miall group began to show signs of concern at working-class aggressiveness. But in this period as a whole the Radical wing of Nonconformity simply took it for granted that it was itself a natural ally for the discontented working classes, and that the demand for Parliamentary reform, and indeed the current working-class demands in general, were part of the same attack on privilege, as exemplified by the restricted franchise, the House of Lords, and the Church of England, which was led by the *Nonconformist*. It did not seem conceivable as yet that Anglican clergymen could be in the forefront of any kind of Radical movement, and the attitude of the *Guardian* shows that it was in fact true that all that Christian Socialism had so far achieved was merely to veil a basically conservative outlook under a liberal mode of expression; the Church of England was on the side of the workers, but it nearly always found the specific demands of the workers' leaders too extreme, or at least inopportune. As for the Roman Catholic Church, it was as yet little interested in English social conflicts, and inclined to discuss them only as illustrative material in debates on Continental, or, much more often, Irish, problems.

2   The Independent Labour Party

After a gap of half a generation the political aspects of the Labour movement again came to the fore in the 'eighties. It was in this decade that the working-class movement in Britain ceased to be a wholly disorganized force and the aspirations of the politically-conscious workers began to crystallize around the bodies which were later, at the end of the century, to coalesce into the Labour Party. In the closing decade of the nineteenth century the most important of these bodies was the Independent Labour Party,

---

[1] *Guardian*, July 25th, August 1st, December 5th, 1866; *Nonconformist*, July 25th, November 28th, December 5th, 1866; January 9th, 1867; *Universe*, August 4th, 1866.

and the I.L.P. was dominated by the somewhat prophetic figure of Keir Hardie. Hardie was in some ways representative of the Christian Socialist tradition, though to say this is perhaps to reinterpret this term out of recognition, for historically Christian Socialism had been Anglican, ecclesiastical in basis, philosophical and scholarly in character. To Hardie, who has been held largely responsible for preventing the alienation of the working-class movement from religion, such a tradition was utterly foreign. The older Christian Socialist outlook was perfectly exemplified in the C.S.U., but

> working-class Christian Socialism has been of quite another character from that of the Christian Social Union. Untheological and even anti-theological, and non-ecclesiastical or even contemptuous of any external organization or expression of religion, it has been essentially a moral humanitarian idealism—derived from Religion and expressing itself in political action. It has owed little or nothing (at any rate consciously) to the Coleridge-Maurice-Westcott tradition of thought; its spiritual ancestry has been almost entirely nonconformist. It has displayed an attachment to the teaching of Jesus and to His example to the almost entire exclusion of devotion to His person.[1]

Hardie grew up in a home where Secularist beliefs were strongly maintained. The family 'did not go to church. Indeed they were not only indifferent to organized religion, they were actively hostile, called themselves atheists and no clergyman or minister entered their door. There was no Bible in the house and the young Hardies were not sent to Sunday School.' Like many other Labour leaders, Keir began with the temperance movement, attending the Band of Hope at the local church and in time graduating to the Good Templars' lodge. In this way he met local ministers, especially Dan Craig, of Hamilton, who persuaded him to go to his church. Later Hardie wrote of Craig that 'he studied the New Testament from the human much more than from the doctrinal standpoint,' and that he was in effect a Socialist, although he did not use the word.[2] Hardie began to attend Craig's church regularly, and in 1879, at the age of twenty-three, he wrote in his diary that he had been converted to Christianity. (It was three years since Beatrice Webb had been converted *from* Christianity, so that two of the outstanding exemplars of the opposed religious tendencies of the

---

[1] Binyon, op. cit., 181.
[2] Emrys Hughes, *Keir Hardie* (1956), 23.

Labour movement passed each other in their spiritual pilgrimage.)
The young Hardie read Renan's humanistic life of Jesus. It was
characteristic of him that he always referred to the New Testament
rather than to the Bible. He joined the Evangelical Union, a
breakaway Church of Congregationalist tendencies, and has been
counted among the heroes of Congregationalism, though he was
not much of a denominationalist.[1] It has been said that he spoke the
language of the Bible and the *Pilgrim's Progress*, and he continued
to be attracted not by Christian theology but by the Sermon on the
Mount. The religion he adopted was not like that which Beatrice
Webb abandoned; indeed in some ways it was more like the
religion she retained—a humanism strongly tinged with Christian
ethics. His parents remained atheists.

This conversion partly undid the effects on Hardie's mind of an
incident which happened when as a child newly at work he was
dismissed without notice for coming to work late at a time when
there was illness at home, the dismissal being by an employer
'noted for his piety.'[2] In his work in the Labour movement he
found that it was advisable to keep his religious references quite
vague. On one occasion, in moving a vote of thanks to Alexander
Macdonald, the miners' leader and Liberal M.P., he compared him
with Luther, to the indignation of the large number of Roman
Catholics in his audience. The minister of the local Evangelical
Union church, which he had joined, was a correspondent for the
local paper, and when he was away ill he asked Hardie to deputize
for him, as he was at the time without work. He was paid £1 per
week, and this job became permanent. He was an active church
member and founded a Good Templar lodge, but his later career
brought him into conflict with church leaders of every breed. At
the 1895 election Roman Catholic priests instructed their people to
vote Conservative or abstain, but not to vote for Hardie, who lost
his seat, although he claimed that there were 'churchmen and
Nonconformists' among his supporters. He offended many church
people by an attack on Lord Overtoun, a Scottish chemical manufacturer, whom he accused of compelling his workers to work on
Sundays under very bad conditions, while campaigning for strict
Sunday observance. He quoted against him Christ's condemnation
of the Pharisees, with the comment that some 'good, pious Christians will be shocked at this "irreverent" quotation of Scripture.'

[1] A. Peel, *A Congregational Two Hundred*, s.v. Hardie.
[2] Hughes, op. cit., 16.

They would approve it as applied to dead hypocrites of long ago, forgetting that Christ spoke it of 'the Lord Overtouns of his day.' He denied that he was attacking the Churches, for he was trying to stir them up to refuse the gifts and services of such men. He received no support from the churches of Glasgow, and in many of them he was denounced from the pulpit. He insisted that it was no use the evangelists D. L. Moody and John McNeill coming for their campaign, since the people's thoughts would be taken up with Lord Overtoun. In 1899 he again came into conflict with some church leaders over his attitude to the South African war, when his paper, the *Labour Leader*, refused to celebrate Christmas as a protest against the war. He attacked the clergy who supported it, and asserted that all sins 'are as virtues compared to the gilded, cold heartlessness of organized Christianity. The proud, bombastic, self-righteous spirit of Phariseeism dominates the Church and all its works.'[1] On his re-election to Parliament (for Merthyr) in 1900 he decided to affirm instead of taking the oath, lest he should kiss the same book as Joseph Chamberlain. In the 1906 election the *Labour Leader* alleged that the Liberals were spreading a whispering campaign that he was an 'atheist and a foreigner,' and that Nonconformist support was ranged behind the Liberals. In Hardie's book *From Serfdom to Socialism* he devoted a chapter to Socialism and Christianity, asserting that the Sermon on the Mount and many other parts of the New Testament were akin to Socialism. In the election campaign of January 1910 he was supported at Merthyr by two ministers, R. J. Campbell and Geoffrey Ramsay, Vicar of Radstock. On one occasion he addressed Dowlais Adult School on 'What think ye of Christ?' In this address he condemned Christians for going to church on Sunday and acting for the rest of the week as though Christ had never lived. He referred to the 'failure of the working class to attend the church,' but said that there was 'no mystery about that. The working class was not interested to know what Christ thought of the Scribes and Pharisees of 1,900 years ago; men and women wanted to know what Christ thought of the Scribes and Pharisees of the beginning of the twentieth century.' He went on to the subjects of the war and poverty. 'It was time there was an Adult School or something else to rescue Christ from the hands of those who did not understand him and restore him to the common people.' Society was based on self-interest and so it was anti-Christian.

[1] Hughes, op. cit., 91ff.

Hardie gave a similar address to a Brotherhood meeting at Browning Hall, London. He defined Christianity as 'sacrifice having its origin in love.' The only way to serve God was by serving humanity; Christ was persecuted because of his love for the poor and his hatred of hypocrisy.[1]

Like so many of his contemporaries Hardie held sincerely and tenaciously to a religious standpoint which would be considered scarcely tenable by either earlier or later generations:

> Like all great creative personalities, Hardie found the inspiration of his life in the deeper things of the spirit. Even when overwhelmed with immediate duties, he would find some secluded and beautiful spot where alone he could refresh his soul by communion with the universal life which he was seeking to express. He was always conscious of a Divine Purpose, and he revered, above all, the life and teachings of Christ, who lived it so completely.
>
> Towards the end of his life he said that were he to live it again he would devote it to the advocacy of the Gospel of Christ . . .[2]

Hardie was a Scot, and his background thus differed to some extent from that of English Labour leaders, though even in Scotland he could fairly be described as 'Nonconformist,' a word normally applicable only in England. The same balance of religious conviction in the Labour movement which is represented by the conversions, in opposite directions, of Beatrice Webb and Keir Hardie, is visible throughout the I.L.P. The Manchester I.L.P. was founded by a partnership of John Trevor, the founder of the Labour Church, and therefore the representative of something like Hardie's ethical and untheological Christianity, with Blatchford, a vigorous spokesman of the Secularist tradition. Again, the foundation conference of the I.L.P. had to make its choice between a resolution demanding 'unsectarian' education and an amendment substituting 'secular,' and chose in favour of the former. The recent author who had made the closest study of the origins of the Labour Party concludes that the breach between the workers and religion was averted in England by Nonconformity rather than by Christian Socialism; this despite plutocratic tendencies in Nonconformity itself, such as pew-rents, and despite an analogy between the C.S.U. and the Fabian Society, both aiming at permeation. But he also notes that there was a strong natural con-

[1] Hughes, op. cit., 202f.

[2] A. Fenner Brockway in *Christian Social Reformers of the Nineteenth Century*, edited by Hugh Martin (1927), 242.

nexion between the Labour movement and the Roman Catholic Church, in that more than any other denomination it drew its support predominantly from the working classes.[1]

Among prominent I.L.P. leaders associated with Nonconformity was Fred Jowett of Bradford. His parents, though not particularly religious, considered themselves 'chapel folk' and were connected with Horton Lane Congregational Church. Many of the Bradford Socialists were Secularists, but 'Fred retained some connexion with chapel folk and helped to bring in converts who later counted a good deal in the Movement.' It is related that on one occasion there were twelve Nonconformist ministers on the platform of the Liberal candidate at an election meeting when Jowett threatened them: 'If you persist in opposing the Labour Movement there will soon be more reason than ever to complain of the absence of working men from your chapels. We shall establish our own Labour Church.'[2]

A striking representative of the religious tradition of the I.L.P. was Margaret McMillan (1860–1931).[3] She was born in America, the daughter of a Scottish immigrant, after whose death the family returned to Britain. She spoke for the dockers during the strike of 1892, and in 1893 she was 'called' to the Labour Church at Bradford and joined the I.L.P., becoming known as the 'labour prophetess of the north.' Her life's work for children's health and education was inspired by religious convictions.

A more direct representative of Nonconformity in the I.L.P. was Charles Leach (1847–1919).[4] He was a Methodist by upbringing and served for two years in the New Connexion ministry before becoming a Congregationalist. While minister at Queen's Park, Harrow Road, he joined the I.L.P. The *British Weekly* found this interesting enough to interview Leach, the interview being published in November 1894 under the heading 'The Independent Labour Party.'[5] While justifying his joining of the party, Leach explained that he disapproved of its methods and of its hostility to the Liberal Party, and thought that Joseph Chamberlain might emerge as head of a Liberal-Labour party—a

[1] Pelling, op. cit., 132ff.

[2] F. Brockway, *Socialism Over Sixty Years* (1946), 26f., 31, 41.

[3] G. A. N. Lowndes, *Margaret McMillan 'The Children's Champion'* (1960), and *Dict. Nat. Biog.* (1931–1940), s.v. McMillan.

[4] Obituary in *Congregational Year Book 1920*, 106.

[5] *British Weekly*, November 1st, 1894.

somewhat belated hope. He believed in the Liberal Nonconformist ideals of Home Rule and Disestablishment, but asked what benefit they would bring to the working classes, in this echoing the general protest of the Labour movement against Liberal policy. He was ready for a wide measure of nationalization and municipal housing. His obituary in the *Congregational Year Book* makes no mention of his connexion with the I.L.P., but relates that in 1910, at the age of about sixty-three, he was elected to Parliament for Colne Valley as a Liberal, remaining a member for a few years till his health broke down. The reason for the transfer of his allegiance is not clear, but it is plainly very likely to have been due to the gradual realization that the I.L.P. was serious in its determination to pursue its own line and not become another 'Lib.-Lab.' group. His joining of the party shows how hard it was even in 1894 to convince men of Radical outlook that Liberalism and Labour were more than different Left-wing emphases, despite the repeated insistence by I.L.P. and Fabian spokesmen that the Liberals were at least as bad as the Tories.

3   *The Last Years of the 'Lib.-Lab.' Era in Nonconformity*

The closing years of the nineteenth century and the first decade of the twentieth were the last period in which Radical Nonconformists could regard themselves as the natural allies of the Labour movement. The alliance did not come to an end with Edward Miall but it was now in danger, from the divergence of interest between traditional Radical ideals and the demands of the working classes. The later 'nineties and the early Edwardian years represented the last attempt to bring together these essentially different forces, and what eventually brought such efforts to an end was the sweeping nature of the Liberal victory in 1906, after which it seemed unnecessary to go very far to meet Labour demands. The Liberal triumph seemed to belie the prognostications of those who had repeatedly warned the Liberal leaders that without a much greater effort to win the mass support of organized Labour the party was doomed, and more than half a generation was to pass before it was revealed that the falsification of their prophecies had only been apparent.

A figure of this Indian summer was Sir Halley Stewart (1838–1937)[1] who from 1863 to 1877 served as a Congregational minister, though he was not ordained. Thereafter he was a newspaper

[1] *Dict. Nat. Biog.* (1931–1940), s.v. Stewart.

editor, a businessman, and a politician. A biographical article describes him as an 'advanced Liberal,' who 'advocated adult suffrage for both sexes, the land for the people, religious equality, and the abolition of hereditary legislators.' He was twice a Liberal M.P. (1887–1895 and 1906–1910), and he established a trust for 'research towards the Christian ideal in all social life.' In London the Nonconformist-Labour alliance was incorporate in the Progressive Party, with Congregationalists Thomas McKinnon Wood (1855–1927) and the brothers Evan and Albert Spicer prominent.

Something of the strength of Nonconformity in public life in this era, even apart from the wholly exceptional position created by the Liberal landslide of 1906, is revealed by statistics given in the *Independent* of Free Church M.P.s sitting on the Liberal side of the House in the 1892–1895 Parliament. (The *Independent* does not give details of any on the Conservative side, either because there were none, or, more likely, because it considered them beneath notice.) The total adds up to 109, made up as follows: 11 Baptists, 27 Congregationalists, 30 Methodists (of assorted kinds), 10 Presbyterians, 10 Quakers, 20 Unitarians, and 1 Swedenborgian. Not only is the overall strength notable, but also the distribution between denominations: the Methodists were far and away the largest body of Nonconformists, if all the Methodists were counted together, but accounted for less than one-third of the M.P.s. The Congregationalists, a very much smaller denomination, were almost as well-represented as the Methodists, and the (religiously) radical wing of Nonconformity, the Unitarians and Quakers, were to be found out of all proportion to their very small numbers. It is safe to say that many of the most active Radicals in Parliament, who were most anxious to reorientate the Liberal Party and to make it the party of the rising working classes, would be found among these 109 members.[1]

4   *The 'Lib.-Lab.' Alliance and the Nonconformist Press in the 'Nineties*

Both the *Nonconformist* (later the *Independent*) and the *British Weekly*, but especially the latter, provided a platform for advocating the alliance of Nonconformist Radicalism and the Labour movement. In 1890 the *British Weekly* alleged that both parties had

[1] *Independent*, July 11th, 1895.

neglected the interests of the workers, and for the Liberals the 'old order' would 'drag along' while Gladstone remained:

> The lesson for Liberal politicians especially is that their time is now, if they are not to be cheated of the fruit of all their labour and sacrifice for the Liberal party. Instead of reducing their programme to one item they should be pressing forward the long arrears for immediate settlement, for they and their questions are in immediate danger of being stranded together.

In the months and years that followed this point of view was often repeated. The Liberal leaders missed the significance of speeches by Lord Randolph Churchill and Joseph Chamberlain on this question, and if Gladstone was only interested in Home Rule he should be replaced. The election to Parliament of John Burns was good, since 'he represents a hundred constituencies besides his own.' Liberals failed to realize that the Labour members were in a position of power, and that 'the working classes are shaping out new politics for themselves, with official co-operation if they can get it, but, otherwise, with fearless independence.' John Morley had alienated Labour, though it was a pity that he should be opposed at a by-election; but this Labour opposition was at least valuable as a test of strength. From the I.L.P. defeat Labour should realize that with a 'little tact' full Radical support could be obtained for Labour demands, while Morley should realize the importance of social questions. There was anger at Liberal disturbance of a Labour meeting at Leeds, and satire for promises to Labour by Churchill, not likely to make Labour trust 'that slippy person.' Burt was a good member of the Government, but he exaggerated the advantages to the working classes of the Liberal Government. A Fabian manifesto was useful as showing the wide difference between Socialists and Liberals, according to the *Independent*, and the Liberal aim should be to capture the working classes from the Socialists. It was true that the workers were not interested in Home Rule, but they ought to remember that however bad the Liberal Government was, the Conservatives would be worse. The *British Weekly* was very pleased at Burns's advice to the electors of Accrington, urging them in the absence of a Labour candidate to vote Liberal, but this was soon followed by a Liberal-Labour clash at Attercliffe. The I.L.P. hated Liberalism even more than Conservatism:

> Many Labour men go further than the advanced Liberal, but the Liberals may come up with them in time. They are parted only by

stages in a journey. A deep gulf, however, lies between Liberals and Socialists, and no amount of coaxing and bullying will bring the average Liberal to accept a Socialist as his representative. Such a comment suggests that despite its enthusiasm for the alliance with Labour, even the *British Weekly* would in time be forced to admit the impossibility of its survival as the leaders of the working classes became more attracted to Socialism. But the same occasion reveals how far the Liberals were from any real effort to come to terms with the Labour movement before such a trend was too far advanced, for the Labour leaders at Attercliffe had understood that one of their own people would be selected as Liberal candidate, and only when this opportunity had been missed did the I.L.P. intervene. There was alarm at the size of the I.L.P. vote at Leicester a few weeks later, and it was urged that there should be a full Liberal-Labour alliance, with constituencies shared out. The Socialists would break away to form a new party, but the Liberals ought not to speak with contempt even of them, for Socialism was 'the creed of many powerful minds, and can be overthrown only by argument.' Liberal-Labour conversations at Sheffield were very satisfactory, and led the *British Weekly* to analyse the Liberal Party into remnants of the upper classes, Nonconformists, and the working classes. Unfortunately control was with the first group. Liberals could go some way even with Socialists, and much further with the rest of the Labour movement. Chamberlain would fail in his efforts to win the workers for the Conservative Party, even though the I.L.P., to the great wrath of the *British Weekly*, preferred Tories to Liberals. A very small Liberal majority in a straight fight with Labour at Bristol obviously implied that Conservative votes had gone to Labour, and the *British Weekly* was momentarily alarmed at the improbable thought of an alliance between Lord Salisbury and Keir Hardie. But a Conservative victory over both other parties at Walworth was comfortingly explained as due to 'the profound depression and hopelessness of the constituency'—as well as to the Liberal Party's failure to do anything for the workers. The *Independent* was reduced to misery by the 1895 election results, and rejected the attempt to find comfort by adding Labour votes to Liberal 'as though we were but different sections of the same party divided by a temporary misunderstanding, but essentially one in principle and aim. This is a sanguine view, and one that seems to us entirely fallacious.' The I.L.P. aimed to destroy the Liberal Party; the response should be to refuse any concessions to Socialism, while embarking on bold reforms. There was another straight fight between Liberal and Labour at Aberdeen in 1896, when Tom Mann came quite near to success; the *British Weekly* attributed this to personalities, and denied that there was a large vote for Socialism. The same year there was satisfaction at a Liberal victory at East Bradford, when Hardie himself finished at the bottom of the poll. The Halifax election the following year was also satisfactory. Convinced Socialists might not be won over, but many I.L.P. voters were 'simply dissatisfied Liberals.' A good Liberal victory at Barnsley suggested a new possibility—though one rejected by the *British Weekly*—that Labour intervention actually took votes from the Conservatives. The South African war confused the issue, for the *British Weekly* surprisingly supported the war, and denounced Morley, previously considered hopelessly Right-wing, for saying he preferred Socialism to militarism—even Liberal militarism.[1]

5   *The Decline of Nonconformist Radicalism*

The Edwardian era saw the last flourish of Nonconformist Radicalism, as indeed of the Liberal Party itself as one of the dominant parties in England. The Labour Party was ultimately destined to replace the Liberal as the alternative to the Conservatives, and in the process the Free Churches, which had been so closely allied with Liberalism, shared in its decline. But for the moment the Labour Party was welcomed as an ally, and the only question was whether the forces of 'reform' and 'progress' ought to be weakened by division. If the Nonconformists had shown some signs of becoming contented and of accepting a position of minor 'establishment' this mood was ended, for the time being, by a number of events early in the twentieth century. The latent pacifism of Nonconformity was roused by the Boer War, and the 1902 Education Act trenched on their own interests. The resulting outcry surprised the Government and created a mood of hostility

[1] *British Weekly*, September 12th, 1890; February 26th, 1891; May 12th, July 14th, July 21st, August 18th, August 25th, September 1st, September 22nd, October 20th, December 29th, 1892; December 21st, 1893; July 5th, September 6th, September 20th, November 20th, December 13th, 1894; March 28th, May 23rd, 1895; May 7th, November 5th, November 12th, 1896; March 11th, November 4th, 1897; June 5th, 1900; *Independent*, November 2nd, 1893; August 1st, 1895.

both to the Conservative Government and to the Church of England, which was attacked in terms which would have delighted Miall himself. For the last time Nonconformists were associated with social rebellion, and offered passive resistance to the Education Act. The 1906 election, producing an enormous majority of Liberals and an abrupt increase in Labour members, brought the most Nonconformist House of Commons there had ever been—at any rate since Cromwellian times—and the number of Free Church members was estimated as high as 200. But time was against them, and this very triumph of the social forces with which Nonconformity was allied took the sting out of it. The first world war brought the Church of England and the Nonconformists together and the dissenting Churches ceased to be aggressively dissident. Then the decline of the Liberals split the Nonconformists between the other two parties, though a remarkable number remained faithful through thick and thin to the Liberals, with whom they no longer had any obvious common interest: so strong is the power of tradition. But in the main the Nonconformist Radicals had had their day. Success tamed them, and then failure broke them.

The Roman Catholics, on the other hand, were a rising force, though they too were divided in their allegiance, and the impact of Catholicism on English politics was still marginal, except when Ireland became involved. Labour successes in 1906 led the *Universe* to envisage an Irish-Labour alliance independent of the Liberals, and to demand extensive social legislation. But more frequently it continued to protest against aspects of Labour policy objectionable to Catholics: 'It is with reluctance we say it, but among the enemies of the Catholic faith in England at the present time, to be reckoned with in any estimate of the forces opposed to us, is the official voice of organized Labour.' The Labour Party showed a tendency to 'go beyond the field of its legitimate activity and interfere in matters of religion.' It was associating itself with Secularism and criticizing Christianity. The symptom of this was its support for secular education, and in the north 'many thousands of Catholic men find themselves torn between conflicting emotions...' Trade unionism for the artisan stood for 'solidarity, for interest, for the sweets of power,' and it gained the support of Catholics. But it forfeited its right to that support when it allowed itself to be captured by Socialists and Secularists 'and employed for purposes of the infidel campaign.' Catholics should

21—TCATLM

fight to keep organized Labour within its rightful bounds, and if they failed, should leave the party.[1]

6   *The Labour Party in Parliament*

Of the Labour heroes of the early twentieth century one of the most outstanding was Will Crooks, victor of a famous by-election in 1903, which presaged the gains soon to be made by the infant Labour Party. Will Crooks (1852–1921)[2] was baptized at Trinity Congregational Church, Poplar and attended Sunday school and church there. As an apprentice he was greatly stirred by the *Iliad* and the *Pilgrim's Progress*, and he was influenced 'like many other members of the Labour Party' by *Unto This Last* and *Alton Locke*. At a later date he numbered among his friends Father Dolling and Dr Chandler, Rector of Poplar, later Bishop of Bloemfontein. He regarded the Labour Party as a religious force; to a crowd he addressed at the dock gates on Sunday mornings he said: 'Labour may be the new force by which God is going to help forward the regeneration of the world.' When a Will Crooks Wages Fund was started to allow him to devote himself to public work the first treasurer was the Rev H. A. Kennedy of All Hallows, Blackwall, and he was followed by Chandler till the latter left the area. On the first executive committee of the Poplar Labour League Kennedy was the only person who was not a trade union leader. Outside supporters included the Barnetts, John Clifford, and Scott Holland. In his by-election campaign in 1903 subscriptions came for Crooks from Adderley, Clifford, Stopford Brooke, and Holland, and 'the churches of nearly every denomination became enthusiastic in his support.' Bishop Talbot wrote a letter of congratulation on his election. Crooks was used to the company of clerics, since in the early 'nineties he had served on a local committee of which all the other members were clergy, on the subject of distress. Nor was his acquaintance confined to any one Church tradition, for the President of the Baptist Union, John Wilson, was 'one of his best supporters in Woolwich,' while he numbered among his friends the Anglo-Catholic Adderley. Two of his own children joined the Church of England, while two became Nonconformists. Crooks regarded the adult school movement as a powerful religious force, saying that he thought it made men take 'a living part in God's work personally—in a word, in striving for

[1] *Universe*, January 26th, 1906; January 17th, 1908.
[2] George Haw, *From Workhouse to Westminster* (1908).

some of Christ's ideals on earth as in Heaven.' Crooks and the Rector of Poplar ran a series of winter addresses at the Town Hall on Sunday afternoons, with one of the two in the Chair:

> The gatherings are not religious in the orthodox sense, nor is any attempt made to teach religion, but I venture to say that they have as much influence for good on the workpeople of Poplar as many of the churches. We nearly always begin with music by singers or players who give their services, and then we have a 'talk,' generally by a public man, on social questions, on education, on books, and authors, and citizenship. Some of our speakers take Biblical subjects . . . The presence of the rector has convinced many, who were formerly hostile to all parsons, Anglican and Nonconformist, that the Churches and Labour can work in harmony. Without pretending to be this, that, or the other, our gatherings have made for the love of one's neighbour, and therefore for the cause of Christ.[1]

Crooks's description of these Sunday afternoon gatherings would fit many of the meetings of the 'Pleasant Sunday Afternoon' type just then at their peak, and Crooks himself was much in demand at such meetings, especially at Whitefield's Tabernacle, the Leysian Mission, and Clifford's Church. In 1906 when the National Free Church Council invited him to address its assembly, the President, Lidgett, said that the invitation was not given lightly, but was a deliberate recognition of the claim which Labour had on the 'thought, energy, and prayer of the Free Churches.' Taking Crooks by the hand he added: 'Thus . . . Labour and the Free Churches are joined in their endeavour to solve some of the great human problems.' In his address Crooks said that many workmen not attending church were still religious, and often indeed they had more faith and works than some of the regular attenders. Soon afterwards he was invited to a banquet at the Hotel Cecil in celebration of the election of a multitude of Nonconformists to the House of Commons. At a time of accusations against the Poplar guardians Crooks received letters of sympathy and support from Holland, the Rev A. Tildsley of Poplar and Bromley Tabernacle, and the Rev H. S. Woolcombe of Oxford House. In view of the prominent part religion played in the life of Will Crooks it is perhaps at first sight surprising to find that the subject is not mentioned in the entry in the *Dictionary of National Biography* on Crooks, written by G. D. H. Cole.

A decade younger than Crooks, but more in the old-established

[1] Haw, op. cit., 259.

Methodist tradition, and much more important in the history of
the Labour Party, was Arthur Henderson (1863–1935). One of the
main architects of the twentieth-century Labour Party, he was a
man guided in all that he did by strong religious convictions:

> The children were, by their mother, brought up on the Bible.
> They went, on Sunday, to the Congregationalist chapel. But when,
> about sixteen, he realized religion, it was in a form intensely personal,
> which came to him with a force that coloured and shaped his whole
> subsequent life. According to his elder brother, 'For Arthur, life
> began with his conversion. Before that, he was just the ordinary boy.'
> He was using the word conversion in its full sense.[1]

Henderson learned the art of public speaking as a Wesleyan lay
preacher, and he attributed to his Christian convictions his success
in face of the varied and highly complex problems he faced in
trade union work, in shaping the Labour Party, and as Foreign
Secretary.

To the rule that most of the founding fathers of the Labour
Party who had religious convictions were Nonconformists the
outstanding exception was George Lansbury (1859–1940). In his
middle twenties he came under the influence of the Christian
Socialist movement, and this influence persisted all his life. His
standpoint was Christian in a very broad and tolerant sense.
Though he was always an Anglican, he was actively interested in
Theosophy and Asiatic religion. He based both his Socialism and
his pacifism on his religious beliefs. In his autobiography he gave
his own account of his religious connexions:

> I also helped to form the Church Socialist League. We were a
> small and very mixed band of adventurers who, some years ago,
> gathered in Egerton Swann's rooms at Paddington. We were all
> rebels against the Capitalist system: this was the one and only thing
> we agreed about. Some of us, like G. K. Chesterton, were strong
> individualists. Others were fanatical Guild Socialists, others Syn-
> dicalists. The Countess of Warwick, Lewis Donaldson, Conrad Noel,
> T. C. Gobat, J. West, Percy Widdrington, and others were Parlia-
> mentarians, but very few had any faith in the Labour Party. At one
> time it looked as if we would become a formidable power in the
> Church. We stirred up the Church Congresses held at Swansea,
> Barrow-in-Furness, Leicester, and elsewhere. Although for some
> years our propaganda meetings were well attended, our numbers
> never grew. I travelled here, there, and everywhere, speaking in

[1] Mary Agnes Hamilton, *Arthur Henderson* (1938), 5.

churches, mission rooms and parish halls. Then came the War, and Christian Socialists became as divided as materialist Socialists. Our God of the human race became in the minds and prayers of some of us God of the British, and so we dwindled and became one of the 'has been' societies. I have also done a considerable amount of lecturing and speaking for the Brotherhood, P.S.A., and similar movements, and many Nonconformist churches.[1]

In 1914 he joined the Theosophical Society, as a result of his contacts with Annie Besant and others, claiming that the only test for membership was that members should work for a universal society, and that people of various religions belonged to it. His own sympathies were wide: 'On all questions of religion and no-religion I have always been more than tolerant.'[2] He admired St Francis and Tolstoy, and but for having a family would have liked to renounce the world. He considered that the greatest influence on his life was the Rev J. Fenwick Kitto, Rector of Whitechapel, and later Vicar of St Martin-in-the-Fields, though he did not say why. He first learned to speak in Whitechapel Church Young Men's Association. As a boy he belonged to the Salvation Army, and admired Catherine Booth, but not William, who was 'much too dictatorial to be a true leader of men.' He himself disliked being regarded as an 'extraordinary specimen' in church assemblies, and criticized clergy who 'talked down' to the working classes, for example by adopting a different accent. He respected Samuel Barnett, but thought his 'whole philosophy of life was all wrong,' in that he avoided all definite opinions. He had no time at all for Toynbee Hall, saying that its 'one solid achievement' was to advance the interests of people who lived there for a time and then turned their backs on the poor and looked after themselves. Moreover, 'my sixty years' experience in East London leaves me quite unable to discover what permanent social influence Toynbee Hall or any other similar settlement has had on the life and labour of the people.' He found in fact a better practical expression of Christianity in the Dew Drop Inn in Whitechapel, kept by Mary Hughes, the daughter of Thomas Hughes: 'Nobody is too wicked or too poor to receive from her the right hand of fellowship and such help as they need.' He contrasted her favourably with Toynbee Hall: 'She teaches the deceitfulness of riches, is definite in her social creed, is a member of the Socialist Party, sits as a Guardian of the Poor and a Borough Councillor in order to help the people.'

[1] George Lansbury, *My Life* (1928), 5f.   [2] Ibid., 8.

Lansbury continued with a vigorous attack on the principles of the Charity Organization Society, to which he declared himself a 'bitter enemy.' Having served on the Archbishop's Committee on the Church and the Labour movement he criticized the other members, except Tawney, for rejecting Socialism, and considered himself a voice in the wilderness on this committee, again except for Tawney, 'and, on occasions, Bishop Gore.' Lansbury was a party man and had little time for the uncommitted, but even so, his judgements on some of the institutions and persons mentioned above are interesting. As a man of the people he was less than enthusiastic for some of the clerical spokesmen of the Christian Socialist movement, and such intentionally non-partisan institutions as Toynbee Hall and the C.S.U. did not inspire him.

Besides Henderson and Lansbury, another man to lead the Labour Party, and the first to lead it in office, was J. Ramsay Macdonald (1866–1937). His religious views were even broader than Lansbury's. His biographer insists that he was a 'deeply religious man,' but he 'worked enthusiastically for some years for the South Place Ethical Society, and was reluctant to have his children baptized.' A streak of rationalism in his nature even in boyhood led him to question the Calvinism by which he was surrounded. At heart he was 'a profoundly religious man, with a mystic's unswerving reverence for "the grand, crowned authority of life," ' though he was

> never a subscriber to sectarian creeds, or, save in Lossiemouth, a regular frequenter of churches. He reverenced all Churches, as embodiments of the life of the spirit, and particularly the Presbyterian Church, because it was the Presbyterian Church which made Scotland what it is—the highest expression, he would have called it, of the Scottish national genius. But neither creeds nor ritual attracted him.[1]

Twice at least religious influences came to bear on him at critical moments. In the first place he went to work for the Rev Mordaunt Crofton, a Bristol clergyman starting a boys' and young men's guild, and in the second place there was his marriage to Margaret Gladstone, whose father was a founder of the Young Men's Christian Association. She had a good deal of influence on him, and after his marriage 'that faint streak of the rationalist, of

[1] Lord Elton, *The Life of James Ramsay Macdonald (1866–1919)*, (1939), 38.

the merely sceptical, which can, I think, be detected in Mac-donald's earlier years, begins to fade out of him.'[1] He was active in the ethical society movement without denying the super-natural, and interpreted his membership as meaning 'that he was not prepared to accept the dogma of any formal church, and that he believed at this time that a secular ethical society might be more active in social reform than any religious organization.'[2] His opposition to religious education was on the grounds that it was inevitably sectarian, and that this led to formalism and the decay of real religion.

Philip Snowden, Viscount Snowden (1864–1937),[3] was a native of Ickornshaw, near Keighley, where the 'atmosphere was strongly radical and Wesleyan Methodist; and the boy imbibed early a familiarity with the Bible and an admiration for Gladstone, neither of which ever left him,' After his conversion to Socialism he achieved a great reputation with 'a particular kind of idealistic, semi-religious eloquence.'

From a religious tradition at the other extreme came John Wheatley (1869–1930).[4] He was born at Waterford, but when he was nine his family moved to Scotland, where he attended a Roman Catholic school. Among various jobs he held was one with a Roman Catholic newspaper. His first political allegiance was to the United Irish League, in Scotland, but in 1908 he joined the Labour Party. He was the founder and first Chairman of the Catholic Socialist Society, 'an organization which did much to win over Irish voters to the Labour party; he engaged in spirited disputations with Catholic clergy, and when he was first elected to the Lanarkshire county council in 1909 ... it was against a sitting Catholic moderate member.' From 1922 to his death he was Member of Parliament for Shettleston and in the first Labour Government was Minister of Health. In his later years he was associated with the I.L.P. attacks on the front bench, and he was left out of the 1929 Government.

It may be mentioned that a still more extreme representative of the Labour Left wing, Victor Grayson, for a time trained for the Unitarian ministry at the denominational college at Manchester.

[1] Elton, op. cit., 79.
[2] Ibid., 94f.
[3] *Dict. Nat. Biog.* (1931–1940), s.v. Snowden.
[4] Ibid. (1922–1930), s.v. Wheatley.

7   The Religious Press and the Labour Party

Neither the *Guardian* nor the *Church Times* took very much interest in the Labour Party. The *Guardian* thought the election of Crooks to Parliament a bad sign for the Liberals, who would receive decreasing support from Labour, though the following year it found it necessary to rebuke Labour for giving too much support, especially on education. On the 1906 election results, there was concern at the 'sudden outcrop of the Labour vote' and the election of 'so large a proportion of men of extreme opinions,' though there was no need to 'take it for granted that the Church must necessarily suffer from the extension of democracy,' and it might even turn out that 'the cause of Christian brotherhood' had been greatly advanced.[1]

In 1903 an article in the *Church Times* forecast that the Labour Party would win 100 seats at the next election, and claimed that Labour supporters were less hostile to Ritualism than the Conservatives, and less friendly to Dissent than the Liberals. True, the Labour Party supported Disestablishment, but Anglo-Catholics were not worried about this.[2]

The *Church Family Newspaper* explained the Woolwich election result as due to local factors, and thought the Labour Party had persistently misrepresented the Conservative candidate. The magnitude of the victory was astonishing, but the Liberals should not rejoice too much, 'because Mr Crooks will disagree with the regular Liberal leaders of both sections of the Party, probably on many more points than he will be in agreement with them.' It is interesting to notice that this newspaper insisted on treating Crooks as a curious kind of Liberal, against the logic of its own argument that he would not support the party. The Government defeat at Devonport the following year was attributed to the Liberal candidate's friendliness to Labour interests. The 1906 election result was attributed primarily to working-class hostility to Protection. The Labour gains were noticed as much as the Liberal landslide, but the Labour Party was still thought of as representing a particular sectional interest, like the Irish, not as a possible rival to the two old parties:

> . . . There will be not merely working men members in Parliament,
> but a bona fide Labour party, which will have to be reckoned with . . .

[1] *Guardian*, August 5th, 1903; August 31st, 1904; January 24th, 1906.
[2] *Church Times*, May 22nd, 1903.

Some timid people appear to be alarmed at this demonstration of organized labour, but if the great masses of working men in the constituencies believe that their political and other interests can be better served by men of their own class than by representatives from the classes which usually supply Parliamentary candidates no harm is likely to follow the gratification of their wish.

The efforts of middle-class journalists to take a sympathetic interest in the Labour Party were apt to produce patronizing and facetious comments, such as the following, on the occasion of the assembly of the new Parliament:

One correspondent tells how tweed garments of unfashionable cut, aggressive red ties, and much unconventionality in the way of head-gear have reminded conventionally attired members of the rise of a new Parliamentary party, and it is stated that one of the new group was actually daring enough to place himself on the Opposition Front Bench where Mr Balfour is to sit. 'Can't I have it till he comes?' he replied when told whose place he was appropriating.

But the good humour wore off, and it was soon noticed that Liberals 'of the older school' were becoming 'restive under the growing arrogance of the Labour demands, especially on the Trade Disputes Bill.' The Labour programme was 'sheer Socialism' and the party would not be 'mollified even by big concessions.' There was particular hostility to Keir Hardie, especially when he compared British rule in India with Turkish atrocities, and the Socialists were urged, in their own interest, to 'depose' him at the first opportunity. It was to be hoped that the Government would 'stand up to the party of Mr Keir Hardie with a little more soul and conscience,' for that party's attitude was 'one of dictatorial arrogance,' though its real 'value' was insignificant. A sweeping Unionist victory in Mid-Essex was a punishment on the Liberals, who, 'by their obvious panderings to sectional interests, their weakness under Socialistic pressure, their readiness to foster class legislation,' had alienated many of their supporters. Two additional curiously-assorted offences on the part of the Labour Party were a protest against a visit by the Tsar, and a threat of the withdrawal of the Miners' Federation backing for the old-established M.P.s, Burt and Fenwick, unless they joined the Labour Party. On the latter occasion this paper made the odd comment that the number of political parties was increasing. The adherence of the two miners to the Labour Party did not increase the number of parties, so the implication would seem to be that the *Church*

Family Newspaper only now noticed that the Labour Party really was a party. Similarly a Unionist victory at Bermondsey brought indignation, shared by the Labour candidate, at the usual Liberal custom of adding Liberal and Labour votes to prove that but for Labour 'intervention' the Government would have held the seat. Labour progress in Wales was looked on with some favour, based on the belief that Labour was much less determined on Welsh disestablishment than the Liberals. But Keir Hardie was getting worse, especially in declaring himself a republican, though despite the 'offensiveness of such expressions to ordinary Englishmen' they were useful in reminding the country of the ambitions of the 'real masters of the present Government.' The demand for the payment of M.P.s was now accepted as reasonable, being pressed by F. E. Smith and other Unionists. If for the moment it was no longer possible to show that the Liberal-Labour alliance was disintegrating, perhaps party capital could be made out of its very firmness—by showing that the Liberals were really Socialists at heart:

> Mr Lloyd George openly proclaimed his alliance with the Socialists in his Mile-end speech on Monday evening. After praising himself as a benefactor of the poor, and abusing the aristocracy for its addiction to idleness and field sports, he urged the Liberals to support Mr George Lansbury, the Socialist candidate for Bow and Bromley, and not to run a representative of their own against him. It will be futile, after this, for Ministerialists, to protest that their ambitions are not Socialistic; and the country will not fail to note that the right of private property is menaced by those who are also assailing the Constitution.

Winston Churchill dared not suppress riots in South Wales 'lest he should thereby alienate the Socialist vote in the approaching elections.' But Liberal-Labour dissension over the Hanley by-election in 1912 revived hopes of the ending of the alliance.[1]

The *British Weekly* also showed a sustained interest in the Labour Party, though of a very different kind. Whatever the Conservative press said about the natural hostility of middle-class Dissenters and the Labour movement, this organ of Dissent took it for granted that the Labour Party was a new expression of

---

[1] *Church Family Newspaper*, March 13th, 1903; June 24th, 1904; January 19th, January 26th, February 16th, August 31st, 1906; October 4th, November 8th, 1907; December 4th, 1908; July 2nd, October 29th, November 5th, 1909; February 18th, May 6th, September 30th, November 25th, 1910; July 5th, 1912.

traditional Radicalism, a Radicalism which Nonconformity had long regarded as its ally. Its policy was that Radicals and Labour must stand together if they were not to be defeated by the Conservatives. A rather untypical comment, at the beginning of the century, was an attack on Irish voters in Lanarkshire, who, by swinging from Liberal to Labour, had let in a Unionist—untypical, because the *British Weekly* was out of sympathy with the Radicals in its coolness on the Irish question. More characteristic was the rejoicing in 1903 at the election of Will Crooks: 'The result indicates what may be done by an alliance between Liberalism and Labour. Nothing could stand before it.' Two other comments in this year were in flagrant contradiction: the defeat of a Labour candidate at Preston who was unsound on education policy showed that Labour was helpless without Liberal support; yet the victory of Henderson at Barnard Castle over both Liberal and Conservative was something even better than a Liberal victory would have been—because the victor was a Nonconformist and a more thorough Free Trader. It was the Liberals who were to blame for the split in the Progressive vote, and they must stop opposing men like Henderson. Progressive victories in the London borough elections again showed the power of the alliance of Liberals, Labour, and Dissent.[1]

Next year brought varied comments. It was satisfactory that Norwich was a Liberal gain, despite the intervention of Labour, but at the General Election the Liberals should support a Labour candidate for one of the two seats, even though he would stand only for Labour, and there should be similar arrangements all over the country. The election of the miners' leader John Johnson at Gateshead was an excellent sign of Liberal-Labour alliance. A Liberal victory over both other parties at North-East Lanarkshire was actually greeted with disappointment, for 'the attitude of Scottish Liberals towards Labourists is distinctly dangerous. The Labour men have a clear right to some seats in Scotland ... They repudiate the name Liberal, but they do not repudiate the thing Liberalism ... As a matter of fact the Labour members in the House of Commons do more for the objects of Liberalism than many of the orthodox profession, and we should rejoice to see their number greatly augmented.' This is an interesting example of the argument that the Liberal tradition was now more fully

[1] *British Weekly*, October 3rd, 1901; March 19th, May 21st, July 30th, November 5th, 1903.

expressed in the Labour Party, an argument to prove very useful to the latter in the days of the Liberal decline. Again the Labour member elected (with Liberal support) for West Monmouth would benefit 'Liberal causes' better than the return of 'a professional Liberal politician.' There was an 'urgent need' for Liberals to assist in the election of 'Labour representatives.' On the other hand the *British Weekly* carried on a campaign against Sidney Webb for supporting the 1902 Education Act, and even turned on the London Progressives, surely the plainest embodiment of the Liberal-Labour alliance, for tolerating him.[1]

The 1906 election result naturally gave great satisfaction, not only because of the Liberal victories, but because of 'the revelation it gives of the mighty power of Labour.' The Liberals should recognize this power, and indeed 'one of the greatest and most reassuring features of the election' was a Labour advance which would ensure that 'the party in power will not be an idle or timid party.' The only Liberal loss was welcomed, on the grounds that 'a great industrial centre like Dundee should have its Labour representative.' Thus Labour success was welcomed as a guarantee that the Liberals would be Radical. During 1906 the Scottish Liberals, the Liberal Whips, and Keir Hardie were criticized for opposition to the alliance, while Shackleton on the one hand and Asquith, Lloyd George, and Churchill on the other were praised for supporting it. The entry of the new Labour members had 'proved most salutary and inspiring.' The working classes would not go Socialist unless the Liberals drove them to it.[2]

The same lines of thought were followed in 1907. The attack on the Progressives continued, and the election of Pete Curran in a four-cornered contest at Jarrow was received with mixed feelings: the Liberal would have been even better, 'but on all the main points Mr Curran, who is a man of marked ability, will support the Liberal programme.' The Tories preferred Labour to Liberal, but the remedy was in the hands of the Liberals: 'Perhaps the Liberals may yet come to see that constituencies like Jarrow would naturally choose, when they can, a Labour representative.' This last quotation is striking for the continuance of the ambiguous use of the word 'Labour,' for it recommends as a safeguard against Liberal

---

[1] *British Weekly*, January 21st, January 28th, February 18th, February 25th, May 12th, August 18th, November 10th, 1904.

[2] Ibid., January 18th, January 25th, February 1st, March 1st, September 20th, October 4th, October 11th, October 18th, 1906.

defeat by 'Labour' (i.e. the Labour Party) the selection by the Liberals of 'Labour' (i.e. working class) candidates. Such ambiguity betrayed a lingering doubt about whether the Labour Party was even now really a distinct 'party.' In the summer the election of a Lib.-Lab. candidate for North-West Staffordshire was satisfactory, and Lord Balfour of Burleigh's plea for a united front against Socialism was dismissed: the good kind (i.e. welfare legislation) would continue, and the bad kind (i.e. Marxism) would be encouraged by a defeat of Liberalism. A narrow Liberal victory, with a split 'Progressive' vote, at West Hull, caused the *British Weekly* to toy with the idea of proportional representation. Even Socialists—of all kinds—were in agreement with the Liberals on the 'next step' in legislation: 'The next step is to tax the rich more heavily.'[1]

The year 1908 was less interesting. Shackleton had declined the leadership of the Labour Party, though there was an interview with the new leader, Henderson. A Labour Party vote in favour of Socialism was not representative of the working classes, and by-election defeats, including that of Churchill, showed the need for Liberal-Labour co-operation. In 1909 such co-operation was credited with victories at Mid-Derbyshire and East Manchester, and there was enthusiasm for a combined Liberal-Labour demonstration in Hyde Park in favour of the Budget, though the failure to achieve a combined candidature at Bermondsey led to Conservative victory. The 1910 General Election brought reiterated pleas for the maintenance of the alliance, criticism of the Government for hesitating over dealing with the House of Lords, on the grounds that this endangered the alliance, and pleasure at a reaffirmation of Labour belief in Free Trade. In 1911 Labour support for the Insurance Bill was welcomed, and the poor Government record in by-elections was attributed to Labour dissatisfaction. The same applied in 1912, and the remedy suggested was 'generous concessions on the part of the Liberals.' But this was immediately followed by great disappointment over Liberal-Labour opposition at Hanley and Crewe. On Hanley the comment was: 'There is not a shadow of doubt that the seat belongs to the Labour party.' The previous member was Labour, though friendly to the Liberals, and the new Labour candidate was ideal, while the Liberal was 'harebrained and we fear quite impossible.' Labour should have more seats, for it was a firm ally of the Government. The Liberal

---

[1] *British Weekly*, January 17th, July 11th, August 8th, October 10th, December 5th, December 19th, 1907.

nevertheless won, and the *British Weekly* had to eat some of its
words: 'We are bound to admit that the Liberal leaders in Hanley
have shown that they knew the minds of the constituency better
than we did.' But this was no encouragement, because 'Liberals
must not forget that the exasperation of Labour will be fatal to their
hopes,' and indeed at Crewe a Conservative was returned, causing
the *British Weekly* to demand from the leaders of both parties a
joint election policy. In some contrast, in the East Carmarthen
election all 'Progressives' were urged to vote Liberal, not Labour,
but the usual appeal for 'an honourable compromise' was made
again after a conflict, and a Conservative victory, at Midlothian,
which was blamed on the Hanley result and the coal settlement.
The resignation of Lansbury, to fight (and lose) on the suffrage
issue, was regarded (as by the Labour leaders) as quixotic. 1913
brought three contrasting election results. There was a Liberal
victory at Houghton-le-Spring in a three-cornered fight, with the
British Weekly commenting: 'But frankly, we do not like these
contests between Liberal and Labourists, and we should be very
glad to see the Labourists getting a seat in return for the seat that
was taken from them at Hanley.' There was also the excellent
victory of a Lib.-Lab. candidate at Chesterfield—a miners' leader
and Primitive Methodist; though to the indignation of the *British
Weekly* the Labour Party disowned him. And another Progressive split lost South Lanark to the Opposition. Early in 1914,
in the case of a Liberal success at North-West Durham, Liberal
and Labour votes were added up to make a huge majority for
Home Rule, and it was hoped that the Labour candidate would
soon find a seat. But other results were bad: Leith was lost through
Labour intervention, but it was all the fault of the Liberals, who
did not treat Labour fairly, and it was especially the consequence of
Hanley, and this affair was blamed again for the loss of North-East
Derbyshire. The Liberal got more votes than Labour, but that was
nothing to do with it: seats had to be found for Labour. It would
be 'a long day' before any conflict emerged between Labour and
the advanced Liberals.[1]

[1] *British Weekly*, January 9th, January 30th, February 6th, April 30th,
1908; July 22nd, July 29th, November 4th, December 30th, 1909; January
6th, January 13th, July 31st, 1910; October 12th, December 28th, 1911;
July 4th, July 11th, July 18th, August 1st, August 22nd, September 12th
September 19th, November 28th, 1912; March 27th, August 28th,
December 18th, 1913; February 5th, March 5th, May 28th, 1914.

This repeated insistence by the *British Weekly* that the future of the Liberals depended on co-operation with Labour looks prescient from a later standpoint, but on closer inspection it is not so impressive. For one thing it blandly ignores the great gulf separating the Lib.-Lab. candidates from the Socialists of the I.L.P., and uses the ambiguous expression 'Labour' to cover a confusion of thought. Parallel to this it insists, or more often takes it for granted, that Labour's aims were the same as the Liberal Party's, for example adding Liberal and Labour votes to make up majorities against tariffs, or in favour of Home Rule. It ignored the fact that the Labour Party was a wholly independent movement, and always spoke as though it was merely a variant form of traditional Radicalism. This was why it was so angry with Socialists like Webb who logically followed out the implications of Labour independence and at times were prepared to support the Conservatives against the Liberals. And yet perhaps the *British Weekly* was not wholly mistaken as against the Fabians: perhaps the Labour Party was in fact a new expression of Radicalism. For most of its spokesmen Marxist theories, even in a revised version, had much less appeal than emotional criticism of what were instinctively felt to be unfair privileges and abuses, and Labour spokesmen often shared also a language with the Left wing of Nonconformist Liberalism.

CHAPTER 7

THE CONTRIBUTION OF THE CHURCHES TO THE LABOUR MOVEMENT DOWN TO 1914

CERTAIN FACTS BECOME CLEAR in the light of the foregoing survey of the relationships of the Churches and the Labour movement. Throughout the period covered a large proportion of the working classes did not belong to the Churches at all, and in 1850 this alienation of the workers, whatever its cause, was by no means new. Unlike most social customs indifference to formal religion tended to spread upwards rather than downwards through the various strata of the social hierarchy, and what at one time had been chiefly a phenomenon of the proletarian areas of London gradually became characteristic of all the large industrial cities. One reason among many why the Churches did not succeed in recovering this lost ground in the period under consideration was that they were absorbed in other matters, which took up most of their attention. Even apart from the great struggles between the Churches themselves—for example over 'Papal aggression' and over education—there was the violently disputed question of Biblical criticism, there were the onslaughts on traditional views from the directions of geology and biology, and for the Established Church there was the continual discord arising from the emergence of Anglo-Catholicism. The Labour movement itself emerged almost simultaneously, and many of those within the Churches who might have grasped the importance of the rising power of the working classes were engaged in mutual warfare.

The Churches tended to patronize the workers rather than to regard them as fully responsible adults, and on the whole they tended to treat them as a mission field to which special campaigns must be directed rather than as potentially active and ordinary members on a par with the middle classes as churchwardens, elders, deacons or stewards. With so many of the workers outside the Churches such an attitude was realistic and honest, but it served to emphasize the gulf which separated the Church and the working classes. The gulf was not of the same dimensions for every part of the Church, for the class character of the various denominations varied widely. The Roman Catholic Church was mainly working class, but since its working-class membership was overwhelmingly Irish—to English city-dwellers quite definitely an alien population—this did not help at all in the approach to the English working classes, at any rate till very late in the period. The Anglican Church obviously had the support and affection of millions of working-class people, but its standing with those groups who created and led the Labour movement was low, and it consistently regarded them—with the kindliest feelings—from a distance. In the parish church there would certainly be some trade union members, but they were rarely sidesmen, and still more rarely churchwardens. The Nonconformist churches were much more firmly rooted in the industrial working class. This is obviously true of the Methodists, especially those who were not Wesleyans, and in particular the miners' and agricultural labourers' unions were Methodist led. On the other hand it would not at first sight seem true of the older Dissenting denominations, which even before 1850 were notoriously middle class; but it is an important fact of social history that for the greater part of this period the working classes received the steady support of a considerable fringe of the lower middle classes in the pursuit of their objectives. The aims of the upper working classes, who directed the Labour movement, and the lower middle classes, were not seen as incompatible, and the kind of alliance which had helped to carry the 1832 Reform Act survived through the century. The lower middle-class allies of the workers were of two main types: Socialists brought up on Owen, or later and less frequently on Marx, who were probably Secularists; and Nonconformist Radicals. From Sturge and Miall at the beginning of this period to Clifford at the end the workers' movement always had firm friends in the Nonconformist churches.

Despite the distractions, the press of the various denominations, with the notable exception of the Roman Catholic, did from time to time give serious attention to the problem of recovering the working classes. Such attention was much more marked in the Anglican press than in the Nonconformist, for two reasons: because the Nonconformists held their own in the working-class areas better than the Anglicans, and because the Church of England was always anxious (especially in face of the disestablishment campaign) to justify its claim to be the Church of the whole English people, while other denominations were sometimes content to make a sectional appeal. The Anglo-Catholics always believed they had special advantages in dealing with the working classes, but in practice the only striking advantage they had from this point of view was that they were not acceptable themselves in many parishes other than the poorest, so that they necessarily made the close acquaintance of the poor. But they suffered the disadvantage which in various ways affected all parties in the Church of England, and in a lesser degree the other denominations too: the working classes they knew were not the working classes who were creating the Labour movement. The slum Ritualists in general were confined to the most depressed classes in the community, and did not meet the active and capable men who were beginning to organize the workers, except in some of the vast working-class areas of the East End, where a huge and poorly-endowed parish might include the whole range of the wage-earning population. The original Christian Socialists were mainly confined to London, while the Church of England as a whole had a very marked rural bias. Not only were there far more churches and clergy, in proportion to population, in rural areas, but the pleasantest country towns were often the best livings, and even the cathedrals, and hence the bishops, were mostly outside the drab industrial areas, till the latter part of the period. The Church was biased towards the countryside and the country towns even more in outlook than in numerical strength. The countryside counted, and so did London and the older universities, but the provincial cities and centres of industry, and the coalfields, the two birthplaces of the Labour movement, did not. The Anglican press, almost to the point of comedy, thought of the working classes in terms of farm labourers, domestic servants, and London craftsmen in those occupations which sometimes brought them into contact with their social superiors. As late as 1911 the greatest objection to the National Insurance scheme, in the eyes of the *Church Family Newspaper*, was the proposal to include domestic servants, and to 'interfere between mistress and maids.'[1] The Roman Catholic press knew all about Lancashire, but Irish immigrants were not the founders of the Labour movement either. Even the Nonconformist press tended to know most about those members of the working classes who were moving out of their class altogether.

[1] See p. 295.

Most of the attempts to win the workers accepted the class structure of society. In the earlier part of the period hierarchical views of society persisted, and one of the tasks of the Church was thought to be the establishment of harmonious relationships between fairly fixed social classes, and the ensuring of fair play for each class. Even a later and apparently more democratic approach, such as was constituted by the Settlement movement, presupposed the permanence of the class system. Places like Toynbee Hall were a means whereby the middle classes could serve the working classes, and it was implicit that there was a fundamental and obvious difference between the two. The same was true of the various 'poor men's Churches,' of various types of missions, of Nonconformist 'institutional Churches.' Once again it might be said that this was a realistic recognition of the existence of the 'two nations'; but such patronage was not the way chosen by the Labour movement. Even the Labour Churches, which were much more nearly a spontaneous creation of the working classes themselves, were open to rather similar objections. A more important objective for the working classes was the securing of full equality within the existing denominations, and to retreat into their own Churches was, as Dr Fairbairn said, 'to run up the flag of surrender.'[1]

On the other hand the separation between the Churches and the working classes was very far from absolute, and throughout the whole of this period millions of working-class people were strongly attached to the Church. In the desolate areas of the new industrial cities an enormous number of new churches was built, and if in general they only kept pace with the increasing population it is worth remembering that at this time the population of England was increasing more rapidly than at any other time in her history. Many of the slum Ritualists filled their churches, overwhelmingly with working-class worshippers; the very classes who were the mainstay of the trade unions were strongly touched by Methodism. In Wales and in parts of the north the older forms of Nonconformity were still a religion of the common people; and the Irish Catholics, if regarded by many as intrusive foreigners, gradually came to constitute a very important section of the working classes of England. The rapid rise of the Salvation Army proved that religion was not merely capable of holding its own among the poor in some circumstances, but even of breaking new ground. In 1914 the Churches and their teachings were still an

[1] See p. 69.

exceedingly powerful influence on the lives of every class of English society.

Turning to a consideration of the degree to which religion contributed to the Labour movement, one must conclude that the contribution was very large, though in the nature of the case such a conclusion cannot be expressed in statistical terms. The Christian contribution was certainly much larger than the Marxist. On the other hand there was an entirely different Socialist tradition in England descending from Owen and the Chartists, non-religious and even anti-religious, but independent of Marx, though later coming increasingly under his influence. In the co-operative movement the Secularist Holyoake, the Christian Socialist Neale and the Nonconformist Mitchell were all important, and each represented a different strand of Labour tradition. In other branches of the Labour movement similar strands could be identified. There is no means of determining which strand was the most important historically, but it can be said with absolute certainty that the Labour movement would have taken a very different form had the Christian share been substantially less, and it is probably true that even in the latter years of this period the victory of Blatchford, and the acceptance of his doctrine that Socialism and irreligion went naturally together, would have been a total disaster for Socialism in England. Of course it might also be maintained that many of the anti-religious Socialists did come themselves from a religious background—Holyoake from Nonconformity, Hyndman from Evangelicalism, and so on; but it would not be wise to press this point. It is always possible to prove that every public man is the product of his early circumstances, because he either reflects them directly or he reacts against them, but such speculation is unprofitable. Yet it may not be altogether unfair to discern in some of them a moral earnestness, and an anxiety to do good, which seems to follow very naturally from the religious circumstances of their upbringing. In any case the direct religious contribution, made by men and women who were not only Christians engaged in the Labour movement, but whose contribution to that movement was inspired and moulded closely and powerfully by their religious convictions, was outstandingly important. It could hardly have been otherwise, for Victorian society was one of the most religious in modern history, and a working-class movement emerging from such a context was bound to be religious too.

There is one very striking aspect of this matter which does not often seem to have been noticed. Late Victorian times and the reign of Edward VII were beyond question an era of religious decline. Enough statistics are available to show that far fewer people attended church in 1914 than in 1850, in proportion to population, and that the impression of decline is not misleading is confirmed by many other details—the recruitment for the ministry, the sales of religious books, and so on. Yet the Labour movement did not cease to include a very strong religious element, and indeed it was in some ways a more religious movement at the end of this period than at the beginning. After all, the term 'Labour movement' as applied to the 'fifties has a primary reference to the declining influence of Chartism and Owenism, and except for the peripheral influence of the Christian Socialists and the still comparatively obscure activities of the Nonconformists who had recently invented a practical form of consumers' co-operation, it tends to suggest Secularists rather than any sort of Christians. Many Owenites and Chartists were Christians, but many were not, and in this respect they stood out in so religious and orthodox an age. But by 1914 the chief organ of the Labour movement was the Labour Party in Parliament, led by men like Lansbury, Henderson, Crooks, Macdonald, and Snowden, all in varying ways religious men. Whatever might be the feeling in the S.D.F. or the Fabian Society the appeal of the Labour Party in the early twentieth century came largely from its associations with that Anglican conscience which was still busy forming settlements and that Nonconformist conscience which was vocal in chapels and trade union branches throughout the industrial areas. With these older forces supplemented by an increasing number of Roman Catholic Labour voters there was at least no prospect whatever that the Labour Party would be against religion, and a strong likelihood that it would continue to talk in strongly (if vaguely) religious accents. Indeed by 1914 the Labour movement was one of the few great national institutions which was not feeling increasingly the draught of indifference and scepticism.

Nevertheless religion was not the force in 1914 which it had been in 1850. It was not merely that the churches were not so full; more important, they were not claiming so much. In 1850 the life of the country was still in many ways—in education, for example— dependent on them. In 1914 they were still important, but by most people were treated as an optional extra item in life for those (still, in fact, a majority) who favoured them. The decline of the religious press was a symptom. A man who read the *Guardian* in the 'fifties received a liberal education, with, for example, very long reviews of the latest works of Dickens and Darwin. In Edwardian times the press was trying to appeal to the ordinary member of the Church as well as to its ministry, but in other respects there was a narrowing. The reader was now more likely to be tempted with a full-page photograph of a new bishop, a drawing of a new church, or a sentimental and edifying tale of the misfortunes of the minister in some quaint Scottish village, written specially for the paper by Barrie or 'Ian Maclaren.' For many reasons the Church had lost confidence, and often it spoke on great issues in the manner of one who does not expect to be heard. The Labour movement, which had at one time seemed to be a large-scale relief organization, aiming at raising the standard of life of the poor, though in danger of exploitation by agitators, was going its own way. Vast numbers of its supporters were members of the Churches, but in practice they decided for themselves what was right, and refused to allow the ecclesiastical authorities to direct them.

Throughout the period one service rendered by the religious press was to keep the issues before the public. At all times these newspapers treated economic questions, including labour relations, as of prime importance. They insisted that the Church must pass a Christian judgement, though in practice they did not know how to do this. With a strong interest in the subject went a great deal of sheer ignorance, especially of the scale of the problems involved. In 1888 the *Church Times* proposed as a solution to the problem of poverty that each church should care for 'three or four old or infirm people' and 'three or four orphans.' The author of such a suggestion was not living in the real world—and that despite the fact that he was supposed to be a spokesman for the party which included the slum Ritualists.

One of the most characteristic features of the age was the substitution of social service for religion. But nothing could illustrate better the surviving strength of religion than that educated people should feel the need for a substitute. It was left to the twentieth century to banish the shadow after the substance had gone. Very representative of the late Victorian age was Beatrice Webb, who pondered at Bacup what 'inspiring motive' could be found to replace religion. Perhaps it is the emphasis on 'inspiration' and ideals which makes even the twentieth-century Labour movement recall so nostalgically the enthusiasms of a past age.

An interesting question is whether the Christian influence in the Labour movement can be identified with the movement's idealistic aspects. In some respects it can. There was something 'other-worldly' about the early Christian Socialist ambition to rid the world of competition, and it corresponds to that search after 'brotherhood' which has constantly reappeared in the movement. The internationalism of the movement, and the desire to improve the lot of the poor, were other aspects strengthened by the extent of Christian influence. But in other ways the Christians were among the hard-headed realists of the movement. The trade union leaders who recalled it on many occasions from remote ideals to the mundane task of increasing wages and reducing hours were in many cases Nonconformists; and conversely some of the most ambitious and elevated schemes for the regeneration of mankind emanated from the Secularist elements. Nor does an analysis into Christian and non-Christian correspond in any way to an analysis into Left and Right, into moderate and extreme. The religiously motivated members in themselves covered the whole range of political opinion to be found among the leaders of the working classes.

A few comments may be made on the religious contribution to specialized departments of the workers' movement. One reason why repeated efforts to bridge the gap between the working classes and the Churches failed was that the agencies created for this purpose tended themselves to lose contact with the Churches. This is strikingly the case with the settlements, which in most cases started as a special aspect of the Church's work in the cities and developed into institutions for general social service. The achievements of the Settlement movement were less than might have been hoped. It provided social service, but in relation to the scale of the problem only in a small way; and it educated a number of young men in the realities of the contemporary world, but again, it was only a few. As a solution to the problems of the age the settlements were not radical enough, like most of the remedies coming from Christian sources. Such comparatively obscure agencies as mechanics' institutes and friendly societies suffered from too much patronage, but they did serve to establish contacts between the Church and some of the more enterprising workers. Such organizations militated against the hope of revolution, especially when they involved the giving of hostages to fortune in the form of working-class savings and investments; but they helped considerably in building up the organization of the working classes in the form it took in England. On the side of co-operation, most spokesmen of the Churches were more interested in co-operative production than in the consumers' movement, and in this way they found themselves in close alliance with anti-religious Secularists, and sometimes opposed to empirically-minded Nonconformists such as Mitchell, for whom the consumers' societies themselves were the ideal. In relation to trade unions, the Christian Socialists gave a good deal of help, especially on the legal side. All the Churches looked with a favourable eye on the 'New Model' trade unionism of the 'seventies and 'eighties, and were annually filled with admiration for the T.U.C. and its 'moderation.' Yet the rise of the more militant 'New Unionism' from 1889 did not at first break the friendly relationship of the Churches and the unions, partly because the leaders, especially Mann, Burns, and Tillett, were men of a character to appeal to religious leaders and partly because of the feeling that at last it was the really downtrodden classes who were making their voice heard, for whom Christian sympathy might be more in place than in the case of the miners or engineers.

After 1900 the Labour Party was welcomed by the Nonconformist Left, partly as an insurance that the Liberals would remain Radical, but there was a persistent refusal to believe, or inability to believe, that the Labour Party really was a party, wholly independent of the others. Thus the *Church Family Newspaper*, Conservative and Anglican, consoled itself on the election of Crooks by anticipating that he would soon find himself in disagreement with the Liberal leadership, as though he was merely an indisciplined Radical, while on the opposite side the *British Weekly* confused its readers by using the term 'Labour' to mean, indiscriminately, the Labour Party and the working classes, in effect recommending that the Liberals should support Labour in order to defeat Labour.

On the developments in the 1906 Parliament, when the Liberals, with Labour support, laid the foundations of the Welfare State, a good deal was heard of the 'thin end of the wedge' in the religious press. To some extent this was nothing more than party politics, but the indignation when the Unionists, still dominated by Chamberlain, supported Government measures, or, even worse, attacked them as inadequate, showed that prominent spokesmen of the Churches were tending to fall into mere reaction.

The relation of the Churches to Socialism also demands some comments. Whatever the defeats suffered by successive generations of Christian Socialists, and however often their tenets had been proved ridiculous, or dangerous, or both, by 1914 Christian Socialism was stronger than ever. The two Archbishops, Davidson of Canterbury and Lang of York, were broadly sympathetic, and in Gore the Christian Socialists had one of the most powerful figures in the Church. But Christian Socialism also suffered from one inherent weakness: no one could say what it was. It had become so vague that almost everyone could be a Christian Socialist, in the same measure that Sir William Harcourt was a Socialist. Throughout the whole of this period, but especially in the middle years, the word 'Socialism' was given an almost infinite variety of definitions, so that most of the arguments about it could have been ended by agreement on a definition. The Church tended to be conservative in the profound sense of taking it for granted that in the main things would remain much as they were. For a time this included the Malthusian and pessimistic assumption that nothing much could be done about the miseries of the poor, but the development of a more sophisticated economics opened the more cheering prospect of a continuous improvement within the existing system. That the whole system should be regarded historically did not occur to many people. Thus from 1850 to 1914 criticisms of Capitalism were answered with the argument that without Capital there would be no employment, despite repeated protests from Socialists that the essence of Capitalism was not the existence of Capital, but the existence of the Capitalist. This conservatism was not peculiar to the Church, and it was not based on religious grounds, except in the special case of the Roman Catholics, who were not thinking of Capitalism at all, but of the historic form of monarchical society. Otherwise the Churches reflected the outlook of their own age. They were usually opposed to Socialism. Apart from mere unthinking conservatism the strongest criticisms of Socialism were usually based upon what must strictly be considered irrelevancies. This was especially true of the High Church and Roman Catholic press, which consistently opposed Socialism because of its association with irreligion and its attacks on the family. Such irrelevance was of course the fault of the Socialists, and from this kind of misinterpretation English Socialism was saved partly by the Christian Socialists and partly by the Fabian Society, whose whole policy was an attempt to stick to the relevant points. Similarly Nonconformists attacked Robert Blatchford more for his warning England that she might be attacked by Germany than for his Socialism or even his scepticism.

A special case of the underlying conservatism of the Churches in relation to Socialism was that they were to a remarkable degree impressed by economic laws and anxious not to appear naïve. To say that something was contrary to economic law seemed as conclusive to mid-Victorian religious leaders as to say to an earlier generation that it was contrary to the Ten Commandments. Economic science had never before had such prestige, and it did not long retain quite so much.

A striking thing about the religious press is that it did not read differently on social issues from the secular press; it did not adopt an independent standpoint, but used all the same arguments, on one side or the other, which were used in purely secular debate. Far from trying to regulate life by theological criteria and neglecting scientific progress, this was a sphere in which the Church tried to be scientific to the neglect of theological judgements. Perhaps this very unusual state of affairs was to be explained, in part at least, by the defeats theology had suffered at the hands of other sciences, and the secret fear of being put in the wrong by the economists as well as by the geologists and the biologists. In reality such a retreat was itself an equally severe defeat for the Church, for even if it was true that many battles, from the time of Copernicus onwards, had been fought on ill-chosen grounds, the refusal of any engagement was a tacit but obvious admission of the abdication of theology from her throne. Nor was this position really scientific, for such a science as political economy, dealing with human relations throughout, did not gain by excluding all consideration of ends. Thus one aspect of the Church's conservatism—its refusal to judge the existing order—arose from a kind of liberalism: the insistence on allowing the full autonomy of a particular intellectual discipline.

Less equivocal features of liberalism were also characteristic of the Church at this time, and contradicted to some extent the underlying conservatism. The idea of development and progress affected all the Churches, in varying degrees. The idea of evolution was abroad, and through Newman's emphasis on development was even applied to the defence of the Roman Catholic Church. Here a way was opened, though Newman would have been horrified to think it, for the Catholic Modernists of a later generation—Loisy,

Tyrrell and Karl Adam, with their interpretation of the Catholic Church as a progressive and evolving institution not bound too closely to the past. Such a development in the Roman Catholic Church was destined to come to a sudden end, but similar ideas overflowed into Protestantism, and reached an extreme in the 'New Theology.' They had their counterpart in some aspects of the Labour movement, especially in the Fabian idea of a slow permeation of an evolving social order, so that it is not surprising to find the exponents of the New Theology sympathetic to Fabian Socialism, and even a more moderate Liberal Protestant like Clifford in the society. The potentially liberal tendencies within the Church gained and the potentially conservative weakened for most of the period here covered, though a further loss of confidence after 1900, especially in face of the Labour unrest of 1911–1912, halted this trend. After about 1870 a doctrinaire attachment to the principles of *laissez-faire* was not a serious impediment to the gradual extension of state interference in economic life, and though spokesmen of the Churches might find obstacles to nearly every case of such interference which was specifically proposed, they rarely offered a thoroughgoing resistance to the whole idea of public intervention.

Indeed the Churches played a part in the growth of a new outlook later in the nineteenth century, an outlook sympathetic to progress, tolerant of social control of economic life, and conscious of the human factors involved. There was a certain recovery of confidence as ethical considerations began to play a larger part in social and political discussions, and there was an era when, instead of regarding the Church as an obstacle to be overcome, those who worked for a new social order demanded somewhat imperiously that the Church should give a lead. Such demands, a regular feature of speeches of such men as Hardie and Tillett, were coupled with stern denunciations of the empirical Church, and were a tribute to the continuing strength of Christian conviction in English life, for they demonstrated that even those who said frankly that they considered the Church reactionary never gave up hope that it might become progressive, and that they considered that in some perhaps undefined way Christianity could be expected to be a progressive force. Reassured by such leaders of the working classes that they had not given up hope of Christian leadership, the Churches did make some effort to rise to the situation. Increasingly they did not oppose Socialism, but only 'false' Socialism, and it became quite a fashion to announce that there was no contradiction between Christianity and 'true' Socialism. This tendency in fact goes all the way back to Maurice himself, for the origin of Christian Socialism can itself be considered an example of such an assertion. The fashion was not very helpful, for it tended to cloud the issue of the Christian's attitude to ordinary Socialism, which in any case was indefinite enough, and it was even made the prelude to announcements that the compatibility of Christianity and 'true' Socialism was so complete that traditional Christianity was by itself a sufficient answer to the problems of the day, no Socialism being needed. On the Socialist side the counterpart of this subtle evasion of the issues was the assertion that Socialism was simply 'applied Christianity.' Both positions indicated an intellectual failure; on the one hand Socialists simply ignored the whole body of Christian doctrine and gave no clue as to how it was supposed to be expressed in Socialism, while on the other Church leaders of progressive tastes equally neglected to show how particular Socialist projects, such as the nationalization of production and distribution, could be directly derived from the New Testament. Not until the Fabian Society appeared did anybody suggest that the argument for Socialism was simply the claim that it worked better than Capitalism. But at least the extreme readiness to see the whole issue in ethical rather than scientific terms, so characteristic of political debate in England, helped to keep the Church and the Socialist movement in touch with each other.

One curious effect of this drastic 'revisionism' was that even those of the Church leaders who were hostile to Socialism rarely realized the strength of the arguments against it. They criticized Socialism on irrelevant grounds—its association with 'free love' or atheism—but they rarely looked very closely at the genuine difficulties involved, except for the problem of incentives in a society without poverty. No one was conscious of the extreme dangers involved in magnifying the powers of the State, and there was little realization of the significance for Socialist theory of the abandonment of the Labour theory of Value. Nor of course did anybody understand the part played by money in the economic problems of the age. The criticisms of Socialism in the *British Weekly* in 1908 were exceptional in their relevance to the real issues.[1] Among the points raised were the quiet drift away from Marx, the vagueness of the limit set to the possible socialization of

[1] See pp. 298f.

property, the equivocal attitude to small property-owners, the danger to individual liberty in the trend to equality, and the confused attitude of Socialists to the question of nationalism and internationalism. After the accession to power of the Liberals in 1906 the issue was complicated by the programme of social legislation undertaken by the Government. The Unionists made the most of the cry of 'Socialism,' and those sections of the Church which were warmly in support of the Government, mostly Nonconformists, were inclined to accept the term, with the usual proviso that this was the 'right kind' of Socialism, so that a considerable body of Christian opinion at least talked a Socialist language in these years.

Those Christians who fully accepted Socialist views tended not to retain orthodox theological convictions. This is shown by the association of Socialism with Liberal Nonconformity, and by the religious attitudes of leading Socialists. In such schools the secularization of religion reached the point of insisting that the prime duty of the Christian was to make a better world; credal orthodoxy, the salvation of the individual soul, the liturgical life of the Church, and many other things were relegated to a secondary place. Such a secularization of religion corresponded to the more radical secularization of idealism exemplified by Beatrice Webb. The progressive, rationalistic, and somewhat hedonistic spirit of the age carried some people out of the Church altogether, to the position that this world was a sufficient 'proper study' for man's ambition, while others found a place for it within the traditional form of the Church. For anyone starting from Beatrice Potter's somewhat other-worldly Evangelicalism there was not much alternative to such a complete break, but it is interesting to reflect that had she come from a Dissenting background she might possibly have been content with the less radical alternative, and become a distinguished lay representative of the 'New Theology.' But it might not have made much difference, since this extreme of Liberal Nonconformity proved rather quickly to be untenable, and Nonconformist Socialists either joined their political beliefs with a more traditional theology or abandoned their Nonconformity. The comparison serves as a reminder that even the most 'secular' Socialists were highly idealistic, brought up on *News from Nowhere* and *Looking Backward*, and that even the Fabians started off from the 'Fellowship of the New Life.'

On the Christian Socialist tradition it is important to remember

that most of the original group were active for the greater part of
this period, having been very young men in 1848, and that much
of their more important work, including the creation of the Working Men's College, the assistance to trade unionism on the legal
side, and the contribution to the growth of the consumers' co-operative movement, was done after Christian Socialism was supposed
to have failed. Their influence was far-reaching, and right down to
1914 no discussion of Christian Socialism was possible without a
consideration of what Maurice and his associates had said and
done. By the later 'seventies most of Maurice's doctrines had been
accepted by large sections of the Church of England, and some of
them by virtually everyone. But the Church at large insisted, and
insisted rightly, that these ideas were not Socialism; and indeed it
is broadly true to say that nobody ever did think the teachings of
the Christian Socialists were Socialism, except perhaps the Christian Socialists themselves. As the ideas of the Christian Socialists
became more fashionable their language was used more and more
vaguely, and the movement suffered the usual fate of revolutionary
doctrines, of being gradually watered down till nothing was left
of the original scandal. By 1914 this process was fairly complete.
But there was also an opposite tendency at work, in that the
Christian Socialists themselves became increasingly radical and
increasingly committed to the Labour movement. While Maurice's
ideas were gradually accepted even by conservative churchmen,
Stewart Headlam was going beyond them. But even he was not
fully involved in the mainstream of the Labour movement. The
first Christian Socialist society so to commit its members was the
Church Socialist League. Thus while the Church caught up with
Maurice new men still found scope for pioneering work. In this
way Christian Socialism remained unrepresentative of the Church
of England. There is not the slightest doubt that in 1914 as in 1850
the main weight of that Church was still ranged behind the Conservative Party, and indeed it would be a moot point at which
date there was the greater unanimity of such support. If there was
far more consciousness of the importance of social reform, and
a much greater degree of acceptance of democratic trends, there
were also the disestablishment of the Welsh Church and the
education dispute to keep the Anglicans in the main solidly
behind the Unionists. The 1908 Pan-Anglican Congress was only
an extreme example of the success of the Christian Socialists in
making more noise than their numbers warranted. The acceptance

of the ideas of Maurice did not break the alliance with the Conservatives, for the radical ideas of 1850 were no obstacle to quite reactionary inclinations in 1914.

The branch of the Church of England which made the most determined efforts to be radical was the Anglo-Catholic party, and although Pusey had once alleged that he and Maurice worshipped different Gods, many Ritualists were disciples of both. For a long time the Christian Socialist movement was dominated by Anglo-Catholics. But it is not true to say that Anglo-Catholicism was captured by the Socialists: the *Church Times* is sufficient disproof. The furthest it went was to try to win support for Anglo-Catholicism by the kudos attaching to the names of such prominent Christian Socialists as Dearmer, Headlam, Donaldson and Adderley, without itself sharing their political views. Despite the prominence of Anglo-Catholics, it seems likely that much of the support for Socialism even in the Church of England came from the opposite extreme of the Church, from the theological liberals such as Llewelyn Davies, or among laymen, Lansbury. During this period Anglo-Catholicism made great gains, but it remained too much of a minority movement to count for a great deal in the relations of two such important bodies as the Church of England and the Labour movement.

The differences between the earlier and the later Christian Socialists are worth emphasizing, for, as so often, continuity of name disguised a radical change of character. The original Christian Socialists were 'patrons' of the working classes. They belonged to an age when it was still just possible for the Anglican clergy to imagine that the shaping of the nation's destiny was in their own hands, and Maurice and his associates were anxious to use that influence to raise the standards of working-class life. The later Christian Socialists were under no such illusions, and simply wished to take their place as one more group among the many which supported the workers' movement. The early Christian Socialists were of a higher intellectual level than the later, and the movement ceased to be so scholarly and became more 'popular'—a parallel to the development of Anglo-Catholicism from Newman and Pusey to the slum Ritualists. From the days of Westcott and Hort the intellectual leadership of the Church tended to be friendly, but not committed, and the real leadership of Christian Socialism passed from the theologians to local activists, though Gore was a marked exception. Until the formation of the Church

Socialist League the whole Christian Socialist movement continued to be an adjunct of the work of the Church rather than a branch of the workers' movement. Even the Guild of St Matthew put first among its objects the defence of the Church against Secularists, and second the promotion of more frequent Communion. It belongs to the history of the Church rather than to the history of the working classes.

With all its limitations, by 1914 Christian Socialism was in a strong position. The prophetic utterances of Maurice had been reduced to commonplaces, but to a large extent this was simply because the movement had achieved so much. On social issues the thinking of the Church of England had made immense progress. Sympathizers with Christian Socialism had risen to high places. To a Conrad Noel, Davidson, Lang, and even Gore were unsatisfactory, but they were much more in touch with the aspirations of the workers than the Victorian bishops. The movement was gaining rather than losing strength. The 1908 Pan-Anglican Congress was only a propaganda victory, but that was far from worthless. There was a diversification of the character of Christian Socialism; it was drifting away from its close alliance with Anglo-Catholicism, to the alarm of Headlam and Noel, but to the advantage of Labour supporters in the Church of England. If the Church of England had not been converted to Socialism many men who had learned from Socialism were in powerful places in that Church, and even thorough and convinced Socialists were no longer merely an occasion of astonishment and ridicule. Christian Socialism was important in the history of the Church. It helped in the recovery of a more corporate interpretation of the Christian religion, linking up ultimately with the Biblical and theological discussion of the meaning of the term 'Kingdom of God.' It changed the idea of the relationship of the Church and the nation. Whatever its influence on the Labour movement, it was theologically and ecclesiastically important.

One more question of primary importance remains to be answered: what kind of Christian tradition contributed most to the Labour movement? Of the three main types of religion in England, there can be no doubt that the Free Churches were far more deeply involved than the Church of England, while the Roman Catholic Church was of minor importance for much of this period. Many poor people belonged to the Church of England, but the kind of men who belonged to the trade unions, organized friendly societies, and built the co-operative movement either attended a Nonconformist chapel or they were likely to be hostile or indifferent to religion. More important than this is the fact that the Nonconformists who have been mentioned in this book have tended to be distinguished figures in the life of their own denominations, while the Anglicans have been members of splinter groups. Congregationalists of the older generation were horrified at the ebullience of Miall, but he lived to become one of the elder statesmen of his denomination. Mid-Victorian Baptists—notably Spurgeon—said harsh things about Clifford, but he became Chairman of the Baptist Union. But it is not on record that anyone suggested Maurice, still less Stewart Headlam or Percy Dearmer or Conrad Noel, for Canterbury. The Nonconformists who were involved in the Labour movement could always count on the applause of their co-religionists, while the Anglicans were more likely to be summoned before the bishop. Despite the efforts of the Anglo-Catholics, the Labour movement through the whole of this period was far more closely linked to Nonconformity than to Anglicanism.

The influence of the Anglo-Catholic Christian Socialists has been exaggerated. Their success in winning the workers to their churches was hindered by their emphasis on authority and on the Church, for the more independent workers wanted to think for themselves and were indifferent to the Church as a historic institution—apart altogether from their being, like most nine-teenth-century Englishmen, natural Protestants. The proportion of women in Ritualist churches was notorious. Nor did these clergy even have the support of their fellow Anglo-Catholics, let alone of the rest of their Church. Liberal and progressive views in politics seemed to most people to go more naturally with liberal and progressive views in religion, and the contribution of the Left-wing of the Church of England to the Labour movement should not be overlooked. Apparently opposite views might come together, as they did in Noel—in the eyes of orthodox churchmen, Papist and Pantheist at once. Anglican 'Modernists,' whether 'Catholic' or not, had something in common with Liberal Non-conformists, and this unorthodox theological trend is important in relation to the Labour movement—more important in some ways than Anglo-Catholicism.

One apparently surprising feature of the age was the Roman Catholic-Nonconformist alliance against the Church of England

and the Conservative Party, though it rested on quite rational foundations. The generous praise in the Nonconformist press for Manning and in the Catholic press for Arch suggested a certain degree of fellow-feeling underneath the formal alliance for political ends. Both Nonconformist and Catholic press gave strong support to the workers, but Catholic enthusiasm for their cause was apt to evaporate rather rapidly in the face of specific demands, because of fear of Socialism. The exception was any occasion when the gain of the working classes was likely to prove a gain for Irish nationalism, as for example in the case of the 1884 Reform Act. This somewhat fanatical antipathy to Socialism continued throughout the period, and it was only towards the end that the realization began to dawn that Manning had been sound, on Catholic grounds, in criticizing Capitalism too, and that there might be advantage in following his example. For nearly all his career Manning, though he became Archbishop of Westminster, was very unrepresentative of the Roman Catholic Church on social affairs, and he won a measure of enthusiasm for his Church which perhaps belonged chiefly to himself as an individual. Yet in a sense this was not unfair, for from another point of view it was Manning rather than lesser spokesmen who spoke for Catholic England, for many Roman Catholics were active in the Labour movement despite the repeated solemn warnings addressed to them in the press— a fact sufficiently attested by the need felt by the *Universe* to condemn Catholics who read the *Clarion*. By the end of the period Roman Catholics were beginning to exercise considerable influence in the Labour Party, as they were bound to do when in certain areas the working-class population was so largely Catholic. At the same time the Catholic population was beginning to rise socially, so that Catholic influence in other respects too was growing.

One feature which Roman Catholics and Nonconformists shared was that politically and socially both groups were partisan and made no pretence of speaking for the whole of society. The Church of England claimed to be a national Church and its press tried, not very successfully, to be impartial on political issues. This was a source of weakness, for while nobody at all really thought the Anglican press anything but Conservative everybody realized that it lacked the polemical vigour of the other papers. The *Universe* and the *Nonconformist* were at least more successful in presenting a party-line than the *Church Times* and the *Church Family Newspaper* were in passing a dispassionate judgement on controversial issues. The great difference between the Roman Catholic press and the Nonconformist was that the former stood for the interests of Catholicism, assuming that in practice this meant the interests of Ireland, while the latter stood for the interests of Nonconformity, assuming that in practice this meant the interests of the working classes. It may have been mistaken in thinking that Nonconformity and the working classes were natural allies, but if so it misinterpreted the whole situation from the beginning of this period to the end, for while the Anglo-Catholic and Roman Catholic press periodically asserted that their respective parties were the best friends of the workers, the Nonconformist press simply took its own alliance with the Labour movement for granted throughout. The mere questioning of this alliance, for example by the Fabian Society, brought something like incredulity. Nonconformity itself changed its character considerably during these years. The last traces of Pietism and other-worldliness fell away into the newer sects which were nonconformist even to Nonconformity, and 'political Dissent' ruled the day. As it was more secular in outlook, so it was in closer sympathy with Labour, though its own social progress was undermining the alliance and beginning to open the way to a Nonconformity which was basically conservative. But the career of the Unionist Governments from 1895 to 1905 provoked this potentially conservative force into a violent Radicalism, so that in Edwardian times vocal Nonconformity stood on the extreme Left of Liberalism and was distinctly friendly to the Labour Party. Apart from the Methodists the Nonconformists were limited in their approach to the workers by their individualist organization, which at times was inclined to decline into anarchy, yet all the main Free Churches won a good deal of support from the working classes, despite the allegation that they were a middle-class religion. Wales was a special case, being traditionally Nonconformist, but such areas as the cotton towns of Lancashire and the woollen area of Yorkshire were strong in the order forms of Dissent, and in these same areas the Labour movement found much of its early strength. The Methodists were dominant in some trade unions, but Methodist trade union leaders tended to be Right-wing and unsympathetic to independent Labour representation. In the Parliamentary sphere the Methodists were by no means dominant. The figures given by the *Independent* for Liberals in the 1892–1895 Parliament[1] showed

[1] See p. 315.

numbers of Congregationalists and Unitarians which were each comparable with the Methodists, although the latter were a far larger denomination, and it was by no means certain that the Methodist Liberals would be nearer to Labour than the others. Again, in the consumers' co-operative movement Nonconformists other than Methodists played a vital part, from the days of the Rochdale Pioneers onwards.

The press comment on trade unionism in the period 1900–1914 surveyed above[1] shows that whatever lip-service the various newspapers gave to the principle only the Nonconformist press was really prepared to give full support to particular union demands. Such a conclusion deserves to be treated with reserve, for the *British Weekly* still regarded the organized working classes as part of the general movement called Liberalism, and in warmly supporting the unions it was doing no more than conducting propaganda for its own party, just as the Anglican press was conducting propaganda for the Conservative Party. But this of course is the real point: the Nonconformists were still able to regard the workers' cause as their own and to support it against 'privilege,' an amorphous system taking in the Conservative Party, the Church of England, the House of Lords, big business and the brewers. There can be no doubt that the Nonconformists were always much more involved in the working-class movement than the other denominations, and this is true not only of the Methodists (still less only of certain types of Methodists), but of Nonconformity as a whole, except for such minor groups as the Presbyterians. The estimate of the actual extent of its contribution to the Labour movement depends upon one's assessment of the relationship between the older Radicalism and the Labour Party. It is true that the Labour movement was influenced considerably by Marx, and still more by Owen and the Chartists, but it was also in many ways continuous with a Radicalism going back beyond Marx and Owen. This Radicalism Nonconformity consistently supported. It is worth noting too that towards the end of the period it was a social Radicalism linking the Liberal Left with Labour rather than the old-fashioned kind represented by Morley, which was favoured. Though the social Radicalism had grown out of the political kind it was a very different movement: for example the one kind was most reluctant to see any widening of state action, while the other warmly welcomed it. The social doctrines expressed by

[1] See pp. 132–147.

leading Nonconformists late in this period were often derived much more from Chamberlain and Dilke than from Morley, though they would have been exceedingly reluctant to admit it. The strong influence of a dilute form of Socialism on Edwardian Nonconformity and allied Radicals is not readily acknowledged today, because of the mythology of the age, which lays it down that Protestantism, especially in such advanced forms as English Dissent, is necessarily individualistic, without social content, and inevitably and inseparably associated with Capitalism. This doctrine has the powerful support of Marxists, Fabians, and Roman Catholics, and historical facts must bow before so impressive a unanimity of theorists.

In brief outline the conclusions drawn from the preceding pages are that in these years all the denominations were to a large extent out of touch with the English working classes, that they shared the current belief that the existing economic system would last for ever, though they were also strongly tinged with contemporary ideas of progress, which weakened the effects of such conservatism; that the Church contributed very substantially to the growth of the Labour movement, even when full recognition is accorded to the influence of non-religious factors; that the Labour movement continued to be subject to a remarkably strong religious influence, even though the Churches were in decline throughout the period; that Christian Socialism flourished right down to 1914, but that while it did a great deal to change the outlook of the Church it tended to stand outside the Labour movement rather than to enter actively into it; that Socialism tended to win the support of unorthodox Christians, even though they might belong to orthodox denominations; and that the kind of Christianity which counted for most in the history of the Labour movement was that kind which found its formal expression in the several denominations of Nonconformity.

EPILOGUE

THE PRECEDING PAGES have traced some of the connexions of the Churches with the Labour movement down to a date from which the expression 'Labour movement' took on a wholly new significance. The reason for this change was not, at least directly, the occurrence of the first world war, but the emergence of the Labour Party as one of the two main parties in the State. Down to 1914 the Labour Party was regarded as a small Parliamentary group voicing the legitimate grievances of the workers while the two traditional parties carried on the serious business of ruling the country. In the election of 1906 and the two of 1910 the group increased to around forty, but in a house of 600 members this was still no serious challenge to the Liberals and the Conservatives. In the 'Coupon Election' of 1918 the Labour membership passed the seventy mark, but this still seemed a secondary consideration in face of the sweeping victory of Lloyd George's coalition. But in 1922 the coalition broke up, with the revolt of the Conservatives, and the Liberals, while holding on to over 100 seats, were split into two equal factions. Labour membership doubled, and it became apparent that a day might soon come when a Labour Prime Minister would hold office—though it could hardly have been anticipated that it would be within a few months. From now on the Labour Party would provide the Government, or, much more frequently, the Opposition.

From the point of view of the Churches the situation was transformed. Until the last years of the nineteenth century the expression 'Labour Party' should have been put in inverted commas. There was no party of this name, and its use served as a forceful, almost paradoxical, assertion of a point of view: the point of view, specifically, that the working classes were not adequately represented by the Liberal and Conservative parties, and in a sense constituted a 'third force.' Few people identified the third force with the I.L.P., and fewer still with the S.D.F.

The key to the debate within the Churches was that support for this so-called 'Labour Party' could be interpreted as a mere extension of the responsibility of Christians—now at last generally recognized—for social reform. The indifference of most church-people to the 'Labour question' seemed to the most committed precisely parallel to the unconcern of earlier generations over slavery or child labour in the mines. Hence the well-established tradition of nagging and hectoring in the press and at Church Assemblies. *Of course* it was a Christian duty to support Labour, as in every other way to uplift the downtrodden.

But it was a very different matter when the Labour Party offered itself as the Government. To help in translating Ramsay Macdonald from the Opposition Front Bench to Downing Street might perhaps be a Christian duty, but no one could suppose it a self-evident one. Moreover a party challenging for power necessarily offered a policy covering the whole range of public life. Hitherto—that is, until the post-war years—everyone assumed that Labour was primarily if not exclusively interested in 'labour' questions, in the other sense of the word: wages, employment, housing, and so on. But now Labour produced programmes on all the issues with which governments have to deal. Was it at all obviously a Christian duty to recognize the Bolshevik government of Russia?—this was one of the issues between the parties.

In the long run the result was to change the basis of appeal from conscience to political conviction. Great numbers of Christians would support Labour—including some very vocal Church leaders—but it would be because they happened to think Labour the best party—best for themselves, or for the country, or for the world; no longer simply because it was a straightforward expression of the Christian ethic. A Christian might well favour nationalization of the railways, but he would be a zealot if he derived it directly from the New Testament. The last Labour Party leader who saw the great issues as simple matters of conscience was George Lansbury, and it was his frequent appeals to conscience which infuriated a man of equal idealism who nevertheless knew that the daily substance of politics is power—Ernest Bevin.

The change in the party's appeal occurred extremely slowly, and only became clear after the second world war, with the Attlee government in power. The reason for this was that a whole series of controversies arose between the wars which did appear to be moral issues. The General Strike could be represented as the revolt of the eternally downtrodden classes, driven at last to desperation; the miseries of the depression were the subject of repeated agonized appeals by prominent clergymen, 'For God's sake, do something'; and in the 'thirties the Labour Party projected an image of itself, in large measure a new image, as the party of Arthur Henderson, the League of Nations party, and so the peace party. On behalf of hungry and desperate miners, the weary and hopeless queue waiting for the 'dole,' and above all on behalf of the cause of peace and internationalism, the Christian conscience of England was still ready to respond. The last relics of the Nonconformist conscience, led gently to alliance with the traditional Tory enemy by the easy route of Liberal Nationalism, contributed something to the appeasement policy of the Chamberlain government; but those lovers of peace who supported the Labour alternative were saved from any comparable misjudgement by lack of opportunity.

For, of course, the Labour Party was still the party of the underdog, in a new sense: it was now not only the party of the working classes, but also the permanent Opposition, fated always to have to sit still and watch the Tories in almost continuous power. The Macdonald governments were mere episodes, the result of Liberal forbearance. Sympathy, in the popular sense, was still a good motive for supporting Labour. It was the victory of 1945 that stopped kind-hearted Christians feeling sorry for Labour.

Since the Churches had throughout the nineteenth century been predominantly middle-class bodies, whose links with Labour rested largely on a basis of guilty conscience, and since after 1918, and especially after 1945, the underdog was never again quite so much in need of sympathy, one might have expected that the long-awaited alienation of Christianity and Labour Party would at last come about.

The fact that in the half-century after 1914 many of the leading spokesmen of Labour were Christians, and that the whole party was permeated with an idealism its opponents saw as woolly sentimentality, surely needs some explaining. By the second half of the twentieth century the Labour Party was one of the few remaining reservoirs of the kind of moral earnestness characteristic of Victorian religious activities. Whether this was to its credit or not was disputed.

It is in any case rather remarkable. If very few ordinary working people went to church before 1914 there is no reason to think that the numbers increased later. The Welsh revival of 1904 was the last of its kind. Between the wars many of the members of the middle classes left the churches too—a rare example of a social custom which spread up the social scale. The favourite Victorian topic: 'Why don't the working classes come to church?' developed in the direction of 'Why doesn't anybody come to church?' Evangelistic efforts continued, with Christian Commando Campaigns during the second world war and visits by Dr Billy Graham after it; but the picture was on the whole of churches sparsely filled, and mostly with middle-class people. Yet the party supported by most of the working classes continued to show many marks of Christian influence. The only churches to contain many members of trade unions were Roman Catholic; yet while most Roman Catholics certainly voted Labour they remained a marginal influence on the party. Protestant Christianity—if the term be stretched to include High Anglicans—became the religion of a minority of the British people, but retained secure strongholds in the ancient universities, the press and radio—and the Labour Party.

It is not possible in this final chapter to deal in detail with this surprisingly tenacious relationship. All that is offered is a selection of samples—a few specimens of the kind of linkage of the Church and the Labour movement which continued in the half-century between the first world war and the accession to power of the government of Harold Wilson.

Anglican Christian Socialism had always been a markedly self-conscious movement, in the sense that it had always taken care that the contributions of prominent Anglicans to the Labour movement received a good deal of public notice. Men like Kingsley, Hughes, Headlam, Dearmer and Noel, whatever their disagreements, all possessed a gift for publicity. The Methodist contribution to the trade union movement, and the general Nonconformist share in the co-operative movement, had in contrast been largely the work of obscure men who did not realize that the association of Christianity with the cause of working-class advancement was anything remarkable. But in the twentieth century Methodism at least became more aware of itself, and the close historical connexion between the Methodist and Labour movements came to be something of a cliché, and even to be exaggerated to the point at which it was sometimes held that the former had given to the latter its form and character.

The continuing influence of Methodism on the Labour movement is described, along with many irrelevancies, in the final volume of Dr Wearmouth's comprehensive survey of the subject.[1] One's impression is, no doubt wrongly, that the Methodist influence in the twentieth century cannot have been very great, if it is necessary, in a volume dealing with this subject, to range over the whole of the nineteenth century, with much repetition from previous volumes, and even to make excursions into the eighteenth. Joseph Arch and Thomas Burt may have lived into the twentieth century, but one was born long before Queen Victoria ascended the throne and the other only just missed that event; and in any case they received a fair share of notice in Dr Wearmouth's previous volume. Nor does an account of Thomas Hepburn, born 1795, belong here.

One's impression that the influence of Methodism may have been exaggerated is encouraged by the fact that Dr Wearmouth's account revolves around County Durham and shrinks to nothing as it moves farther away from that area. It is questionable whether anyone really wants to know the names, faithfully set down, of the forty-seven Methodists who served on the Darlington council in the first half of the twentieth century.

Some of the Methodists who have been referred to in earlier chapters do indeed belong also to the period after 1914. It was between the wars that Arthur Henderson served as Foreign Secretary and Philip Snowden as Chancellor of the Exchequer. Such men had their successors. Jack Lawson, born in 1882 in a two-roomed house in Whitehaven, was brought up by a bullying and illiterate mother in Durham. At twelve he left school to go down the pit, and by his twenties he was a Wesleyan local preacher and a speaker for the I.L.P. Through trade union and political service, and a spell at Ruskin College, he worked his way up to County Councillor, and, in 1919, to Parliament as member for Chester-le-Street. After holding junior office in the Macdonald governments he became Secretary for War in 1945, and in 1950 a peer. Methodists and miners had not yet supplied so many recruits to the Upper House that his arrival was an event to pass without notice.

William Whiteley, another Durham miner, associated with the New Connexion tradition rather than the Wesleyan, joined the Labour Party early in the twentieth century, and held at one time

[1] Robert F. Wearmouth, *The Social and Political Influence of Methodism in the Twentieth Century* (1957).

or another such unusually-associated offices as Secretary, Treasurer, Sunday School Superintendent, Choir Master and Trustee of his local church, and Lord Commissioner of the Treasury, Comptroller of the Royal Household, and, in the Attlee government, Chief Whip.

Neither Lawson nor Whiteley made so much impression on the public at large as Ellen Wilkinson, who seemed in the 1930s and 1940s to personify the spirit of an earlier era of Labour history. From leading a hunger-march from Jarrow to London she progressed to the Attlee Cabinet as Minister of Education, and at the time of the 1945 election campaign and in the years immediately following she was one of the Labour leaders most widely respected by people of all political persuasions. In her combination of convinced Methodism and outspoken Socialism she had perhaps something of a successor in the Wilson government in the person of Mr George Thomas.

Yet the influence of Methodism at the national level has not been comparable with that in particular areas. In the forty-seven years from 1905 to 1951 Methodists served as chairmen of the Durham County Council on thirty-three occasions; but of the more than 600 members of the 1951 House of Commons only twenty-seven were Methodists, of whom twenty-two were Labour. (One of the minority was Mr Selwyn Lloyd, a Methodist who achieved the remarkable distinction of becoming a *Conservative* Cabinet Minister, a social revolution indeed.)

In the trade union world Methodists continued, as before, to be prominent in particular areas and industries. Dr Wearmouth laments that in the twentieth century Wesleyanism 'developed rather rapidly into a middle-class ecclesiastical system.' Wesleyanism had on the whole been middle class for a long time. In the twentieth century the rest of Methodism became middle class too, though there is no reason to suppose that the rapid disappearance of the characteristics of the smaller Methodist bodies was a result of Methodist union. The transformation of the uncouth vitality of proletarian Churches into bourgeois respectability is a familiar enough phenomenon everywhere in the Protestant world, and especially in America.

But at least in the north-east the old tradition survived. William Straker (1855–1941) will do as one example (from many given by Dr Wearmouth) of the miners' leader who lived on into the new era, when the Labour Party was the alternative government. He was a small boy at work in the fields before Gladstone became Premier for the first time, and not many years afterwards a miner and a Primitive Methodist local preacher. As a union official he adapted himself to changing circumstances, and from being a spokesman of the *laissez-faire* attitude of the north-eastern miners, hostile to the political Labour movement and legislative interference, he moved towards Socialism, fighting for the nationalization of the mines. In the *Monthly Circular* which he edited, a trade union paper, he wrote of the women at the tomb of Jesus on Easter morning, and of the shepherds on the Judean hills at Christmas time, and quoted hymns. In Roman Catholic countries the use of religious language in secular contexts seems to be familiar; in Protestant England it breaks out only occasionally in relatively unsophisticated areas of society.

Straker lived on till the 1940s. In the post-1945 world another Methodist, Sam Watson, enjoyed a power and influence among the miners of the north-east sufficient to make his name nationally known, though for some reason it does not appear in Dr Wearmouth's pages.

Straker and Watson belong to the traditional world of Methodist trade unionism. A quite different type of leader is exemplified by Ronald Gould, a Methodist local preacher who became secretary of the National Union of Teachers and an international figure in the world of education. The world of education is a white-collar world (though the whitest collars belong to other teachers' organizations) but the N.U.T. is nevertheless a trade union, though not currently affiliated to the T.U.C.

A quite different specimen again is Percy Belcher, leader of the Tobacco Workers, in youth a Baptist and during the second world war a Communist, who was converted in 1943 by a Christian Commando Campaign, becoming a Methodist local preacher and a lay pastor.

Throughout the history of the Labour Movement Methodism has made considerable contributions, but it is an exaggeration to say, in words which have now become a cliché, that it has been a movement more Methodist than Marxist, if by this is meant that more has been done for the political Labour Movement by men under the influence of Methodism than by men under some sort of Marxian influence, direct or indirect. It is doubtful whether the Methodist influence has in fact been any greater than that of the older Dissenting bodies, and more than doubtful if it has been greater than the Anglican influence, even when purely nominal Anglicanism is discounted. Of course the ethos of the Labour Party has been much more like that of Methodism than that of international Communism; but that is not due so much to direct derivation as to the intimate connexions of both with the social classes on the borderline of the middle-class and working-class worlds, and no doubt much of the same ethos also pervades pigeon racing and brass-band contests.

Methodist trade unionism bore something of the character of a survival from earlier days. There is a much more modern flavour about the attempt to create a Christian Sociology. Sociology sounds rather like Socialism, but there is in fact little resemblance between them. The characteristic spokesman of the one is the modern prophet, of the other the scholar. But Christian Sociology in England is at any rate an offshoot of Christian Socialism. Its chief propagandists were Dr V. A. Demant, who gave a series of Scott Holland lectures in 1949, published in 1952 as *Religion and the Decline of Capitalism*, a deliberate sequel to Tawney's famous *Religion and the Rise of Capitalism;* and Maurice Reckitt, whose *Maurice to Temple* (1947) is sub-titled *A Century of the Social Movement in the Church of England*, and whose autobiography of 1941 bears the same title as that later used by Attlee—*As It Happened*.

Reckitt himself was at Oxford in the years before 1914 and was one of the numerous company who embraced the Socialist creed. He followed his own variety, in alliance with G. D. H. Cole, promoting the cause of Guild Socialism. This was the very mild and pacific English version of Syndicalism, currently popular in France, and took issue with Labour Party policy on the grounds that it was designed to replace private Capitalism by state Capitalism, rather than by true Socialism, which was held to consist in workers' control of industry. It was a principle which had an obvious appeal to a Christian Socialist, in that it was a return to a new form of the original ideals of Ludlow and Maurice, but it was one to which the Labour Party consistently refused to commit itself.

After the war Reckitt left his Socialist beliefs behind and embraced the Social Credit doctrines of Major Douglas, which he rather unexpectedly held to be an expression of Christian Sociology. In due course he left this movement too, as others did, because he found the authoritarian methods of Douglas intolerable. Another affiliation was with G. K. Chesterton's Distributivism.

From Guild Socialist days onward Reckitt was a lively commentator on the movement to create a Christian Sociology. Its originator was P. E. T. Widdrington, of the Church Socialist League, the first Christian Socialist organization to be affiliated officially to the Labour Party, which had enjoyed a reasonably substantial popularity between 1906 and 1914.

The outbreak of war was a great shock to the Christian Socialists, as to the Churches in general. In 1916 the Church of England organized a National Mission of Repentance and Hope. The demagogue Horatio Bottomley denounced the whole idea that the British people, engaged in a black and white conflict with German evil, needed any repentance; correspondingly the Christian Socialists saw the mission as a partial vindication of their witness and a hopeful sign for the future. A committee appointed to follow it up produced a report on Christianity and Industrial Problems; it was a committee largely composed of C.S.U. members and it was said that the report was largely written by R. H. Tawney. It was a characteristic product of the C.S.U. outlook, demanding a change in the spirit of the industrial system—which anyone who wished might interpret as implying also a change in the industrial system itself. To the old principle of the 'living wage' Christian thought now added the demand, a partial move in the Guild Socialist direction, that the workers should share in the control of industry. The report was accepted by the Lambeth Conference of 1920.

In 1918 Scott Holland had died. For a long time he and Gore had been the leading figures in the C.S.U., and it seemed the right time to adopt a new policy. The C.S.U. was therefore amalgamated with the Navvy Mission, an evangelistic agency, to form the Industrial Christian Fellowship. In this the chief figure was Geoffrey Studdert Kennedy, most famous of army chaplains, who interpreted the Fellowship's primary purpose as evangelistic, though he always bore in mind the social as well as the individualistic aspect of Christianity. The I.C.F. worked chiefly through lay agents, who spoke on street corners and in factory canteens, opened centres for the unemployed, and conducted periodical 'Crusades' in particular districts.

The war brought a crisis also to the Church Socialist League. The enthusiasms and Utopianism of the pre-1914 years now seemed intolerably naïve. It had become clear that the reconstruction of society was not to be achieved by the passing of resolutions. The League came round to the conviction always held by the Union that the first necessity was study. The progressive and Modernist theology of the earlier years also went into decline, and the League's supporters were more than ever thoroughgoing Anglo-Catholics. The Dearmer tradition of looking back to the Middle Ages, the era of Christendom, before the Reformation ushered in Capitalism and removed the Church's fatherly guidance from the economic sphere, revived. It was mooted that a Christian Sociology might well be built up on the traditional bases of widespread private property, the doctrine of the just price, and Guild Socialism. The Church Socialist League became the League of the Kingdom of God; as Widdrington put it, 'we disentangled ourselves from political parties.' Writing in 1945 he explains that the break was because Socialism had become more and more Secularist and had lost its early idealism. But the change was also in himself and in his associates, who had lost faith in partisan solutions and preferred the leisurely techniques of research and conferences. In 1922 as 'A Group of Churchmen' they produced a preliminary book of essays entitled *The Return of Christendom*, a rather unhappily chosen title conveying, perhaps unjustly, the suggestion of wishing to put the clock back.

The emergence of what became known as the Christendom group was part of the process by which Anglican social concern was more prominently before the public in the 1920s than ever before. The Anglo-Catholic Summer School of Sociology, beginning in 1925, 'COPEC' (the Conference on Christian Politics, Economics, and Citizenship), the General Strike, with Archbishop Davidson, though critical of the strike leaders, working for a compromise and being subjected to a veto by the Government, which resisted his wish to broadcast, the long efforts of several bishops on behalf of the miners after the General Strike failed—Stanley Baldwin asked how they would like it if he asked the Iron and Steel Federation to revise the Athanasian Creed— the valiant efforts for better housing, made in St Pancras by Basil Jellicoe, who died worn out at the age of 36, and by Charles Jenkinson in Leeds; all this helped to keep alive some sort of Christian Socialist tradition. The Malvern Conference of 1941 and subsequent discussions led to a successor to *The Return of Christendom*, in the shape of *Prospect for Christendom* (1945), edited by Reckitt. But the transition which had begun when the C.S.L. set out to rethink its position during the first world war was now complete, and one of the most influential members of the group was the right-wing T. S. Eliot, whose *Idea of a Christian Society* (1939) was by many regarded as a thoroughly reactionary work, nostalgically seeking a renewal of theological, and perhaps clerical, control of society. (A vigorous answer by D. L. Munby appeared twenty-four years later entitled *The Idea of a Secular Society* (1963) claiming that the so-called secularization of society was something to be welcomed rather than deprecated by Christians.) The academic detachment of *Prospect for Christendom* is indicated by the titles of some of the essays in it: V. A. Demant wrote on *The Idea of a Natural Order*; E. L. Mascall on *The Person and the Family*; T. S. Eliot on *Cultural Forces in the Human Order*. The attempt to ground Christian pronouncements firmly on a reasoned theory of society is one which can hardly be faulted; but by the 1960s it was difficult to see that Christian sociologists had as yet had much influence, and Munby's book seemed one symptom of a widespread revaluation of secular society evident in very influential writers on both sides of the Atlantic: a revaluation quite at variance with the attempt to re-create 'Christendom.'

Meanwhile in the 1930s the long-established Christian Socialist tradition in the Church of England reached its climax when one of its most influential leaders became Archbishop of Canterbury. How this event would have appeared to the mid-Victorian age one can hardly imagine, yet the event itself was greater even than the simple statement of it conveys, for William Temple was not only Archbishop of Canterbury but by general consensus one of the outstanding holders of that office and the unquestioned leader of his Church, which his predecessors had not always been.

Temple was born in 1881, the son of Frederick Temple, Bishop of Exeter, who was sixty years old, and who, before William was grown up, had been translated first to London, and then to Canterbury. William grew up in the atmosphere of Fulham Palace and then Lambeth, with as promising a prospect of succeeding to an Archbishopric as a boy could have. The prospect was realized, and Temple in due course became Bishop of Manchester, Archbishop of York, and Archbishop of Canterbury. In his early youth he would have been the best bet one could hope to find to enjoy such a career. More surprising in a way was his lifelong devotion to the cause of Christian Socialism; more surprising until it is remembered that he grew up in the period around 1900 when a

Christian Socialist was a very natural thing for a young Anglican of upper-class origins to become. It is a mark of the achievements of the movement, especially in the version of it formulated by Gore and the C.S.U., that no one seemed surprised that Frederick Temple's son should be a Socialist, and that his convictions seem to have forwarded rather than hindered his career. Perhaps the decisive point was his appointment to the diocese of Manchester, and his association with working-class movements seemed an obvious qualification, just as Fraser's advanced Liberalism had seemed to qualify him for the same post. Once a bishop, Temple's great gifts and influence marked him out for further promotion.

Temple was outstanding in several ways. As a philosopher he at least stood out among bishops, though it seems doubtful whether his works have had any very lasting influence. He was an extraordinarily able chairman, possessing in an almost unique degree the chairman's gift of finding a formula. He was no great administrator, but his charm and effectiveness in personal contacts supplied any deficiency. But he is likely to be remembered in history for two particular reasons: his contribution to the Ecumenical Movement and the founding of the World Council of Churches and his embodiment of the Anglican Christian Socialist tradition.

The background of his Christian Socialism was, as for so many of his generation, the Settlement movement. He was sent to Rugby, of which his father had been headmaster, and while there and at Oxford he took part in the work of the Rugby Settlement, Toynbee Hall, Oxford House, and the Oxford Medical Mission. From such experience his political opinions evolved gently in the direction of Socialism. In youth he favoured Protection, as against the current Free Trade ethos, not on Imperialist grounds, but as a means of insulating the national economy so that it might be directed towards social reform. This was an attitude which would have won him the sympathy of the Fabian Society, and indeed alarmed complaints were made to his father of his enthusiasm for Bernard Shaw.

It has been described as axiomatic of Temple that he was always on the side of the underdog. An early expression of his sympathy was his share in organizing the sweated industries exhibition in 1907; another was his chairmanship of an S.C.M. conference at Matlock on 'Christianity and Social Problems' in 1909.

These were transient events, but a lifelong allegiance was with the Workers' Educational Association. Apart from his share in founding the movement, he served as its chairman for sixteen years, from 1908 to 1924, and it remained thereafter one of the causes to which he was most ready to sacrifice his time. In this particular allegiance there is something typical not only of Temple, but of Anglican Christian Socialism as a whole. The members of the W.E.A. were always very unrepresentative specimens of the working classes as a whole, and the movement served as an effective means by which a comparatively few men with ambition and determination could in effect rise into the middle classes. This was not at all the wish of most workers; cynical Tories knew this very well, and so did secular and Marxist Socialists; but it took well-meaning churchmen like Temple some time to find out.

From 1910 to 1914 Temple was head of Repton, without greatly adding to his reputation. He had little understanding of boys, except a select few of the exceptionally able and earnest sixth formers, and was remembered for his geniality rather than for his inspiration. One is bound to ask what relation is to be found between his headship of an expensive and exclusive public school and his Socialism. The answer is disappointing. Before his appointment he warned the governors that he was opposed to the class divisions represented by public schools and hoped to diminish them. Bravely, and commendably, the governors still appointed him; but no revolution occurred, and Repton continued much as before. Four years is too short a time to reform a school, but Temple had a gift for getting much done in a short time when he knew what he wanted, and it was quickly apparent that he had no idea what he wanted to do at Repton. This is significant, because the traditional expression of progressiveness and a social conscience in the English public school is still the heritage of Arnold: the inculcation on the pupils of the conviction that because they are the natural leaders of society they must learn to serve—in ways chosen of course by themselves—all classes of society. This is the way Temple looked at Repton. It is better than nothing, and of course in Arnold's day, when public school men really were the natural leaders of society, it was wholly right. But by the twentieth century the conception of a self-appointed Samurai trained in a few exclusive schools to do good to the rest of mankind was an anachronism. Temple's headship is a reminder of the cultivated paternalism always characteristic of the Church of England.

During the first world war Temple, now rector of the fashionable parish of St James's, Piccadilly, edited an Anglican paper called the *Challenge*, which represented reforming and radical movements of several kinds, Christian Socialism prominent among them. It was sympathetic to the problems and demands of the working classes, notably in relation to their suspicion of the 'dilution of labour' (i.e. the drafting of large numbers of new workers into war industry without due regard to the interests of long-standing skilled workers).

In 1918 Temple joined the Labour Party. He left after seven years because of a disagreement over foreign policy, but continued to give general support to the party. But though he exercised a greater influence over the working classes than any other Church leader of his day his relations with their political party were not altogether cordial. He shared the idealistic hopes that it would be a movement of social and moral reform rather than the instrument of a class-interest, and he was suspicious of Socialist hopes that the Church as a whole would adopt a Socialist programme. It is impossible to acquit Temple of the charge of a certain naïvety and other-worldliness even in his social gospel.

The S.C.M. conference of 1909 led on, with the usual ecclesiastical leisureliness, to the Conference on Politics, Economics and Citizenship of 1924, when Temple chaired a gathering of 1,500 delegates, eighty of them from abroad, representing six European countries, China and Japan. The conference represented the triumph of the principle proclaimed in 1889 with the foundation of the C.S.U., that the Church had a right and duty to concern itself with political and economic issues. This was an achievement, but it is a little difficult to say what else Copec achieved, beyond unusually voluminous reports. One thing it did succeed in doing was to establish Temple himself as the Church of England's champion chairman. It reveals the limitations of what had by now become the main method of Christian social policy, the compiling of reports on a basis of inquiry and conference, as though problems will solve themselves once they are correctly diagnosed.

Temple was abroad at the time of the General Strike, but returned in time to take part in a highly controversial intervention in the coal stoppage which continued after it, in that he was a member of an interdenominational group which attempted to negotiate. It was widely accused of misleading the miners into thinking that they had the general support of the Churches and so stiffening their resistance as to prolong the dispute, to the ultimate disadvantage of all concerned. Temple was the spokesman who wrote to *The Times* to deny the allegation of bias, but it is difficult to avoid the conclusion that the intervention of unofficial groups on such occasions did give a misleading impression. Temple's biographer considered that something was nevertheless achieved: 'One result at least had been achieved by the Churches' group. Coming as it did immediately after the Archbishop's action in the General Strike, its intervention changed completely the miners' attitude to the Churches. By organized labour organized religion had hitherto been held to embody the reactionary spirit of a privileged caste and to be consistently opposed to the welfare and progress of the workers; notable leaders of the Churches had now come into the open with an independent and unprejudiced outlook.'[1]

A comment like this needs to be taken with a pinch of salt. Even if true, it amounts to saying that the Churches' intervention on behalf of the miners did the miners no good, but no matter, it did some good for the Churches; but in any case the sweeping claim that the miners' whole attitude to the Church was changed lacks evidence. One thing which was certainly achieved was a further development of Temple's reputation as a leading churchman on the side of the workers; but there is every reason to suppose that the latter considered him a rare specimen, and his elevation to York and Canterbury as little short of a miracle.

In the 'thirties the great issue was unemployment. In 1934 Temple clashed with the Chancellor of the Exchequer, Neville Chamberlain, by writing to *The Times* to suggest that any budget surplus should go to the relief of the unemployed rather than to cut taxes. The incident illustrates the difficulty of making moral contributions to political debate, for under some circumstances tax cuts might be the most effective remedy for unemployment.

Temple was well aware that letters to *The Times* (of which he wrote a fair number) are not the final solution of social problems. He also called together a group of friends, financed by the Pilgrim Trust, to undertake a thorough investigation of the condition of the unemployed. Here was an example of yet another problem

[1] F. A. Iremonger, *William Temple* (1948), 343f.

confronting the social reformer: the report did not appear till 1938, when, although warmly received, it was obviously out of date.

During the second world war social questions came even more to the fore, with the insistence from the start, and even in the darkest days, that a new society should be planned for the post-war era. The Industrial Christian Fellowship raised its voice, and Temple was invited to preside over the conference of Anglicans at Malvern, early in 1941. The delegates were honoured with a star-studded cast including Middleton Murry, T. S. Eliot, Dorothy Sayers, Sir Richard Acland, Kenneth Ingram, Donald Mackinnon, H. A. Hodges, V. A. Demant, and W. G. Peck, with a paper sent along by Maurice Reckitt, who was ill. Not surprisingly this group of brilliant individualists did not produce an agreed programme for the post-war world. To Acland, most vocal of a vocal gathering, it seemed that Christianity obviously involved public ownership of the means of production, and surprised onlookers over-hastily formed the impression that the Church of England had gone over to Socialism. Temple was not unsympathetic to Acland, but other members of the conference were not altogether convinced that private ownership of industry 'is' a stumbling-block to Christianity, though they were persuaded to accept Temple's very characteristic compromise, that it 'may be.' Reckitt and others later co-operated in the study of Christian sociology which led to *Prospect for Christendom*, while Temple wrote *Christianity and Social Order* (1942), a little book starting from the traditional Christian concept of Natural Law and justifying the intervention of the Church in economic life. It sold 139,000 copies.

It would have been intriguing to see what kind of relationship Temple formed with the Attlee government after the war. Unfortunately he did not live to see it, but died very suddenly at a time when the hopes of a post-war Utopia were still bright.

Temple is the logical conclusion of the Christian Socialist movement begun by Maurice and organized by the C.S.U. Certainly it had its limitations, not least the survival of the idea that the Church's function in relation to social problems begins with a fatherly and benevolent hand on the shoulder and issues in investigations reported to conferences. Still, with all his limitations Temple was as distinguished a Church leader as his age produced anywhere in the world, and the man of whom this must be said was a convinced Christian Socialist who firmly supported the Labour Party.

Throughout the half-century beginning in 1914 Christian Socialism continued to bear its witness in public life, as ever in many forms. Dr Hewlett Johnson (b. 1874) maintained a faithful allegiance to the cause of Soviet Communism in improbable places—as incumbent of a very prosperous Manchester suburb, and from 1931 as Dean of Canterbury. He held this office to a very advanced age and to the embarrassment of a succession of Archbishops. That a spokesman of minority views should occupy a platform of such prominence and survive so many attacks in the Conservative press and the House of Lords is a tribute to the Anglican system; but unfortunately the Dean's usefulness in this respect was minimized by the naïvety of his devotion to Stalinist orthodoxy through all its deviations. However, in the post-war years of the Cold War he did at least voice an alternative form of nonsense to that currently fashionable.

In Parliament Christian Socialism was as ever protean in its variations of form. Sir Richard Acland was a vociferous spokesman of the view that political programmes must be based on moral and ultimately on religious foundations. During the second world war he left the Labour Party to found Commonwealth, a political movement consciously advocating Socialism as an expression of Christian principle. In the abnormal political conditions of the last phase of the war, when the British electorate was becoming bored with the suspension of party politics, Commonwealth won several seats in by-elections, among them some (notably Eddisbury, a large rural constituency in Cheshire) which would normally have been safely Conservative. All the Commonwealth M.P.s, including Acland himself, either lost their seats or joined the Labour Party after the war. Acland later left the Labour Party again and lost his seat in Parliament over his opposition to the development of the Hydrogen Bomb.

Christian Socialists in Parliament have generally stood on the l eft of the Labour Party and advocated a thorough-going Socialism. Socialism has been for them, as for nineteenth-century pioneers, the expression of Christian idealism, an interpretation of the Kingdom of God, and they have resisted the temptation to compromise with a capitalist system they have regarded as fundamentally unjust.

After 1945 a Christian Socialist group existed in Parliament and was for a time large and active, but it suffered severely in the 1950 election. Its main strength was Anglican.

A union of Christian Socialist organizations in 1960 brought into being the Christian Socialist Movement, with headquarters at Kingsway Hall, London, a Methodist church. The chairman was Dr Donald Soper, minister of the church, who had for many years previously been an outspoken advocate of Socialism and Pacifism, and it is perhaps worth noting that even in the more conservative mood of Nonconformity in the twentieth century this had not prevented his becoming President of Conference. The initial conference of the Christian Socialist Movement agreed on the following aims:

> Believing that human society should be grounded in the Christian Faith, and that Socialism is the political expression of the quest for the Kingdom of God on earth, the members of the Christian Socialist Movement pledge themselves to work
> for the common ownership of the major resources of the world,
> for a classless and just society,
> for human and racial equality,
> for the unity of all Christian people,
> for friendship between East and West,
> for the abolition of nuclear weapons,
> for disarmament and for world peace,
> and to study, to give, and to pray for these ends.

A leaflet issued for the 1964 election spoke in the historic accents of the Christian Socialist tradition:

> *The popular idea* of religion as something apart from politics is an invention of the ruling classes foisted upon the people to conceal the truth. It has no justification in Christ's teaching or in history . . .
> *Christians are commanded* to pray that God's Kingdom may come on Earth as in Heaven. There can be no room in that Kingdom for exploitation, for tyranny, greed or inequality . . .
> *Capitalism* is based on the motive of avarice and the finance of usury—the payment of interest without service. Usury was condemned as deadly sin by the Law and the Prophets and by the Church for 1,800 years. Christians must see industry as a service, to be run by the community to meet men's needs, in which they earn their living by serving their fellows. That is socialism; the application of Christian principles to industrial life. In the modern world there is no Christian alternative. Those who say 'NO to nationalization' say Yes

to industrial autocracy, privilege and profiteering; though nationalization is not the only way to secure public ownership . . .

The leaflet goes on to deal with international issues, including the
need to reduce the difference in living standards between advanced and backward nations, the dangers occasioned by national
and racial prejudice, and so on. Such a publication might be
dismissed as superficial if it were forgotten that election literature
is never a satisfactory medium for the presentation of a profoundly
reasoned case.

The Christian Socialist Movement carried out a survey of its
members by questionnaire, including a question on denominational
affiliation. The figures are interesting, though two provisos must
be borne in mind: that they cover only something over 20% of the
membership, and that denomination was never a major factor in
the life of the movement. No disagreements followed denominational lines; still, it is useful to know which Church traditions
supplied members. The details are as follows:

Anglican (including Scottish Episcopal)	84
Methodist	53
Congregational	16
Society of Friends	12
Baptists	7
Presbyterian	4
Salvation Army	3
Church of Scotland	3
'Old Roman Catholic'	2
Unitarian	1
Roman Catholic	1
Non-denominational	3

'Anglican' referred in the great majority of cases to High Churchmen, or at least 'middle' Anglicans; the 'Low Church' tradition
was conspicuously lacking. The dominance of High Anglicans and
Methodists is of course in the usual Christian Socialist tradition,
but the small Congregationalist denomination and the tiny body of
the Quakers seem to be well represented. Proportionately to size
there are very few members of the Church of Scotland, which
perhaps represents a regional weakness, and, very markedly, of
Roman Catholics, even including the two 'old' (? lapsed) Catholics.
But this last fact may reflect Roman Catholic reluctance to join

societies which sit lightly to denominational differences rather than a genuine lack of support.[1]

Many leaders of the Labour Party after the second world war continued to be active in Christian work. Perhaps the first place in the immediate post-war generation should be given to Sir Stafford Cripps, one of the most distinguished and colourful figures in the record of Christian Socialism. His father, C. A. Cripps, might himself be included in the record. A great lawyer, he was married to Beatrice Webb's sister, and as a devout Anglican played a leading part in the movement for the self-government of the Church of England, which led to the setting up of the Church Assembly. He became a Conservative M.P., but his party allegiance was always lukewarm, and when, as a judge, he became Lord Parmoor, he virtually broke his party ties. In the first Labour government he accepted office as Lord President of the Council, with special responsibility for League of Nations affairs, though, like some other members of that government, he was never much of a Socialist.

Richard Stafford Cripps was born in 1889 and followed his father into the legal profession, building up a successful practice after 1918. He followed his father in other ways too, notably in devoting himself assiduously to Christian work. He was especially active in the newly-formed World Alliance for Promoting International Friendship through the Churches, and, consequently, in the rapidly developing ecumenical movement, undertaking a good deal of speaking and preaching on its behalf.

Cripps did not join the Labour Party till 1929, so that, while he is one more example of the prosperous middle-class Christian Socialist, he is most unusual in having a father who preceded him into Labour allegiance. Apart from Parmoor the great influence on him was his school, Winchester, which had begun to produce a remarkable number of Socialists, though Cripps was admittedly late in his conversion. (There was to come a day when a Wykehamist triumvirate of Cripps, Hugh Gaitskell and Douglas Jay was to control the economic policy of a Labour government.) It was direct Christian conviction which led Cripps to Labour in 1929, and within a few months he found himself with a platform of

---

[1] For information about the Christian Socialist Movement, and for some other details in this chapter, I should like to express my thanks to the officers of the Movement, and especially to the treasurer, Mr Charles Record.

high prominence for the expression of his Christian Socialist beliefs, in his appointment as Solicitor-General in the second Labour government.

In the 'thirties Cripps moved steadily to the left. Christian idealism and a keen awareness of the dangers of Nazism led him to vigorous advocacy of a Popular Front of Socialists, Communists, Liberals, and anyone else prepared to join them. Such doctrines were as unpopular with many party leaders as Churchill's warnings with the Conservative leadership, and Cripps's refusal to accept party discipline on this issue led to his expulsion from the party in 1939. It is a remarkable tribute to his political calibre that after being expelled from his own party he was accepted as one of the few figures of really national, and indeed international, stature during the second world war, serving as a member of the war Cabinet and in vital missions overseas. Strong Christian principle continued to be his guiding motive, and the same independence in pursuit of what he believed to be right which had brought about his expulsion from his party led him to denounce demands for a policy of hatred and revenge against the German nation, and so earned him the spite of the more irresponsible sections of the press.

After the war Cripps rose to the position of Chancellor of the Exchequer, and at the end of the 1940s was one of the three dominant figures in the government, along with Attlee and Bevin. His illness during the latter days of the Attlee regime (he died in 1952), along with the death of Bevin, was an undoubted reason for the marked decline in effectiveness of the Government after the 1950 election.

As Chancellor Cripps found it necessary to pursue a rigid economic policy which greatly disappointed the left of the party, with memories of his radicalism in the 'thirties, and his reputation for asceticism—he neither smoked nor drank—enabled hostile newspapers to represent him as a humourless Puritan; though in reality he was of a lively disposition and his abstentions were for reasons of health. In 1949 Cripps devalued the pound after giving definite assurance that its value would be maintained; although reasonable men conceded, as they were bound to do, that it was essential to refute anticipations of devaluation if they were not to provoke financial disaster, the occasion proved irresistible for gleeful denunciation of a Socialist who preached both in pulpits and from political platforms the necessity for a Christian basis for society, and yet could be accused of public and solemn prevarication. It was an occasion seized not only by organs of the press never noted for balanced judgement, but regrettably, by Churchill in Parliament.

The incident, and Cripps's career as a whole, is an interesting commentary on the problematic relationship between Christian idealism and political realities. The attempt to found political action on religious principles can result in policies which blithely ignore the realities of power. Such had been the experience of Christians over and over again, not least in the history of Christian Socialism itself. To the leaders of the Labour Party in the late 'thirties, men like Attlee, Bevin, and Herbert Morrison, Cripps's advocacy of a Popular Front seemed fully in line with this tradition. The outbreak of war and the forced alliance with the Soviet Union seemed to show that the idealists had after all proved themselves the true realists; but the post-war years, and especially the fate of the Social Democrats in other countries who tried to apply the doctrine of the Popular Front, gave a very different impression, and some of Cripps's pre-war colleagues found themselves expelled from the Labour Party again. But in the meantime Cripps, along with another hero of the pre-war left, Aneurin Bevan, had shown that they could live with political realities in a world of power politics and economic stress. Bevan's record continued to be one of only partially contained dissidence, but Cripps showed himself a thorough realist, and even seemed to be a man of the Labour right. The devaluation incident showed that political action invariably involves compromise with things in theory excluded by the highest moral standards. Perhaps it was his willingness to accept such compromise which provoked his enemies to portray him as a hypocrite; but the British people as a whole seemed to possess enough political sophistication to see through the portrayal, and to respect him as a truly good man.

One or two Methodists who belonged to the Attlee administration have been mentioned. To them should be added George Tomlinson, George Isaacs, and the younger Arthur Henderson. Other forms of Nonconformity were represented by James Griffiths and Harold Wilson, Congregationalists; by A. V. Alexander (later Lord Alexander of Hillsborough), a Baptist; and Chuter Ede, a Unitarian. The Noel Bakers (Philip, winner of a Nobel Peace Prize, and later Francis, his son) were prominent Quaker M.P.s; while Roman Catholicism was represented by R. R. Stokes and by Lord Pakenham, later the Earl of Longford and Labour leader in the Lords, a very notable Roman Catholic convert and an accepted leader in his chosen Church.

Ernest Bevin and Aneurin Bevan were both lapsed Nonconformists. It is not suggested that Nonconformity can claim credit for the achievements of those whom it failed to hold, or even positively repelled, but in the case of these two men the Nonconformist element in their background cannot be ignored.

Ernest Bevin had, like so many of his generation (he was born in 1881) first learned his public speaking through the scope given to laymen by Nonconformity, in his case as a Baptist lay-preacher. He had in fact been sufficiently active in Church work at one time to consider the possibility of entering the Baptist ministry. He belongs to the generation which came to maturity in the 1890s, when Nonconformity was still producing and training men who became statesmen; producing and training them, but then alienating them by ethical and cultural narrowness.

Aneurin Bevan was Welsh and born half a generation later (in 1897), two differences which help to account for his more complete revolt from Nonconformity. His father, to whom he was devoted, was a Baptist, his mother a Methodist, and they met as members of a chapel choral society: 'The family background was that of Welsh nonconformity in its heyday . . .'[1] But the drift from this tradition was already beginning a generation earlier, for Bevan's father, once a keen member of his chapel, gradually drifted away. Bevan himself was never in the slightest degree enamoured of the world of the chapel. As a boy he was already a sufficiently vocal critic of the Biblical literalism of the Baptist chapel to be transferred to the comparatively liberal Congregationalists, but he formed no firm attachment there either, though his biographer somewhat speculatively attributes to his Nonconformist background a Puritan streak which rather surprisingly persisted in him.

The alienation of men like Bevin and Bevan was a symptom of the failure of Nonconformity—a failure which was related to its success in the struggle for social recognition. A generation earlier a man like Bevin would have been an honoured guest at Baptist assemblies and rallies, publicly displayed as evidence of what Nonconformity could do for a man; in any generation, and in any society, Bevan would have been a dissident; but it might have happened in the past that he would have been found urging his eloquent protests and denouncing unjustifiable privilege from the

[1] Michael Foot, *Aneurin Bevan*, I (1962), 15.

floor of the Congregational Union assembly, or preaching a
stimulating mixture of political revolution and liberal religion in
one of John Trevor's Labour Churches. But Bevan reached adult
years in the days of the first world war, when such intriguing
prospects had long passed away.[1]

The several varieties of religious conviction discernible in the
history of the English Labour movement are rather neatly exemplified by the first three Labour Party leaders to serve as Prime
Minister.

Ramsay Macdonald represents the kind of diffuse religiosity
which appeared in mid-Victorian times, and on the whole was
dissipated by the first world war. In his acceptance of the simple
and vague creed that life has a spiritual basis, a creed so simple and
vague that almost everyone might readily accept it according to
manifold possible interpretations, he resembled the adolescent
Beatrice Webb and a whole generation of Victorians. There has
been a religious tradition in Labour which has found uplifting
expression in singing 'These things shall be!' and 'And did those
feet in ancient time' without pressing too urgently for meanings,
as there has been a very mild Marxism which has delighted in
'The Red Flag,' and as the most pacific Tories have put heart and
soul into rendering the indefinite Imperialist aspirations of 'Land
of Hope and Glory.' Criticism of Macdonald is too easy and a
wasting asset, but it is fair to say that his religion was little more
than the lingering echo of a more dogmatic faith which now
seemed to be untenable. Such generalized Theism was merely the
expression of nostalgia for the vanished certainties of a lost age.

The second Labour Premier was in every way a more solid
character. In religious terms he represents a second tradition of the
Labour movement: Anglican Christian Socialism. It is true that in
his charming autobiography[2] he tells his readers little about his
religious beliefs; but then he tells them little about most things.
Attlee belonged to the prosperous, more-or-less Conservative
middle class from which other Christian Socialists emerged—his
father was a highly successful solicitor. 'Our family,' he writes,
'were strong supporters of the Church of England and Sunday was

---

[1] The first time I heard Aneurin Bevan speak was in an 'institutional
church' belonging to the Congregationalists. It served simply as a hall
booked for an election meeting, but I sensed a certain anachronistic
symbolism.

[2] C. R. Attlee, *As It Happened* (1954).

strictly observed. There was much church-going, special reading and no games. Walks were the only relaxation on Sundays in our days though this Puritanism was later relaxed.'[1]

But while it is evident that Attlee writes without enthusiasm of this late-Victorian Sabbatarianism he and his brothers and sisters continued to live in an Anglican atmosphere, a brother becoming a clergyman and a sister a missionary.

At Oxford Attlee found the atmosphere Tory and Socialism little discussed, but he finds it worth mentioning that among the undergraduates were such notable future leaders of Christian Socialism as William Temple and R. H. Tawney.

Even in his family tradition religion was held to imply duties in the sphere of social service. His mother was a district visitor for the Church and an aunt had gone to live in a poor street in Wandsworth over a club, which she ran, for factory girls. His own school, Haileybury, ran a boys' club in Stepney, and Attlee, starting with casual visits, took over as manager, and lived in the East End for fourteen years, part of the time living at Toynbee Hall, of which he became secretary.

It was from this initiation into social work in the Settlement movement that Attlee embarked on a reasonably straight course which made him mayor of Stepney, a Member of Parliament, and Prime Minister. His accession to office in 1945, along with Temple's appointment as Archbishop of Canterbury in 1942, marked the zenith of achievement of the Anglican Christian Socialist movement which had begun with Maurice and been revived and developed by the C.S.U. With a representative of this tradition nearly simultaneously at Lambeth Palace and at Downing Street there seemed few worlds left to conquer. (*The Times* held out, but its fate was sometimes in doubt.) Temple and Attlee were both men of prosperous background; both went to public schools and to Oxford; both were converted to Socialism by shame at the social conditions of the pre-1914 world, and always influenced in the character of their Socialism by their indelible recollections of that era; both, despite—or because of?—their prosperous *bourgeois* background, were unquestioningly accepted as leaders and heroes of the English working classes. It should perhaps have been anticipated that when the Church of England, the public schools and Oxford all shared in fashioning Socialists they would be the leading Socialists of their time.

[1] Attlee, op. cit., 4.

The third Labour Prime Minister came from a different religious tradition again, that of English Nonconformity, which had played so large a part in creating the Labour movement over the past 100 years. It is interesting that he belonged not to Methodism, whose share in Labour politics was so generally recognized, but to Congregationalism. Born in a lower middle-class home and brought up in the West Riding and on Merseyside, progressing by means of scholarships from local grammar school to Oxford, Harold Wilson marked the ultimate, long-delayed triumph of that tradition of English Dissenting Radicalism which had been for Gladstone in the eighteen-seventies, for Lloyd George in the Edwardian era, and now found a natural home in the Labour Party. Nothing could be more characteristic of such a man than to meet his wife (a minister's daughter) through attending a Congregational church—nor, it must be added, more characteristic of Congregational churches than the fact that the two attended for some time without meeting, one being a morning and the other an evening attender. As residents of Hampstead the Wilsons belonged to the United Free Church there; and so, while of Congregational origins, and married in a Congregational College chapel, they could in a sense rightly be claimed by all the denominations of historic Dissent. In background, character, and religious affiliation Wilson resembled neither of his predecessors, but represented another major religious tradition in English Socialism. It remained an extraordinary feature of English life that the Socialist movement, to which Marxian—and Owenite—sceptics and Secularists had contributed so much, produced as its first three premiers a sincere if obscure Theist, a solid Anglican, and a representative Nonconformist.

It is not altogether a paradox to claim that the twenty years following the second world war were a period of great success for the Labour Party, despite the fact that for most of the period the Conservatives were in office. For one thing, in the six general elections of this period and the by-elections between them the Labour Party received towards a million more votes than the Conservatives and their allies. The fact that the Conservatives nevertheless held office for two-thirds of the period constituted in their eyes a peculiar excellence of the system. (If the calculation is started from the 1950 election the Conservatives did, it is true, win 3% or 4% more votes than Labour down to the 1964 election, inclusive; they also held office for nearly 90% of the period.) The extreme disproportion between election results and tenure of office was not due to any deliberate bias in the electoral system, but to a number of fortuitous factors: a slight *accidental* bias due to the accumulation of 'wasted' Labour votes in some industrial areas; the fact that at the end of the period the Labour victory in 1964 had not yet been 'used up,' a Labour government being in office; and a good deal of sheer luck. The Conservatives' near-monopoly of power in the nineteen-fifties and early nineteen-sixties bore a superficial resemblance to their dominance between the wars; but a fundamental change had occurred in that Labour had now approximately caught up with their opponents in terms of votes, though the latter by accident still ruled the nation nearly continuously. It seemed improbable that this disproportion (unlike the still more extreme under-representation of the Liberals) could continue indefinitely.

A more remarkable advance recorded by the Labour Party after 1945 was in the conversion of the Conservative Party to its own views. The most surprising feature was the wide measure of Conservative acceptance of Socialism, using that imprecise word in one of its commoner senses, to mean the intervention of public authority in economic and social life. The necessities of party warfare required that the Conservatives should continue to denounce Socialism, but in fact the British economy was scarcely less Socialist in 1964 than in 1951, before thirteen years of continuous Conservative rule. Of the widespread measures of nationalization carried through by the Attlee government only the iron and steel industry (and not quite the whole of that) and a part of road transport had been denationalized. The Budget was used as an instrument of social regulation by Conservative much as by Labour Chancellors. No attack had been made on the Welfare State, including the National Health Service, despite Conservative suspicion of the legislation establishing it. Towards the end of the long Conservative reign the party leaders vied with Labour in proclaiming their devotion to modernization and planning. The Conservative Party had a long record of quiet acceptance of changes at first bitterly resisted, but it was an unexpected development that Conservative England was nearly as Socialist as Labour England, and that so little protest was raised from the back benches and the constituencies.

The same is true of Imperial and international issues. Labour policy of giving independence to the colonies was adopted with enthusiasm by the Conservatives, often after a token period of denunciation and imprisonment for the local leaders; the Macmillan government boasted of its policy of *rapprochement* with the Soviet Union—a policy for whose support men were expelled from the Labour Party in the nineteen-forties; and in the service of internationalism, even if necessary by the sacrifice of Imperial interests, the Conservatives overtook Labour by seeking entrance to the European Common Market. In this department of policy there was indeed some resistance: a League of Empire Loyalists was formed, whose members vociferously denounced Harold Macmillan as a traitor, till silenced by physical violence, and there were occasional scarcely noticed resignations from Conservative governments, including that of Lord Salisbury; and a variety of ineffective groups appeared on the Parliamentary right wing. Beyond this marginal resistance by defenders of traditional Conservative policies the revolution was complete.

In other respects the conversion was not so complete. The Conservative Party in Parliament remained fundamentally a class party, led predominantly by men who had been born into prosperous homes and educated at expensive public schools; a generalization not invalidated by the existence of a small minority of leading Conservatives of lower middle-class origins and perhaps one or two of working class. The Parliamentary Labour Party included a substantial number of wealthy public school men; but it also represented every other sizeable group in the community.

There was another aspect of the Labour Party which was at first sight rather curious: it was the party of humanitarian reform. This was so well established a fact that its strangeness received little comment; yet it was not easy to account for the fact that a party which had originated in the demands of the working classes for a fuller share in the good things of the world, and which had at times half-heartedly committed itself to a doctrine of class war, should be a main agency of doctrines of tolerance and humanitarianism. Parties whose Socialism had a more Marxian tone in no way emulated this example. According to one psychological analysis, the Labour Party represented the 'tender-minded,' the Conservatives the 'tough-minded'; if so it was not surprising that Khrushchev, not notably tender-minded, openly preferred the latter.

Whatever the explanation, the facts can hardly be disputed, and it must be admitted that this was a sphere in which the conversion of the Conservative Party had made less progress. The man who wished to engage in some latter-day humanitarian campaign in the grand tradition of Wilberforce or Shaftesbury would not have joined the Conservative Party. There seems no very obvious reason why the line of division on steel nationalization should coincide with the line of division on the death penalty, but until the nineteen-sixties the correspondence was fairly close, and even then the reformers could count on virtually unanimous Labour support but only a relatively small minority of Conservatives. Incidentally every Conservative insistence that the abolition of hanging would not be popular emphasized the more clearly the almost unique situation of a party in power embarking on a policy for purely moral reasons while recognizing that it was contrary to its own self-interest. For one of the two great parties in the state consciously to prefer morality to self-interest was a remarkable development, and it would perhaps have been Utopian to expect it of both simultaneously.

The same division occurred on other issues of a humanitarian kind. It would have been untrue to assert without qualification that the Conservatives were illiberal, or at any rate equivocal, on the issue of racial prejudice; but it is quite certain that a campaign against racialism, whether at home or abroad, would look immediately and naturally to Labour as an obvious source of support. The cause of underdeveloped nations; prison reform; and in fact all matters concerning the oppressed, the unfortunate, and the underdog, including those matters calculated to lose votes and even seats (as Mr Gordon Walker found in 1964), could rely on Labour support; and equally on Conservative opposition, normally with a small dissenting group prepared to face the wrath of constituency committees.[1] It is fair to add that on all these issues the Liberal Party would be found fighting staunchly side by side with Labour.

The fact that the party of the wealthy and cultured, who had from earliest years enjoyed the benefits of a gracious home life and the most expensive education available, should have shown so little enthusiasm for movements of liberal and humanistic reform, while the party which found a place also for the much criticized

---

[1] In the mid-sixties there were signs of a change. During the 1966 election the new Conservative leader, Mr. Edward Heath, condemned the appeal to racial prejudice by any candidate; and in the Parliaments preceding and following this election a growing body of Conservative members supported the abolition of capital punishment.

petit bourgeois Philistine and the manual worker with little opportunity for educational advancement or delicate civility stood in the forefront of such movements, needs some explanation.

On the Labour side historical factors must have been relevant, and among them the influence of certain forms of Christian tradition. This is not contradicted by the fact that the Churches themselves were not, in the mid-twentieth century, very prominent in the cause of humanitarian reform. On few of the matters mentioned here were the Churches in the van; perhaps one might pick out racialism as an issue on which the Churches as official bodies were nearer to Labour and the Liberals (and the Conservative dissidents) than to most Conservatives. But while the hypothetical successor of Wilberforce or Shaftesbury would have been surprised to receive official help from the Churches, he could be certain that his most active and enthusiastic coadjutors would include men and women whose Christian principles brought them into his movement; they would be relatively more numerous in his committees and in canvassing support than the church-going habits of the nation would have suggested; and they would be much more likely to vote Labour or Liberal than Conservative. Such 'tender-minded' Christians and their sympathizers might in fact account for a fair proportion of the middle-class Labour vote, in alliance (as always since Robert Owen's day) with atheists and agnostics with whom they shared a common enthusiasm for the betterment of human society.

It is not at all suggested that the strange devotion of Labour to what were essentially moral causes, even when they brought no party profit, was wholly due to Christian influence. Many of the policies which to the onlooker seem a reasonably accurate political interpretation of the Christian ethic were passionately advocated by men indifferent or hostile to religion, while they were equally passionately resisted by many regular church-goers; but it has never been orthodox Christian doctrine that the Holy Spirit could use for his purposes only those officially enrolled on ecclesiastical lists; nor that officially recognized church members would always be found on the side subsequently regarded as their obvious allegiance. It would be particularly ungenerous not to recognize that the protagonists of good causes have consistently included people of Jewish race and often Jewish religion. Indeed the latter-day Shaftesbury might very reasonably have his hopes raised higher by discerning a Jewish name (such as Silverman) than by hearing that a man was a churchwarden or deacon, or even entitled to the prefix 'Reverend.' But when due credit has been given elsewhere and due acknowledgement made of the apathy and worse than apathy of Churches the fact remains that reforming movements of the twentieth century, like those of earlier times, drew into their service many who found their place in them because of their Christian principles; many who through this continuing idealism, historically derived from Jesus Christ, were led to identify their causes and themselves with the Labour Party.

APPENDIX I: *LUX MUNDI*

The following passages from *Lux Mundi* (1889) indicate in some measure why this work came with a revolutionary impact to a Church which for many years had been absorbed with ecclesiastical and theological questions to the neglect of social issues.

Extract 1: from Section II, *Christianity and Politics*, by W. J. H. Campion. Pp. 328f. in twelfth edition (1891).

The same emphasis on higher motives is characteristic of Christian treatment of the questions connected with property. Christianity is certainly not pledged to uphold any particular form of property as such. Whether property had better be held by individuals, or by small groups, as in the case of the primitive Teutonic villages, or of the modern Russian or Indian village communities, or again by the State, as is the proposal of Socialists, is a matter for experience and common sense to decide. But where Christian ethics steps in is, firstly, to show that property is secondary and not primary, a means and not an end. Thus, in so far as Socialism looks to the moral regeneration of society by a merely mechanical alteration of the distribution of the products of industry or of the mode of holding property, it has to be reminded that a change of heart and will is the only true starting-point of moral improvement. On the other hand, it cannot be too often asserted that the accumulation of riches is not in itself a good at all. Neither riches nor poverty make men better in themselves. Their effect on character depends on the use made of them, though no doubt the responsibility of those who have property is greater, because they have one instrument the more for the purposes of life. And so, secondly, Christianity urges that *if* there is private property, its true character as a trust shall be recognized, its rights respected and its attendant duties performed. These truths it keeps steadily before men's eyes by the perpetual object-lesson of the life of the early Church of Jerusalem, in which those who had property sold it, and brought the proceeds and laid them at the Apostles' feet, and distribution was made unto every man according to his needs, an object-lesson enforced and renewed by the example of the monastic communities, with their vow of voluntary poverty, and their common purse. So strongly did the early Fathers insist on the duty, almost the debt, of the rich to the poor, that isolated passages may be quoted which read like a condemnation of all private property, but this was not their real drift. The obligation which they urged was the obligation of charity.

Extract 2: From Appendix I (*On Some Aspects of Christian Duty*) to Section 12, *Christian Ethics,* by R. L. Ottley. P. 385 in twelfth edition (1891).

As to the social sphere generally, we begin by remarking that, from the Christian standpoint, *every transaction* between man and man is to be regarded as *personal,* and therefore *ethical.* The most significant fact perhaps of our time is the process of transition from (so-called) political to ethical economics. To reason rightly on social problems we must ever have regard to *personality.* For ethical purposes the abstract terms Capital, Labour, Production, Wealth, etc., must be replaced by *personal* terms, Employer, Employê, Producer, Man of Wealth, etc. Our problem is how to supersede the technical and legal relation by the personal.

This being our fundamental point of view, we find that ethics will treat equally of rights and duties. A Christian theory of *rights* is required. The prevailing view of them is *individualistic.* It is forgotten that the rights of one man have their ground in the obligations of another; they are limited by the claims of other personalities on our own; 'right' is, in fact, a condition making possible the fulfilment of duty. It is thus a matter of Christian concern (to suggest mere examples) that workers should attain to the possibility of free self-development: healthy conditions of work, the enjoyment of domestic life, security of maintenance, perhaps permanence of contract, opportunities of recreation and culture—everything, in fact, which will give them a fair chance of healthful and worthy human life. Christianity can be content with nothing short of this.

On the other hand *duties* call for notice. Modern capitalists form a class whose responsibilities it is difficult adequately to measure. The general principle, however, is easily repeated: that it is the duty of the wealthy, or those who employ workers, to respect the personality of their employees, to treat them not as machines, but as men. Thomas Carlyle well describes the aim that should guide this influential class: 'to be a noble master among noble workers, the first ambition: to be a rich master, only the second.'

Industrial development indeed brings into prominence many questions of duty and right, which can only be solved by deeper apprehension of the Christian standpoint: and of 'morality as an industrial force':[1] for the ties which bind men in the relation of brotherhood and sonhood are the noblest and strongest.

APPENDIX II: WORKS OF ANDREW REID

The era when Christian Socialism and the religious aspects of the Labour movement were marked more by fervour than by clarity and precision of thought is accurately exemplified in two books of the mid-'nineties edited by Andrew Reid. *Vox Clamantium: the Gospel of the People, by Writers, Preachers, and Workers. Brought together by Andrew Reid,* appeared in 1894, with contributions by Hall Caine, S. R. Crockett,

[1] A footnote in the original explains that this phrase is a chapter-heading in T. E. Brown: *Studies in Modern Socialism and Labour Problems.*

James Adderley, Grant Allen, A. R. Wallace, C. L. Marson, Henry Arthur Jones, Tom Mann and C. W. Stubbs, among others. The following are three representative extracts:

(1) By Frank Smith: 'But what shall we do? Attack those who make sin, as well as damn the sinner. Let the prophets of God in these days be as uncompromising as they were of old. Thunder out the truth that the earth is the Lord's, and *not* the landlord's. Trumpet that the earth, and all that is in it, is the gift of the Creator to all men, and that they who rob men of, or hinder them in any way from enjoying, the full use and benefit of the Divine gift, are enemies of humanity of the worse[1] kind.'[2]

(2) By Tom Mann: 'A little less time spent at orthodox mission meetings, and more time spent in helping on effective industrial organization, to ensure right-doing in the business of life, is sadly needed just now. This orthodox mission work is exactly what our exploiting plutocrats rejoice in. It is so gracious of them to give an occasional ten pounds to keep a mission going, that they may with reasonable safety exploit an additional twenty from their employêes,[3] and still receive the praise and blessings of the faithful.'[4]

(3) By Tom Mann: 'Democracy is learning how to provide for itself, and never was the democracy so truly religious as now. And it is gradually getting more so. This religious evolution will increase as the bad environment is altered on the one side, and the ethical gospel is lifted up and followed truthfully on the other.'[5]

A further volume of essays, edited by Reid, appeared in 1895 in a popular edition (at the not particularly popular price of 2/6d.) It was entitled *The New Party*, and referred to the 'New Party and National Union of Socialists,' also called the 'Isocratic Party,' an attempt to draw together Socialists of various kinds, whose aim, according to the editor, was to become 'the most comprehensive, picturesque, historical, ideal, ethical, political party which has ever stepped foot upon God's earth.'[6] As this quotation is a fair specimen of the rather prophetic style of the volume it is not easy to read, at any rate after the lapse of two generations. After eighteen preliminary quotations, varying in authorship from St Luke and Aristotle to Lord Salisbury and John Morley, there are twenty-nine essays by representatives of many aspects of contemporary Socialism. Notes on one or two of these are added below.

The Mission of the Churches, by the Dean of Durham (G. W. Kitchin). This traces the social changes currently in progress: 'In town and country alike the future is in the wage-earner's hands: Churches will rise or fall as they accept this fact.'[7] Religious leaders, regrettably, often talked as if the Church was a Capitalist's Church. Yet parallel to the statesman's slogan of 'one man one vote' the churchman proclaimed 'one man one soul,' 'and with this he proclaims the essential equality of men.'[8] In the coming age

---

[1] Sic.   [2] Op. cit., 287.   [3] Sic.   [4] Op. cit., 301 f.   [5] Ibid., 306.
[6] *The New Party, described by some of its Members.* Edited by Andrew Reid (Popular edition, 1895), preface, p. vi.   [7] Ibid., 41.   [8] Ibid., 45.

of prosperity and freedom the Church must protect the workers from new temptations.

The Church and the Democratic Idea, by C. L. Marson. The traditional opposition of the Anglican clergy to the Liberal Party had now been justified, for 'the Liberal Party is simply the Plutocratic Party, a worse foe to progress even than the courtlier tyranny which it fought against and overcame.'[1] In the Roman Empire the Church was notoriously democratic, and the Fathers, such as St Basil ('a consistent Socialist') expressed many collectivist ideas. True collectivism could not be wholly a matter of legislation, for there were many things the law could not do, but must depend upon voluntary social service.

Christus Invictus, by R. F. Horton. Horton is largely concerned to defend the address to the Congregational Union by Dr Barrett on 'The Secularisation of the Pulpit'[2] against the misunderstanding that Barrett was opposed to social reform by the Church. He goes on to attack existing conditions:

> The industrial structure and the social system in England today are not based on religion. They are based upon Adam Smith and such gospel as he had to deliver to mankind; and Adam Smith derived his good news from the French Encyclopaedists. It was a very dubious gospel, and one in most respects the precise reverse of what had been understood to be the Gospel of Jesus Christ.[3]

The world must be warned to distinguish between Christ and the Church, for the latter was often worldly. The Democracy was often impatient with the Church—and rightly so; but it must not turn from Christ.

The Social Work of the Undivided Church, by Percy Dearmer. The Church was not founded at the Reformation, as Protestants imagined, and it could not be accused of being indifferent to democracy:

> For as a matter of fact the Church has been founding a Christian democracy ever since the Divine Democrat of Nazareth founded her, and set a handful of working men to preside over her interests.[4]

All the troubles of the day were due to Individualism, and Individualism was itself due to Protestantism: 'It was the spirit of schism which destroyed at the Reformation the socialism which the Church was building up.'[5]

A divided Church could never be socially effective; for one thing 'sects can never rise above class and national distinctions,' and for another the energy of the Church was absorbed in internal struggles. Until the Reformation the Church was collectivist in outlook, it was the centre of art for all, and it protected the agricultural labourer. The era when Protestantism was strongest saw the longest hours and the lowest wages

[1] *The New Party*, 50.   [2] See p. 67.
[3] *The New Party*, 64.   [4] Ibid., 199.   [5] Ibid., 200.

for the labourer. Trade unionism flourished under the protection of the medieval Church, but collapsed and was prohibited under Protestantism. In the middle ages there were many holidays, there were no standing armies or nationalism, and there were no unemployed. It is true that there were class divisions, and there was the aristocracy:

> But it must be remembered that the Church had only been at work for ten centuries, and that class distinctions, unavoidable under any system but that of perfect and long-established socialism, were a necessity in a state that was being slowly redeemed from barbarism.

But there was no rigid *separation* of classes, such as now existed. Avarice was condemned, as was usury, and the religious orders maintained an example of communism.

The Advance of the People, by P. H. Wicksteed. Although Wicksteed was a Unitarian minister, his essay was of a fairly secular kind, being an argument against the necessity of a leisured class. It then went on to claim that the Labour movement was not merely based on selfish and materialistic ambitions, but that even if it were, it would still deserve support, being a plea for justice. The test of the morality of the British Democracy would be the degree of its concern for the oppressed races as it gained its own freedom and increased its power.[1]

The summing-up by the editor seemed to make the whole movement an expression of Christian Socialism:

'The three old parties have three "lords" to lead them, and many of our Christian Isocrats may be tempted to say, "Our Leader is the Lord Jesus." And verily I believe that *through the New Party* that strange and wild-looking saying will come true:

"AND I, IF I BE LIFTED UP FROM THE EARTH, WILL DRAW ALL MEN UNTO ME." '[2]

[1] *The New Party*, 232–244.   [2] Ibid., 289.

BIBLIOGRAPHY

BIBLIOGRAPHY

Altrincham, Lord: *Two Anglican Essays* (1958).
Attlee, C. R.: *As It Happened* (1954).
Baernreither, Josef Maria: *English Associations of Working Men*. English edition, trans. Alice Taylor, (1893).
Barker, John Thomas (ed.): *The Life of Joseph Barker, written by himsel* (1880).
Beck, G. A. (ed.): *The English Catholics 1850–1950* (1950).
Beer, M.: *History of British Socialism*, (New edition, 1929).
Begbie, Harold: *The Life of General William Booth* (1920).
Beith, Gilbert (ed.): *Edward Carpenter: In Appreciation* (1931).
Bell, G. K. A.: *Randall Davidson, Archbishop of Canterbury* (1935).
Bettany, F. G.: *Stewart Headlam* (1926).
Binyon, Gilbert Clive: *The Christian Socialist Movement in England* (1931).
Blaug, Mark: *Ricardian Economics* (1958).
Bonner, Hypatia Bradlaugh: *Charles Bradlaugh: A Record of his Life and Work* (7th edition, 1908).
Booth, William: *In Darkest England and the Way Out* (1890).
Brinton, Crane: *English Political Thought in the Nineteenth Century* (1933).
Brockway, Fenner: *Socialism over Sixty Years* (1946).
Carpenter, S. C.: *Church and People, 1789–1889* (1933).
Clapham, J. S.: *An Economic History of Modern Britain* (Vol. 2, 1932).
Clayton, J.: *Father Dolling: A Memoir* (1902).
Cole, G. D. H.: *A Short History of the British Working Class Movement, 1789–1927* (Vol. 2, 1926, Vol. 3, 1927).
Cole, G. D. H. and Raymond Postgate: *The Common People* (1938).
Cole, Margaret: *Beatrice Webb* (1945).
Cole, Margaret: *Makers of the Labour Movement* (1948).
Cooper, Thomas: *The Life of Thomas Cooper, written by Himself* (1877 edition).
Cunningham, William: *Christianity and Social Questions* (1910).
Dale, R. W.: *A History of English Congregationalism* (1907).
Davies, Rupert E.: *John Scott Lidgett* (1957).
Demant, V. A.: *Religion and the Decline of Capitalism* (1952).
Elliott-Binns, L. E.: *English Thought 1860–1900. The Theological Aspect* (1956).
Elton, Godfrey: *'England, Arise!' A Study of the Pioneering Days of the Labour Movement* (1931).
Elton, Lord: *The Life of James Ramsay Macdonald (1866–1919)* (1939).
Ensor, R. C. K.: *England 1870–1914* (1936).

Evans, E. W.: *Mabon (William Abraham 1842–1922): A Study in Trade Union Leadership* (1959).

Evans, Joan: *John Ruskin* (1954).

Fabian Tracts (from 1884).

Fay, Charles Ryle: *Great Britain from Adam Smith to the Present Day* (1928).

Fay, Charles Ryle: *Life and Labour in the Nineteenth Century* (1920).

Foot, Michael: *Aneurin Bevan*, Vol. I (1962).

Frederick James Furnivall: A Volume of Personal Record (1911).

Gillespie, Frances Emma: *Labor and Politics in England: 1850–1867* (1927).

Gore, Charles (ed.): *Lux Mundi: A Series of Studies in the Religion of the Incarnation* (Twelfth edition, 1891).

Grant, John W.: *Free Churchmanship in England 1870–1940* (no date).

Graves, Charles L.: *Life and Letters of Alexander Macmillan* (1910).

Gretton, R. H.: *A Modern History of the English People: 1880–1922* (1930 edition).

'Group of Churchmen, A': *The Return of Christendom* (1922).

Halévy, Élie: *A History of the English People in the Nineteenth Century: IV. Victorian Years 1841–1895* (1951); *V. Imperialism and the Rise of Labour 1895–1905* (Second edition, 1951).

Hamilton, Mary Agnes: *Arthur Henderson* (1938).

Hammerton, H. J.: *This Turbulent Priest* (1952).

Harrison, J. F. C.: *A History of the Working Men's College 1864–1954* (1954).

Haw, George: *From Workhouse to Westminster* (1908).

Hodder, Edwin: *The Life of Samuel Morley* (Second edition, 1887).

Holt, Raymond V.: *The Unitarian Contribution to Social Progress in England* (Second edition, 1952).

Holyoake, G. J.: *The History of Co-operation in England* (1906).

Holyoake, G. J.: *Sixty Years of an Agitator's Life* (Fourth impression, 1900).

Hort, Arthur Fenton: *Life and Letters of Fenton John Anthony Hort* (1896)

Hovell, Mark: *The Chartist Movement* (Second edition, 1925).

Howell, George: *Labour Legislation, Labour Movements, and Labour Leaders* (1902).

Hughes, Emrys: *Keir Hardie* (1956).

Hughes, Thomas: *James Fraser, Second Bishop of Manchester* (1887).

Hughes, Thomas: *Memoir of Daniel Macmillan* (1883).

Hughes, Thomas: *Rugby, Tennessee* (1881).

Hutchinson, Keith: *The Decline and Fall of British Capitalism* (1951).

Inglis, K. S.: *Churches and the Working Classes in Victorian England* (1963).

Iremonger, F. A.: *William Temple* (1948).

Jones, Lloyd: *The Life, Times, and Labours of Robert Owen* (Second edition 1895).

Kendall, G.: *Charles Kingsley and his Ideas* (?1946).

Lansbury, George: *My Life* (1928).

Leslie, Shane: *Henry Edward Manning* (1953 edition).

Lindsay, Donald, and E. S. Washington: *A Portrait of Britain between the Exhibitions 1851–1951* (1952).

Lloyd, Roger: *The Church of England in the Twentieth Century* (Vol. I, 1946).

London Trades Council 1860–1950 (1950).

Lowndes, G. A. N.: *Margaret McMillan 'The Children's Champion'* (1960).

Lynd, Helen Merrell: *England in the Eighteen-Eighties* (1945).

Maccoby, S.: *English Radicalism, 1853–1886* (1938).

Maccoby, S.: *English Radicalism, 1886–1914* (1953).

Macdonald, Greville: *George Macdonald and his Wife* (1924).

Macfadyen, Dugald: *Sir Ebenezer Howard and the Town Planning Movement* (1933).

Mack, Edward C., and W. H. G. Armytage: *Thomas Hughes: The Life of the Author of 'Tom Brown's Schooldays'* (1952).

Mackail, J. W.: *The Life of William Morris* (1899).

Marchant, James: *Alfred Russel Wallace: Letters and Reminiscences* (1916).

Marchant, James: *Dr. John Clifford, C. H.: Life, Letters and Reminiscences* (1924).

Martin, Hugh (ed.): *Christian Social Reformers of the Nineteenth Century* (1927).

Martindale, C. C.: *Bernard Vaughan, S. J.* (1923).

Masterman, C. F. G.: *Frederick Denison Maurice* (1907).

Meech, Thomas Cox: *From Mine to Ministry: The Life and Times of Thomas Burt, M.P.* (no date).

Miall, Arthur: *The Life of Edward Miall* (1884).

Miles, Susan: *Portrait of a Parson* (1955).

Noel, Conrad: *Autobiography* (ed. Sidney Dark, 1945).

Packe, Michael St John: *The Life of John Stuart Mill* (1954).

Paget, Stephen (ed.): *Henry Scott Holland: Memoir and Letters* (1921).

Pankhurst, Richard K. P.: *The Saint Simonians Mill and Carlyle* (no date).

Paul, C. Kegan: *Memories* (1899).

Pease, Edward R.: *The History of the Fabian Society* (1916).

Peel, Albert: *The Congregational Two Hundred 1530–1948* (1948).

Pelling, Henry: *The Origins of the Labour Party 1880–1900* (1954).

Pimlott, J. A. R.: *Toynbee Hall* (1935).

Prestige, G. L.: *The Life of Charles Gore* (1935).

Raven, C. E.: *Christian Socialism 1848–1854* (1920).

Reckitt, M. B.: *As It Happened* (1941).

Reckitt, M. B. (ed.): *Prospect for Christendom* (1945).

Reckitt, M. B.: *Maurice to Temple* (1947).

Redfern, P.: *The New History of the C.W.S.* (1938).

Reid, Sir T. W.: *Life of the Right Honourable William Edward Forster* (1888).

Richard, Henry: *Memoirs of Joseph Sturge* (1864).

Ritchie, D. G.: *Philosophical Studies* (1905).

Sabine, George H.: *A History of Political Theory* (Third edition, 1951).

Sandall, Robert: *History of the Salvation Army* (1950).

Saville, John (ed.): *Democracy and the Labour Movement* (1954).

Search, Pamela: *Happy Warriors. The Story of the Social Work of the Salvation Army* (1956).

Sommer, Dudley: *Haldane of Cloan: His Life and Times 1856–1928* (1960).

Stocks, Mary: *The Workers' Educational Association* (1953).

Swann, Tom: *Edward Carpenter: The Man and his Message* (Revised edition, 1922).

Temple, William: *Christianity and Social Order* (1942).

Thompson, L.: *Robert Blatchford: Portrait of an Englishman* (1951).

Trevelyan, G. M.: *British History in the Nineteenth Century 1782–1901* (1922).

Trevelyan, G. M.: *English Social History* (Third edition, 1946).

Trevelyan, Janet Penrose: *The Life of Mrs Humphry Ward* (1923).

Underwood, A. C.: *A History of the English Baptists* (1947).

Vaughan, Bernard: *Socialism from the Christian Standpoint* (1912).

Wagner, Donald O.: *The Church of England and Social Reform since 1854* (1930).

Ward, J. T.: *Revolutionary Tory: The Life of Joseph Rayner Stephens of Ashton-under-Lyne (1805–1879)*, in the *Transactions of the Lancashire and Cheshire Antiquarian Society*, Vol. LXVIII, 1958.

Waugh, T.: *The "Clarion" or the Bible* (no date).

Wearmouth, R. F.: *Methodism and the Struggle of the Working Classes 1850–1900* (1954).

Wearmouth, R. F.: *The Social and Political Influence of Methodism in the Twentieth Century* (1957).

Webb, Beatrice: *My Apprenticeship* (1926).

Webb, Sidney and Beatrice: *History of Trade Unionism* (Revised edition, 1920).

Whibley, Charles: *Lord John Manners and his Friends* (1925).

Wickham, E. R.: *Church and People in an Industrial City* (1957).

Williams, Francis: *Fifty Years' March* (1949).

Wolf, Lucien: *Life of the First Marquess of Ripon* (1921).

Young, G. M.: *Victorian England: Portrait of an Age*, 1936.

Newspapers:
    British Weekly
    Church Family Newspaper
    Church Times
    Guardian
    Nonconformist (from September 1890 called the *Independent*).
    Tablet
    Universe

INDEX

INDEX

Aberdeen (4th Earl), 279
Abraham, William, 115
Acland, A. H. D., 57
Acland, Sir Richard, 372 f.
Adam, Karl, 345
Adderley, J. G., 24, 188, 200 f., 203, 207 f., 233–236, 299, 320, 349, 391
Alexander II, Tsar, 273
Alexander, A. V. (Earl Alexander of Hillsborough), 378
Alexander, William (Bishop of Derry), 193
Alienation from religion, scepticism, secularism, 9, 16, 19, 21–28, 36, 47–49, 74–79, 156 f., 188, 195, 207 f., 249, 293, 301, 311 f., 319, 334 f., 338–342, 359 f.
Allen, Grant, 391
Allen, William, 172
Ambrose, St, 228
Anderson, K. C., 39, 72
Anglo-Catholics, Oxford Movement, Tractarians, 12, 17, 19, 24 f., 31–34, 37, 42–45, 73, 78, 95, 105, 122, 124, 186–188, 193 197, 200, 205, 212, 215–217, 224, 231, 236, 240–244, 265, 289, 302, 326, 334, 336 f., 343, 349, 351, 353, 360, 366, 375
Arch, Joseph, 99–106, 132, 148, 184, 216, 352, 361
Aristotle, 250, 391
Arnold, Matthew, 23
Arnold, Thomas, 13, 186, 283, 369
Ashley, Lord: see Shaftesbury, 7th Earl of
Ashley, W. J., 57, 252
Ashurst, W. H., 155 f.

Askwith, Sir George, 143
Asquith, H. H. (1st Earl of Oxford and Asquith), 118, 138, 140 f., 216, 293, 295, 330.
Atherton, Canon, 50
Attlee, C. R. (1st Earl Attlee), 358, 362, 364, 372, 377 f., 380 f., 383
Austin, Alfred, 274
Aveling, Edward, 274
Aveling, Eleanor Marx-, 261, 274

Babeuf, F. N., 192
Baker, Francis, Noel-, 378
Baker, Philip Noel-, 378
Bakunin, Michael, 271
Baldwin, Stanley (1st Earl Baldwin of Bewdley), 366
Balfour, A. J. (1st Earl of Balfour), 297, 327
Balfour of Burleigh, Lord, 331
Ball, John, 106, 192
Ball, Sidney, 66, 230, 256
Ballard, F. H., 296
Barker, Joseph, 19,21
Barmby, J. G., 156
Barnett, Henrietta O., 55 f., 58, 60, 261 f., 320
Barnett, Canon, S.A., 55–66, 175, 217, 261 f., 320, 323
Barrett, G. S., 67 f., 392
Barrie, J. M., 340
Baur, F. C., 19
Bax, Belfort, 301
Bayley, R. S., 172 f.
Bebel, August, 291, 300
Becher, J. T., 159
Bedford, 9th Duke of, 209
Beesly, E. S., 174
Belcher, Percy, 363
Bell, J., 98

Bell, R., 139
Bellamy, Edward, 282
Belloc, Hilaire, 229
Benson, E. W. (Archbishop of Canterbury), 64
Benthamites, 11
Bergson, H., 72
Bernstein, E., 298, 300
Besant, Mrs Annie, 21, 191, 204, 255, 260, 274, 279, 323
Best, Samuel, 159
Bevan, Aneurin, 378–380
Beveridge, W. H. (later Lord), 138
Bevin, Ernest, 358, 377–379
Biblical criticism, 19, 185
Bickersteth, Cyril, 201
Binney, Thomas, 14 (note), 182
Binyon, G. C., 225
Birrell, Augustine, 107
Bismarck, Prince, 273, 286
Black, Hugh, 287
Blanc, Louis, 166, 170, 250, 267, 270
Bland, Hubert, 255, 260
Blanqui, L. A., 250, 270
Blatchford, Robert, 27, 212, 235 f., 282, 291–293, 295–297, 299, 301, 303, 312, 338, 344
Blaung, M., 252 (note)
Blazeby, William, 154
Blomfield, C. J. (Bishop of London), 10, 28, 34 f., 54
Bokouswine: see Bakunin
Booth, Catherine, 323
Booth, Charles, 27 f., 54, 70, 109
Booth, William, 47 (note), 49–51, 54 f., 61, 63, 75, 251, 289, 323
Bottomley, Horatio, 365
Bowley, A. L., 219
Bowring, Sir John, 246
Bradby, Dr, 55
Bradlaugh, Charles, 21, 123, 268, 274, 301
Bradley, A. C., 56
Bray, Charles, 246
Brewer, J. S., 174
Briggs, Archibald, 176
Bright, John, 46, 96, 136, 258, 280, 307

Broad Church, Liberal Anglicanism, 12 f., 183, 186 f.
Broadhead, William, 178
Broadhurst, Henry, 92, 97 f., 123, 127
Brocklehurst, Fred, 228
Brooke, Stopford, 125, 320
Brougham, Henry (1st Lord Brougham and Vaux), 161
Brown, Hugh S., 160
Browne, G. F. (Bishop of Bristol), 221
Bryce, James (1st Viscount Bryce), 57
Buchanan, R., 245 f.
Bull, Paul, 225, 233
Burdett-Coutts, Baroness, 126
Burke, Edmund, 258
Burne-Jones, Sir Edward, 243
Burns, John, 58, 110 f., 120 f., 126, 128, 137 f., 151, 158, 192, 217, 285, 316, 342
Burt, Andrew, 98
Burt, Robert, 98
Burt, Thomas, 98, 327, 361
Butler, H. M., 216
Buxton, Sydney (1st Earl Buxton), 111, 253

Caine, Hall, 390
Cairnes, J. E., 252 (note)
Cairns, Lord, 24
Campbell, Archibald, 173
Campbell, R. J., 72, 209, 233, 241, 292, 311
Campbell, W. H. P., 194
Campion, W. J. H., 196 f., 389
Carlile, Wilson, 50
Carlyle, A. J., 200
Carlyle, Thomas, 54, 243, 245 (note), 258, 283, 390
Carpenter, E., 195, 264
Carter, John, 201, 208 (note)
Cartwright, John, 247
Catholic Crusade, 226, 230 f.
Cecil, Lord William, 227
Census of Religion, 1851, 13, 17, 21 f., 25

Chamberlain, Joseph, 126 f., 277, 281, 294, 311, 314, 316, 342, 355
Chamberlain, Neville, 371
Champion, H. H., 190, 192, 204, 288
Champneys, W. B., 162
Champneys, W. W., 162 f.
Chandler, Bishop Arthur, 320
Charity Organization Society, 55, 60 f., 261, 276, 324
Chartism, 14 f., 19, 45 f., 49, 87, 161, 164 f., 167 f., 174, 184, 206, 246–251, 280, 304–306, 338 f., 354
Chesterton, Cecil, 225
Chesterton, Frances, 229
Chesterton, G. K., 225, 229, 322, 364
Christendom Group, 366 f.
Christian Social Union, 181, 194, 196-203, 207–209, 216–225, 227, 229, 234, 236–238, 309, 312, 324, 365, 368, 370, 372, 381
Christian Socialism, 20 f., 34, 53, 55–57, 80 f., 101, 125, 148, 150, 152, 154, 156 f., 165–242, 246, 261, 265, 267, 273, 276–278, 280 f., 287, 291–293, 298–300, 302, 305 f., 308 f., 312, 322, 324, 336, 338 f., 341–343, 346–351, 360, 364 f., 367–370, 372–376, 378, 380 f., 393
Christian Socialist Movement (1960), 374–376
Christmas, T., 170
Church, R. W., 31
Church accommodation and building, 10, 28–31, 78, 337
Church Socialist League, 194, 223–231, 233 f., 322 f., 348, 350, 365 f.
Churchill, Lord Randolph, 274, 316
Churchill, Sir Winston, 138 f., 290, 328, 330, 377
Clayton, Joseph, 203
Clifford, John, 15, 110, 203, 205 f., 209–212, 215, 241, 281, 290, 320, 335, 345, 351

Cobbett, William, 247
Cobden, Richard, 136, 258, 307
Cole, G. D. H., 176, 320, 364
Colenso, Bishop J. W., 19, 179
Coleridge, S. T., 198, 309
Collins, J., 246
Commune of Paris, 1871, 251, 267–271, 273, 276, 280, 288
Community of the Resurrection, 225
Complete Suffrage Movement, 304–306
Compton-Rickett, Sir J., 140
Comte, A., 72, 259
Conciliation, Industrial, 82, 121 f., 218 f.
Conference on Politics, Economics and Citizenship (COPEC), 370
Cook, E. T., 57
Cooper, Thomas, 15, 206, 248 f., 287
Cooper, Walter, 166, 170, 174
Co-operation, 20, 59 f., 82, 152–157, 165–170, 175–177, 180 f., 207, 217 f., 225 f., 246, 263, 271 f., 277, 284–286, 296, 302, 307, 338 f., 342, 348, 351, 354, 360
Copernicus, 344
Corbet, R. W., 194
Cory, W. J.: see William Johnson
Cowey, Ned, 98
Cox, J. C., 102
Craig, Dan, 309
Crawford, W. Sharman, 249
Creighton, Mandell (Bishop of Peterborough; later of London), 114
Cripps, C. A. (Lord Parmoor), 376
Cripps, Sir Stafford, 376–378
Crockett, S. R., 390
Crofton, Mordaunt, 324
Crompton, Henry, 174
Cromwell, Oliver, 183
Crooks, Will, 137, 320 f., 326, 329, 339, 342
Crosskey, R. W., 86, 162
Cunningham, William, 57, 222 f., 238, 252

Curran, Pete, 330
Cyprian, St, 228

Dale, R. W., 20, 28
Dante, 116
Darboy, Georges (Archbishop of Paris), 267
Darwin, Charles, 19, 23, 266, 340
Davidson, Randall (Archbishop of Canterbury), 25, 220 f., 232, 343, 350, 366
Davidson, Thomas, 190
Davies, J. Llewelyn, 36, 102, 104, 173 f., 183, 185–187, 349
Davitt, M., 124, 188
Dawson, George, 86, 155
Dawson, Mrs, 60
Dearmer, Percy, 188, 198, 200, 203, 207, 212–216, 220, 228 f., 234–236, 255, 289, 292, 349, 351, 360, 366, 392
Debs, E., 118
Demant, V. A., 364, 367, 372
Denison, Edward, 54
Devonport, Lord (1st Viscount), 142
Dickens, Charles, 12, 340
Dickinson, G. Lowes, 173
Dilke, Charles, 116, 355
Dilke, Lady Emilia, 116
Disraeli, B. (1st Earl Beaconsfield), 32, 96, 183, 243 f., 258
Dods, Marcus, 287
Dolling, Robert, 44, 194, 228, 320
Domestic servants, 93 f.
Donaldson, F. Lewis, 199, 201, 223, 225, 227, 233 f., 236, 322, 349
Douglas, Major C. H., 364
Dungannon, Lord (3rd Viscount), 35
Dunn, C. B., 156

Ede, Chuter, 378
Education, 24 f.
Edward I, 90
Edward VII, 24, 339
Edwards, Enoch, 98

'Eliot, George' (Marian Evans), 116, 260
Eliot, T. S., 367, 372
Ellicott, C. J. (Bishop of Gloucester), 101–103, 105 f., 258
Elliott, Ebenezer, 206, 246
Elliott, Robert, 154
Employer's liability, 96 f., 126
Engels, F., 288, 291
Essays and Reviews, 19
Evangelicals, 11 f., 24, 34 f., 85, 186, 229, 231, 242 f., 265, 289, 338, 347

Faber, F. W., 244
Fabian Society, 118, 189–192, 203–206, 209–216, 231, 234, 240 f., 252, 254–257, 280 f., 284, 286, 289–292, 312, 314, 316, 333, 339, 343–347, 353, 355, 368
Factory Reform, 87
Fairbairn, A. M., 68, 281, 337
Farn, J. C., 154
Farquhar, J. W., 195
Farrar, F. W., 51
Fels, Joseph, 61
Fenians, 87, 89, 271, 307
Fenwick, C., 327
Ferre, T., 270
Fielden, J., 246
Figgis, J. N., 225
Finney, S., 98
First International, 89, 92, 96, 251, 267, 271
Fletcher, C. G., 201
Flint, Robert, 205, 284
Forster, W. E., 248
Forsyth, P. T., 71
Fourier, C., 170, 245, 268
Francis, St, 323
Fraser, James (Bishop of Manchester), 13, 40 f., 48, 91 f., 95, 101–104, 148, 185, 193, 252 f., 281, 368
Free Trade, Protection, 133 f., 137, 150, 184, 326, 329, 331, 368
Frere, W. H., 225
Friendly Societies, 157–160, 341 f., 351

Frost, J., 250
Fry, T. C., 216
Furness, Sir Christopher, 120 f.
Furnivall, F. J., 173 f., 181 f.

Gaitskell, Hugh, 376
Gardiner, Thory, 57
Gaskell, Elizabeth, 164
Gaskell, W., 164
Gell, P. L., 56
George V, 138
George, David Lloyd (1st Earl Lloyd George of Dwyfor), 89, 139–141, 302, 328, 330, 357, 382
George, Henry, 189 f., 193, 229, 253, 277, 279, 281, 302
Gibbons, Cardinal, 112, 253
Giffen, R., 274
Girdlestone, E., 101 f.
Gladstone, W. E., 32, 36, 45, 47, 103, 136, 178, 183, 307, 316, 325, 363, 382
Glasier, Bruce, 296
Gobat, T. C., 223, 322
Goderich, Viscount (Prime Minister): see Earl of Ripon
Goderich, Viscount (son of preceding): see 1st Marquess of Ripon
Gore, Charles (Bishop successively of Worcester, Birmingham and Oxford), 24, 65 f., 73, 136, 143, 196–200, 202, 208, 216–221, 223, 225, 230, 236, 240, 324, 343, 349 f., 368
Gould, Ronald, 363
Graham, W., 284
Graham, W. (Dr Billy Graham), 360
Gray, B. K., 282
Grayson, Victor, 137, 297, 325
Green, E. J., 101
Green, J. R., 54
Green, T. H., 56, 283
Greening, E. O., 154
Greenwood, J. G., 164
Gregory, I, Pope, 228
Grey, A., 56
Griffiths, James, 378

Gronlund, L., 274
Grove, George, 174
Guild of St Matthew, 188–198, 200, 203, 217, 223–227, 229, 233, 237, 240, 254, 276, 350
Guild Socialism, 225 f., 322, 364, 366

Haldane, J. A., 231
Haldane, Richard, 231
Haldane, R. B. (1st Viscount Haldane), 58, 231 f.
Hall, Leonard, 228
Hancock, T., 188, 192, 194, 204
Hansard, S., 43, 174, 187
Harcourt, Sir William, 343
Hardie, Keir, 14, 67, 120, 128 f., 137, 140, 224, 257, 285, 287 f., 296 f., 299, 301, 309–312, 317 f., 327 f., 330, 345
Hardy, Thomas, 260
Harker, B. J., 67
Harmer, J. R. (Bishop of Rochester), 221
Harney, G. J., 168
Harrison, Frederic, 90, 174, 178, 259, 274
Hartley, William P., 98, 138
Hartshorn, Vernon, 239 f.
Harvey, T. E., 64
Harwood, G., 273
Hatherley, Lord, 24
Hawkins, A. H. ('Anthony Hope'), 57
Hawkins, E. C., 54
Headlam, S. D., 24, 44, 56, 63, 180, 187–195, 197, 203–205, 215–217, 220, 223 f., 229, 233, 237, 254 f., 274, 279–281, 289, 292, 348–351, 360
Heath, Edward, 385 (note)
Henderson, Arthur, sen., 322, 324, 329, 331, 339, 359, 361
Henderson, Arthur, jun., 378
Hennell, C. C., 246
Hennell, M., 246
Henson, Hensley (Bishop of Durham), 207, 222
Hepburn, Thomas, 361

Herbert, Auberon, 274
Heywood, Sir Benjamin, 160
Hicks, E. L. (Bishop of Lincoln), 228
Hill, Octavia, 172
Hobhouse, L. T., 217
Hodges, H. A., 372
Hodgson, B. H., 259
Holland, H. Scott, 24, 110, 124, 187, 194, 196–203, 208, 216–219, 223, 227, 230, 320, 365
Holyoake, G. J., 20 f., 47, 153–157, 175 f., 195, 206, 279, 284, 296, 338
Hopkins, Evan, 50
Hopps, J. P., 154
Horne, C. Sylvester, 64, 70 f.
Hort, F. J. A., 185–187, 195, 263, 281, 349
Horton, R. F., 40, 124, 281 f., 392
Hose, H. J., 174
Hoskyns Sir Edwyn (Bishop of Southwell), 221
Houldsworth, Sir William, 117
House of Lords, 96 f., 126, 139, 157, 188, 193, 211, 221, 240, 280, 308, 331, 354, 373
How, W. W. (Bishop of Bedford), 54 f., 57
Howard, A., 194
Howard, Sir Ebenezer, 282
Howick, Viscount, later 3rd Earl Grey, 244
Hughes, Hugh Price, 48
Hughes, Mary, 323
Hughes, Thomas, 13, 21, 43, 84, 90 f., 104, 169 f., 173, 175 f., 178 f., 180–183, 185, 208, 271, 307, 323, 360
Hunt, Henry, 247
Hutton, Hugh, 20
Huxley, Thomas, 23, 52, 175
Hyndman, H. M., 45, 195, 204, 236, 251, 264, 273, 276 f., 284, 297, 338

Independent Labour Party, 67, 126, 201, 208, 223, 233, 282, 285, 291, 295, 301–303, 308–314, 316–318, 325, 333, 357, 361

Industrial Christian Fellowship, 365, 372
Inge, W. R., 222, 232
Ingersoll, Col. Robert, 301
Ingham (Oxford House), 203
Ingram, K., 372
Irish Home Rule, 183, 276, 314, 316, 329, 332 f.
Irish immigration, 17
Irving, Edward, 163
Isaacs, George, 378
Isham (Christian Socialist), 170
Italian question, 82–84, 270

James, J. A., 20
Jaurès, J., 300
Jay, Douglas, 376
Jayne, F. J. (Bishop of Chester), 228
Jellicoe, Basil, 366
Jenkinson, Charles, 229 f., 366
Jevons, W. S., 154, 252 (note)
Johnson, Hewlett, 373
Johnson, John, 98, 329
Johnson, William (W. J. Cory), 173, 187, 200
Jones, Ernest, 46 f., 167 f., 250
Jones, H. A., 391
Jones, Henry, 102
Jones, Lloyd, 154 f., 157, 166 f., 169
Jowett, Benjamin, 56
Jowett, Fred, 301, 313
Jowett, J. H., 64
Joynes, J. L. (sen.), 190
Joynes, J. L. (jun.), 190

Kautsky, K., 284, 297 f., 300
Kempis, Thomas à, 116
Kempthorne, Dr, 199
Kennedy, G. Studdert, 365
Kennedy, H. A., 320
Keynes, J. M. (Lord Keynes), 222
Khrushchev, N., 384
King, Bolton, 57
King, John, 155
King, William, 155, 245

Kingsley, Charles, 34, 163, 170–173, 176, 179 f., 183–185, 204, 211, 227, 237, 243, 265, 271, 280, 305, 360
Kipling, Rudyard, 69
Kirkup, T., 274, 286 f.
Kitchin, G. W., 66, 391
Kitto, J. F., 323
Knox, 'Driver,' 143
Kossuth, L., 250
Kropotkin, Prince Peter, 279

Labouchere, H., 263
Labour Churches, 66-69, 312 f., 337
Lacordaire, J. P. H., 43
Lambert, Brooke, 54, 57
Lambeth Conferences, 221, 225, 276, 365
Lang, C. G. (Archbishop of York), 57, 220 f., 231 f., 343, 350
Langford, J. A., 155
Lansbury, George, 137, 223–225, 230 f., 322, 324, 328, 332, 339, 349, 358
Larkin, J., 143–145
Lassalle, F., 192, 204, 273, 277
Latimer, Hugh (Bishop of Worcester), 218
Laurie, A. P., 58
Law, Bonar, 135
Law, William, 249
Lawson, Jack, 361 f.
Leach, Charles, 313 f.
League of the Kingdom of God, 366
Ledru-Rollin, A. A., 250
Lee, Peter, 98
Leo XIII, Pope, 39 f., 253, 286, 288, 291
Leonard, G., 70
Liberal Anglicans: see Broad Church
Liberation Society, 29
Lichfield, 2nd Earl of, 178
Liddon, H. P., 31, 217
Lidgett, J. Scott, 65, 320
Liebknecht, W., 291, 300

Lightfoot, J. B. (Bishop of Durham), 185 f., 195
Lilley, A. L., 229
Linnell, A., 192
Litchfield, R. B., 173
Lloyd, Selwyn, 362
Lodge, Sir Oliver, 256
Lofft, C., 248 f.
Loisy, A., 72, 344
London County Council, 201, 284, 287, 295, 329 f.
Londonderry, 6th Marquess of, 125
Longford, 7th Earl of, 378
Lovett, W., 46, 206, 305
Lowder, C., 43, 45, 54
Ludlow, J. M., 155 f., 166 f., 169 f., 172 f., 175–177, 179–181, 183, 185 f., 199, 305, 364
Lushington, G., 174
Lushington, V., 174
Luther, M., 310
Lux Mundi, 186, 196 f., 217
Lyell, Sir Charles, 19
Lynch, T. T., 174

McDonald, A., 98, 310
Macdonald, George, 282
McDonald, J. M., 57
Macdonald, J. Ramsay, 135, 142, 220, 224, 230, 240, 291, 299–301, 303, 324, 339, 358 f., 380
Macdonald, Margaret, 324
Macdonald, T. M., 20
McGlynn, Dr, 253
Mackinnon, Donald, 372
Mackonochie, A., 43 f.
Maclaren, A., 15
'Maclaren, Ian' (John Watson), 340
Macmillan, A., 174, 182
Macmillan, D., 182
Macmillan, Harold, 384
Macmillan, Margaret, 313
McNeill, John, 311
Magee, W. C. (Bishop of Peterborough, later Archbishop of York), 103, 206
Malthus, T. R., 278

Mann, Tom, 58, 111, 113, 121, 124, 130, 145, 149, 158, 217, 284 f., 318, 342, 391

Manners, Lord John (later 7th Duke of Rutland), 244

Manning, Cardinal H. E., 17–19, 39 f., 48, 51 f., 75, 103 f., 106, 108, 110–114, 117, 133, 145, 162, 207, 209, 217, 242, 253, 258, 266, 279, 281, 352

Mansbridge, Alfred, 65 f.

Mansfield, C. B., 170, 172, 174, 179 f.

Marriott, Joseph, 156

Marshall, Alfred, 57, 186, 222, 284

Marson, C. L., 200, 203, 254, 391 f.

Marx, Karl, 32, 165, 192, 204, 211, 251, 271, 273, 280, 284, 291, 298–301, 303, 335, 338, 346, 354

Mascall, E. L., 367

Massey, Gerald, 166, 168

Maurice, F. D., 13, 24, 34, 36 f., 53, 57, 65, 70 f., 152, 155, 157, 165 f., 169–175, 177–186, 188 f., 193–195, 198, 202, 204, 207, 211, 216, 220, 223, 226 f., 230, 237, 248, 252, 263–265, 271, 280–282, 298, 309, 346, 348–351, 364, 372, 381

Maxted, E. G., 230

Mazzini, G., 250

Mearns, A., 56

Mechanics' Institutes, 160–164, 341 f.

Meyer, F. B., 140

Miall, E., 20 f., 29, 37, 46 f., 53, 132, 206, 212, 305 f., 308, 314, 319, 335, 351

Mill, J. S., 96, 245 (note), 250, 267

Millbank, Joseph, 174

Mills, H. V., 274

Mills, M., 258

Milner, Alfred (1st Viscount), 55 f., 136

Mitchell, J. T. W., 153 f., 156, 175 f., 338, 342

Mitchell, William, 154

Molesworth, Sir William, 46

Molesworth, W. N., 154

Moll, W. E., 223 f., 228, 254

Montague, F. C., 56, 274

Moody, D. L., 311

Morgan, J. M., 166, 245

Morley, John (1st Viscount), 280, 316, 318, 354 f., 391

Morley, Samuel, 47, 50, 91, 104

Morris, J. W., 246

Morris, William, 67, 204, 243 f., 264, 266, 301

Morris, W. A., 228

Morrison, Herbert (Lord Morrison of Lambeth), 378

Moulton, W. F., 65

Munby, D. L., 367

Mundella, A. J., 95, 178

Murry, Middleton, 372

Napoleon III, Emperor, 82, 250

National Agricultural Labourers' Union, 99–106, 230

Neale, E. V., 156, 166, 169 f., 172, 174–177, 181 f., 185, 338

Nettleship, R. L., 56

Newman, Cardinal J. H., 12, 17, 32, 42, 205, 242 f., 258, 344, 349

Newton, John, 85

Newton, William, 172

Nicholas II, Tsar, 327

Nicholls, J. A., 163

Nicholson, J. S., 284

Nightingale, Florence, 23

Noel, Conrad, 188, 223–231, 235 f., 322, 350 f., 360

Noel-Baker, Francis: see Baker, Francis Noel-

Noel-Baker, Philip: see Baker, Philip Noel-

Nonconformists, 13–19, 22–25, 27–31, 36 f., 45–49, 53, 57, 65, 69–72, 75, 77 f., 86 f., 97–99, 104–106, 111 f., 114, 141, 151, 154, 157, 159 f., 162 f., 180, 205 f., 215 f., 241, 248 f., 251, 258, 262 f., 281 f., 289 f., 296, 303–306, 308–315, 317–323, 326, 328 f., 333, 335–339, 341 f., 344, 347, 350–355, 359–364, 374 f., 378–380, 382

Nunn, T. H., 57

Oastler, Richard, 87
O'Brien, James (Bronterre), 46
O'Connell, Daniel, 249
O'Connor, F., 49, 87, 206, 247
Odger, George, 195
O'Grady, James, 129
Old Age Pensions, 61, 290, 293, 295, 298
Olivier, S., 190, 254,
O'Neill, A., 246 f.
Orange, A. R., 176
Ordination statistics, 23 f.
Osborne Judgement, 134 f., 150
Ottley, R. L., 197, 390
Overtoun, Lord, 310 f.
Owen, Robert, 80, 152, 155 f., 166 f., 170, 177, 211, 244 f., 248, 268, 285, 335, 338, 354, 386
Oxford Movement: see Anglo-Catholics

Paine, Tom, 247
Palmerston, Viscount, 46
Pankhurst, Emmeline, 228
Parish system, 9
Parker, Joseph, 282
Paton, J. B., 51, 281
Pattison, Mark, 116
Paul, C. Kegan, 174, 184
Pearson, Karl, 299
Pease, E. R., 254
Peck, W. G., 372
Peel, Sir Robert, 243 f.
Penrhyn, Lord (2nd Baron), 119 f., 138
Penty, A. J., 176, 225
Percival, J. (Bishop of Hereford), 66, 221
Peto, Sir Morton, 15
Phelps, L. C., 56
Phillips, W. A., 274
Phillips, W. L., 254
Pickard, Ben, 116, 130
Pickard, J. (Christian Socialist), 170
Place, Francis, 87
Plater, C. D., 75 f.
Plimsoll, Samuel, 96, 128
Podmore, F., 254
Poor Law, 87 f.

Preston, G. C., 56
Priestley, Joseph, 21
Pringle-Pattison, Seth, 231 f.
Protection: see Free Trade
Proudhon, P. J., 192, 250, 268
Pulsford, J., 195
Pusey, E. B., 12, 42, 349

Rabone, J., 156
Rae, J., 122, 274
Ramsay, G., 311
Rashdall, H., 202, 223
Raven, C. R., 175
Reade, Charles, 89
Reade, Winwood, 259
Reckitt, Maurice, 176, 225, 364–366, 372
Redhead, Father, 228
Reform Acts, 185, 304–308
Reid, Andrew, 390 f.
Renan, E., 310
Ricardo, D., 202
Richmond, Wilfred, 217
Ripon, 1st Earl of (Lord Goderich), 183
Ripon, 1st Marquess of (Lord Goderich), 173, 177, 183, 272
Ritchie, D. G., 283
Ritchie, George, 283
Ritchie, R. D. B., 128
Roberts, W. C., 230 f.
Roberts, W. P., 87
Robertson, F. W., 34, 264
Robinson, W., 64
Roebuck, J., 174
Rogers, A., 58
Rogers, F., 57
Rogers, T., 273
Roman Catholics, 17–19, 22, 25, 30 f., 74–76, 78, 83 f., 104, 106, 108 f., 111–114, 116, 144 f., 147 f., 150, 162, 183 f., 208 f., 240–244, 249–251, 253, 260, 266, 270 f., 273, 283, 286, 290–293, 295, 299–303, 308, 310, 312 f., 319 f., 325, 335–337, 339, 343–345, 350–353, 355, 360, 375 f.
Rosebery, 5th Earl of, 118, 297 f.
Rossetti, D. G., 174, 265

Rowley, Charles, 53
Royal Commission on Trade Unions, 80, 89 f., 178
Ruskin, John, 54, 56, 174, 181, 193, 200, 213, 243, 250, 252, 265 f., 281, 284
Russell, 1st Earl (Lord John Russell), 307
Ryle, H. E. (Bishop of Exeter), 228

Sabbatarianism, 11, 174, 181, 187, 306, 310, 380 f.
Sadler, M., 57, 87
St Simon, Comte de, 245 (note)
Sala, G. A., 280
Salisbury, 3rd Marquess of, 108, 125, 274, 317, 391
Salisbury, 5th Marquess of, 384
Salt, Sir Titus, 83, 159
Salvation Army, 25, 49-54, 75, 77, 323, 337
Sanderson, Richard Burdon-, 231
Sarson, G., 189, 194
Sayers, Dorothy, 372
Scepticism: see Alienation from religion
Schäffle, A., 284
Scott, A. J., 163 f.
Scott, B., 163
Secularism: see Alienation from religion
Seeley, J. R., 57, 202
Selborne, 1st Earl of, 24
Settlement Movement, 53-66, 78, 202, 230, 283 f., 312, 323 f., 337, 339, 341
Sexton, James, 147
Shackleton, D. J., 330 f.
Shaftesbury, 7th Earl of, 11 f., 14, 35, 50, 91, 136, 207, 244, 385 f.
Shaw, G. B., 122, 190 f., 193, 233, 240, 252, 254 f., 289, 368
Sheffield outrages, 80, 88 f., 97, 178
Shorter, T., 174
Shuttleworth, H. C., 188 f., 193 f., 208
Sims, G. R., 56
Slaney, R. A., 169
Slessor, H., 225

Smith, Adam, 152, 392
Smith, C. S., 223
Smith, F. E. (1st Earl of Birkenhead), 328
Smith, Frank, 391
Smith, H. Ll., 58
Smith, J. E., 244 f.
Smith, Mudie, 25
Snowden, Philip (1st Viscount), 238, 297, 325, 339, 361
Social Democratic Federation, 189, 191, 251 f., 291, 295, 339, 357
Social distinctions among the clergy, 10 f.
Socialist League, 191
Solly, Henry, 154, 161 f., 246
Soper, Donald (Lord Soper), 374
South African War, 130, 134, 311, 318
Spencer, Herbert, 258-260, 284, 301
Spencer, T., 306
Spender, J. A., 57
Spicer, A., 315
Spicer, E., 315
Spurgeon, C. H., 15, 110, 351
Stalin, J., 257
Stanhope, Lord (5th Earl), 48
Stanley, A. P. (Dean of Westminster), 13
Stansfeld, J., 246
Stanton, A., 43-45, 187, 189
Stead, W. T., 51, 56, 286
Steinthal, S. A., 154
Stephens, G., 87
Stephens, J. R., 87 f.
Stewart, Sir Halley, 314 f.
Stokes, R. R., 378
Strachey, Lytton, 264
Straker, William, 362 f.
Strikes, 80-84, 86, 92, 95 f., 101-106, 109-113, 116-122, 132-134, 138-146, 149-151, 218-220, 230, 239 f., 253, 358 f., 366, 370 f.
Stubbs, C. W. (Bishop of Truro), 188, 208, 391
Stubbs, William (Bishop of Oxford), 217
Sturge, Joseph, 46, 248, 305, 335

Sumner, J. B. (Archbishop of Canterbury), 35
Swann, N. E. E., 223, 322
Sweating, 219, 229, 368
Symes, J. E., 189
Symons, B. P., 55
Syndicalism, 140–142, 145, 151, 302, 364

Taff Vale case, 132–134, 150
Taine, H. A., 33
Tait, A. C. (Bishop of London; Archbishop of Canterbury), 36
Talbot, E. (Bishop of Southwark), 218, 221, 320
Tansley, G., 174
Tawney, R. H., 176, 225, 324, 364 f., 381
Taylor, P. A., 162
Taylor, S., 57
Temperance movement, 158, 228, 247 f., 293, 297, 309 f.
Temple, F. (Bishop of London; Archbishop of Canterbury), 110, 114, 192, 201, 367 f.
Temple, William (Bishop of Manchester, Archbishop of York, Archbishop of Canterbury), 66, 223, 227, 367–373, 381
Ten Hours' agitation, 83
Thiers, L. A., 267 f.
Thomas, D. A., 142, 151
Thomas, T. G., 362
Thorne, Will, 116
Thorold, A. W., 35
Tildsley, A., 320
Tillett, Ben, 14, 38 f., 58, 68, 110–112, 142, 145, 149, 158, 217, 253, 342, 345
Tillich, Paul, 212 (note)
Tithes, 10
Tolpuddle Martyrs, 86
Tolstoy, Count L., 323
Tomlinson, George, 378
Touche, Rose la, 266
Toynbee, Arnold, 56, 175, 195, 252, 281, 283
Toynbee, G., 56

Tozer, T. M., 228
Tractarians: see Anglo-Catholics
Trade unions, 80–151, 167, 178, 219, 222, 234, 239, 267, 290, 302, 319, 335, 339, 341 f., 348, 350, 353 f., 360–364, 392 f.
Trench, R. C. (Dean of Westminster), 36, 174
Trevor, John, 66 f., 312, 380
Tuckwell, W., 195
Turquand, P. J., 64
Tyrell, George, 72, 345

Unemployment, 108 f., 124, 126, 131, 136–138, 149–151, 199, 223, 275, 290, 359, 371 f.
Unitarians, 20 f., 85 f., 98, 154, 161 f., 184, 246, 251 f., 258, 282, 304, 315, 325, 354, 393

Vansittart, A. A., 170
Vaughan, B. J., 75, 290–293
Vaughan, D. J., 173
Vaughan, Cardinal H., 75, 290
Verinder, F., 193, 203
Victoria, Queen, 11, 75, 152, 361
Vincent, Henry, 46, 87, 206, 246–248

Wade, A. S., 245
Walker, P. C. Gordon, 385
Wallace, A. R., 266, 391
Wallace, J. B., 67
Walmsley, Sir Joshua, 306
Ward, Mrs Humphry, 23, 283
Ward, W. G., 43
Warren, T. H., 56
Warwick, Frances, Countess of, 225, 229, 322
Watson, R. A., 287
Watson, Sam, 363
Watts, Isaac, 20
Wearmouth, R. F., 15, 86, 97 f., 361 f.
Webb, Beatrice, 55, 61, 125, 232, 258–264, 284, 287, 289, 309 f., 312, 340, 347, 376, 380

Webb, Sidney, 58, 61, 125, 167, 190 f., 232, 255–257, 261, 278, 280, 284, 287, 289
Webster, F. S., 50
Welldon, J. E. C., 239
Wells, H. G., 191, 210 f., 291, 295, 299
Wemyss, 10th Earl of, 125
Wesley, John, 15 f., 35, 249
West, G. A., 223 f.
West, J. (possibly=preceding), 322
Westcott, B. F. (Bishop of Durham), 24, 114, 117, 185–187, 195, 197 f., 201 f., 217 f., 281, 292, 309, 349
Westlake, J., 173
Whalley, G. H., 269
Wheatley, John, 325
White, the Rev. Edward, 37
Whiteley, William, 361 f.
Whitman, Walt, 264, 283
Wickham, E. R. (Bishop of Middleton), 22
Wicksteed, P. H., 66, 252, 393
Widdrington, P. E. T., 223–225, 228, 322, 365 f.
Wilberforce, Samuel (Bishop of Oxford, later of Winchester), 184

Wilberforce, William, 12, 385 f.
Wilkinson, Ellen, 362
Williams, C. Fleming, 288
Williams, T. Rhondda, 72
Williamson, H., 86
Wilson, Havelock, 121
Wilson, John (Unitarian minister), 154
Wilson, John (Miners' leader), 98
Wilson, John (Baptist leader), 320
Wilson, J. Harold, 360, 362, 378, 382
Wilson, J. Stitt, 226
Wiseman, Cardinal N. P. S., 19
Wodehouse, T., 187
Wood, T. M., 315
Woolcombe, H. S., 320
Woolman, John, 203
Woolsey, Theodore D., 273
Workers' Educational Association, 65 f., 216, 219, 232, 369
Working Men's College, 172–175, 232, 265, 348
Wrigley, Isaac, 154
Wrigley, W., 246
Wylie, Alexander, 274

Young England, 14, 183, 242–244, 305